Comparative Matters

Comparative Matters

The Renaissance of Comparative Constitutional Law

Ran Hirschl

OXFORD
UNIVERSITY PRESS

OXFORD
UNIVERSITY PRESS

Great Clarendon Street, Oxford, OX2 6DP,
United Kingdom

Oxford University Press is a department of the University of Oxford.
It furthers the University's objective of excellence in research, scholarship,
and education by publishing worldwide. Oxford is a registered trade mark of
Oxford University Press in the UK and in certain other countries

First published 2014
First published in paperback 2016

Published in the United States of America by Oxford University Press
198 Madison Avenue, New York, NY 10016, United States of America

British Library Cataloguing in Publication Data
Data available

Library of Congress Cataloging in Publication Data
Data available

ISBN 978-0-19-871451-4 (Hbk.)
ISBN 978-0-19-871452-1 (Pbk.)

Acknowledgments

This voyage across the seven seas of comparative constitutionalism is the third and final part of a longer tri-partite expedition into the intersecting worlds of constitutional law and comparative politics, past and present, with side-trips into religion, economics, sociology, and legal theory. It has been the intellectual journey of a lifetime. *Towards Juristorcracy* (Harvard University Press, 2004) was the expedition's beginning, followed by *Constitutional Theocracy* (Harvard University Press, 2010); I now conclude with *Comparative Matters*.

Writing this wide-ranging book and meditating upon its interdisciplinary themes has been a true labor of love for me. However, it could not have been completed without the support of many friends and colleagues who provided valuable references, pinpoint citations, insightful examples, thoughtful new directions, or simply overall good advice.

First, thanks must go to the many scholars, jurists, and students who have helped to turn the study of comparative constitutionalism into one of the most intellectually vibrant areas of contemporary legal scholarship. It is largely due to the field's tremendous growth that a book of this scope and nature could have been written.

My work on this book began while I was a Maimonides Fellow at NYU's Institute for the Advanced Study of Law and Justice then headed by Joseph H. H. Weiler. It is my hope that a distant echo of the fellowship namesake's intellectual grandeur and striking combination of the universal and the particular may still be heard in these pages.

A generous Killam Research Fellowship by the Canada Council for the Arts provided the precious time necessary for the completion of a book of this "Odyssean" scope. The Canada Research Chair program provided essential research funding without which this project could not have been completed. Three academic leaders at the University of Toronto—David Cameron, Lou Pauly, and Ryan Balot—created an institutional environment that is conducive to original thinking and quality scholarship. I am indebted to Ana-Maria Bejarano, David Fontana, Ruth Gavison, Kenneth Green, Sooin Kim, Rebecca Kingston, Daniel Lee, Mariana Mota Prado, and Mark Tushnet for their insightful suggestions and thoughtful responses to my queries, pointed or broad as they might have been. My mother, Naomi Ernst-Hirschl, helped with sound judgment and with instilling a genuine thirst for knowledge. Conversations with Mark Graber, Tom Ginsburg, Gary Jacobsohn, and Sanford Levinson—outstanding scholars and constant sources of inspiration—stimulated the mind and set the expectations bar suitably high. At OUP, Alex Flach, Natasha Flemming, Briony Ryles, and Joy Ruskin-Tompkins provided attentive service and excellent editorial guidance. Comments by OUP's anonymous reviewers are greatly appreciated. Alexander Barroca, Evan Rosevear, Padraic Ryan, and Samantha Ahn helped at various stages with dedicated research assistance. Craig Mullins and Jennie Rubio provided meticulous editorial comments and suggestions that made the final product considerably better. I benefited from questions and comments by participants in workshops and conferences held at the 2010 World Congress of the International Association of Constitutional Law (Mexico City), the 2011 Annual Meeting of the American Political Science Association, the Center for the Constitution at James Madison's Montpelier (the Montpelier Roundtable in Comparative Constitutional Law), the Hertie School of Governance (Berlin), Columbia University Law School, the 2014 AALS Annual Meeting Symposium on constitutional change, and NYU's Center for Constitutional Transitions.

I am grateful to the following journals for publishing my earlier articles related to the issues and topics discussed in this book, including: Ran Hirschl, "The Question of Case Selection in Comparative Constitutional Law," *American Journal of Comparative Law* 53 (2005): 125–55; Ran Hirschl, "Comparative Constitutional Law: Thoughts on Substance and Method," *Indian Journal of Constitutional Law* 2 (2008): 11–37; and Ran Hirschl, "From Comparative Constitutional Law to

Comparative Constitutional Studies," *International Journal of Constitutional Law* 11 (2013): 1–12.

Most of all, I thank my much better half, Ayelet Shachar, and our dazzling son, Shai, two true and amazing lifetime companions— brilliant, funny, and spirited—who have enriched my world in so many wonderful, indescribable ways.

Ran Hirschl
April 2014

Contents

List of Abbreviations   x

Introduction: The C Word   1

1. The View from the Bench: Where the Comparative
   Judicial Imagination Travels   20

2. Early Engagements with the Constitutive Laws of Others:
   Lessons from Pre-Modern Religion Law   77

3. Engaging the Constitutive Laws of Others: Necessities,
   Ideas, Interests   112

4. From Comparative Constitutional Law to Comparative
   Constitutional Studies   151

5. How Universal is Comparative Constitutional Law?   192

6. Case Selection and Research Design in Comparative
   Constitutional Studies   224

Epilogue: Comparative Constitutional Law, Quo Vadis?   282

Table of Cases   285
Index   291

List of Abbreviations

AIR	All India Reporter [India]
AKP	Adalet ve Kalkınma Partisi (Justice and Development Party [Turkey])
ALAC	American Laws for American Court
BJP	Bharatiya Janata Party
BRICS	Brazil, Russia, India, China, and South Africa
BVerfG	Bundesverfassungsgericht [Decisions of the German Federal Constitutional Court]
C.A.	Court of Appeal [Israel]
CCSA	Constitutional Court, South Africa
CFA	Court of Final Appeal [Hong Kong]
CFI	Court of Final Appeal [Hong Kong]
CLJ	Current Law Journal [Malaysia]
ECHR	European Convention on Human Rights [Council of Europe]
ECtHR	European Court of Human Rights [Council of Europe]
ESRs	economic and social rights
EUI	European University Institute
G.R.	General Register [Philippines]
HCJ	High Court of Justice [Israel]
HDI	Human Development Index
IMF	International Monetary Fund
IsrLR	Israel Law Review [Israel]
MLJ	Malaysia Law Journal [Malaysia]
NWFP	North-West Frontier Province

P.D.	Piskei Din [Israel]
PEI	Prince Edward Island
P.L.D.	All Pakistan Legal Decisions [Pakistan]
PPP	Pakistan People's Party
SC	Supreme Court [India]
SCC	Supreme Constitutional Court [Egypt] Supreme Court Cases [India] Supreme Court of Canada [Canada]
SCI	Supreme Court of Israel [Israel]
SCR	Supreme Court Reports [Canada]
TakEl	Takdin Elyon, Supreme Court Law Reports [Israel]
TCC	Turkish Constitutional Court [Turkey]
UGSC	Uganda Supreme Court [Uganda]
UKHL	United Kingdom House of Lords [United Kingdom]
UKSC	United Kingdom Supreme Court [United Kingdom]
UNDP	United Nations Development Programme
U.S.	U.S. Supreme Court reports [United States]

Introduction
The C Word

In the late 1990s, when I was writing my PhD dissertation at Yale University, comparative constitutional law was still at its early revival stages. News about the constitutional transformation of Europe or dilemmas of constitutional design in the post-communist world made headlines. But what was not then obvious to many was the full extent of the astounding global spread of constitutionalism and judicial review, and the ever-increasing reliance on constitutional courts worldwide for addressing some of the most fundamental predicaments a polity can contemplate.[1] Likewise, the profound understanding, now quite common, that this is one of the most noteworthy developments in late 20th- and early 21st-century government was still in its infancy.

The field's early-day difficulties were readily evident. Very few relevant sources were available online, and those that were had to be accessed through a complex dial-in process using a large, noisy, and unreliable modem (we called it the "old unfaithful")—by far the most expensive item in our rather modest graduate housing unit. To access and review constitutional jurisprudence by courts overseas, I had to borrow a rusty master key from the chief librarian, and travel some 20 miles southwest to a mid-size gray office building in the rather unspectacular city of Bridgeport, CT, where Yale Law Library stored its comparative law collection at the time. A slow, squeaky elevator ride took me to the ninth floor, where executive ordinances from Botswana, Indian legislation from the 1960s, and landmark rulings from Germany, were packed in huge carton boxes. To peruse the comparative constitutional law materials not available at that storage site

---

[1] In the European context, J. H. H. Weiler's influential article, "The Transformation of Europe," *Yale Law Journal* 100 (1991): 2403–83 is widely considered an early game changer. In the global context things are less clear, but Bruce Ackerman's "The Rise of World Constitutionalism," *Virginia Law Review* 83 (1997): 771–97, may be considered an early field definer.

required traveling to Cambridge, MA, where the law library of that other great university is located. I can recall countless train rides from New Haven to Boston and back to eagerly read court rulings from New Zealand, Israel, Hungary, or South Africa—many of which were freshly catalogued, although the decisions they contained had been made and subsequently published many months earlier. This was an intellectually gratifying labor of love, yet not the most user-friendly experience. It served as a mundane, small-scale testament to the difficulty of making comparative constitutional law an accessible and exciting endeavor for the greater majority of lawyers, judges, and scholars. Back at my New Haven "home court," the razor-sharp, genuinely cosmopolitan, and knowledge-thirsty intellectual community was incredibly supportive. Yet even with the most generous conversation companions who were truly interested in listening to my enthusiastic accounts of what some British scholars or Canadian jurists had to say about the parts of the constitutional universe that lie beyond US territory, the conversation quickly reverted back to familiar home turf.

This intellectual pursuit has, of course, changed considerably. Over the last few decades, the world has witnessed the rapid spread of constitutionalism and judicial review. Over 150 countries and several supranational entities across the globe can boast the recent adoption of a constitution or a constitutional revision that contains a bill of justiciable rights and enshrines some form of active judicial review. Consequently, constitutional courts and judges have emerged as key translators of constitutional provisions into guidelines for public life, in many instances determining core moral quandaries and matters of utmost political significance that define and divide the polity.

This global transformation has brought about an ever-expanding interest among scholars, judges, practitioners, and policymakers in the constitutional law and institutions of other countries, and in the transnational migration of constitutional ideas more generally. From its beginnings as a relatively obscure and exotic subject studied by a devoted few, comparative constitutionalism has developed into one of the more fashionable subjects in contemporary legal scholarship, and has become a cornerstone of constitutional jurisprudence and constitution-making in an increasing number of countries worldwide.[2]

---

[2] For a compact introduction to the field's main themes and theoretical advances over the past few decades presented by one of the field's pre-eminent scholars, see Mark Tushnet, *Advanced Introduction to Comparative Constitutional Law* (Hart Publishing, 2014).

Everyday indicators of this unprecedented comparative turn are many. Virtually all reputable peak courts across the globe maintain websites where thousands of rulings, including those released earlier the same day, may be browsed with ease and downloaded within seconds. New world-wide-web portals allow jurists, scholars, and policymakers to retrieve and compare the entire corpus of constitutional texts around the world, from the late 18th century to the present. Lively discussions about current developments in constitutional law, theory, and design feature centrally in blogs devoted exclusively to comparative constitutionalism. And the comparative revolution has certainly not been limited to the digital world: scholarly books dealing with comparative constitutional law are no longer considered a rarity; new periodicals and symposia are dedicated to the comparative study of constitutions and constitutionalism; and top-ranked law schools in the United States and elsewhere have begun to introduce their students to a distinctly more cosmopolitan and comparatively informed view of constitutional law and legal institutions. Meanwhile, prominent constitutional court judges commonly lecture about, write on, and refer to the constitutional laws of others. And constitutional drafters from Latin America to the Middle East openly debate comparative constitutional experiences in making their choices about what constitutional features to adopt or to avoid. In many respects, then, these are the heydays of comparative constitutionalism.

And yet, despite this tremendous renaissance, the "comparative" aspect of the enterprise, as a method and a project, remains undertheorized and blurry. Fundamental questions concerning the very meaning and purpose of comparative constitutional inquiry, and how it is to be undertaken, remain largely outside the purview of canonical scholarship.[3] Colloquially, the word "comparative" is often used in the sense of "relative to" (e.g. "he returned to the comparative comfort of his home") or to refer to words that imply comparison (e.g. "better," "faster," etc.). The scientific use of "comparative" is defined in the *Oxford English Dictionary* as "involving the systematic observation of the similarities or dissimilarities between two or more branches of science

---

[3] A few initial attempts to deal with these questions are: Vicki Jackson, "Methodological Challenges in Comparative Constitutional Law," *Penn State International Law Review* 28 (2010): 319–26; Ran Hirschl, "The Question of Case Selection in Comparative Constitutional Law," *American Journal of Comparative Law* 53 (2005): 125–55; Mark Tushnet, "The Possibilities of Comparative Constitutional Law," *Yale Law Journal* 108 (1999): 1225–309.

or subjects of study." These definitions seem intuitive enough—yet, the meaning of the *comparative* in comparative constitutional law has proven quite difficult to pin down.

Since its birth, comparative constitutionalism has struggled with questions of identity. There is considerable confusion about its aims and purposes, and even about its subject—is it about constitutional systems, constitutional jurisprudence, constitutional courts, or constitutional government and politics? It also remains unclear whether comparative constitutional law is or ought to be treated as a subfield of comparative law, a subfield of constitutional law, or an altogether independent area of inquiry. Is the age-old debate in comparative law between "universalists" and "culturalists" relevant to the study of phenomena as widespread as constitutionalism and judicial review, and if so, how? Is there a conceptual affinity between comparative constitutional law and other comparative disciplines (e.g. comparative politics, comparative literature, comparative religion, comparative biochemistry and physiology; comparative psychology)? And what to make of the fact that the constitutional lawyer, the judge, the law professor, the normative legal theorist, and the social scientist all engage in comparison with different ends in mind?

Adding to the confusion is that self-professed "comparativism" sometimes amounts to little more than a passing reference to the constitution of a country other than the scholar's own or to a small number of overanalyzed, "usual suspect" constitutional settings or court rulings. The constitutional experiences of entire regions—from the Nordic countries to sub-Saharan Africa to Central and South East Asia—remain largely uncharted terrain, understudied and generally overlooked.[4] Selection biases abound. The result is that purportedly

---

[4] For conscious attempts to expand the circle of studied cases, see, e.g., Albert Chen, ed., *Constitutionalism in Asia in the Early Twenty-First Century* (Cambridge University Press, 2014); Rosalind Dixon and Tom Ginsburg, eds., *Comparative Constitutional Law in Asia* (Edward Elgar, 2014); Roberto Gargarella, *Latin American Constitutionalism* (Oxford University Press, 2013); "Perspectives on African Constitutionalism," *International Journal of Constitutional Law* 11 (2013): 382–446; Ran Hirschl, "The Nordic Counter-Narrative: Democracy, Human Development and Judicial Review," *International Journal of Constitutional Law* 9 (2011): 449–69; Jiunn-rong Yeh and Wen-Chen Chang, "The Emergence of East Asian Constitutionalism: Features in Comparison," *American Journal of Comparative Law* 59 (2011): 805–39; Ran Hirschl, *Constitutional Theocracy* (Harvard University Press, 2010); and "Symposium: The Changing Landscape of Asian Constitutionalism," *International Journal of Constitutional Law* 8 (2010): 766–976.

universal insights are based on a handful of frequently studied and not always representative settings or cases. Instrumentalist considerations such as availability of data or career planning often determine which cases are considered. Descriptive, taxonomical, normative, and explanatory accounts are often conflated, and epistemological views and methodological practices vary considerably. Some leading works in the field continue to lag behind in their ability to engage in controlled comparison or trace causal links among germane variables and, consequently, in their ability to advance, substantiate, or refute testable hypotheses. The field's potential to produce generalizable conclusions, or other forms of nomothetic, ideally transportable knowledge is thus hindered. Meanwhile, comparative constitutional scholarship that favors contextual, idiographic knowledge seldom amounts to a true, inherently holistic, "thick description" the way Clifford Geertz—a grand champion of thorough, contextual "symbolic interpretation"—perceived it and preached for. Given the prevalence of "armchair" constitutional research carried out with little or no fieldwork or systematic data collection, and the absence of an established tradition of rigorous and anonymous peer review in many leading law reviews, it is no surprise that the outcome is a loose and under-defined epistemic and methodological framework that seems to be held together by a rather thin intellectual thread: interest of some sort or another in the constitutional law of polity or polities other than the observer's own.

This book, then, takes as its premise a simple fact: the unprecedented revival of comparative constitutional studies rides on a fuzzy and rather incoherent epistemological and methodological matrix. In fact, comparative constitutional studies lack a core work that clarifies the essence of the term "comparative" as a project and a method. My hope—from the outset, an ambitious one—is that this book will help to fill that gap. In what follows, I chart the intellectual history and analytical underpinnings of comparative constitutional inquiry, probe the various types, aims, and methodologies of engagement with the constitutive laws of others through the ages, and explore how and why comparative constitutional inquiry has been, and perhaps ought to be more extensively, pursued by academics and jurists worldwide.

Structure of the book: what drives comparative constitutional inquiry and how are we to study it?

The book is divided into two main parts, each comprising three chapters. In the first part (Chapters 1 to 3) I explore what may be learned by looking into the rich history of engagement with the constitutive laws of others. What has driven comparative constitutional journeys through the ages? And why, at given times and places, have certain communities, thinkers, or courts embarked on them, while others have rejected them? Convergence, resistance, and selective engagement (to paraphrase Vicki Jackson's terminology) with the constitutive laws of others, past and present, reflect broader tensions between particularism and universalism, and mirror struggles over competing visions of who "we" are, and who we wish to be as a political community. Comparative constitutional encounters are thus at least as much a humanist and sociopolitical phenomenon as they are a juridical one. Specifically, I identify the interplay between the core factors of *necessity*, *inquisitiveness*, and *politics* in advancing comparative engagement with the constitutive laws of others through the ages. The second part (Chapters 4 to 6) revisits the disciplinary boundaries between comparative constitutional law and the social sciences. Drawing on insights from social theory, religion, political science, and public law, I argue for an interdisciplinary study of comparative constitutionalism, an approach that would be both richer and more fitting for understanding the studied phenomenon than accounts of "comparative constitutional law" and "comparative politics" as two separate entities. The future of comparative constitutional inquiry as a field of study, I argue, lies in relaxing the sharp divide between constitutional law and the social sciences, in order to enrich both.

The first main focus of this book is to highlight the interplay between necessity, inquisitiveness, and politics that surrounds the formal constitutional sphere in advancing comparative engagement with the constitutive laws of others through the ages. Constitutional journeys are driven by the same rationales as other types of journey. Hunter-gatherers are constantly on the go in search of food, water, and shelter. Their forays are driven by necessity. Likewise, few would sneak through the Mexico–US border or gamble their lives on the rough Australian seas without being driven by economic or physical survival instincts or, more generally, by a quest for better life opportunities. What seems to be common to Copernicus' study of the skies, Charles Darwin's journey to the Galápagos Islands, and Thor Heyerdahl's voyage across the Pacific Ocean onboard his self-built raft (Kon-Tiki), are driven largely by sheer intellectual curiosity and scientific inquisitiveness. The space race of the 1960s and 1970s involved a series of risky voyages driven by a thirst for new knowledge alongside easily identifiable political interests and a quest for domination.

Similar rationales seem to have driven constitutional voyages. Survival instincts may push minority communities to develop a matrix for selective engagement with the laws of others in order to maintain their identity in the face of powerful convergence pressures. Intellectual curiosity may drive scholars to investigate new constitutional settings and develop novel concepts, arguments, and ideas with respect to the constitutional universe. Comparative engagement may also be— indeed, often is—driven by a desire to advance a concrete political agenda or an ideological outlook.

Of these three rationales for comparative constitutional engagement, politics is a crucial and yet infrequently acknowledged feature, a background setting that may seem to be invisible unless it is brought to the fore. From Jean Bodin's quest to transform the political and legal landscape of 16th-century France via comparative public law inquiry to Simón Bolívar's love–hate relations with French and American constitutional ideals, and to the Israeli Supreme Court's attempt to define the country's collective identity by making voluntary reference to foreign precedents, comparative constitutional inquiries are as much a political enterprise as they are a scholarly or a jurisprudential one. More broadly, I argue that the specific scope and nature of engagement with the constitutive laws of others in a given polity at a given time cannot be meaningfully understood independent of the concrete sociopolitical struggles, ideological agendas, and "culture wars" shaping that polity at that time.

This argument is pursued in three steps: (i) an exploration of how constitutional courts and judges conceive of the discipline of comparative constitutional law, what weight they accord to it, and how, why, and when they use it; (ii) a sketch of doctrinal innovation and adaptation in the pre- and early-modern, predominantly religious world as a response to encounters with the constitutive laws of others; and (iii) a thumbnail history of constitutional comparisons from the birth of the systematic study of constitutions across polities in the mid-16th century to contemporary debates about the legitimacy and usefulness of comparative constitutional law.

Chapter 1, "The View from the Bench: Where the Comparative Judicial Imagination Travels," explores how constitutional courts and judges—the key purveyors and consumers of comparative constitutional jurisprudence—conceive of the discipline of comparative constitutional law, what methods they use to engage with it, and how and why they vary in their approach to it. I begin by outlining the key empirical findings on *voluntary* foreign citations and examine what these findings may tell us about how and why constitutional courts engage with comparative constitutional law. The evidence with respect to foreign citation patterns is surprisingly scarce, and draws on the experience of only a handful of peak courts. However, the evidence does suggest that certain courts refer to foreign jurisprudence more frequently than others. It shows that there are areas of constitutional jurisprudence that are more informed by national idiosyncrasies and contingencies than others. In the area of rights, it would appear, cross-jurisdictional reference is more likely to occur than it is in areas such as aspirational or organic features of the constitution. The evidence also points to a decline in the status of British and American constitutional cases as common points of reference for constitutional courts worldwide, and perhaps to a corresponding rise in the international stature of other peak courts—most notably the Supreme Court of Canada, the German Federal Constitutional Court, and the European Court of Human Rights.

What explains the judicial thinking behind the selection of a reference to a given foreign court? The general literature on the subject stresses the importance of factors that include the following: global convergence and the inevitability of engagement with foreign jurisprudence; judicial prestige- or legitimacy-enhancing factors; and structural features (e.g. constitutional provisions that call for foreign citations, linguistic permeability, a legal tradition or trajectory of legal education that affects a given apex court's ability and willingness to cite foreign jurisprudence). Whereas these accounts provide illuminating explanations for the rise and variance in the practice of global judicial dialogue, they leave out a crucial factor: the sociopolitical context within which constitutional courts and judges operate, and how this affects whether and where the judicial mind travels in its search for pertinent foreign sources to reference.

Instances of strategic, ad hoc judicial recourse to foreign law are obviously inseparable from the concrete political settings within which they take place. In post-authoritarian or newly created constitutional settings, such choices can signal a judicial commitment to breaking with a nation's less-than-dazzling past or to belong to a certain group of polities. Such choices may likewise help courts and their backers to advance certain worldviews and policy preferences that may be otherwise contested in majoritarian decision-making arenas. Alongside more traditional factors, the foreign references that peak courts in discordant constitutional settings select, reject, or ignore reflect the judicial position vis-à-vis the nation's contested collective identity quandaries.

The Supreme Court of Israel, to pick one court that I investigate in detail in Chapter 1, regularly refers to case law and scholarly commentary from the United States, Canada, Germany, and the United Kingdom, as well as to various European and international sources of law. However, rarely if ever does it refer to the law of countries such as India that share a similar experience of deep identity and ethnic-religious rifts. Likewise, it never cites rulings by the national high courts of Pakistan, Turkey, or Malaysia, even though the tensions between secularism and religiosity informing these countries' constitutional landscapes resemble tensions embedded in Israel's self-definition as a "Jewish and democratic" state. It is equally telling that Israeli secular judges (who make up the vast majority of those appointed to the bench) hardly ever treat Jewish law as a relevant source of comparative insight, despite the fact that it is actually the sole source to which the law refers judges when they encounter a lacuna. Instead, the Israeli judge prefers to look to "the West," and so to affirm the state's desire to be included in the liberal-democratic club of nations. Similar patterns of selective reference are evident in other discordant constitutional settings, from 19th-century Argentina to present-day India. These choices reflect considerable case selection biases ("cherry-picking") and other methodological difficulties. They also raise questions concerning how "comparative" a practice really is that draws on the constitutional experience of a small group of mostly liberal-democratic countries but seldom refers to constitutional experience, law, and institutions elsewhere. As I show, the "identity" dimension—the attempt to define who "we" are as a political community, and to articulate in a public way what "our image" or "our place" in the world is or should be—inevitably influences comparative jurisprudence and acts as a key factor explaining judicial choices of reference sources. Voluntary reference to foreign precedents is at least as much a political phenomenon as it is a juridical one.

Chapter 2, "Early Engagements with the Constitutive Laws of Others: Lessons from Pre-Modern Religion Law," explores the birth of two core concepts that are cardinal for understanding the philosophy of comparative constitutional studies today: (i) acknowledgment of the legitimacy and integrity of the constitutive laws of others; and (ii) doctrinal innovation in response to a necessity-based or ideologically driven impulse to respond to or incorporate such laws. Contemporary discussions in comparative constitutional law often proceed as if there is no past, only a present and a future. However, many of the purportedly new debates in comparative constitutional law (e.g. the debates over the migration of constitutional ideas, judicial recourse to foreign law, and the emergence of a multiplicity of legal orders alongside powerful transnational convergence vectors) have early equivalents, some of which date back over two millennia. And many of these equivalents are found in religion law—Jewish law, to pick one example, provides an ideal context for studying the tension between two opposing tendencies. There may be an objection on principle to the recognition of another system's legitimacy; however, this objection may come into conflict with a pragmatist acknowledgment of the inevitability of dealing with extra-communal law. For thousands of years Jewish law has evolved as an autonomous legal tradition without political sovereignty. Because of its near-permanent "diasporic" state, Jewish law has developed a complex relationship with its legal surroundings, oscillating between principled estrangement and pragmatic engagement. Pre-modern canon and Shari'a law also grappled with aspects of engagement with the outer legal universe, leading to rifts between inward-looking, "originalist," "textualist," or otherwise strict interpretive approaches on the one hand, and more cosmopolitan or adaptive interpretive schools on the other. The wealth of knowledge and degree of theoretical sophistication found in this body of pre-modern opinions, essentially a *terra incognita* for today's scholars of comparative constitutionalism, allow us to consider contemporary debates about engagement with the constitutive laws of others from a new angle.

The chapter outlines some specific doctrinal innovations in respect of engagement with the foreign laws that emerged in the ancient and pre-modern world. Examples include the official policy of legal diversity introduced in Ptolemaic (Hellenic) Egypt; the Roman Republic's *praetor peregrinus*, a municipal officer who engaged in legal comparisons to settle disputes to which non-citizens were party; and novel approaches in medieval Jewish law to governing encounters with the often hostile "outer" world. These diverse examples are not meant to provide an exhaustive or even near-exhaustive survey of areas where pre-modern, religion-infused law may enrich or shed new light on discourses on contemporary comparative constitutional studies. Taken as a whole, however, these examples suggest that the history of engagement with the constitutive laws of others is much longer and thicker than that of the current trend of constitutional convergence. Moreover, these examples illustrate that alongside inquisitiveness per se, instrumentalist factors—from community survival to political economy—matter a great deal in explaining purportedly principled, doctrinal debates over openness toward, or rejection of, the constitutive laws of others, past and present.

Chapter 3, "Engaging the Constitutive Laws of Others: Necessities, Ideas, Interests," explores a few key junctures in the intellectual history of comparative public law in the early-modern and modern eras. I highlight how the interplay between intellectual inquisitiveness and instrumentalism has influenced many of the field's epistemological leaps, from the first attempts to delineate a universal public law and to study comparative government in a methodical fashion, to the current renaissance of comparative constitutional inquiry. Many political and legal thinkers have contributed to the birth of what is now termed comparative public law. A detailed intellectual history of this field would occupy several volumes and many hundreds of pages, so the analysis here is intentionally stylized and bounded in scope. To that end, I focus on several pre-eminent figures and substantive transformations, each of which exemplifies the main intellectual and political challenges of its time.

Following the early engagements of religious legal systems with comparative challenges, our intellectual journey fast-tracks to early modern Europe. Here the changing political and intellectual landscape led thinkers such as Jean Bodin, Francis Bacon, Hugo Grotius, Samuel von Pufendorf, John Selden, Gottfried Wilhelm Leibniz, Gottfried Achenwall, and notably Montesquieu to take an interest in comparing the laws of nations in a systematic way. I start by examining the epistemological and methodological innovation in the early-modern public law comparisons of Jean Bodin (16th century), John Selden (17th century), and Montesquieu (18th century), all of whom emerged in and responded to a monarchical setting troubled by political instability and religious transformation. Bodin's *Six livres de la république* (*Six Books of the Commonwealth*, 1576), Selden's *De Iure Naturali et Gentium Juxta Desciplinam Ebraeorum* (*On Natural Law and Nations, according to the Teaching of the Jews*, 1640), and Montesquieu's *Lettres persanes* (*Persian Letters*, 1721) and *De l'esprit des lois* (*The Spirit of the Laws*, 1748) are all masterpieces (some acknowledged more than others) of early comparative public law scholarship. I then move on to the early 19th century, an age of nationalism and modern state formation. There emerged at this time much interest in constitutions as effective means of social and political design. Perhaps no one represents this era of constitutional thought better than Simón Bolívar, the great liberator of Spanish South America, an influential figure in the framing of a host of independence constitutions in Latin America, and one of the first political leaders of the new era to devote considerable thought to the reconciliation of local traditions with foreign constitutional models.

The chapter continues its intellectual journey into the 20th century—an era dominated by the global spread of constitutional courts, judicial review, and bills of rights as the centerpieces of the comparative constitutional universe. The voluminous scholarship on these matters is written predominantly from an American or European standpoint. However, it is the less-often studied Canadian constitutional landscape that provides a paradigmatic illustration of all the embodiments and preoccupations of comparative constitutionalism in the past century. Canada entered the 20th century as a living exemplar of deferential, British-style constitutional tradition; it emerged out of that century with a very different constitutional culture, featuring active judicial review, an acclaimed constitutional bill of rights (the Charter of Rights and Freedoms), a pervasive rights discourse, and one of the most frequently cited peak courts in the world. What is more, as part of its 1982 constitutional revolution, constitutional innovations such as a commitment to bilingualism, multiculturalism, indigenous peoples' rights, proportionality (via the Charter's section 1, the "limitation clause"), and majority rule (via section 33, the "override clause") were introduced, and later analyzed and emulated abroad. Canada's transformed constitutional terrain, and its reflection of changing Canadian politics and society, thus serves as the fifth focal point of my thumbnail history of modern constitutional comparisons. (The reader may think of this choice as akin to the award of the Nobel Peace Prize to an institution or organization—say *Médecins Sans Frontières*—rather than to an individual). I close the chapter with an account of the current controversy in the United States concerning reference to constitutional jurisprudence of other countries. Three forces become significant here: the 'inevitability of encounters with foreign legal materials in an age of globalization; the tremendous brainpower of the American legal academia; and, above all, the deep political divide in contemporary United States. These three forces, I argue, have converged to generate a vehement debate about the status of comparative constitutional law in a polity that sees its own constitution as one of its most revered markers of collective identity. The contrast between the Canadian openness toward comparative constitutional endeavors and the contentious American approach to that same enterprise serves to illustrate that ultimately attitudes toward the "laws of others" reflect social processes, political ideologies, and national meta-narratives that are broader than the constitutional sphere itself.

These examples all illustrate that comparative constitutional inquiry is best understood as being driven by a combination of intellectual innovation and a compatible political agenda or ideological outlook— what I have earlier termed the trio of necessity, inquisitiveness, and politics. In some instances, intellectual pursuit led the way with an instrumentalist goal or ideological agenda providing added impetus. In other instances, comparative constitutional inquiry was more directly driven by political interests, ambitions, and aspirations, writ small or large.

The journey continues in Chapter 4, "From Comparative Constitutional Law to Comparative Constitutional Studies." Here I argue for an interdisciplinary approach to comparative constitutional inquiry that is methodologically and substantively preferable to mere doctrinal accounts. In a nutshell, I suggest that for historical, analytical, and methodological reasons, maintaining the disciplinary divide between comparative constitutional law and other closely related disciplines that study various aspects of the same constitutional phenomena artificially and unnecessarily limits our horizons. It also restricts the kind of questions we ask as well as the range of answers we are able to provide. The traditional disciplinary boundaries, both substantive and methodological, between comparative (public) law and the social sciences continue to impede the development of comparative constitutional studies as an ambitious, coherent, and theoretically robust area of inquiry. To establish a stable, thriving research tradition in an interdisciplinary endeavor, we should strive to construct "shared, enduring, foundational commitments to a set of beliefs about what sorts of entities and processes make up the domain of inquiry; and to a set of epistemic and methodological norms about how the domain is to be investigated, how theories are to be tested, how data are to be collected, and the like."[5]

Heart health has more to it than mere anatomy, consisting as it does of far more than its sum of arteries, valves, and atriums. It involves interconnected physiological systems and complex biochemistry, genetics, preventive medicine, and healthy lifestyle. Car production is not merely assembling a collection of gears, engines, and chassis. It is also a matter of design and style, energy consumption, comfort, pricing, and marketing. Comparative constitutional law professors, to follow the metaphor, will continue to hold a professional advantage in their ability to identify, dissect, and scrutinize the work of courts and to critically assess the persuasive power of a given judge's opinion. No one is better positioned than they are to trace the relationship between patterns of convergence and the persisting divergence in constitutional jurisprudence across polities, or to advance the research on how constitutional courts interact with the broader, transnational legal environment within which an increasing number of them operate. But theorizing about the constitutional domain as part of the outer world requires more than this. It requires the study of judicial behaviour (an overwhelming body of evidence suggests that extrajudicial factors play a key role in constitutional court decision-making); an understanding of the origins of constitutional change and stalemate (a variety of theories point to the significant role of ideational and strategic factors in both); the promises and pitfalls of various constitutional designs (the relevance of the social, political, and cultural context in settings where such designs are deployed is obvious); and the study of the actual capacity of constitutional jurisprudence to induce real, on-the-ground change, independently or in association with other factors (the social sciences are essential for studying the actual effects of constitutions beyond the courtroom). Above all, the field's potential to produce generalizable conclusions, or other forms of nomothetic, presumably transportable

[5] Larry Laudan, *Beyond Positivism and Relativism: Theory, Method, and Evidence* (Westview, 1996), 83; cited in Rudra Sil and Peter J. Katzenstein, "Analytic Eclecticism in the Study of World Politics: Reconfiguring Problems and Mechanisms across Research Traditions," *Perspectives on Politics* 8 (2010): 411–31, 413.

knowledge requires familiarity with basic concepts of social science research design and case-selection principles.

Many of the tools needed to engage in the systematic study of constitutionalism across polities can be found in the social sciences. Despite (or perhaps because of) bitter debates about approaches and methods, the social sciences have developed a rich and sophisticated framework for guiding serious comparative work. A close look at the philosophical foundations of comparative social research and the gamut of pertinent social science methods and approaches could suggest a toolkit of methodological considerations essential to comparative constitutional inquiry. It would effectively support a spectrum of comparative constitutional studies, qualitative and quantitative, inference-oriented or hermeneutic.

In fact, I would argue that for both analytical and methodological reasons there cannot be a coherent positivist (as in "is," not "ought") study of comparative constitutional law without the social sciences in general, and political science in particular. I suggest that the time has come to go beyond analyses of court rulings (or comparative constitutional *law*) toward a more holistic approach to the study of constitutions across polities (comparative constitutional *studies*). The intellectual foundations of such an approach are already in place; indeed, a close look at the "cosmology" of comparative constitutional studies as reflected in the seminal works of many of its grandmasters indicates that comparative constitutionalism as an area of inquiry is at its best when it crosses disciplinary boundaries in both substance and method.

Chapter 5, "How Universal is Comparative Constitutional Law?" addresses two issues at the heart of comparative constitutional law's epistemological and methodological domain. First, I consider the very possibility of transhistorical and transgeographical comparisons of constitutional law and institutions. In particular, I am thinking here of the debate between "universalists," who emphasize the common elements of legal (and constitutional) systems across time and place, and "particularists" who emphasize the unique and idiosyncratic nature of any given legal (and constitutional) system. Second, I consider the "global south" critique in comparative constitutional law. Or, put differently, how truly "comparative," universal, or generalizable are the lessons of a body of knowledge that draws almost exclusively on a small—and not necessarily representative—set of frequently studied jurisdictions and court rulings to advance what is portrayed as general knowledge.

The debate between "universalists" (who emphasize the common and the similar among legal systems) and "particularists" (who pay heed to the unique and different in each system) has long plagued the field of comparative law; it has been debated using hyperbolic terms, often ad nauseam, and at times at the expense of generating actual comparative law scholarship per se. In comparative constitutional law, things have developed in a more productive direction. From the cultural defense in criminal law to dilemmas of religious accommodation, tensions between general norms and local traditions have been centrally featured in jurisprudence, constitutional or otherwise. Supranational tribunals and quasi-constitutional entities such as the European Court of Human Rights and the Court of Justice of the European Union make a living out of adjudicating particularism-versus-universalism conundrums. Meanwhile, within the world of new constitutionalism, we see a substantial convergence and consequent increase in similarity of constitutional ideas, structures, and practices; at the same time we observe patterns of persisting divergence among constitutional systems. This has created ideal, living laboratory-like conditions for comparative constitutional scholarship. There is now sufficient unity within the constitutional universe to allow for credible comparisons, combined with a healthy measure of plurality that makes comparisons meaningful and worthwhile.

As any North American sports fan knows, the finals of Major League Baseball is called rather boldly "The World Series." In the second part of this chapter, I address what may be termed the "World Series" syndrome in comparative constitutional law: the presumption that insights based on the constitutional experience of a small set of "usual suspect" settings—all prosperous, stable constitutional democracies of the "global north"—are truly representative of the wide variety of constitutional experiences worldwide, and constitute a "gold standard" for its understanding and assessment. In this section, I unpack and evaluate the various claims raised by proponents of such a "global south" critique of comparative constitutional law, and assess the relevance of each of these claims to the epistemological and methodological challenges of comparative constitutional inquiry.

From this, other questions follow. Might it be that the focus on the constitutional "north" betrays not only certain epistemological and methodological choices but also a normative preference for some concrete set of values the northern setting is perceived to uphold? I suggest that it does, absolutely. The near-exclusive focus on a dozen liberal democracies in comparative constitutional law reflects the field's deep liberal bent. But moving away from its normative facet to the positivist, real-life one, the relevance of the global south critique becomes more qualified. Does the selective "northern" (or "western") emphasis in comparative constitutional law limit the applicability or value of canonical scholarship in the field? I argue that the answer hinges on the specific question that is being posed. A given constitutional setting may belong to the "global south" in one context or comparative dimension, but not in another.

Chapter 6, "Case Selection and Research Design in Comparative Constitutional Studies," continues the critical examination of the field's epistemology and methodologies by addressing three additional aspects. I identify the various meanings, purposes, and modes of comparative inquiry in contemporary comparative constitutional studies. Importantly, I argue that while each of the purposes and modes of this inquiry is useful and advances knowledge in an important way, shifting from engagement with a given purpose of comparative work to engaging with another requires thoughtful adjustment of case-selection principles. I go on to suggest that while the study of comparative constitutional law has generated sophisticated taxonomies, concept formations that lead to theory building, and valuable normative accounts of comparative constitutionalism, it has for the most part fallen short of advancing knowledge through inference-oriented, controlled comparison that permits both in-depth understanding of the studied phenomena and the development of general explanatory principles.

I further discuss a few basic principles of case selection that may be employed in inference-oriented small-N studies in the field of comparative constitutional studies: (i) the "most similar cases" principle; (ii) the "most different cases" principle; (iii) the "prototypical cases" principle; (iv) the "most difficult case" principle; and (v) the "outlier cases" principle. While commonly deployed in comparative politics, these case-selection principles are often overlooked in comparative studies of constitutional law. I subsequently illustrate the successful application of these principles by examining a few recently published and genuinely comparative works dealing with the foundations, practice, and consequences of constitutionalization worldwide. Comparative constitutional scholarship that strives to advance causal arguments, I argue, should look more like these works.

Finally, I explore the emerging world of multivariate, large-N studies of comparative constitutionalism. The trend of works that attempt to capture the commonalities of the constitutional universe by drawing on statistical analyses of large data sets, Bayesian probability, and correlation is still in its early days. It may be argued that these studies suffer from most of the shortcomings of a-contextual social science, and may be seen by those who favor historical or cultural explanations as being overly shallow. But for the intellectually curious observer, large-N studies appear to introduce a novel, refreshing dimension to comparative constitutional studies. One reason for this is that these studies often make a conscious effort to avoid conflating positive ("factual") and normative claims. They also pay close attention to research design, formulation of hypotheses, and data analysis. Perhaps most importantly, by treating constitutional law as a universal phenomenon with multiple manifestations worldwide, these studies signal a departure from the field's traditional overreliance on a handful of frequently discussed examples. The result is that this mode of comparative constitutional inquiry empirically tests some of the core insights of post-WWII constitutional theory.

No research method enjoys an a priori advantage over any other without taking into account the scope and nature of the studied phenomenon or the question the research purports to address. For this reason, I argue that attempts to outline an "official" comparative method, or calls for the adoption of a stringent, "correct" approach to research methods, are not only unrealistic but also unwise. I argue that, by way of an alternative, comparative constitutionalists should settle on a set of four more sensible guiding principles: scholars should: (i) define clearly the study's aim—descriptive, taxonomical, explanatory, and/or normative; (ii) articulate clearly the study's intended level of generalization and applicability, which may range from the most context-specific to the most universal and abstract; (iii) encourage methodological pluralism and analytical eclecticism when appropriate; and (iv) ensure that the research design and methods of comparison reflect the analytical aims or intellectual goals of specific studies, so that a rational, analytically adaptive connection exists between the research questions and the comparative methods used. The Epilogue, "Comparative Constitutional Studies: Quo Vadis?," brings together the main elements of the book—past and present, near and far—in order to assess the challenges that must be overcome for the 21st century to live up to its billing as the "era of comparative law," and in particular as the era of comparative public law.

These are far from purely academic matters. Today, comparative study has emerged as the new frontier of constitutional law scholarship as well as being an important aspect of constitutional adjudication. Increasingly, jurists, scholars, legislators, and constitution drafters worldwide are accepting that "we are all comparativists now." Precisely because the concern with the a-systematic "cherry-picking" of "friendly" examples (often raised by opponents of comparative inquiry) may not be easily dismissed, those who wish to engage in valuable comparative work ought to pay closer attention to research methods, and the philosophy of comparative inquiry more broadly. The response to the "cherry-picking" concern is not to abandon comparative work; rather, it is to engage in comparative work while being mindful of key historical foundations, epistemological directions, and methodological considerations.

This book, then, aims to fill a critical gap by charting the intellectual history and philosophical underpinnings of comparative constitutional inquiry, and by probing the different types, purposes, meanings, and methodologies of engagement with the constitutive laws of others through the ages. It explores how and why comparative constitutional inquiry has been, and ought to be, pursued by academics and jurists worldwide. I then consider a few key junctures in the intellectual history of comparative public law in the early-modern and modern eras, highlighting how the interplay between intellectual inquisitiveness and instrumentalism has influenced many of the field's epistemological leaps, from its early attempts to delineate a universal public law and study comparative government in a methodical fashion to the current renaissance of comparative constitutional inquiry. It is my keen hope that what follows will make a contribution to the comparative study of constitutional law and courts, as well as to our understanding of the historical development and political parameters of one of the most intellectually vibrant subjects in contemporary public law.

1

The View from the Bench

Where the Comparative Judicial Imagination Travels

"Every time I describe a city I am saying something about Venice"
Marco Polo to Kublai Khan (Italo Calvino, *Invisible Cities*)

The rise of a global constitutional dialogue, and the corresponding emergence of an international epistemic community of courts and judges, is a phenomenon that has attracted much attention among scholars and jurists alike. Whether there has been a significant increase in foreign citations in recent years is an open question; the empirical data concerning the actual scope and nature of these trends is inconclusive and quite thin considering the normative polemics and scholarly buzz the phenomenon has attracted of late. One thing is clear, however: comparative constitutional law is at least as much a judge-made enterprise as it is an academic one. In this chapter, I explore how constitutional courts and judges—the key purveyors and consumers of comparative constitutional jurisprudence—conceive of the discipline of comparative constitutional law. To this end, I will detail the methods they use to engage with it, as well as how and why they vary in their approach to it. I will also discuss which countries and courts are typically cited and relied upon, and by whom. In other words, I will track where and how the judicial imagination travels in its search for comparative reference, while teasing out why it travels where it does.

I address these questions in three steps. First, I outline the key empirical findings on foreign citations and examine what these findings may tell us with respect to *how* and *why* constitutional courts engage with comparative constitutional law. The evidence with respect to foreign citation patterns is surprisingly scarce, and draws on the experience of only a handful of peak courts.[1] It suggests that certain courts refer to foreign jurisprudence more frequently than others. It shows that there are areas of constitutional jurisprudence—most notably rights—where cross-jurisdictional reference is more likely to occur than it is in areas such as the more aspirational or organic (e.g. structural or separation of powers) features of the constitution, where national idiosyncrasies and contingencies are more prevalent. The evidence also points to a decline in the status of British and American constitutional cases as common points of reference for constitutional courts worldwide, and perhaps to a corresponding rise in the international stature of other peak courts, most notably the Supreme Court of Canada, the German Federal Constitutional Court, and the European Court of Human Rights. With respect to the "global constitutional dialogue" phenomenon, the literature offers a number of explanations, most notably: global convergence and the inevitability of engagement with foreign jurisprudence in an era of globalization and increased inter-connectivity;[2] instrumentalism (e.g. reference to foreign law as an authority- or legitimacy-enhancing practice, or as an efficient cost-reducing means);[3] the importance of the professional networks that judges operate in (e.g. judicial urge to join or be associated with an international epistemic community of cosmopolitan jurists);[4] and structural features (e.g. constitutional provisions that call for foreign citations, linguistic permeability, or a legal tradition or trajectory of legal education that affects a given apex court's ability and willingness to cite foreign jurisprudence).[5] Whereas these accounts provide illuminating explanations for the rise and variance in the practice of global judicial dialogue, they leave out a crucial factor: the sociopolitical context within which constitutional courts and judges operate, and how this

---

[1] For an initial assessment of foreign citation trends and their possible causes, see Christopher McCrudden, "A Common Law of Human Rights? Transnational Judicial Conversations on Constitutional Rights," *Oxford Journal of Legal Studies* 20 (2000): 499–532.

[2] See, e.g., Mark Tushnet, "The Inevitable Globalization of Constitutional Law," *Virginia Journal of International Law* 49 (2009): 985–1006.

[3] See, e.g., P. K. Tripathi, "Foreign Precedents and Constitutional Law," *Columbia Law Review* 57 (1957): 319–47.

[4] Anne-Marie Slaughter, "A Typology of Transjudicial Communication," *University of Richmond Law Review* 29 (1994): 99–137; Anne-Marie Slaughter, "A Global Community of Courts," *Harvard International Law Journal* 44 (2003): 191–219.

[5] David Law and Wen-Chen Chang, "The Limits of Global Judicial Dialogue," *Washington University Law Review* 86 (2011): 523–77.

affects whether and where the judicial mind travels in its search for pertinent foreign sources to reference.[6]

In the realm of voluntary reference to foreign law, judicial choices as to what to cite and what not to cite cannot be understood in isolation from the views of constitutional courts and judges with respect to the interplay between the "domestic" and the "foreign," the "particular" and the "universal," the "traditional" and the "modern." What constitutional courts and judges regard as "relevant" or "irrelevant" sources of reference reflects in no small part their vision of a concrete set of values they wish their country to be associated with and the "right" club of nations to which they prefer their country to belong. In other words, a court's position and how it views its role with respect to sociopolitical struggles over the polity's collective identity is at least as significant a factor in explaining judicial choices of foreign reference as any structural, linguistic, or legal factor. Voluntary reference to foreign precedents is at least as much a political phenomenon as it is a juridical one.

In the chapter's second part, I explore in considerable detail patterns of foreign reference in Israel—a perfectly situated constitutional jurisdiction for the purposes of our discussion. Israel is a bastion of Western constitutional thought in the Middle East, as well as a country that has long been torn between its particular ("Jewish") and universal ("democratic") aspirations. Importantly, Israel's legal system is informed by both an amalgam of legal traditions (largely common law, with facets of civil and Ottoman law) and the presence of legislated jurisdictional enclaves for recognized religious communities, so that the Israeli legal system reflects the territory's rich legal history and the polity's diverse demographic composition. Israel's leading jurists have long been well-versed in German and American legal thought, and the Supreme Court of Israel was led until recently by CJ Aharon Barak—one of the most prominent jurists in Israel's history, a leading intellectual in the comparative constitutional world, and a member of honor in the emerging global epistemic community of judges.

---

[6] See Gary J. Jacobsohn, "The Permeability of Constitutional Borders," *Texas Law Review* 82 (2004): 1763–819. Jacobsohn argues that proper constitutional borrowing requires careful consideration of the social and political contexts of *both* of the countries involved. This is so because constitutional arrangements are "manifestations of key attributes of national identity." In his view, this does not outright preclude constitutional borrowing, but rather is an important consideration that must always inform it.

The Supreme Court of Israel regularly refers to case law and scholarly commentary from the United States, Canada, Germany, the United Kingdom, and various European and international sources of law. However, it seldom refers to countries, such as India, that share a similar experience of identity-based and ethnic–religious rifts. Likewise, it rarely, if ever, cites rulings by the national high courts of Pakistan, Turkey, Malaysia, or Ireland even though the tensions between secularism and religiosity in these countries' constitutional landscapes resemble tensions embedded in Israel's self-definition as a "Jewish and democratic" state.[7] It is equally telling that Israeli secular judges (who represent the vast majority of those appointed to the bench) hardly ever treat Jewish law as a relevant source of comparative insight, despite Israel being the sole Jewish country in existence, the explicit constitutional emphasis of the country's Jewish character, and the fact that Jewish law is one of the main sources to which the law itself refers judges when they encounter a lacuna.[8] Instead, the typical secular Israeli judge prefers to look to "the West" as a source of comparative and international law, and in doing so to affirm the state's desire to be included in the liberal-democratic club of nations. As I show later, similar trends manifest themselves in other constitutionally discordant settings, including Pakistan, Turkey, Malaysia, and India, where peak court judges are frequently called upon to determine disputes that deal with foundational state and religion, and broader national identity, dilemmas. Their choices of which foreign precedent or persuasive authority to turn to from abroad, and which to reject, denote not only legal doctrinal considerations but also the judges' positionality in their own respective society, and their view of its place in the world.

These choices reflect considerable case selection biases ("cherry-picking") and other methodological difficulties. They also raise vital questions concerning how "comparative" a practice really is that draws on the constitutional experience of a small group of mostly liberal-democratic countries but seldom refers to constitutional experience, law, and institutions elsewhere. Above all, the selective choices made by judges provide a rare insight into where the judicial imagination

---

[7] For further discussion, see Ran Hirschl, *Constitutional Theocracy* (Harvard University Press, 2010).

[8] See *Hok Yesodot Ha'Mishpat* ("Act for the Foundations of Law"), 1980 [Israel], discussed later in greater detail.

travels when it seeks to find instructive comparative cases to serve as persuasive authority in resolving a specific dispute. As I hope to show, the "identity" dimension—the attempt to define who "we" are as a political community, and to articulate in a public way what "our image" or "place" in the world is or should be—inevitably influences comparative jurisprudence and acts as a key factor explaining judicial choices of reference sources.[9] Instances of strategic, ad hoc judicial recourse to foreign law (e.g. Romania, Uganda) are obviously inseparable from the concrete political settings within which they take place. In post-authoritarian or newly created constitutional settings (e.g. South Africa, Timor-Leste), such choices can signal a judicial commitment to breaking with a nation's less-than-dazzling past or to belong to a certain group of polities. They may likewise help courts and their backers to advance certain worldviews and policy preferences that may be otherwise contested in majoritarian decision-making arenas. More than anything else, the foreign references that courts in discordant constitutional settings—the focus on my analysis in this chapter—select, reject, or ignore reflect the judicial position and aspiration vis-à-vis the nation's contested collective identity quandaries.

The empirical dimension: what is actually known about patterns of foreign reference?

Before we proceed any further, two key distinctions must be made. First, cross-jurisdictional constitutional "pollination" can refer to three different objects of migration: constitutional structure—the very architecture of a given constitutional system and its organs; constitutional methods—interpretive techniques and modes of analysis (e.g. originalism, purposive interpretation, proportionality); and comparative jurisprudence—concrete constitutional court rulings, precedents, and legal analysis. I will touch upon the diffusion of constitutional structures and design in Chapter 4. The migration of interpretive methods evades easy delineation for a host of definitional, methodological, and operational reasons; at any rate, observers agree that "virtually every effective system of constitutional justice in the world with the partial

---

[9] On the identity dimension, see Jacobsohn, "The Permeability of Constitutional Borders" (n 6); and more generally, Gary J. Jacobsohn, *Constitutional Identity* (Harvard University Press, 2010).

exception of the United States has embraced the main tenets of proportionality analysis," so that proportionality has become "a foundational tenet of global constitutionalism."[10] To maximize the intellectual yield of the analysis, I focus on the main component of the actual international migration of constitutional ideas: judicial reference to foreign constitutional jurisprudence.

Second, there are several types of recourse to foreign law by courts: mandatory or binding use of foreign law (e.g. when courts are legally obliged to use foreign legal rules or to follow rulings of foreign tribunals in a domestic forum); advisable but non-binding use of foreign law (e.g. when the foreign law has clear normative and reputational value that makes reference to it alluring, as with, for example, international human rights norms); and voluntary or optional use of foreign law (e.g. where there is no requirement, expectation, or authority in the domestic legal order for the reference to foreign law, but it is made nonetheless).[11] In the latter scenario, foreign law may be used as a "persuasive authority" or an interpretive aid (so that the ruling does not appear arbitrary), as a testament to a given rule's functionality in other jurisdictions, as a benchmark against which to compare a given constitutional system's take on the issue at stake, or simply for "beautification" or "decorative" purposes.[12] The discussion herein addresses this third type of recourse to the laws of others: *voluntary* reference to the constitutional jurisprudence of other polities.

Despite the ever-increasing interest in the international migration of constitutional ideas, detailed analyses of the practice of constitutional court recourse to foreign sources—including a breakdown of precisely which countries' courts are cited the most or the least by other high courts—are quite difficult to come by. Very little is known about the scope of the practice in entire regions, most notably Latin America, Africa, and large parts of Asia, a point which I will return to in Chapter 5. However, initial insights into the changing patterns of non-binding foreign reference are now available in about a dozen

[10] Alec Stone Sweet and Jud Mathews, "Proportionality Balancing and Global Constitutionalism," *Columbia Journal of Transnational Law* 47 (2008): 73–165. See generally, Aharon Barak, *Proportionality: Constitutional Rights and their Limitations* (Cambridge University Press, 2012).
[11] For a detailed and illuminating discussion of this typology, see Michal Bobek, *Comparative Reasoning in European Supreme Courts* (Oxford University Press, 2013), 19–35.
[12] The term "persuasive authority" is drawn from H. Patrick Glenn, "Persuasive Authority," *McGill Law Journal* 32 (1987): 261–98.

countries, and this is a fast-growing and proliferating area of comparative constitutional research.

It has become a near-cliché to mention that in its landmark 1995 ruling determining the unconstitutionality of the death penalty, in the *Makwanyane* case, the newly established South African Constitutional Court examined in detail pertinent jurisprudence from Botswana, Canada, Germany, Hong Kong, Hungary, India, Jamaica, Tanzania, the United States, Zimbabwe, the European Court of Human Rights, and the United Nations Committee on Human Rights.[13] In total, it refers to no fewer than 220 foreign case citations from 11 national and three supranational courts.[14] This seems indicative of a broader pattern; foreign law has been cited or referenced in more than half of the South African Constitutional Court rulings since 1994.[15] Observers often point out that Section 39 of the South African Constitution explicitly permits courts to look to foreign jurisprudence and in fact mandates that they consult international law when dealing with rights cases. It is hardly surprising that Justice Dikgang Moseneke, Deputy Chief Justice of South Africa, stated in 2010 that: "[I]t is no exaggeration to observe that our decisions read like works of comparative constitutional law and where appropriate we have not avoided relying on foreign judicial dicta or academic legal writings in support of the reasoning we resort to or conclusions we reach."[16] Even the US Supreme Court—often considered (though perhaps incorrectly) the last bastion of principled resistance to foreign citations among the world's leading national high courts—has hesitantly joined the comparative reference trend. As is well known, in several rulings rendered since the turn of the century, most notably *Lawrence v. Texas* (2003) and *Roper v. Simmons* (2005), the

---

[13] *S v. Makwanyane*, 1995 (3) SA 391 (CC) [South Africa].

[14] See generally, Christa Rautenbach and Lourens du Plessis, "In the Name of Comparative Constitutional Jurisprudence: The Consideration of German Precedents by South Africa Constitutional Court Judges," *German Law Journal* 14 (2013): 1539–77.

[15] Ursula Bentele, "Mining for Gold: The Constitutional Court of South Africa's Experience with Comparative Constitutional Law," *Georgia Journal of International and Comparative Law* 37 (2009): 219–40.

[16] Dikgang Moseneke, "The Role of Comparative and Public International Law in Domestic Legal Systems: A South African Perspective," *Advocate* (Dec. 2010), 63–6, 63. Moseneke went on to suggest (at 65) that: "it is fair to say that our burgeoning jurisprudence owes much debt to judicial reasoning emanating from other democratic jurisdictions and in particular, the Commonwealth, the European Court of Human Rights, the European Court of Justice and certain African jurisdictions."

US Supreme Court's majority cited foreign judgments to support their decisions.[17]

On the supply side, too, things appear to have changed considerably. In 1957, Indian scholar P. K. Tripathi astutely observed (in a piece published in the prestigious Columbia Law Review) that as of the mid-20th century, the main point of foreign reference had shifted from the United Kingdom to the United States, even in former British colonies such as Australia, Canada, and India, and the territories under its rule such as Israel.[18] Over half a century later, there seems to have been yet another shift, this time around a decline (the extent of which is not entirely clear) in the significance of American constitutional jurisprudence overseas.[19] Some studies suggest that landmark judgments such as *Brown v. Board of Education* are referenced by only a small number of apex courts (e.g. in South Africa, India, Canada, and Israel), mainly to help to justify the transformative role of those courts in equality-related matters.[20] Other studies identify an increasing reference to certain elements of American constitutional jurisprudence as negative examples used by courts for distinction and contrast purposes.[21] At any rate, it is safe to say that the current "global market" of citation sources offers considerably more choices to potential "consumers" than was the case 50 years ago. Accordingly, the Supreme Court of Canada, the German Federal Constitutional Court, and the European Court of Human Rights have emerged as three of the most frequently cited courts in the world. In New Zealand, for instance, Canadian decisions were cited far more than those of any other nation in civil rights cases.[22] The Chief Justice

---

[17] *Lawrence v. Texas*, 539 U.S. 558 (2003) [United States]; *Roper v. Simmons*, 543 U.S. 551 (2005) [United States]. In *Atkins v. Virginia*, 536 U.S. 304 (2002) [United States], the majority opinion referred in a footnote to an amicus brief by the European Union. The reference supported a factual statement that: "within the world community, the imposition of the death penalty for crimes committed by mentally retarded offenders is overwhelmingly disapproved."

[18] Tripathi, "Foreign Precedents and Constitutional Law" (n 3).

[19] David Law and Mila Versteeg, "The Declining Influence of the United States Constitution," *NYU Law Review* 87 (2012): 762–858.

[20] See Sheldon B. Lyke, "Brown Abroad: An Empirical Analysis of Foreign Judicial Citation and the Metaphor of Cosmopolitan Conversation," *Vanderbilt Journal of Transnational Law* 45 (2012): 83–144.

[21] Sujit Choudhry, "The Lochner Era and Comparative Constitutionalism," *I-CON International Journal of Constitutional Law* 2 (2004): 1–55; Kim Lane Scheppele, "Aspirational and Aversive Constitutionalism: The Case for Studying Cross-Constitutional Influence through Negative Models," *I-CON International Journal of Constitutional Law* 1 (2003): 296–324.

[22] James Allan et al., "The Citation of Overseas Authority in Rights Litigation in New Zealand: How Much Bark? How Much Bite?," *Otago Law Review* 11 (2007): 433–69.

of the Supreme Court of Canada recently observed that "Canadian decisions are routinely cited by courts in South Africa, New Zealand, Israel, the United Kingdom, Australia and India, and by the European Court of Human Rights."[23] The Supreme Court of Canada itself used to cite decisions of the American Supreme Court approximately a dozen times a year, but over the recent years the annual citation rate has fallen by more than half, reflecting both the declining relevance of the jurisprudence of the latter and the increasing confidence of the former.[24]

But let us delve deeper into the concrete evidence on reference to foreign law. A familiar starting point is the United States. There, David Zaring's extensive study of the foreign citation practices of all federal American courts supports the general notion that American courts are reluctant to refer to foreign case law.[25] Zaring's central conclusion is that foreign citations are rare and that their effect on case outcomes is negligible: "American courts rarely cite foreign courts," he writes, "they do so no more now than they did in the past, and on those few occasions where they do cite foreign courts, it is usually not to help them interpret domestic law."[26] Zaring reports that between 1995 and 2006, "the federal courts [in all districts] made 145 foreign citations in total." Interestingly, he finds that the courts most likely to cite foreign decisions were the Supreme Court and the lower federal courts based in New York City (Zaring does not speculate on why this is the case, but it may well be, one might think, that the New York area's self-professed cosmopolitanism is among the reasons for this trend).[27] In keeping with patterns of voluntary reference to foreign law elsewhere, Zaring finds that "the courts most likely to be cited were those from Canada and Western Europe."[28]

---

[23] Beverley McLachlin, "The Canadian Charter of Rights and Freedoms' First 30 Years: A Good Beginning," in Errol Mendes and Stephane Beaulac, eds., *Canadian Charter of Rights and Freedoms* (5th edn, LexisNexis, 2013), 41.

[24] Adam Liptak, "U.S. Court is Now Guiding Fewer Nations," *New York Times* (Sept. 17, 2008). See also Gianluca Gentili, "Canada: Protecting Rights in a Worldwide Rights Culture," in Tania Groppi and Marie-Claire Ponthoreau, eds., *The Use of Foreign Precedents by Constitutional Judges* (Hart Publishing, 2013), 39–67.

[25] David Zaring, "The Use of Foreign Decisions by Federal Courts: An Empirical Analysis," *Journal of Empirical Legal Studies* 3 (2006): 297–331.

[26] Zaring, "The Use of Foreign Decisions by Federal Courts" (n 25), 298.

[27] Zaring, "The Use of Foreign Decisions by Federal Courts" (n 25), 303.

[28] Zaring, "The Use of Foreign Decisions by Federal Courts" (n 25).

Calabresi and Zindahl examine in detail the US Supreme Court's citation of foreign law from 1789 through 2005.[29] They notice that the Court tends to turn to foreign sources of law in certain cases in particular: when it must make a determination of reasonableness; when it faces "the problem of making sense of an ambiguous phrase"; when it seeks to provide "logical reinforcement for its decisions"; and when it seeks "to provide empirical support for assertions that are made about the likely consequences of legal reforms that are being advocated for the United States."[30] The authors conclude that the Court's citation of foreign sources of law in recent years is not "unprecedented," but is increasing in the modern era in ways that they view as quite problematic.

It should be noted, however, that what Calabresi and Zindahl describe as a "dramatic increase in the frequency with which the Court turns to foreign sources of law, especially in the realm of the criminal law, and in progressively more controversial and ground-breaking cases" amounts to less than two dozen decisions that refer to foreign law over a 65-year period (1940–2005)—a small fraction of the thousands of cases decided by the US Supreme Court over that period, and a very low number compared to most other leading apex courts. Indeed, a more recent study of foreign citation patterns in the Court concludes that the practice is very rare. References to foreign precedents were found in 0.3 percent of all decisions rendered by the Rehnquist Court (1986–2004), and in no decisions at all from the first few years of the Roberts Court (2005 onward).[31]

The general skepticism in the United States toward foreign citations is also evidenced by the overwhelming reaction of the legal academy and the media to early signs that the US Supreme Court was increasingly citing foreign law. This has led to a vigorous debate (discussed in detail in Chapter 3) among critics—mostly from the political right—and proponents of the practice over the appropriateness and legitimacy

[29] Steven Calabresi and Stephanie Dotson Zimdahl, "The Supreme Court and Foreign Sources of Law: Two Hundred Years of Practice and the Juvenile Death Penalty Decision," *William and Mary Law Review* 47 (2005): 743–910, 753.
[30] Calabresi and Zimdahl, "The Supreme Court and Foreign Sources of Law" (n 29), 784.
[31] Angioletta Sperti, "The United States of America: First Cautious Attempts of Judicial Use of Foreign Precedents in the Supreme Court's Jurisprudence," in Groppi and Ponthoreau, eds., *The Use of Foreign Precedents by Constitutional Judges* (n 24), 393–410.

of the US Supreme Court's reliance on the constitutional jurisprudence of other nations' courts.[32]

In neighboring Canada, there has been considerably less resistance to
foreign citations by the Supreme Court. In fact, the practice has never
been seriously contested within Canada's legal academia, let alone in
the popular media or the broader political sphere. As one observer
suggested: "the Supreme Court of Canada's use of foreign jurisprudence and international instruments in its Charter jurisprudence
reflects an open-minded approach that remains receptive to new
approaches to universal concepts like human rights, even while
remaining strongly grounded in the cultural, historical, and political
particularities of Canada's domestic law."[33] In his comprehensive studies of the Supreme Court of Canada's (SCC's) citation practices from
2000 onward, Peter McCormick concludes that "[t]he McLachlin
Court has made just over 1,500 citations to non-Canadian judicial
authority, this comprising roughly one-tenth of all judicial citations."[34]
The SCC referred to foreign law in three of 12 (25 percent) constitutional cases it addressed during that term; and of the 69 total decisions
rendered by the Court in 2008, 15 (or 22 percent) contained citations
to foreign authorities.[35]

Over 800 of the SCC's foreign citations from 1949 onward were
to UK authority. With respect to citations to the United States,
McCormick observes that "we are seeing less of a sustained intellectual
exploration of American ideas than an occasional selective raid."[36] Of
the 13,602 total citations to judicial authority (including foreign and
domestic) the SCC made between 2000 and 2008, a relatively small
percentage (476 or 3.5 percent) were to American authorities. Whereas

[32] See, e.g., Norman Dorsen, "The Relevance of Foreign Legal Materials in U.S.
Constitutional Cases: A Conversation between Justice Antonin Scalia and Justice Stephen
Breyer," *International Journal of Constitutional Law* 3 (2005): 519–41. See generally, Vicki
Jackson, *Constitutional Engagement in a Transnational Era* (Oxford University Press, 2010).

[33] Bijon Roy, "An Empirical Survey of Foreign Jurisprudence and International Instru-
ments in Charter Litigation," *University of Toronto Faculty of Law Review* 62 (2004): 99–148.
See also C. L. Ostberg, Matthew Wetstein, and Craig R. Ducat, "Attitudes, Precedents and
Cultural Change: Explaining the Citation of Foreign Precedents by the Supreme Court of
Canada," *Canadian Journal of Political Science* 34 (2001): 377–99.

[34] Peter McCormick, "Waiting for Globalization: An Empirical Study of the McLachlin
Court's Foreign Judicial Citations," *Ottawa Law Review* 41 (2009): 209–43.

[35] Adam Dodek, "Comparative Law at the Supreme Court of Canada in 2008: Limited
Engagement and Missed Opportunities," *Supreme Court Law Review* 47 (2009): 445–73, 447.

[36] Peter McCormick, "American Citations and the McLachlin Court: An Empirical
Study," *Osgoode Hall Law Journal* 47 (2009): 83–129.

use of American authority rose sharply in the early Charter era, it "has now fallen back to its modest pre-Charter levels, [the Court's foreign] references failing to reflect more recent American jurisprudence." Claire L'Heureux-Dubé (Justice of the Supreme Court of Canada, 1987–2002) observed that "an informal analysis of Canadian Supreme Court decisions since 1986 revealed that the Rehnquist court was cited in fewer than one-half as many cases as the Warren Court, and in just under one-third the number of Burger Court cases."[37] Citations to authority from countries other than the United Kingdom or the United States, McCormick reports, "have always been present, but they have always occurred at a very modest level...[B]efore the Charter era, they typically accounted for just over one percent of total judicial citations; since then, they comprise just under two per-cent."[38] A more recent survey of SCC foreign citation patterns in constitutional cases reports a total of 1,826 such citations from 1982 to 2010, of which 1,144 (about 62.5 percent) were to US cases, 502 (27.5 percent) to UK cases, and about 10 percent to rulings from other jurisdictions, most notably Australia, New Zealand, and the European Court of Human Rights. The majority of references to American court rulings were made in the first 15 years of the Charter, with a considerable decline in citation of American sources since the late 1990s.[39]

These findings are in line with a broader trend discussed earlier: the waning in global influence of the US Supreme Court. At the same time, American constitutional jurisprudence is still widely cited in most common law countries, including in rarely studied ones such as the Philippines. While it is true that the proliferation of constitutionalism and comparative constitutional jurisprudence has gradually eroded the status of American constitutional law as the ultimate source for constitutional borrowing, the groundbreaking ideas of the Founding Fathers (as expressed in the seminal *Federalist Papers* and elsewhere) are still studied widely worldwide. The limitation of government powers and protection of fundamental civil liberties entrenched in the US Constitution are still considered quintessential tenets of modern constitutionalism. Famous figures of American constitutional theory

---

[37] Claire L'Heureux-Dubé, "The Importance of Dialogue: Globalization and the International Impact of the Rehnquist Court," *Tulsa Law Journal* 34 (1998): 15–40, 29.

[38] McCormick, "Waiting for Globalization" (n 34), 225.

[39] Gianluca Gentili, "Canada: Protecting Rights in a Worldwide Rights Culture," in Groppi and Ponthoreau, eds., *The Use of Foreign Precedents by Constitutional Judges* (n 24), 39–67.

(e.g. Bickel, Ely, Dworkin) are responsible even today for much of what is seen as the global canon of constitutional theory and interpretation. The legacy of the Warren Court era remains widely admired worldwide; in some jurisdictions, *Brown v. Board of Education* (1954) is still a constitutional event of near-mythic proportion, although as mentioned earlier, it is not as frequently cited as the legend may have it. Many US Supreme Court rulings on freedom of expression, property rights, and above all criminal due process protections—think classics such as *Miranda v. Arizona* or *Mapp v. Ohio*—are widely perceived as cornerstones of 20th-century rights jurisprudence.

What is more, American influence over constitutional jurisprudence abroad may also be understood as extending beyond direct citations. It has been argued, for instance, that Canadian constitutional jurisprudence has been characterized by extensive "Americanization" of Canada's rights discourse and of Canada's perception of what makes for a good society.[40] In a similar vein, there seem to be deep ideological links, yet to be fully fleshed out, between the shrinkage of the Keynesian welfare state, lenient regulation, the small-state economic and social thought prevalent in the decades prior to the economic meltdown of 2008, and the conceptualization—prevalent in American constitutional thought—of rights as essentially negative liberties that shield the private sphere from the long arm of the encroaching state. The dominant notion of rights as negative freedoms is based on a view of society as composed of an unencumbered, autonomous, and self-sufficient private sphere, whose members' full realization of freedom is constantly threatened by paternalistic or otherwise unwarranted state intervention. Deregulation and privatization, so-called free and flexible markets (i.e. markets with low wage and welfare safety nets, disincentives for collective bargaining, minimal job security, and removal of trade shields), economic efficiency, and fiscal responsibility (often perceived as a call for reduced public spending on social programs) are all fundamentals of the 1980s and 1990s orthodoxy of economic neo-liberalism. These objectives are rooted in concepts of individualism, social atomism, and existential fear of a big-brother state, all of which inform the current hegemonic discourses of rights.[41] At a deep,

---

[40] See, e.g., David Schneiderman, "Exchanging Constitutions: Constitutional Bricolage in Canada," *Osgoode Hall Law Review* 40 (2002): 401–24.

[41] Joel Bakan, *Just Words: Constitutional Rights and Social Wrongs* (University of Toronto Press, 1997). For a comparative assessment, see Ran Hirschl, *Towards Juristocracy: The Origins and Consequences of the New Constitutionalism* (Harvard University Press, 2004), 100–48.

ideological level, rights talk of the type often associated with American political and constitutional thought appear to have triumphed.[42]

The ostensive decline in direct reference to American constitutional jurisprudence, at least in Canada, Australia, and other similarly situated countries, may also be the result of greater confidence by the borrower side rather than of a decline by the supplier side. We may call it the "jurisprudential maturation" factor: the more established a given constitutional court is or the more developed its jurisprudence, the lesser the likelihood it will refer to foreign precedents. As Aaron Aft argues, "the dip in U.S. citations in [Canada in] the early twenty-first century is better explained by a maturing SCC jurisprudence, rather than an effect caused by U.S. hostility to comparative exercise, or political disagreements."[43] He suggests that "when facing novel constitutional cases, a court might be more inclined to look abroad to more experienced tribunals for guidance. One would anticipate an increase in the citation to the U.S. Supreme Court when addressing novel constitutional instruments or issues, and that such citations would recede in favor of reliance on domestic precedent once it is established."[44]

In his study of the influence of the Canadian Charter in Hong Kong's development of human rights jurisprudence after returning to China in 1997, Simon Young finds support for the "maturation" point.[45] Young speculates that as Hong Kong's rights jurisprudence evolves, thickens, and becomes more confident, reliance on foreign jurisprudence will decline. Canadian influence on Hong Kong's rights jurisprudence has traditionally been strong in part because Canadians were involved in the early days of the Hong Kong Bill of Rights (essentially a transplant of the International Covenant on Civil and Political Rights), which was adopted in 1991. Adding to this is that Hong Kong's post-1997 constitution—the Basic Law—has foreign reference built into it, and includes a mechanism (Section 92) through which judges from other common law jurisdictions can be appointed

---

[42] See, generally, Mary Ann Glendon, *Rights Talk: The Impoverishment of Political Discourse* (Free Press, 1993).

[43] Aaron B. Aft, "Respect My Authority: Analyzing Claims of Diminished U.S. Supreme Court Influence Abroad," *Indiana Journal of Global Legal Studies* 18 (2011): 421–54, 439.

[44] Aft, "Respect My Authority" (n 43), 453.

[45] Simon N. M. Young, "The Canadian Charter of Rights and Freedoms in Hong Kong Jurisprudence," paper presented at the University of Toronto, Faculty of Law, Oct. 12, 2012; on file with author.

by the Chief Executive of Hong Kong to sit on the newly formed
Court of Final Appeal (CFA) alongside the Court's permanent judges.
Thus, Young states, it was unsurprising to find from a review of post-
1997 decisions that when Charter law was cited (in over 40 cases) it was
generally treated positively or neutrally by Hong Kong courts. There
were only a few instances when Charter law was explicitly rejected and
these were generally cases in which the SCC judges were themselves
divided. Charter law has been cited positively in many areas including
constitutional remedies, freedom of expression, freedom of thought,
equality, right to vote, right to counsel, fair trial rights, right to silence,
language rights, and freedom from cruel, inhuman, or degrading
punishment. However, Young finds signs of a recent decline in the
Charter's influence in Hong Kong. Of the 70 CFA human rights
decisions, only 15 (or 21 percent) cited Charter case law, of which
ten showed positive attitudes toward Canadian jurisprudence. And in
the 14 rights cases decided over the 2010–12 period, only two Charter
decisions were cited. This is indicative, Young suggests, of an increasing trend toward a more indigenous approach to rights, due either
to the existence of constitutional problems unique to Hong Kong
(e.g. right of abode cases) or to the tendency to develop a distinct
approach after having canvassed different and varied common law
approaches.

   The maturation effect seems also to be present in continental Europe. Newly established constitutional courts in post-authoritarian or
post-communist Europe make more frequent reference to foreign
precedent that the more established constitutional courts in Europe
(e.g. the German Federal Constitutional Court, the Italian Constitutional Court, or the Austrian Constitutional Court).[46] Roughly similar
evidence emanates from India. Although approximately a quarter of
the 15,000 rulings rendered by the Supreme Court of India from 1950
to 2005 cited foreign sources, the use of foreign jurisprudence has
varied considerably over the years.[47] In fact, the data suggest that the
use of foreign law has undergone a drastic decline: while approximately
65 percent of the Supreme Court of India's rulings relied on foreign

[46] Wen-Chen Chang and Jiunn-Rong Yeh, "The Internationalization of Constitutional
Law," in Michel Rosenfeld and András Sajó, eds., *The Oxford Handbook of Comparative
Constitutional Law* (Oxford University Press, 2012), 1165–84, 1175.

[47] Adam Smith, "Making Itself at Home: Understanding Foreign Law in Domestic
Jurisprudence—The Indian Case," *Berkeley Journal of International Law* 24 (2006): 218–72.

citations in the 1950s, less than 10 percent did so by the mid-1990s. Equally telling is that whereas reference to American constitutional jurisprudence has remained largely unchanged over that period, there has been a constant decline in reference to UK law and jurisprudence—the colonial bedrock of India's legal system. The maturation factor may also explain the resistance to foreign citation by the US Supreme Court—arguably the most established national high court in the world.

Legal tradition (common law, civil law, and so on) offers another explanation for variance in sources of reference. Generally, courts tend to cite rulings from jurisdictions with a legal tradition similar to their own. This is due to the relative equivalence of terms and concepts across jurisdictions that share the same legal tradition, as well as similarities in how they understand the role of the judiciary and the nature of judging.[48] The concept of precedent-following and reference (often leading to analogy, contrast, and modification) has been one of the cornerstones of the common law tradition, and in particular of what may be called Anglo-American law, with British legal tradition at its core. The practice of referring to British precedents was further aided by the legal institutions of colonialism. Beginning in the 19th century, judicial bodies of transnational entities such as the British Commonwealth and the Privy Council resorted to foreign precedents as a matter of common practice. Canada, to pick one example, cut its ties with the Privy Council in 1949; Australia eliminated Privy Council appeals in 1986, although the practice had been practically dead for years before that; New Zealand followed suit in 2004. The Privy Council's extensive reliance on UK precedents "deeply influenced the development of law in countries such as New Zealand, Australia, India, South Africa, Hong Kong, Caribbean countries and Canada, along with other countries in the colonial area of East and Southern Africa."[49] Until the mid-20th century, the Judicial Committee of the Privy Council served as the court of final appeal for British colonies and dominions, a function that it continues to perform with respect to a small number of Caribbean countries. It is thus hardly surprising that cross-reference among peak courts of these countries is quite common.

[48] See, generally, H. Patrick Glenn, *Legal Traditions of the World* (4th edn, Oxford University Press, 2010).
[49] Andrea Lollini, "The South African Constitutional Court Experience: Reasoning Patterns Based on Foreign Law," *Utrecht Law Review* 8 (2012): 55–87, 56.

Cheryl Saunders reports that "foreign law was cited in the majority of constitutional cases decided by the Australian High Court between 1998 and 2008."[50] Nicholas Aroney observes that although the Australian High Court has in recent years become increasingly open to the citation of foreign cases from a range of countries:

British and American case-law has remained easily the most common. Generally speaking, the next most prevalent have been decisions of other countries within or to some extent associated with the British Commonwealth, most notably Canada, India, South Africa and Ireland, followed lastly by jurisprudence of European civil law countries, especially Germany, and the European Union.[51]

Michael Kirby, Justice of the High Court of Australia (1996–2009), confirms that the High Court of Australia often looks to "the Supreme Court of India, or the Court of Appeal in New Zealand or the Constitutional Court of South Africa" for inspiration.[52] Aroney suggests that:

[w]hile proportionately more comparative case law can be found in judgments of the High Court compared to those of the [U.S.] Supreme Court, when the rationales justifying the use of comparative jurisprudence are examined, the differences in attitude are not so great. Both Courts are entirely open to the use of comparative law in the form of the traditional principles of the common law enunciated by English courts.[53]

These findings are confirmed by Russell Smyth's comprehensive study of foreign citations in the Australian State Supreme Courts over the period 1905 to 2005. While there has been a decline in the proportion of English cases cited, says Smyth, "the proportion of citations of foreign precedent from countries other than England has remained consistently low."[54] Smyth suggests that Australian courts cite non-English

---

[50] Cheryl Saunders, "Judicial Engagement with Comparative Law," in Tom Ginsburg and Rosalind Dixon, eds., *Comparative Constitutional Law* (Edward Elgar, 2011), 573.

[51] Nicholas Aroney, "Comparative Law in Australian Constitutional Jurisprudence," *University of Queensland Law Journal* 26 (2007): 317–40, 331.

[52] Michael Kirby, "Think Globally," 4 *Green Bag* 2D, Spring 2001, 287.

[53] Aroney, "Comparative Law in Australian Constitutional Jurisprudence" (n 51), 339.

[54] Russell Smyth, "Citations of Foreign Decisions in Australian State Supreme Courts over the Course of the Twentieth Century: An Empirical Analysis" (June 2008) (unpublished manuscript available at <http://works.bepress.com/russell_smyth/1>).

foreign courts infrequently due to "the different economic and social contexts in which other legal systems are situated," as well as "the pervasive influence of English law."[55]

Michal Bobek's study of foreign citation patterns in the courts of five European countries (England, the Czech Republic, Slovakia, Germany, and France) confirms the significance of the legal tradition factor.[56] Of these five countries, England is the one in which courts are most open to voluntary foreign citations (almost exclusively from other common law countries), whereas France is the least open to such practice, to the extent that it is nearly non-existent. Germany places in between those two ends. Newer constitutional courts (those in the Czech Republic and Slovakia) seem more inclined to refer to foreign law than their more established German counterpart. Overall, Bobek finds that the practice of non-mandatory foreign reference is not as common as a reader of the heated debates about the legitimacy of the practice might be led to believe. Either way, Bobek correctly notes that in deciding a case, a judge on an EU member state high court must consider the constitutional law of her own country, as well as relevant provisions of EU law, the European Convention on Human Rights, and international law, before she can turn her mind to voluntary use of non-binding foreign law.

Support for the legal tradition factor is also found in foreign citation patterns in British courts. At the UK Supreme Court, Elaine Mak finds, "the first criterion for the selection of foreign judgments concerns the legal family, in the sense of the shared background with other common law systems."[57] Sources most often referred to come from Commonwealth legal systems, most notably Australia, Canada, and New Zealand, as well as from the US legal system. The availability of

---

[55] Smyth, "Citations of Foreign Decisions in Australian State Supreme Courts" (n 54), 16–17.

[56] See Bobek, *Comparative Reasoning in European Supreme Courts* (n 11); Michal Bobek, "Comparative Law in European Supreme Courts: Why is Nobody Interested in Originalism?," paper presented at the Constitutional Roundtable, University of Toronto, Mar. 14, 2012; on file with author.

[57] Elaine Mak, "Reference to Foreign Law in the Supreme Courts of Britain and the Netherlands: Explaining the Development of Judicial Practices," *Utrecht Law Review* 8 (2012): 20–34, 30–1. Elsewhere, Mak notes that references to foreign law are quite rare in the published judgments of the Dutch Hoge Raad, either because of the lack of foreign citation tradition, the more "economic" style of Dutch rulings compared with the common law tradition, and perhaps also due to concerns of court authority and legitimacy. See Elaine Mak, *Judicial Decision-Making in a Globalized World* (Hart Publishing, 2013), 160–1.

these sources, Mak notes, "forms an extra reason for the judges to look at these foreign sources first."[58]

In a comprehensive study of cross-citation by national high courts in Europe, Gelter and Siems analyzed all decisions (over 600,000) of ten high appeals courts (not constitutional courts!) for the period between 2000 and 2007.[59] In total, they found 1,430 cross-citations. Strikingly, they found that "Austria has cited Germany 459 times, and Ireland has cited England 456 times."[60] In other words, of the 1,430 cross-citations, 915 (64 percent) came from two citation trails alone—a textbook illustration of the "national identity" thesis developed in this chapter's second part. As the authors note in another paper of theirs, "Austria and Ireland, which stand in an asymmetric relationship with Germany and England respectively, seem to be particularly receptive to foreign influence on their legal systems."[61] Other citation trails found are citations of Dutch rulings (58) and Swiss rulings (45) by the German Bundesgerichtshof, and citation of 41 Belgian decisions by the French Cour de Cassation. The authors note that:

seven out of the ten courts have a favourite court accounting for more than 50% of its foreign citations. These are the Irish citations to England (98%), the Austrians to Germany (94%), the Spanish to Germany (88%), the Germans to Austria (83%), the Belgians to France (70%), the Swiss to Germany (70%), and the Italians to France (67%). In contrast to this, the citations of the English, French and Dutch high courts are more evenly split.[62]

Gelter and Siems speculate that language transferability and perhaps also similarity in legal culture more generally are important factors in explaining these pairings.[63] In short, there seems to be fairly solid

---

[58] Mak, *Judicial Decision-Making in a Globalized World* (n 57).

[59] Martin Gelter and Matthias Siems, "Networks, Dialogue or One-Way Traffic? An Empirical Analysis of Cross-Citations between Ten of Europe's Highest Courts," *Utrecht Law Review* 8 (2012): 88–99.

[60] Gelter and Siems, "Networks, Dialogue or One-Way Traffic?" (n 59), 91.

[61] Martin Gelter and Matthias Siems, "Language, Legal Origins, and Culture before the Courts: Cross-Citations between Supreme Courts in Europe," *Supreme Court Economic Review* 21 (2013).

[62] Gelter and Siems, "Networks, Dialogue or One-Way Traffic?" (n 59), 93.

[63] Gelter and Siems, "Language, Legal Origins, and Culture before the Courts" (n 61). See also, Daphna Barak-Erez, "The Institutional Aspects of Comparative Law," *Columbia Journal of European Law* 15 (2009): 477–94.

evidence, albeit based on a relatively small number of countries, to support the importance of the legal origins and language factors in explaining where apex courts look for reference.

When we move away from the handful of "usual suspect" Western constitutional democracies, evidence on patterns of foreign reference by peak courts becomes scant. The few works that do address patterns of citation in these countries point to an array of rather idiosyncratic or context-specific determinants. Legal "patriotism" and formalism render citation of foreign cases by the Russian Constitutional Court nearly non-existent.[64] Direct citation of foreign precedents is also very rare in Romania; of the 13,234 cases decided by the Romanian Constitutional Court from 1992 to 2011, merely 14 engaged in the practice.[65] Based on a careful analysis of all of the Supreme Court of Japan's rulings from 1990 to 2008, Akiko Ejima points to some detectable indirect influences of American constitutional tests and concepts on the Court's rulings in several landmark cases, and argues that "the Supreme Court of Japan accepted universalism of human rights as an ideal or a principle," but ultimately concludes that there have been very few direct references to foreign law by the Court.[66] Likewise, in Mexico, legal tradition renders direct foreign citation a rare practice. That said, the latent or indirect effects of foreign case law and doctrine may be detected.[67] In Singapore, reports Arun Kumar Thiruvengadam, courts have adhered to a national-formalist approach that sees the country's constitution as reflecting its unique heritage and its deep-rootedness in its particular history and political traditions.[68] Although reference to foreign law is not uncommon in Singapore, it is modest relative to

[64] Sergey A. Belov, "Using of Foreign Constitutional Precedents by the Russian Constitutional Court: Explicit Citations and Implicit Influence," paper presented at the XIII World Congress of the International Association of Constitutional Law, Mexico City, Dec. 2010.

[65] Elena Simina Tanasescu and Stefan Deaconu, "Romania: Analogical Reasoning as a Dialectical Instrument," in Groppi and Ponthoreau, eds., *The Use of Foreign Precedents by Constitutional Judges* (n 24), 321–45, 330–2.

[66] Akiko Ejima, "Enigmatic Attitude of the Supreme Court of Japan towards Foreign Precedents: Refusal at the Front Door and Admission at the Back Door," *Meiji Law Journal* 16 (2009): 19–44.

[67] Eduardo Ferrer Mac-Gregor and Ruben Sanchez-Gil, "Foreign Precedent in Mexican Constitutional Adjudication," *Mexican Law Review* 4 (2012): 293–307.

[68] Arun Kumar Thiruvengadam, "Comparative Law and Constitutional Interpretation in Singapore: Insights from Constitutional Theory," in Kevin Tan and Thio Li-ann, eds., *Evolution of a Revolution: 40 years of the Singapore Constitution* (Routledge, 2009), 114–52.

other common law jurisdictions.[69] This approach may also reflect the so-called "four corners" doctrine, still followed in Singapore, according to which no external evidence may be drawn upon to challenge a document that appears on its face to be complete. In Taiwan, by contrast, the Constitutional Court "nearly always engages in extensive comparative constitutional analysis, either expressly or implicitly, when rendering its decisions."[70] Whereas direct, explicit citation in majority opinions is rare, it is considerably more common in individual concurring (approximately 16 percent) or dissenting opinions (approximately 9.5 percent).[71] As Law and Chang explain, the structure of legal education and the legal profession in Taiwan incentivizes judges and academics to possess expertise in foreign law (unlike, say, in the United States, where there is almost no incentive for jurists to possess such expertise). "Openness on the part of individual [U.S.] justices to foreign law," they argue, "ultimately cannot compensate for the fact that the hiring and instructional practices of American law schools neither demand nor reward the possession of foreign legal expertise."[72]

In summary, the extant literature concerning constitutional court engagement with foreign law points in three main directions. First, despite the tremendous scholarly interest in the international migration of constitutional ideas, the actual empirical evidence on the nature and scope of reference to foreign law across polities remains thin. The studies that do exist address a dozen "usual suspect" courts; the evidence on patterns of foreign reference in other jurisdictions varies from scant and a-systematic to virtually non-existent. Second, the evidence suggests that significant variation still exists across jurisdictions with respect both to the frequency of voluntary jurisprudential reference to the laws of others and to the source of reference. Whereas in some jurisdictions constitutional court reference to foreign rulings is a relatively common practice, in other jurisdictions it is rare. To the extent that an international canon of referenced rulings has emerged, it

---

[69] Despite this trend, cases involving rights claims and related issues tend to engender more vibrant reference to foreign jurisprudence. For a recent illustration, see *Ramalingam Ravinthram v. Attorney General* [2012] SGCA 2 [Singapore]—an "equality before the law" case.

[70] David Law and Wen-Chen Chang, "The Limits of Global Judicial Dialogue," *Washington Law Review* 86 (2011): 523–77.

[71] Wen-Chen Chang and Jiunn-Rong Yeh, "Judges as Discursive Agents," paper presented at the XIII World Congress of the International Association of Constitutional Law, Mexico City, Dec. 2010.

[72] Law and Chang, "The Limits of Global Judicial Dialogue" (n 70), 524.

includes landmark cases from Germany, Canada, South Africa, the European Court of Human Rights, and to a lesser degree India, Australia, and occasionally several other smaller jurisdictions, such as pre-1999 Hungary.[73] American and British constitutional jurisprudence is still prominent, although there is some evidence indicating a decline in its overall global stature. Third, the literature identifies several factors that explain the choice of which courts to reference, most notably language, legal tradition and education, regional proximity, substantive "sameness," and court newness.

The identity construction factor: Israel as a test case

An often overlooked aspect of the foreign reference phenomenon is the identity-construction factor, itself embedded in and reflective of a given society's foundational tensions and struggles as captured by competing facets of its political sociology. The constitutional domain does not develop in a vacuum and cannot be analyzed separately from the concrete social and political struggles that shape the environment within which it operates. Indeed, it is an integral part and an important manifestation of those struggles, and so cannot be understood in isolation from them. Any attempt to portray the constitutional domain as exclusively legal, rather than imbued in the social or political arena, is destined to yield thin, overly doctrinal or formalistic accounts of the origins, nature, and consequences of constitutional law.

Perhaps nowhere in the constitutional domain is this insight truer than in the area of constitutional interpretation, where the text itself is often vague or deliberately open-ended and can support a range of understandings or interpretive approaches. Interpretation cannot plausibly avoid or insulate itself completely from broad ideological processes that limit the range of meanings that are likely to be attributed to the constitutional text by its interpreters. Selective, opinionated interpretation not only seems likely, but also stands in contrast to legalistic views that see constitutional interpretation as an objective, value-free,

[73] From its inception in 1990 until 1998, the Hungarian Constitutional Court under the presidency of László Sólyom was considered one of the more progressive peak courts in the world, let alone in the post-communist world. Political interference has stripped much of the Court's international clout and liberal-progressive reputation since that time.

quasi-scientific process. What is more, an overwhelming body of empirical evidence suggests that extrajudicial factors play a key role in constitutional court decision-making patterns.[74] Constitutional courts and judges may speak the language of legal doctrine but, consciously or not, their actual decision-making patterns are correlated with policy preferences and ideological or attitudinal tilts, and appear to reflect strategic considerations vis-à-vis their political surroundings, panel compositions, their professional peers, or the public as a whole.[75] This can be explained by reference to the costs that judges as individuals or courts as institutions may incur as a result of adverse reactions to unwelcome decisions, or the various benefits they may acquire through the rendering of welcome ones.[76] A wide array of empirically grounded studies suggests that a harsh political response to unwelcome activism or interventions on the part of the courts, or even the credible threat of such a response, can have a chilling effect on judicial decision-making patterns. Other works point to judges' relations with their epistemic communities of reference (the "network of jurists"), or their concern with the court's legacy, reputation, and public stature—both domestically and internationally—as important determinants of judicial behavior, particularly in politically significant cases. In any event, of all the types and elements of judicial interpretation, the open-ended area of voluntary reference to foreign law, where the judicial mind is supposedly unbound and free to travel virtually anywhere in time and space, is arguably most conducive to influence and to the application of such extrajudicial considerations.[77]

---

[74] For a sample of court-specific studies, see, e.g., Jeffrey Staton, *Judicial Power and Strategic Communication in Mexico* (Cambridge University Press, 2010); Gretchen Helmke, *Courts Under Constraints: Judges, Generals and Presidents in Argentina* (Cambridge University Press, 2005); Alexei Trochev, *Judging Russia: The Role of the Constitutional Court in Russian Politics 1990–2006* (Cambridge University Press, 2008); Diana Kapiszewski, "Tactical Balancing: High Court Decision Making on Politically Crucial Cases," *Law and Society Review* 45 (2011): 471–506; Wen-Chen Chang, "Strategic Judicial Responses in Politically Charged Cases: East Asian Experiences," *International Journal of Constitutional Law* 8 (2010): 885–910.

[75] A well-known exposition of the so-called "attitudinal" model of judicial behavior in the US context is Jeffrey A. Segal and Harold J. Spaeth, *The Supreme Court and the Attitudinal Model Revisited* (Cambridge University Press, 2002).

[76] For an overview of this approach, see Lee Epstein and Tonja Jacobi, "The Strategic Analysis of Judicial Decisions," *Annual Review of Law and Social Science* 6 (2010): 341–58.

[77] See Tripathi, "Foreign Precedents and Constitutional Law" (n 3). Tripathi suggests that courts and judges use foreign precedents instrumentally in order to support or legitimize the preconceived adjudicative results they wish to advance. This is particularly true, he suggests, in the fairly open-ended realm of constitutional jurisprudence.

In polities where cultural orientations, political affiliations, and collective identities are intensely contested, the choices courts and judges make with respect to foreign reference—which bodies of foreign law are referred to and cited as authoritative and which are decried or ignored—are an important indicator of their ideological and strategic preferences with respect to the polity's social, cultural, and political divisions. These choices are sociopolitical, not juridical. They signal commitment to and advancement of certain worldviews, aspirations, and visions of the "right" way of life and of the polity's place in the world.

Patterns of foreign reference by the Supreme Court of Israel (SCI) provide a textbook illustration of this logic at work. Foreign reference is a common practice in Israeli courts. Various studies suggest that the SCI refers to comparative precedents in approximately one-fifth of all its rulings, and perhaps even at a higher rate in its constitutional law decisions.[78] The data also suggests that approximately 10 percent of all case citations are composed of foreign law sources. Such citations appear more common in landmark cases: 75 of the 100 most frequently cited cases in Israeli law between 1948 and 2000 refer to foreign law. Moreover, the SCI refers to foreign sources in all 50 constitutional law cases included in that 100 most-cited cases list.[79] American, Canadian, British, and German rulings are frequently referred to, and occasional references are also made to other jurisdictions, such as Australia, South Africa, and New Zealand, as well as to some continental European jurisprudence.[80] These sources are often invoked and dealt with by the Court in a "dialogical" fashion (as opposed to a "universalist" fashion), to borrow Sujit Choudhry's analytical concept;[81] the Court claims that comparative materials help it to identify and enforce principles

---

[78] See Miron Gross, Ron Haris, and Yoram Schachar, "References Patterns of the Supreme Court in Israel-Quantitative Analysis," *Hebrew University Law Review* 26 (1996): 115–217.

[79] See Chanan Goldschmit, Miron Gross, and Yoram Shachar, "100 Leading Precedents of the Supreme Court—A Quantitative Analysis," *Haifa University Law Review* 7 (2004): 243–303; Iddo Porat, "The Use of Foreign Law in Israeli Constitutional Adjudication," paper presented at the conference Israeli Constitutional Law in the Making—Comparative and Global Perspectives, Tel-Aviv University, 2011.

[80] Suzie Navot, "Israel: Creating a Constitution-Use of Foreign Precedents by the Supreme Court (1994–2010)," in Groppi and Ponthoreau, eds., *The Use of Foreign Precedents by Constitutional Judges* (n 24), 129–53, 145.

[81] See Sujit Choudhry, "Globalization in Search of Justification: Toward a Theory of Comparative Constitutional Interpretation," *Indiana Law Journal* 74 (1999): 819–92; Sujit Choudhry, "Migration as a New Metaphor in Comparative Constitutional Law," in Sujit Choudhry, ed., *The Migration of Constitutional Ideas* (Cambridge University Press, 2006), 1–36.

embedded in the Israeli constitutional order. In practice, however, comparative materials are often used in a "universalist" fashion, whereby they are taken to represent an external "gold standard" that the country's constitutional jurisprudence ought to follow or else risk being left behind.

There are many illustrative examples of these reference choices. In its most significant ruling to date, the *United Mizrahi Bank* case (1995)—the "Israeli *Marbury v. Madison*," as observers of the Israeli legal system have described it—wherein the SCI formally asserted its authority to exercise judicial review over acts of the Knesset, the Court made reference to 123 relevant precedents: 76 of its own rulings, along with decisions by the US Supreme Court (17), the UK House of Lords (5), the Supreme Court of Canada (3), Australia's High Court (3), the German Federal Constitutional Court (2), and the Supreme Court of India (1).[82] It also referred to eight Jewish law sources. (It is also interesting to note than in 1995, the year the *United Mizrahi Bank* case was decided, over 50 percent of the constitutional cases (13 of 24) decided by the Court cited foreign cases).

Again, in what many view as the Court's most significant ruling of the last decade—the *Citizenship Law/Family Unification* case (2006), wherein a divided 6:5 bench essentially gave priority to Israel's "Jewish" constitutional pillar of collective identity over the "democratic" one—the Court made reference to 246 judicial decisions: 183 of its own, as well as rulings of apex courts in the United States (30), Canada (9), the European Court of Human Rights (8), the United Kingdom (6), South Africa (3), Germany (3), and Ireland (1). Although this legal dispute cannot be understood outside the foundational, if not existential, tensions between the competing particularist and universalist visions of the polity, no reference whatsoever was made to other discordant constitutional jurisdictions that struggle with related challenges. For instance, the Malaysian and Pakistani constitutional courts have had to deal with similar conundrums growing out of the constitutionally enshrined sectarian (there, "Muslim") and universal values operating as the main tenets of their collective (and constitutional) identity.[83] Likewise, no reference was made to countries such as Serbia,

---

[82] C.A. 6821/93 *United Mizrahi Bank v. Migdal Cooperative Village*, 49(4) P.D. 221 (1995) [Israel].

[83] For a discussion of the jurisprudential strategies adopted by these courts in addressing such tensions, see Hirschl, *Constitutional Theocracy* (n 7).

Thailand, or Nepal where religion, ethnicity, and nationhood are closely entangled. And no reference was made either to the many predominantly Catholic polities (e.g. Poland, Slovakia, Italy, the Philippines, or the entirety of Latin America), despite the fact that in many of these countries, religious affiliation, symbolism, and morality all remain central markers of collective identity and public discourse while often colliding with constitutional rights provisions.

The distribution of foreign references in the *Citizenship Law/Family Unification* case is telling. In this ruling, the SCI upheld a temporary amendment to the new Citizenship and Entry to Israel Law that imposed age restrictions on the granting of Israeli citizenship and residency permits to Arab residents of the Occupied Territories who marry Israeli citizens.[84] Because the practice of marrying Palestinians is far more common among Israel's Arab minority, the law limiting family unification and spousal naturalization effectively singled out Arab citizens while maintaining the demographic balance in favor of members of Israel's Jewish population, who seldom marry Palestinians and whose non-citizen spouses are often naturalized by way of marriage to an Israeli (Jewish) citizen. Interestingly, the majority of six justices prioritized the first tenet in Israel's self-definition as a *Jewish* and *democratic* state, while the other five sitting justices (including then-Chief Justice Aharon Barak) gave priority to the second. Both the majority and minority opinions are exceptionally erudite, and cite a variety of iconic sources, including Greek philosophers and Roman poets (though not Muslim thinkers or Hindi authors, to be sure). But when it comes to references to constitutional cases overseas, there is a clear division: of the 63 references made in the ruling to foreign constitutional cases, 58 (92 percent) are made in the dissenting opinion (the pro-"Democratic" tenet opinion), while only 5 (8 percent) are made in the majority opinion (the pro-"Jewish" tenet opinion). The first paragraph of the majority opinion (authored by then-Deputy Chief Justice Mishael Cheshin) seems to capture neatly the majority opinion's attitude toward the consideration, or even preliminary relevance, of foreign sources in core cases such as this when it says that CJ Barak's opinion, while perhaps applicable to the imagined "State of Utopia," is not applicable to the State of Israel.[85]

---

[84] HCJ 7052/03 *Adalah v. Minister of Interior*, [2006] 2 TakEl 1754 [Israel].

[85] Within the Israeli legal academia, a vocal critic of the Court's judicial activism in the 1990s and 2000s, and incidentally, of the practice of Israeli judges who "go foreign" for

In 2012, the SCI upheld (6:5) the final version of the Citizenship Law.[86] The majority ruled that "the right to a family life does not necessarily have to be realized within the borders of Israel." The Court's incoming Chief Justice, Asher Grunis, wrote that "human rights cannot be enacted at the price of national suicide" (referring to what has been termed in Israeli public discourse as "the demographic threat" to the Jewish character of the state). In its 230-page ruling, the Court made reference to numerous scholarly works of North American and European jurists, including Antonin Scalia (US Supreme Court Justice), Dieter Grimm (former judge of the German Federal Constitutional Court), and András Sajó (judge of the European Court of Human Rights). It also cited 47 foreign court decisions, of which 26 were US Supreme Court rulings; the others included decisions from the European Court of Human Rights (9 decisions), the European Court of Justice (4), and the peak courts of Canada (4), the United Kingdom (2), and Germany (2).

A similar foreign citation pattern is evident in civil cases decided by the Court. *Ettinger Estate v. Jewish Quarter Company*, a typical tort law case, came before the SCI in 2004.[87] It involved a suit for liability in tort by the estate of a 12-year-old boy who died after falling into an unfenced pit at an archaeological site located near a playground in the Old City of Jerusalem. The main issue considered was whether the estate was entitled to compensation for loss of the deceased's earning capacity for the years of working life that the deceased lost because he died as a result of the respondents' negligence. A second issue was whether the respondents should have been found liable to pay punitive damages.[88] The appeal was heard by an extended bench of five

reinforcements to pursue their liberal goals, is Ruth Gavison—a distinguished (now retired) law professor at the Hebrew University. In the early 2000s, Gavison was among the leading candidates for a Supreme Court appointment; an unusually outspoken campaign by CJ Barak and others, alongside ministerial portfolio changes in the Israeli government, effectively prevented the appointment.

[86] HCJ 466/07 *MK Zahava Gal-On (Meretz-Yahad) et al. v. Attorney General et al.* (decision delivered on Jan. 11, 2012) [Israel].

[87] C.A. 140/00 *Ettinger Estate v. Jewish Quarter Co.* [2004] IsrLR 97 [Israel].

[88] The Supreme Court held in a nutshell that where a person dies as a result of a tortious act, his claim to compensation for the loss of earning capacity in the "lost years" passes to his estate. If the deceased has dependants who are awarded compensation for loss of support in the lost years, this compensation is deducted from the compensation payable to the estate for loss of the deceased's earning capacity in the "lost years" to prevent double liability being imposed on the tortfeasor. The Court left undecided the question whether Israeli courts have the power to award punitive damages, since the facts of this case did not warrant them.

Supreme Court judges, including President Aharon Barak and Vice-President Theodor Or. In its 85-page decision, the Court referred to 165 rulings in total: 77 of its own decisions, as well as British cases (27), US Supreme Court decisions (26), Supreme Court of Canada rulings (21), Irish cases (3), Australian rulings (2), South African cases (2), and a decision from New Zealand.

How legitimate or relevant judicial reference is to foreign constitutional jurisprudence is an interesting and widely debated question. But even when we leave aside (or for that matter accept) the legitimacy and relevance of foreign citations, the repertoire of sources itself presents us with a puzzle. Naturally, none of these cited courts' jurisprudence is written in Hebrew. The United States, United Kingdom, Canada, and Australia are common law jurisdictions, but Germany and other continental European jurisdictions are not. None of these countries is in Israel's region, however broadly defined. (The SCI has never cited a single ruling of any of its neighbor countries, or any other predominantly Muslim country in Northern Africa or in Asia). The "learning from the experience of others" explanation seems forced; none of the source countries the SCI refers to faces a fundamental constitutional disharmony (to borrow Gary Jacobsohn's phrase) stemming from a constitutional commitment to two apparently contradictory tenets.[89] The "new court" factor is not relevant either; the SCI was established some 65 years ago. Its cumulative body of jurisprudence is very rich, and its landmark rulings carry great symbolic weight in Israel and abroad. What is more, the German Federal Constitutional Court—established at the same time as its Israeli counterpart—seldom cites foreign precedents, and "has developed a style of reasoning where it basically cites only its own precedents."[90] In short, none of the common explanations for extensive judicial recourse to foreign law—language, legal tradition, region, "sameness," or court newness—applies to this case. How are we to explain the Israeli case? Or, put differently, what general conclusions may be drawn from the Israeli case, and perhaps from other similarly situated cases, on the motives

[89] See generally, Gary J. Jacobsohn, "The Disharmonic Constitution," in Stephen Macedo and Jeffrey Tulis, eds., *The Limits of Constitutional Democracy* (Princeton University Press, 2010), 47–65.

[90] Brun-Otto Bryde, "The Constitutional Judge and the International Constitutional Dialogue," in Basil Markesinis and Jorg Fedtke, eds., *Judicial Recourse to Foreign Law* (Routledge, 2006), 298.

behind a court's decision whether and where to look for foreign reference?

In his masterful treatise *The Judge in a Democracy*, Aharon Barak praises comparative law as providing "great assistance in realizing [his] role as judge."[91] Comparative law, he suggests, "acts as an experienced friend."[92] It allows "for greater self-knowledge," enriches the options available, and expands the judge's "horizon and the interpretive field of vision," and is thus "a good source . . . for cross-fertilization of ideas."[93] Ultimately, Barak argues that "comparative law can help judges determine the objective purpose of a constitution" and that it is "an important tool with which judges fulfill their role in a democracy." With respect to concrete comparative sources, Barak states that "the case law of the courts of the United States, Australia, Canada, the United Kingdom, and Germany have helped [him] significantly in finding the right path to follow,"[94] and that "reference to the United States law, United Kingdom law, Canadian law, and Australian law is commonplace" in Israeli courts.[95] He goes on to praise the Supreme Court of Canada for being "particularly noteworthy for its frequent and fruitful use of comparative law. As such, Canadian law serves as a source of inspiration for many countries around the world."[96] Elsewhere, Barak states that "the constitutional law of Germany—and the judgments of the German Federal Constitutional Court—are central for anyone interested in comparative constitutional law."[97] And what makes Canadian or German law suitable for citation by the Israeli judge? According to Barak, the answer is twofold: joint democratic principles ("many of the basic principles of democracy are common to democratic countries, [so] there is good reason to compare them");[98] and historical development and social conditions that are sufficiently similar to allow for a valid comparison.[99]

These are somewhat forced justifications. Common democratic principles? Sufficiently similar historical development? Israel and

---

[91] Aharon Barak, *The Judge in A Democracy* (Princeton University Press, 2006), 197.
[92] Barak, *The Judge in A Democracy* (n 91), 198.
[93] Barak, *The Judge in A Democracy* (n 91), 200.
[94] Barak, *The Judge in A Democracy* (n 91), 197.
[95] Barak, *The Judge in A Democracy* (n 91), 202.
[96] Barak, *The Judge in A Democracy* (n 91), 203.
[97] Aharon Barak, endorsement of Donald Kommers and Russell Miller, *The Constitutional Jurisprudence of the Federal Republic of Germany* (3rd edn, Duke University Press, 2012).
[98] Barak, *The Judge in A Democracy* (n 91), 203.
[99] Barak, *The Judge in A Democracy* (n 91), 201.

Germany? In fact, one would be hard-pressed to find a better illustration of wishful judicial thinking, for there cannot be two countries in
the democratic world whose constitutional histories, social conditions,
and political realities are less similar than Israel and Germany. There is
no commonality in language or legal tradition. The systems of government are different. The range of pertinent political issues is poles
apart. As everybody knows, less than 70 years ago, Germany was set to
terminate the Jewish people, and continues to pay billions in reparation
moneys to Holocaust survivors and their descendants. It underwent a
major constitutional reconstruction in the mid-20th century, absorbed
the former East Germany into its constitutional order in the early
1990s, and is now a key component of a major transnational legal
order that subjects certain elements of its constitutional sovereignty
to supranational scrutiny. None of these core characteristics has even a
remote parallel in Israel, which is steeped in its own geopolitical
difficulties, social struggles, and constitutional idiosyncrasies.

And what to say about the stark differences between Canada and
Israel? The former is a peaceful, stable, and thriving democracy that has
not known war since its independence in 1867, and that is politically
and constitutionally committed to bilingualism and multiculturalism.
Israel, by contrast, defines itself in sectarian terms, cherishes its role as
fortress and homeland for the entire world's Jewry, exists in a permanent sense of threat from its hostile neighbors, and has a checkered
history with respect to its treatment of Palestinians and Arab Israelis
alike. In short, Barak's constitutional vision aside, few countries in the
democratic world are as dissimilar to Israel as Canada. It may well be—
and is quite understandable—that Barak and the social groups whose
worldviews he shares and promotes would like Israel to be like Canada.
And it may also be the case that there are similar yearnings that define
the views and behavior of particular segments of the Israeli society and
that enjoy a broader consensus in Canada. But to claim that it is the
similarity of the two countries that validates recourse to Canadian
jurisprudence in Israel seems a bit of a stretch.[100]

---

[100] Interestingly, the Chief Justice of the Supreme Court of Canada herself reflected on
the practice of voluntary reference and the use of Canadian Charter jurisprudence in foreign
courts, stating that "the Charter and our jurisprudence cannot be imported wholesale by
other states. Nor am I suggesting it should be. Each time a country looks to the constitutional
jurisprudence of another country for inspiration, it must determine whether that jurisprudence is compatible with its domestic constitution, its own political and social context, and its

In many important respects, Malaysia or India (and dare I say, Pakistan, Sri Lanka, or Turkey) have much more in common with Israel, constitutionally speaking, than the United States, Canada, or Germany. Both India and Malaysia are democracies by any standard definition. Their legal traditions and constitutional development are considerably closer to those of Israel. Most importantly, both countries, like Israel, face constitutional challenges revolving around secularism, modernism, and the centrality of religion and ethnicity in collective identity and public life. Learning from these countries' constitutional experience, or even "exchanging notes," is guaranteed to be a more useful exercise than looking at Canadian or German jurisprudence. Yet despite these similarities—considerably more substantive similarities than the advertised "shared democratic values" sound-bite that is supposed to justify the Court's turn to Canada or Germany—the Supreme Court of Israel seldom cites rulings of the Supreme Court of India and has never made a reference to the jurisprudence of the Federal Court of Malaysia, let alone that of peak courts in Pakistan, Bangladesh, Sri Lanka, Poland, Turkey, or Kenya—all countries that share at least as many characteristics of Israel's political and constitutional identity as do Germany or Canada.

How are we to explain these selective citation trends? At the outset, there may be an "educational" motive at work here—an attempt to bind what may be seen as a transitional society to a certain group of states, or a "self-consciously pedagogical commitment premised on the felt need to instill habits of Western democracies participation in a body politic that on the whole is inexperienced in the ways of democracy."[101] However, such attempts to advance a certain vision of the good society or to define what our right place in the world should be— all while operating in a polity that is divided precisely along the lines of that very question—are never purely "pedagogical" in the "consensus curriculum/happy classroom/dedicated teacher/keen students" sense of the term. It is incomplete without an understanding of the concrete social tensions, political struggles, and culture wars that are conducive to the development of such judicial motivations, or that nourish judges'

---

aspirations as a state." See McLachlin, "The Canadian Charter of Rights and Freedoms' First 30 Years" (n 23), 43.

[101] Gary J. Jacobsohn, *Apple of Gold: Constitutionalism in Israel and the United States* (Princeton University Press, 1993), 224–5.

self-perceptions as "national educators", "collective ideologues," or "social oracles" of one type or another.

Referring to the Israeli case, Gary Jacobsohn argues cogently that judicial choices to cite jurisprudence from several Western democracies (he does not address directly the flip side of the same coin—the rejection of alternative sources), are driven by a quest for constitutional harmony. Jacobsohn suggests that "[t]he deep division over the most basic questions of national identity ... has encouraged members of the Israeli Supreme Court to complete the task of constitutional closure with the aid of examples taken from places where constitutional development has progressed less problematically in fulfillment of liberal democratic aspirations."[102] While there is much to this analysis, I suggest that deeper matters of political sociology, and the Court's position with respect to those matters—that is, its preference for a specific vision of the good society or its quest to portray an actual "disharmony" as "harmony"—not merely an abstract pursuit of harmony per se, is what drives its choice of references.[103]

A quotation from Hannah Arendt's letter to Karl Jaspers, in which she describes her "ethnographic" impression of the atmosphere in and surrounding the courthouse in Jerusalem where the famous Eichmann trial took place, seems to capture it all:

Impression: On the top, the judges, the best of German Jewry. Below them, the prosecutors, Galicians, but still Europeans. Everything is organized by a police force that gives me the creeps, speaks only Hebrew and looks Arabic. Some downright brutal types among them ... And outside the doors, the oriental mob, as if one were in Istanbul or some other half-Asiatic country.[104]

Fifty years later, few descriptions capture more accurately the existential fear Israel's old Ashkenazi bourgeoisie holds toward the non-European aspects of everyday life, or the extent to which it sees the

---

[102] Jacobsohn, "The Permeability of Constitutional Borders" (n 6), 1767.

[103] Jacobsohn acknowledges that aspect in claiming that the rift over the value of comparative law "threatens to undermine the Israeli Court's ability to function as an effective arbiter of constitutional questions." See Jacobsohn, "The Permeability of Constitutional Borders" (n 6), 1768.

[104] Hannah Arendt and Karl Jaspers, *Correspondence 1926–1969* (Harvest Books, 1993), 443. Note that Moshe Landau, the judge who presided over the Eichmann trial, was born in Danzig, Germany (now Gdansk, Poland).

Court as a beacon of "reasonableness" operating amid a rather "Levantine" sociopolitical context. This is the social setting against which judicial choices of reference sources take place and are to be understood.

In a famous medieval poem written in 12th-century al-Andalus, Yehudah Ha-Levi, a Jewish physician, poet, and philosopher, memorably wrote: "My heart is in the East and I am at the edge of the West" reflecting the unremitting yearning of a diasporic people for their ancestral homeland, the land of Israel (or Zion, as Ha-Levi refers to it in other poems). Paradoxically, today, when the SCI is back in Zion, and located in Jerusalem, we can paraphrase Ha-Levi to say that the choice of foreign references by Israel's jurists reflects a new post-independence reality: "My heart is in West and I am at the edge of the East." This expresses a deep and perhaps understandable desire to connect to the global "*bon ton*," while at the same time residing in a conflict-ridden and deeply divided society, whereby judges with cosmopolitan and liberal leanings wish to differentiate themselves—and project on to the world—an image of their country that is removed from those local "masses" that, half a century earlier, gave Arendt, in her own words, "the creeps." Despite all the apparent differences, judicial reference to Canadian or German cases but not Pakistani or Indian cases may be driven by the same "my heart is in the West," impulse, just as members of the same sociopolitical constituency in Israel are keen on skiing in the Swiss Alps, shopping in New York, or going to the opera in Berlin.

Israeli elites' rejection and denial of their surrounding culture ("we are not in the Middle East" ["*anakhnu lo ba'mizrakh ha'tikhon*"] as a hit song in the 1990s exclaimed) also manifests itself in a refusal to learn their neighboring nations' languages, in presenting oriental culture as unrefined and "lowbrow," and in amplifying the significance of Israel's membership of organizations such as the European Football Association (UEFA) and the European Basketball Association (FIBA Europe), or its participation in the Eurovision song contest—a widely watched and much discussed annual song competition held among member countries of the European Broadcasting Union.

Sociologists, anthropologists, and political scientists have long been fascinated by the role played by "cultural capital" (*le capital culturel*, French) in social and symbolic construction of identity and differentiation.[105] As Ernest Gellner famously observed, the ruling classes in transitional societies often control state institutions and use artifacts like high culture or modernism to underwrite social structure, distancing themselves from non-members of the national elite.[106] Luxury goods, as both sociologists and savvy marketing agents are quick to note, often carry a connotation of social status. From Louis Vuitton handbags and Mercedes-Benz cars to private yachts and exclusive vacation destinations, the rich (and perhaps even more so the nouveau riche) have always found ways to signal their affluence by expensive possessions. The "objective" functional or economic difference between most such goods and cheaper equivalents is questionable, but the symbolic or reputational value that they carry links them to a certain social stratum. A similar differentiation impulse is evident with respect to abstract choices such as a proclivity for "high culture" and aesthetics. In his *Distinction: A Social Critique of the Judgement of Taste*, renowned French sociologist Pierre Bourdieu shows how social class often determines a person's penchants, interests, and artistic and cultural preferences, and how these distinctions are reinforced in popular culture in order to maintain the social stratification that created them in the first place.[107] Certain supposedly "refined" aesthetic choices (say, consumption of classical music or high literature) actively distance those who belong to one class from others who do not (as indicated by their supposed "crude" or "vulgar" taste). The application to Israel's "culture wars," and by extension to choice of foreign references by the SCI, seems obvious.

The Court's reference to a near-canonical group of courts and body of jurisprudence brings to mind the emulation dynamics that exist in what John Meyer and other thinkers of the so-called Stanford School termed "world culture."[108] Despite striking differences in socioeconomic conditions and cultural particularities, modern states paradoxically adopt similar policies and institutions.[109] For instance,

[105] The classic articulation is offered by Pierre Bourdieu and Jean-Claude Passeron, *Reproduction in Education, Society and Culture* (Richard Nice, trans., Sage, 1977).

[106] Ernest Gellner, *Nations and Nationalism* (Cornell University Press, 1983).

[107] Pierre Bourdieu, *Distinction: A Social Critique of the Judgement of Taste* (Harvard University Press, 1984).

[108] See generally, Didem Buhari-Gulmez, "Stanford School on Sociological Institutionalism: A Global Cultural Approach," *International Political Sociology* 4 (2010): 253–70.

[109] See, e.g., John W. Meyer et al., "World Society and the Nation-State," *American Journal of Sociology* 103 (1997): 144–81.

in many countries that do not share common characteristics, national constitutions outlaw ethnic and racial discrimination, embrace similar understandings of rights, and call for largely similar commitments to justice and equality.[110] Likewise, despite having little in common in any pertinent respect, constitutional courts in different places refer to a roughly similar set of jurisdictions and to the world canon, "*le bon ton*," or fashionable mode, of comparative constitutional law. This could be explained by a world culture whose values are ontologically prior to nation-states and their cultural idiosyncrasies. Or it may reflect a process of diffusion in which reference choices of one court affect the choice set and the calculus of others. Either way, both reference to and emulation of these supposedly global values increase the borrower's legitimacy and sense of timeless universalism and cosmopolitanism vis-à-vis its social surroundings.

Expanding the discussion beyond the focus on Israel, accounts of strategic incorporation of international standards into domestic law may have some explanatory bite here too. Several studies suggest that such incorporation by new or volatile democracies may be aimed at "locking-in" or signaling commitment to liberal or democratic world-views and policy preferences, in particular at times of political transition or uncertainty as to the future of democracy in a given polity.[111] Having defeated President Musharraf in the February 2008 election, and anticipating a phoenix-like rise from the ashes of a military regime, the newly elected government of Pakistan, led by the Pakistan People's Party (PPP), quickly ratified the International Covenant on Economic, Social and Cultural Rights and signed the International Covenant on Civil and Political Rights. A similar logic may explain the 1994 incorporation of ten international human rights covenants into Argentine constitutional law following years of military rule, and perhaps also the 1991 constitutionalization of rights in British-ruled Hong Kong that took place shortly after the British Parliament had ratified the Joint Declaration on the Question of Hong Kong, whereby Britain was to restore Hong Kong to China in July 1997. Such measures commit future governments to certain democratic and human rights standards,

---

[110] See, e.g., Colin Beck, Gili S. Drori, and John W. Meyer, "World Influences on Human Rights Language in Constitutions: A Cross-National Study," *International Sociology* 27 (2012): 483–501.

[111] Andrew Moravcsik, "The Origins of Human Rights Regimes," *International Organization* 54 (2000): 217–52; Tom Ginsburg, "Locking in Democracy: Constitutions, Commitment, and International Law," *Journal of International Law and Politics* 38 (2006): 707–59.

and may also signal the "right" message to the international community and to important domestic interest groups.

Judicial application of these commitments may likewise allow courts to demonstrate to both domestic and international observers that they are willing to adopt widely shared best practices and are serious about the rule of law. In Uganda (as well as in other countries in transition), argues Johanna Kalb, reference to foreign sources may be seen as a strategic "public relations" practice that signals the court's independence, legitimacy, and accountability to the outer world.[112] As with the incorporation of international law standards, such reference to the "right" set of foreign laws may communicate that the new, post-transition court should be taken seriously by the international community. This in turn may suggest that a given court's selective reference to the constitutional jurisprudence of a small group of liberal-democratic countries may not be explained in isolation from that court's position and role, real or self-professed, with respect to the foundational political and social struggles of the country it serves.

Selective recourse to foreign law may also be driven by an ad hoc judicial calculus, or by a deeper ideational commitment to a certain vision of the good society. A recent study suggests that the Supreme Court of India's extensive reference to foreign (almost exclusively Western) constitutional precedent helped the Court to bolster its political significance and position itself as the ultimate guardian of the rights of the accused against police abuse.[113] Many lesser known illustrations of strategic judicial use of foreign references are equally telling. The Supreme Court of Uganda legitimized the results of that country's 2001 and 2006 presidential elections (both won by Yoweri Museveni, uninterrupted ruler of Uganda since 1986) despite having acknowledged massive problems with the electoral process and gross violations of key constitutional principles.[114] In both rulings the Court found that election malpractices committed by state agents had not been committed with Museveni's knowledge or approval. As to who

---

[112] Johanna Kalb, "The Judicial Role in New Democracies: A Strategic Account of Comparative Citation," *Yale Journal of International Law* 38 (2013): 423–65.

[113] Sam F. Halabi, "Constitutional Borrowing as Jurisprudential and Political Doctrine in *Shri D. K. Basi v. State of West Bengal*," *Notre Dame Journal of International and Comparative Law* 3 (2013): 73–121.

[114] Election Petition 1/2001, *Rtd. Col. Dr. Besigye Kiiza v. Yoweri Kaguta Museveni & The Electoral Commission* [Uganda]; Election Petition 1/2006, *Rtd. Col. Dr. Kizza Besigye v. Electoral Commission, Yoweri Kaguta Museveni* [2007] UGSC 24 [Uganda].

in fact was responsible for the systematic, wide-ranging violations it identified, the Court did not speculate. An invisible hand, perhaps. (The reader can make an educated guess at Museveni's reaction had the Court ruled otherwise). To reach its decision in both cases, the Court drew on British jurisprudence on evidence and on elections law; sources such as *Phipson on Evidence*, quotations from Lord Denning, the *Hackney Case* (1874), and the *Halsbury's Laws of England* on elections anchor both rulings. The questionable relevance of British evidence or election rules, some of which were designed to apply to elections in rural communities in 19th-century England, to a Uganda ruled by a 30-year leader who for 19 years banned the entire party system, who amended the constitution to remove a two-term limit, who forced his main political rival (the petitioner in the two cases) into exile, and who has otherwise clung to power by all means available to him, did not seem to bother the judges at all. The Court treats their recourse to British law that evolved within a very different political context as a natural, seamless choice, as if these two settings are perfectly comparable. Nowhere in the election appeal rulings can a reader find reference to the fact that Britain is a stable democracy with routine, free, and open elections whereas Uganda has been under authoritarian or semi-authoritarian rule for most of its post-colonial life.

A similar ad hoc selectivity with respect to foreign sources can be seen in Romania, where party politics has occasionally escalated into all-out constitutional war. In 2012, the Romanian Constitutional Court ruled that the impeachment of President Traian Băsescu through a national referendum was invalid, since only 46 percent of the electorate had cast their vote—69 percent support for removal in parliament and 87.5 percent support in the national referendum were deemed insufficient by the Court.[115] This decision triggered a massive political backlash against the Court, a backlash orchestrated by Prime Minister Victor Ponta, Băsescu's main political rival and the clear winner of the December 2012 parliamentary elections. And so, in July 2013, less than

---

[115] For a thorough analysis of the Romanian constitutional crisis, see Vlad Perju, "The Fragility of Constitutinalism: An Analysis of Romania's 2012 Constitutional Crisis," paper presented at the Symposium on Constitutionalism in Central and Eastern Europe, Boston College, Oct. 2013; on file with author. See also, Bianca Selejan-Guţan, "The Illusion of the Romanian Constitution?," *I-CONnect: International Journal of Constitution Law Blog* (Dec. 7, 2012), <http://www.iconnectblog.com/2012/12/the-illusion-of-the-romanian-constitution>; and Kim Lane Scheppele and Vlad Perju, "Guest Post: Separating Law and Politics in Romania," *New York Times* (July 12, 2012).

a year after its initial ruling on the matter, the reconstructed Court (now including three new Ponta-appointed judges) approved a proposed amendment to the referendum law that lowers the validity threshold to 30 percent of the electorate.[116] The main basis for the 2013 decision was respect for "the sovereignty of the Romanian people." The Court did not explain why this was such an important principle in 2013 but not in 2012. To support its ruling, the Court drew heavily on the Council of Europe's Venice Commission Code of Good Practice on Referendums 2007, which strongly disapproves of the imposition of a participation quorum. In 2012, by contrast, the then pro-Băsescu Court disregarded the recommendation of the Venice Commission Code altogether.

These instances of strategic judicial recourse to foreign law are obviously inseparable from the concrete political settings within which they take place. But the consistent, decades-long recourse to a particular set of foreign sources as we have seen in Israel and other similarly situated polities stems from a deeper ideational commitment to a certain vision of the good society and of the polity's cultural orientation and place in the international family of nations.

To further illustrate this point, let us consider another important facet of the "to cite or not to cite" quandary in Israel: the glaring oversight of Jewish law. In a Jewish state—the only one in existence—where Hebrew and not English or German is the law's language and the people's, and where serving as homeland for the entire world's Jewry is a foundational moral and legal commitment, the only credible external legal source that shares Israel's uniqueness, language, and tradition is frequently overlooked and sometimes proactively discredited as a relevant source of reference. Indeed, when Jewish law is referenced, it is largely for ornamental or decorative purposes, not substantive ones. Even in those rare cases in which Jewish law is cited, the SCI has often provided its own "modernist" reading of Jewish law, either by taking it out of context or by reading contemporary legal ideas and concepts into it.[117]

---

[116] For further analysis, see Bianca Selejan-Guțan, "One Year After: How the Romanian Constitutional Court Changed Its Mind," *I-CONnect: International Journal of Constitutional Law Blog* (July 14, 2013), <http://www.iconnectblog.com/2013/07/oneyearafter>.

[117] Steven F. Friedell, "Some Observations about Jewish Law in Israel's Supreme Court," *Washington University Global Studies Law Review* 8 (2009): 659–700.

The evidence is plain but telling.[118] In 1980, the potentially far-reaching law *Hok Yesodot Ha'Mishpat* ("Act for the Foundations of Law") was passed, officially making Jewish Law (*Mishpat Ivri*, literally "Hebrew Law") a formal source of interpretation in instances involving lack of precedent or legal lacunae.[119] Despite this legislative milestone, the SCI rarely turns to Jewish law in its rulings. In 27 of the 30 years from 1978 to 2007, the number of Supreme Court decisions that referred to foreign law significantly exceeded the number of decisions that referred to Jewish law sources. In several of these years, the ratio of foreign citations to Jewish law citations was 5:1 or higher. In 1986, to pick one example, the Court referred to foreign law in 18.5 percent of its rulings, and to Jewish law in 2.1 percent of its rulings. In its 201 rulings reported in the official gazette (*Piskei Din*, P.D.) in 2003, the SCI references 176 foreign sources alongside 23 Jewish law sources (a ratio of 8:1). References to Jewish law sources peaked in the 1990s with more than 7 percent of the decisions in each of the years from 1993 to 1997 citing Jewish law sources, before falling back markedly in the mid-2000s (e.g. 1 percent in 2005; 2.3 percent in 2006).

Individual judges' attitudes toward Jewish law make a difference; the handful of religious judges who have been appointed to the SCI over the years—most notably Menchem Elon, a noted professor of Jewish law who served as Justice on the Court from 1977 to 1994, and Elyakim Rubinstein, who was appointed to the Court in 2004—are more inclined than their non-religious peers to cite Jewish law sources. Elon cited Jewish law sources in the majority of his rulings; Rubinstein did so in approximately one-third of his judgments. Other, not expressly religious judges (e.g. Mishael Cheshin, Justice 1992–2006) are also relatively likely to quote Jewish sources; these judges express respect for Jewish law sources, and are not outspoken proponents of reference to Western law. (For example, Cheshin led the majority opinion in the *Citizenship Law/Family Unification* case discussed previously, where, as explained earlier, a divided 6:5 bench essentially gave priority to Israel's "Jewish" constitutional pillar of collective identity over the "democratic" one). By contrast, Aharon Barak (Justice 1978–95;

---

[118] The data in this paragraph draws on Yuval Sinai, *Application of Jewish Law in the Israeli Courts* [Hebrew: *Yisum Ha'Mishpat Ha'Ivri Be'vatei Ha'Mishpat Be'Israel*] (The Israeli Bar Association, 2009), 4–32.

[119] On the transformation of Jewish law in the pre-state years, see Assaf Likhovski, "The Invention of 'Hebrew Law' in Mandatory Palestine," *American Journal of Comparative Law* 46 (1998): 339–73.

Chief Justice 1995–2006) cited Jewish law in less than 6 percent of his rulings, and the context of these references is telling: he argues that the Jewish law principles he does cite are universal principles of justice incorporated into Jewish law and not unique principles of Jewish law per se, thereby giving Jewish law a universalistic reading and stripping it of much of its particularity. Eliezer Rivlin (Justice 2000–6; Deputy Chief Justice 2006–12) quoted Jewish sources only twice throughout his years on the bench. Dorit Beinisch (Justice 1995–2005; Chief Justice 2006–12) seldom cited Jewish law at all, and went on record occasionally to denounce the quotation of Biblical and Talmudic verses by some of her colleagues on the bench.

One of history's little ironies, as we will see in the next chapter, is that unlike the SCI, major legal thinkers of the 16th and 17th centuries—think Erastus, Grotius, and Selden, none of whom, needless to say, were Jewish—viewed Jewish law in what they termed the "Hebrew Republic" as an authoritative source of foreign reference, indeed as an ideal-type benchmark against which to develop their theories of toleration and state control of religious affairs.[120] Their high regard for Jewish law was unflagging. In arguing that the church lacks an independent power of excommunication (*Treaties of Erastus*, 1589), Erastus—a Swiss theologian—regarded the "commonwealth" of the Hebrews as an expression of God's own political preferences. Accordingly, he announces that "that Church is most worthily and wisely ordered, which cometh nearest to the constitution of the Jewish Church."[121] Likewise, in his search for a God-given constitution against which to evaluate the relations between civil and religious authority of his time, Hugo Grotius invokes the laws of the Jews as a prime example. "If, however, there is somehow to be found a republic which could rightly point to the true God as its founder," Grotius writes, "then this must clearly be the one that all other ones should set themselves to imitate and seek to resemble as closely as they can." From this, notes historian of political thought Eric Nelson, it follows that "if

---

[120] On the significant impact of Jewish sources, biblical and rabbinical, on European political thought in the 17th and 18th century, see Eric Nelson, *The Hebrew Republic: Jewish Sources and the Transformation of European Political Thought* (Harvard University Press, 2010). Earlier accounts pointed to the possible influence of Jewish sources on the development of international law. See, e.g., Shabtai Rosenne, "The Influence of Judaism on the Development of International Law," *Netherlands Law Review* 5 (1958): 119–49.

[121] See Eric Nelson, "The Religious Origins of Religious Toleration," *The Templeton Lecture on Religion and World Affairs* (Foreign Policy Research Institute, 2011), 5–6.

God himself had designed a commonwealth, then the constitution of that republic would be perfect and authoritative. And, as Grotius promptly adds, God did design such a commonwealth: the republic of the Hebrews."[122] Ironically, in present-day Israel, as they are located on the edge of the East, its judges seem to express a yearning to belong to—or, in Ha-Levi's terms, "have their hearts in"—the West. Canadian and German case law, the prime exemplars of the post-WWII cosmopolitan constitutional worldview, not Jewish law, which in Israeli politics is associated with the traditional and conservative, not the modern and the progressive, have come to gain priority and preference, and indeed now constitute the gold standard for comparative reference.

Understanding why the Court makes very limited reference to Jewish law despite having the legal framework to do so requires understanding the Court's position as a cosmopolitan, liberalizing force within the social and political context in which it operates. Since the establishment of the State of Israel, a fundamental—and unresolved—collective-identity issue has been whether the country is a *medinat hok* (a state based on civil or secular law) or a *medinat halakhah* (a state based on Jewish law). Israel's constitutional system is based on two fundamental tenets: that the state is *Jewish* and *democratic*. It is this commitment to the creation of an ideologically plausible and politically feasible synthesis between particularistic (Jewish) and universalistic (democratic) values that has proved to be the major constitutional challenge faced by Israel since its foundation. Reaching such a synthesis is especially problematic given that non-Jews—primarily Muslims, Christians, and Druze—constitute approximately one-fifth of Israel's citizenry (excluding the Palestinian residents of the West Bank and Gaza Strip).

Even within the Jewish population, the exact meaning of Israel as a "Jewish" state has been highly contested. Not only do opinions differ sharply on whether Jews are citizens of a nation, members of a people, participants in a culture, or coreligionists, but even among adherents of the last opinion—arguably the most established of these constructions—there are widely divergent beliefs and degrees of practice. These adherents range from the ultra-Orthodox to millions who define themselves as "traditional" (*Masorti* or *Shomer Masoret*), and

---

[122] Nelson, "The Religious Origins of Religious Toleration" (n 121), 7.

THE VIEW FROM THE BENCH 61

include those who pursue a fully secular lifestyle yet celebrate their children's bar/bat mitzvah and acknowledge the Jewish high holidays. Nevertheless, for a host of historical and political reasons, the Orthodox stream of the Jewish religion has long enjoyed the status of being the sole branch of Judaism formally recognized by the state. This exclusive status has enabled the Orthodox community to establish a near monopoly over the supply of religious services—a lucrative business entailing countless civil service jobs at the national and municipal levels, monitoring of business compliance with legalized, religion-infused standards, and handling of religious ceremonies ranging from circumcisions to weddings to burials. It has also enabled the Orthodox community to impose rigid standards on the process of determining who is a Jew—a question that has crucial symbolic and practical implications because, according to Israel's Law of Return, Jews who immigrate to Israel are entitled to a variety of benefits, including the right to immediate full citizenship.[123] All of this has taken place even though over two-thirds of the world's Jews, on whom Israel relies for essential symbolic, material, and strategic support, continue to live outside Israel and do not subscribe to the Orthodox stream of Judaism.

The close entanglement of state and religion in Israel is perhaps best shown by looking at a few everyday examples that are ordinary to Israelis but will seem quite unusual to others. First, as any traveler's guidebook about Israel will mention, El Al—Israel's national airline—serves only kosher food and does not operate on Saturdays or on Jewish holidays. Less well known is that the SCI ruled in 1994, in one of the first and most progressive rulings of its kind in the world (the *Danilowitch* case), that El Al had to provide same-sex employees (and their partners) the same benefits it provided to opposite-sex employees and their partners. (Interestingly, the *Danilowitch* landmark ruling cited 17 cases from foreign jurisdictions, and one Jewish law source).[124] Second, in Tel-Aviv, Israel's largest city and its center of business and

---

[123] For an accessible introduction to some of the main aspects of the "who is a Jew" question, see "Who is a Jew?," *The Economist* (Jan. 11, 2014), 51–2.

[124] HCJ 721/94 *El Al Airlines Ltd. v. Danilowitch et al.*, 48(5) P.D. 749 (1995) [Israel]. This act of progressive jurisprudence is not exceptional. E.g., in Dec. 2012 an Israeli court approved the nation's first same-sex divorce even though the country does not officially recognize same-sex marriage. Not allowing the separation, the court reasoned, would violate the couple's fundamental rights. Because rabbinical courts' refusal to deal with same-sex marriage and divorce is to be honored, ruled the court, an ordinary court can claim jurisdiction over the matter.

commerce, public transportation comes to a complete halt on Friday at dusk and does not resume until nightfall on Saturday, at the end of the Jewish Sabbath. By contrast, in the city of Haifa—Israel's third largest city, located less than 60 miles north of Tel-Aviv—public transportation is fully operative throughout Friday and Saturday. Why this difference? In 1947 the secular leadership of the Zionist movement in pre-state Israel and leaders of the religious Jewish community concluded an informal agreement that created a framework for the establishment of the country. The agreement, known as the "status quo agreement," laid out ground rules for the relationship between state and religion in four major areas: education, *kashrut* (Jewish dietary rules), matrimonial law, and Shabbat (including the operation of public transportation). The deal froze the common practice at the time with respect to these four realms, and so froze the operation of public transportation in Tel-Aviv and Haifa as they were at that time. And finally, a third, equally telling anecdote: in 2004 Professors Avram Hershko and Aaron Ciechanover of the Technion in Haifa won the Nobel Prize in Chemistry for their discovery of ubiquitin-mediated protein degradation. This was the first-ever Nobel Prize awarded to a scientist working in an Israeli university and undoubtedly a historic event for Israel's scientific community.[125] The Swedish Royal Academy, however, happened to announce Hershko and Ciechanover's prize on a Jewish holiday. Instead of holding a major press conference at the Technion, as one would expect given the moment's grandeur, Technion authorities had to host the press conference with the two laureates at Hershko's home. It was later revealed that the Technion's rabbi would not allow the university to hold a press conference on the university's premises during the Jewish holiday because by law all public institutions must remain closed on such days. Not even a historic Nobel Prize could change that divine call. These episodes reveal the reality of what is arguably one of the most complex settings for studying the charged relations between religion and constitutionalism.

To further complicate things, over the last four decades there has been a continuous decline in the political power and representation of

---

[125] Israelis had won Nobel Prizes in Literature and Peace; Daniel Kahneman, an Israeli, won the Nobel Prize in Economic Sciences while he was working at Princeton. Israeli scientists have since won the Nobel Prize on three additional occasions: in Economic Sciences in 2005, and in Chemistry in 2009 and in 2011. An Israeli-born and educated chemist (now at UCLA) won the Nobel Prize in Chemistry in 2013.

Israel's historically hegemonic, secular-socialist Ashkenazi constituencies (mostly Jews of European descent, often with Western cultural propensities, and—at least during the first few decades of statehood— better off socioeconomically compared with Mizrahi Jews, who are mostly of North African and Middle Eastern origin). This decline of the Ashkenazi cultural and political establishment was accompanied by a corresponding rise of new or hitherto marginalized groups, some of which (most notably residents of Jewish settlements in the West Bank and religious Mizrahi residents of development towns and socioeconomically underdeveloped urban neighborhoods) are strong advocates for Jewish tradition.[126] The expansion of the electorate by the addition of approximately one million newly arrived immigrants from the former Soviet Union and elsewhere (roughly 15 percent of Israel's population)—many of whom support extreme nationalist parties—also contributed to destabilizing the Labor movement's historical grip on political power. As the largely secular Ashkenazi elite's disproportionate influence over the country's important political decision-making arenas has been increasingly challenged, its willingness (if not eagerness) to transfer crucial religion-and-state questions from the political arena to the SCI has likewise increased.[127] Given the Court's record of adjudication, as well as its judges' educational backgrounds and cultural propensities, Israel's left-leaning, relatively cosmopolitan bourgeoisie can safely assume that its worldviews and policy preferences with regard to constitutive questions of religion and state will be less effectively contested. This has resulted in the transformation of the SCI into a (if not *the*) crucial present-day forum for addressing the country's most fundamental collective-identity quandaries.

Over the last few decades, the Supreme Court has become a bastion of "reason" and "sanity" for Israel's "enlightened public"—a group frequently referred to by the SCI throughout the 1990s when determining the "reasonableness" of specific acts. This court-constructed "enlightened public" closely conforms to the characteristics of the old Ashkenazi establishment at the center of the Zionist consensus, and shares its worldviews and policy preferences. Since the late 1980s, the

---

[126] On the origins and various legal manifestations of Israel's internal social rifts and culture wars, see Menachem Mautner, *Law and the Culture of Israel* (Oxford University Press, 2011).

[127] See Ran Hirschl, *Towards Juristocracy: The Origins and Consequences of the New Constitutionalism* (Harvard University Press, 2004); Ran Hirschl, "The Socio-Political Origins of Israel's Juristocracy," *Constellations* 16 (2009): 476–92.

Court has pursued a distinctly liberalizing agenda in core matters of religion and state, ranging from the curtailment of the exclusive jurisdiction of the rabbinical courts in matters of personal status and the erosion of the Orthodox monopoly over the provision of religious services to the liberalization of rules pertaining to commercial activity on the Jewish Sabbath, the right to pray in holy sites, the solemnization of marriage, *shmita* (land sabbatical) laws, and *kashrut* (kosher; meaning "fit" or "legitimate" for consumption according to Jewish dietary and food-preparation restrictions). In an important case involving a blatant ethnic segregation policy by an ultra-Orthodox girls' school (the segregation was justified by school authorities as addressing the distinct needs of two separate religious streams), the Court ruled (2009) that although the right to cultural pluralism in education is recognized by Israeli law, religious affiliation as a basis for autonomous schooling is not an absolute right when it collides with the overarching right to equality.[128] (Curiously, the newly established United Kingdom Supreme Court drew on the same general logic and cited the SCI ruling in a case involving a selective, some say discriminatory, admissions policy by a North London Jewish school).[129] In 2011, the Court held in another landmark case that gender segregation on public buses operating in several ultra-Orthodox towns was unlawful.[130] Bus companies offering services in religious neighborhoods were ordered to carry anti-segregation signs indicating that all passengers were allowed to choose any seat, except seats designated for the disabled.

Proponents of secular policies have also scored victories because of the Court's relatively progressive treatment of the issue of non-Orthodox conversion to Judaism and the related question "Who is a Jew?" In a landmark ruling on the subject (2005), the Court agreed (7:4) to recognize non-Orthodox "bypass" conversions to Judaism performed de jure abroad but de facto in Israel.[131] It held that a person will be considered Jewish who comes to Israel as a non-Jew and, during a period of lawful residence there, undergoes conversion in a recognized Jewish community abroad. In its judgment the Court stated that: "The Jewish nation is one … It is dispersed around the world, in

---

[128] HCJ 1067/08 *Noar Ke'Halacha v. Ministry of Education* [2009] IsrLR 84 (decision released on Aug. 6, 2009) [Israel].

[129] See *R(E) v. Governing Body of JFS* [2009] UKSC 15 [United Kingdom].

[130] HCJ 746/07 *Ragen v. Ministry of Transport* (decision released on Jan. 5, 2011) [Israel].

[131] HCJ 2597/99 *Thais-Rodriguez Tushbaim v. Minister of Interior*, 59(6) P.D. (2005) [Israel].

communities. Whoever converted to Judaism in one of these communities overseas has joined the Jewish nation by so doing, and is to be seen as a 'Jew' under the Law of Return. This can encourage immigration to Israel and maintain the unity of the Jewish nation in the Diaspora and in Israel." Few would articulate the non-Orthodox view of Judaism in present-day Israel more potently.

A pinnacle of the SCI's liberalizing jurisprudence in matters of religion and state is its subjection of the religious courts' jurisprudential autonomy in matters of personal status to general principles of administrative and constitutional law, most notably due process and gender equality. This has had far-reaching implications in areas as diverse as family and personal-status law, representation in statutory religious bodies, and gender equality in the religious labor market. In Israel, no unified civil law applies to all citizens in matters of marriage and divorce. Instead, for various political and historical reasons (the roots of contemporary Israeli family law go back as far as the Ottoman Empire's pre-modern *millet* system), the courts of the different religious communities hold exclusive jurisdiction over marriage, divorce, and directly associated personal-status matters. A number of other personal-status matters may be adjudicated through the rabbinical court system (controlled by Orthodox Judaism) if the involved parties consent to such extended jurisdiction. Muslim, Christian, and Druze courts also have exclusive jurisdiction over the personal-status affairs of their respective communities.

Since the mid-1990s, the SCI has gradually been attempting to limit the authority exercised by religious courts. The most important SCI judgment regarding this matter was rendered in 1995 in the *Bavli* case.[132] In several earlier decisions, the SCI had ruled that religious tribunals must comply with provisions of concrete laws pertinent to their operation and jurisdictional boundaries. In its ruling in *Bavli* the SCI expanded considerably its overarching review of religious tribunals' jurisprudence by holding that all religious tribunals, including the Great Rabbinical Court, are statutory bodies established by law and funded by the state; in principle, all aspects of their judgments are thus subject to review by the SCI. Although the SCI recognized the special jurisdictional mandate awarded to Jewish, Muslim, Christian, and

---

[132] HCJ 1000/92 *Bavli v. The Great Rabbinical Court*, 48(2) P.D. 6 (1995) [Israel]. On Shari'a court jurisdiction, see C.A. 3077/90 *Plonit ("Jane Doe") v. Ploni ("John Doe")*, 49(2) P.D. 578 (1996) [Israel].

Druze courts by the legislature, it nevertheless asserted its power to impose fundamental constitutional norms on their exercise of authority. Rabbinical court officials have responded by publicly asserting their resistance to the idea that the SCI, as a secular entity, possesses the authority to review their adjudication, which rests on religious law. Some have gone so far as to declare their intention to ignore the Court's ruling in *Bavli*, which they perceive as an illegitimate intrusion into their exclusive jurisdictional sphere. The SCI has not been impressed by this reaction. On the basis of its landmark decision in *Bavli*, it has gone on to overturn at least two dozen other rabbinical court and Shari'a court rulings for not conforming with general principles of Israel's constitutional and administrative law, including gender equality, reasonableness, proportionality, natural justice, and procedural fairness.

In *Katz* (1996), the Court held that the rabbinical courts were not authorized to declare an individual who refused to have a civil matter adjudicated by the rabbinical court excommunicated or ostracized. The majority opinion stated that since the rabbinical court system is a public organ that exists by force of law and draws its authority from the law, it can only exercise those prerogatives vested in it by law.[133] A year later, the Court overturned a rabbinical court decision that held that a divorced father who had become religious was entitled to decide where his children would be educated, even though his wife, who remained secular, had been granted custody of the children.[134] In 1998, the Court overturned another rabbinical court decision that had forced a divorcee to send her son to a religious school at the demand of her ex-husband.[135] In a similar spirit, the Court ruled in 2001 that the rabbinical courts were unauthorized to decide on a request by a man to prohibit his ex-wife from letting their children spend time with her lesbian partner.[136]

A fascinating recent illustration of this trend is the Court's ruling in *Plonit ("Jane Doe") v. The Great Rabbinical Court* (2008).[137] Section 5 of

---

[133] HCJ 3269/95 *Katz v. Jerusalem Regional Rabbinical Court*, 50(4) P.D. 590 (1996) [Israel].

[134] HCJ 5507/96 *Amir v. Haifa District Court*, 50(3) P.D. 321 (1997) [Israel].

[135] HCJ 5227/97 *David v. Great Rabbinical Court*, 55(1) P.D. 453 (1998) [Israel]. Matters of marriage and divorce fall under the exclusive jurisdiction of rabbinical courts. Matters of children's education are not within the rabbinical courts' jurisdiction, unless "bound up" expressly in a suit to the rabbinical court.

[136] HCJ 293/00 *Plonit ("Jane Doe") v. Great Rabbinical Court*, 55(3) P.D. 318 (2001) [Israel].

[137] HCJ 8928/06 *Plonit ("Jane Doe") v. The Great Rabbinical Court* (decision released on Oct. 8, 2008) [Israel].

the Property Relations between Spouses Law (*Hok Yahasei Mammon bein Bnei Zug* 1973, amended in 1995) states that in the case of divorce, the couple's assets will be split evenly between the two spouses regardless of the formal registration status of these assets. However, Section 8 of that law grants courts the authority to determine "special circumstances" in which an uneven split may be justified. In *Plonit*, a woman who married her husband in 1985 had an extramarital affair in 2003 that eventually brought about the breakup of her marriage. The Great Rabbinical Court ruled that the wife's unfaithful behavior constituted "special circumstances," and that the husband was entitled to more than half of the couple's assets, in this case, pension moneys owed to him.

On appeal, the SCI used its reasoning in *Bavli* to overturn the ruling. It accepted the wife's argument that the Great Rabbinical Court ruling did not comply with earlier SCI decisions which stated that adulterous behavior may justify neither a departure from the presumption of an even split nor a retroactive negation of the adulterous spouse's rights to accumulated property in the years before his or her extramarital affair. Even more importantly, the SCI rejected the husband's claim that the law assigned to either the rabbinical court or the general court dealing with the matter the authority to decide what "special circumstances" were in this context. The SCI stated decisively that the two systems are not parallel, but unitary. Rulings of the rabbinical court system, including rulings of the Great Rabbinical Court, are subject to review by the SCI and must comply with pertinent jurisprudential principles established by the SCI over the years. One can hardly think of a greater blow to the rabbinical court system's jurisdictional autonomy. Rabbinical courts have not been indifferent to what they see as "interventions and restrictions" by the SCI, and have occasionally responded by adopting an ultra-conservative position in defiance of the rulings of the SCI.[138] It is little wonder that religious parties, led by Shas, vow to pass laws that expand the jurisdiction of the rabbinical court system and exempt it from the SCI's scrutiny.

Given its clear jurisprudential position on religion-and-state matters, the Court's rejection of Jewish law as a viable source of reference and as a useful interpretive tool, indeed its penchant for Western constitutional jurisprudence more broadly, is hardly surprising. These preferences are

---

[138] Daphna Hacker, "Religious Tribunals in Democratic States: Lessons from the Israeli Rabbinical Courts," *Journal of Law and Religion* 27 (2012): 59–81, 64.

not explained solely or even primarily by legal tradition factors, and certainly not by language, regional diffusion, or court newness, but by the SCI's ideological standing with respect to Israel's contested collective identity and culture wars.

Similar trends elsewhere

A quick look at patterns of foreign reference in other countries where a constitutional court has positioned itself as a bastion of universalism and cosmopolitanism (at least relative to the context within which it operates) supports the idea that selective foreign reference has a socio-political foundation.

Since gaining its independence in 1947, Pakistan has been grappling with what may be called an identity crisis, reflecting existential uncertainty with respect to its relation to Islam. Although from a formal standpoint, notes Farzana Shaikh, Pakistan was created as the first self-professed homeland for Muslims, neither Pakistanis nor their governments have ever been able to reach a consensus over the precise role and meaning of Islam.[139] In the foundational Constituent Assembly debates, Mohammad Ali Jinnah ("the Father of the Nation") articulated a vision of collective identity that prioritized political citizenship over religious affiliation. However, Islam has always remained a major marker of collective identity in Pakistan.

The process of formal "Islamization" of Pakistani constitutional law goes back to 1973 and has known many twists and turns. The preamble to the 1973 Constitution states, inter alia: "Whereas sovereignty over the entire universe belongs to Allah Almighty alone and the authority which He has delegated to the State of Pakistan through its people for being exercised within the limits prescribed by Him is a sacred trust ... Wherein the principles of democracy, freedom, equality, tolerance and social justice as enunciated by Islam shall be fully observed; Wherein the Muslims shall be enable to order their lives in the individual and collective spheres in accordance with the teachings and requirements of Islam as set out in the Holy *Qur'an* and the *Sunnah.*"

---

[139] Farzana Shaikh, *Making Sense of Pakistan* (Columbia University Press, 2009).

Article 1 of the current constitution declares that Pakistan's official name shall be the Islamic Republic of Pakistan, and Article 2 declares Islam the state religion. In 1978, President Zia-ul-Haq established the Shari'at Benches at the provincial High Courts, and in 1980 the Federal Shari'at Court, as well as the Shari'at Appellate Bench at the Supreme Court; each of these would be responsible for ensuring the appropriate implementation of Shari'a law. In 1985, a set of amendments to the constitution was introduced, effectively stipulating: "All existing laws shall be brought in conformity with the Injunctions of Islam as laid down in the Holy Qur'an and Sunna, in this Part referred to as the Injunctions of Islam, and no law shall be enacted which is repugnant to such Injunctions." In theory, this means that legislation must be in full compliance with principles of Shari'a. The Supreme Court of Pakistan, however, has begged to differ.

In response to the possible conclusiveness of the Islamization reforms, the Court developed its "harmonization doctrine," according to which no specific provision of the constitution stands above any other provision. In a landmark ruling in 1992 (*Hakim Khan v. Government of Pakistan*), the Supreme Court held that the "Islamization amendment" shall not prevail over the other articles of the constitution, as the amendment possessed the same weight and status as the other articles of the constitution and therefore "could not be placed on a higher pedestal or treated as a *grund norm*."[140] The Court's subsequent judgments of this key issue have firmly precluded and strongly warned against an interpretation of the Islamization amendments that would "raise it to the point of being a litmus test for gauging, evaluating, and potentially justifying the judiciary to strike down any other constitutional provisions."[141] Any reading of the amendments as elevated "special clauses" would undermine the entire constitution. The constitution as a whole must be interpreted in a harmonious fashion so that specific provisions are read as an integral part of the entire constitution, not as standing above it. In the words of the Court: "It may be observed that the principles for interpreting constitutional documents as laid down by this Court are that all provisions should be read

[140] *Hakim Khan v. Government of Pakistan*, P.L.D. 1992 S.C. 595 [Pakistan]. See Ajmal Mian, *A Judge Speaks Out* (Oxford University Press, 2004), 135.

[141] Osama Siddique and Zahra Hayat, "Unholy Speech and Holy Laws: Blasphemy Laws in Pakistan—Controversial Origins, Design Defects, and Free Speech Implication," *Minnesota Journal of International Law* 17 (2008): 303–85, 368.

together and harmonious construction should be placed on such provisions so that no provision is rendered nugatory."[142] In addition to its
refusal to accept the Islamization amendments as a supra-constitutional
norm, the Court has consistently retained its overarching jurisdictional
authority, including its de facto appellate capacity over the Shari'at
Appellate Bench at the Supreme Court. This has proved time and again
to be a safety valve for secular interests.

Inasmuch as the Supreme Court of Pakistan sees itself as a stronghold
of reason and modernism operating in a religion-infused constitutional
and political sphere, it is hardly surprising that it commonly cites
English and other Western case law, occasionally refers to Supreme
Court of India rulings, but almost never engages with jurisprudence
from predominantly Muslim countries that much like Pakistan itself
have constitutionally entrenched the status of Islam as the official state
religion and as "a" or "the" source of legislation. Ajmal Mian, Chief
Justice of Pakistan from 1997 to 1999 and the judge who authored the
majority opinion in the leading "harmonization" ruling described
previously, refers to the influence of global constitutionalism on Pakistani constitutional jurisprudence in his memoirs.[143] Notably, Mian
takes great pride in the fact that Justice Claire L'Heureux-Dubé of the
Supreme Court of Canada (1987–2002)—a major proponent of international constitutional cross-fertilization—visited the Supreme Court
of Pakistan and expressed keen interest in its jurisprudence on constitutional matters.

In post-conflict Afghanistan, President Hamid Karzai opted for a
shake-up of the newly established Supreme Court's composition following more than two years of conservative jurisprudence, rife with
citation of verses from the Qur'an, on religious matters. In 2006, Karzai
appointed several new, more moderate jurists to the Court. In addition, the reappointment of Chief Justice Faisal Ahmad Shinwari—a
conservative Islamic cleric with questionable educational credentials—did
not pass the parliamentary vote. Karzai then chose his own legal
counsel Abdul Salam Azimi, a former professor at the University of
Nebraska at Omaha who was educated in the United States, to succeed
Shinwari. In August 2006 the new, distinctly more moderate court was
sworn in. A wave of citations of Western law followed.

---

[142] *Qazi Hussain Ahmed et al. v. General Pervez Musharraf, Chief Executive and Another*, P.L.
D. 2002 S.C. 853 [Pakistan].
[143] Mian, *A Judge Speaks Out* (n 140).

THE VIEW FROM THE BENCH 71

Despite the strong secularist and modernist agenda established by Kemalist reformism and its constitution, Turkey has witnessed a dramatic resurgence of political Islam over the last few decades. Since 2002, the country has been governed by the pro-religious Justice and Development Party (AKP). Yet at least until the recent alteration of its composition by the AKP-led government, the Turkish Constitutional Court has served as a bastion of Kemalist interests in their fight to curb the influence of popular political Islam. Having dissolved two pro-Islamist parties in 1998 (the Welfare [Refah] Party) and 2001 (the Virtue [Fazilet] Party), the Court came very close in 2008 to banning the AKP; six of the 11 judges—one vote shy of the necessary seven votes—found the AKP platform unconstitutional.[144] In so doing, the judges signaled that no further Islamization would be tolerated by the Court and its secularist and military establishment backers. A few weeks later, the Court declared unconstitutional a constitutional amendment that had been passed legally by the AKP-controlled parliament that would have lifted the ban on the wearing of the Muslim headscarf (*hijab*) by Islamist female students in public universities.[145]

Interestingly, despite their geographical proximity, and even though Israel and Turkey are facing similar societal conflicts over secularism and religion, as well as comparable culture wars between Mediterranean and European propensities, there is no citation whatsoever of Israeli Supreme Court cases by the Turkish Constitutional Court (or vice versa), a trend that is not likely to change anytime soon given the sour political climate between the two countries. What is more, in its decision to disband the Refah Party, for example, the Turkish Constitutional Court stated that in modern secular states such as Turkey (Turkey is often cited as one of the three most religious democracies in the world alongside the United States and India), religious creed is a private matter, "saved from politicization, taken out of being a tool of administration, and is kept in its real, respectable place which is the conscience of the people."[146] In such countries, modernity has become

---

[144] TCC Decision 1/1998 (Welfare [Refah] Party Dissolution case), Jan. 16, 1998 [Turkey]; and TCC Decision 57/2001 (Virtue [Fazilet] Party Dissolution case), June 21, 2001 [Turkey].

[145] TCC Decision 116/2008 (Unconstitutional Constitutional Amendment Case), decision released June 5, 2008; legal reasoning released Oct. 22, 2008 [Turkey].

[146] See, generally, Dicle Kogacioglu, "Dissolution of Political Parties by the Constitutional Court in Turkey: Judicial Delimitation of the Political Domain," *International Sociology* 18 (2003): 258–76, 268.

"the basic building block of transforming the people from an ummah [religious community] to a nation."[147] These statements were backed by reference to Enlightenment philosophy as well as to French, American, and German jurisprudence. No reference was made to any Mediterranean or Middle Eastern jurisdiction. Switzerland on the Bosphorus.

Similarly, apex courts in Taiwan and Hong Kong seldom cite court rulings from mainland China. The Supreme Court of Ireland and the Court of Judicature of Northern Ireland (until 2009 the Supreme Court of Judicature), very rarely cite each other. The Seychelles Court of Appeal frequently cites UK cases as well as rulings of the US and Indian Supreme Courts, but seldom if ever refers to rulings from continental Africa, from which it aspires to distinguish itself.[148] The Supreme Court of Appeal of Timor-Leste (East Timor) frequently cites jurisprudence from Portugal and Europe more generally; reference to Indonesian court rulings is a political nonstarter.[149] In Korea, reference to German rulings is far more prevalent than reference to Japanese law.[150] The Malaysian Federal Court—Malaysia's peak constitutional tribunal—has found English constitutional cases to be more persuasive and relevant to its interpretive framework than Indian cases, even though the Malaysian constitution is nearer in content and structure to the Indian constitution than to the constitutional laws and principles of Britain, and even though the tensions of ethnicity, religion, and federalism in Malaysia are far closer to those in India or Indonesia than to those in Britain.[151] At a time when the very essence of Malaysia as an Islamic state is hotly contested in the political sphere, the Malaysian Federal Court seldom references the constitutional jurisprudence of other predominantly Muslim countries.

---

[147] Kogacioglu, "Dissolution of Political Parties by the Constitutional Court in Turkey" (n 146).

[148] See A. H. Angelo, ed., *Leading Cases of the Seychelles Court of Appeals 1988–2010* (Bar Association of Seychelles, 2010).

[149] In 2003, the newly established Timorese Supreme Court of Appeal ruled that law in the new nation should be based on Portuguese legal heritage, not Indonesian. Because Indonesia's occupation (1975–2002) was unlawful, the Court ruled, the United Nations-drafted legal system adopted after independence (which left many Indonesian legal structures intact) was invalid.

[150] See David Law, "Judicial Comparativism and Judicial Diplomacy," *University of Pennsylvania Law Review* 163 (2015): 927–1036.

[151] See Andrew Harding, *The Constitution of Malaysia: A Contextual Analysis* (Hart Publishing, 2012), 206.

The Supreme Court of India itself makes considerably more extensive use of foreign jurisprudence in periods when it wishes to advance more socially progressive rights jurisprudence.[152] In its 2014 ruling recognizing transgender constitutional rights of equality as "third gender," to pick a recent example, the Supreme Court of India cited cases and legislation from Argentina, Australia, Canada, the Council of Europe, the European Court of Human Rights, Germany, Malaysia, Nepal, the Netherlands, New Zealand, South Africa, United Kingdom, and the United States; the apex courts of Illinois, Massachusetts, and New South Wales (Australia); a host of international covenants including the Universal Declaration of Human Rights; as well as the writings and ideas of Aristotle, John Locke, Immanuel Kant, and John Rawls.[153] Likewise, in its much discussed decision in the *Naz Foundation* case (2009), the High Court of Delhi drew extensively on foreign rulings in support of arguments from equality, privacy, and dignity to strike down India's sodomy laws.[154]

And vice versa: in its landmark ruling in *Koushal v. NAZ Foundation* (2013), the Supreme Court of India reversed the 2009 decision of the Delhi High Court that Section 377 of the Indian Penal Code was unconstitutional under the Indian Constitution and upheld India's sodomy law as constitutional. A presumption of constitutionality ought to be applied, ruled the Supreme Court in this atypically conservative ruling, given the "importance of separation of powers and out of a sense of deference to the value of democracy that parliamentary acts embody." The Court's opinion lambasts the Delhi court's extensive reliance on foreign sources to support its progressive ruling. Justice Singhvi who authored the opinion did not mince words in stating that:

In its anxiety to protect the so-called rights of LGBT [lesbian, gay, bisexual, and transgender] persons and to declare that Section 377 violates the right to

---

[152] Adam Smith, "Making Itself at Home: Understanding Foreign Law in Domestic Jurisprudence—The Indian Case," *Berkeley Journal of International Law* 24 (2006): 218–72.

[153] Writ Petition (Civil) 400/2012 and Writ Petition (Civil) 604/2013, *National Legal Services Authority v. Union of India and others* (decision released Apr. 15, 2014) [India].

[154] On the sophisticated, possibly even strategic use of comparative constitutional law in this ruling, see Sujit Choudhry, "How to do Comparative Constitutional Law in India: *Naz Foundation*, Same Sex Rights, and Dialogical Interpretation," in Sunil Khilnani, Vikram Raghavan, and Arun K. Thiruvengadam, eds., *Comparative Constitutionalism in South Asia* (Oxford University Press, 2013), 45–85.

privacy, autonomy and dignity, the High Court has extensively relied upon the judgments of other jurisdictions. Though these judgments shed considerable light on various aspects of this right and are informative in relation to the plight of sexual minorities, we feel that they cannot be applied blindfolded for deciding the constitutionality of the law enacted by the Indian legislature.[155]

In other words, much like in Israel, the United States, and elsewhere, foreign reference is more likely to fly in support of a universalist position, much like a rejection of such sources is more likely in support of a particularist position. There are, to be sure, notable exceptions to this trend, but as prominent Polish scholar Wiktor Osiatynski puts it, "culture usually tends to resist borrowing."[156]

In neighboring Sri Lanka, Gary Jacobsohn and Shylashri Shankar find, the Supreme Court commonly cites Indian rulings, albeit sometimes in a selective, even opportunistic way that is "consistent with the larger judicial effort to secure the constitutional moorings upon which the identity of the Sri Lankan state was tethered, chief among which is Sinhalese Buddhism."[157] Courts in late 19th-century and early 20th-century Argentina borrowed extensively and sometimes blindly from the US constitutional model and jurisprudence to advance the interests of new economic and political elites and assist with the centrist conquest of the hinterlands; in this way, Argentina's constitutional domain, during a critical period in the country's history, depended on the prestige of its US model for its international legitimacy and reputation.[158] An aspiration to rejoin the family of "enlightened"

---

[155] Civil Appeal 10972/2013 *Koushal v. NAZ Foundation* (decision released Dec. 11, 2013) [India]. On Jan. 28, 2014, the Supreme Court of India declined a petition to revisit the matter, and left the Dec. 2013 ruling intact. See *Suresh Kumar Koushal and another v. Naz Foundation and others* (2014) 1 SCC 1 [India].

[156] See Wiktor Osiatynski, "Paradoxes of Constitutional Borrowing," *International Journal of Constitutional Law* 1 (2003): 244–68, 261; cited in Jacobsohn, "The Permeability of Constitutional Borders" (n 6), 1776. For an example of reliance on comparative materials to advance a conservative agenda one might think of Mary Ann Glendon's work on abortion, and her critique of the American notion of the "lone rights bearer." That said, Glendon has been outspoken about the need to restrict the practice of foreign citations in the United States. See, e.g., her essay "Comparative Law in the Age of Globalization," *Duquesne Law Review* 52 (2013): 1–24.

[157] Gary J. Jacobsohn and Shylashri Shankar, "Constitutional Borrowing in South Asia: India, Sri Lanka, and Constitutional Identity," in Khilnani et al., eds., *Comparative Constitutionalism in South Asia* (n 154), 180–218.

[158] Jonathan Miller, *Borrowing a Constitution: The U.S. Constitution in Argentina and the Heyday of the Argentine Supreme Court 1853–1930*, unpublished book manuscript; on file with author.

nations surely informed the work of South African Constitutional Court judges as they extensively referenced Western law in the post-apartheid years. Finally, as mentioned earlier, the vociferous debate in the United States concerning citation of foreign constitutional jurisprudence is intimately related to wider struggles over competing visions of the United States' place in the world.

Conclusion

Patterns of non-mandatory reference to foreign law tell us a great deal about *how* and *why* constitutional courts engage with comparative constitutional law. Unlike the legally binding and warranted application of other bodies of law, this practice is purely voluntary and may stem from a variety of goals and aspirations; it thus reflects authentic judicial views and preferences with respect to the laws of others. Existing accounts of constitutional court reference to the laws of others suggest the practice is more common (and less contested) in some jurisdictions than in others. That said, the actual frequency and scope of such references around the world is very much an open question, primarily because existing studies focus on a relatively small (and not necessarily representative) set of countries; little is known about the actual scope and nature of voluntary reference to foreign law in the vast majority of countries. Systematic, reliable data is hard to come by with respect to constitutional courts in much of Latin America, Africa, Asia, and the Pacific. At least with respect to the supply side—the courts whose jurisprudence is frequently cited elsewhere—it seems indisputable that American and British jurisprudence no longer enjoy exclusive status as sources of frequently referenced rulings. Other courts, most notably the European Court of Human Rights, the German Federal Constitutional Court, and the Supreme Court of Canada, and to a somewhat lesser degree peak courts of half a dozen other countries, have become credible "providers" of internationally cited jurisprudence.

What explains judicial choice of which courts to reference? Like any other major socio-legal phenomenon, the international migration of constitutional ideas, including voluntary reference to foreign law, results from a confluence of factors rather than any single cause. As Jacobsohn and Shankar astutely observe, "the practice of constitutional borrowing, like other judicial practices, cannot be readily reduced to any single motivation . . . Ultimately borrowing results from a mix of motives—opportunistic, self-reflective and sometimes unreflective. Which one dominates may be less a function of judges themselves, and more a function of the institutional balance between the executive and the judiciary."[159] And, one might add: a function of a given court's position with respect to fundamental collective identity challenges that face the polity within which it operates.

Works that attempt to explain (not merely describe) voluntary constitutional court engagement with the emerging global constitutional canon point to various factors ranging from institutional prestige and court newness to convergence along the lines of linguistics and legal tradition. Like any other institutional choices, however, judicial decisions with respect to what body of foreign judgments to cite or not to cite cannot be understood in isolation from the sociopolitical context within which these decisions are made, and more specifically in isolation from the positions, preferences, and beliefs of those who make these choices. As we have seen, a given constitutional court's normative and strategic standing with respect to key collective identity quandaries that preoccupy the polity within which it operates is a key determinant of judicial choices with respect to foreign citations, especially when such choices cannot be explained by other commonly cited factors. The distinctions courts make between "pertinent" and "irrelevant" comparators may well reflect the objective or reputational value of these sources, but more often they reflect the judicial image of the "right" culture and "suitable" set of values the borrowing polity ought to follow. Thus, voluntary judicial engagement with the laws of others, certainly in transitional or discordant constitutional settings, is at least as much an identity-constructing political phenomenon as it is a juridical one.

---

[159] Jacobsohn and Shankar, "Constitutional Borrowing in South Asia" (n 157), 218.

2

Early Engagements with the Constitutive Laws of Others
Lessons from Pre-Modern Religion Law

"Can you see anything?"
"Yes, wonderful things!"

(Howard Carter, archaeologist, in response to
Lord Carnarvon, his patron, on Carter first
stepping into Tutankhamun's tomb, Valley of
the Kings, Egypt, November 26, 1922)

Contemporary discussions in comparative constitutional law often proceed as if there is no past, only present and future. The underlying assumption is that contemporary intellectual endeavors in the field constitute a necessary advance over previous ones. When the past *is* referenced, the focus is often on the introduction of the US Constitution or the constitutional aftermath of World War II. As a result, many of the debates that take place within the field are presented as being grounded in ideas or situations that are fresh and hitherto unknown to mankind. The migration of constitutional ideas, judicial recourse to foreign law, and the emergence of a multiplicity of legal orders alongside powerful transnational convergence vectors are some of the exciting constitutional developments that have inspired such debates in the last few decades. However, the world was created before 1945, and even before 1787. The reality is that critical encounters with the constitutive laws of others have been taking place since well before the late 18th century. Many of the purportedly new debates in comparative constitutional law have early equivalents, some of which date back over two millennia.

There has been much debate in contemporary constitutional law about the unique nature of each polity's constitutional heritage and its prospects for withstanding pressures of global convergence, and in particular about what, if any, external constitutional and transnational sources may be referred to in interpreting a given country's constitutional texts. Such debates, however, are anything but novel when considered against the history of pre-modern community-constituting law, most notably religious law. Jewish law, to continue a thread of discussion from the previous chapter, provides an ideal context for studying the tension between principled objection to recognizing the legitimacy of other legal systems and the pragmatist acknowledgment of the inevitability of dealing with extra-communal law. For thousands of years Jewish law has evolved as an autonomous legal tradition without political sovereignty. Because of the near-permanent "diasporic" state of the Jewish people, Jewish law has developed a complex relationship with its legal surroundings, oscillating between principled estrangement and pragmatic engagement.

The Halakha generally takes a negative attitude toward other legal systems: although it recognizes non-Jewish law, it designates courts that base their rulings on such law as illegitimate institutions. At the same time, the variety of social, economic, and political realities the Jews have been through since *c.* 70 CE has given rise to a notably more pragmatic approach to non-Jewish law. The struggle between "authentic," "Hellenized," and later "Romanized" Judaism characterized the days of the Hasmonean dynasty, King Herod, and the Jewish–Roman wars. The *Tannai'm* (sages of the Mishna, *c.* 30–200 CE) addressed the relationship between Jewish law and the Roman legal system; the Babylonian *Amorai'm* (the sages of the Gemara, *c.* 200–500 CE) contemplated measures to cope with petitions by Jews to Persian courts; and their successors, the *Ge'onim* of Babylonia (*c.* 600–1050 CE), dealt with Islamic law and its courts. Subsequent generations stretching all the way to Maimonides (in 12th-century Spain) and the 16th-century *Shulkhan Arukh* (a codification of Halakha) by Rabbi Yosef Caro also frequently addressed the "principled pragmatism" duality informing Jewish law's approach to the laws of others. Even within each of these periods, considerable variance existed among Jewish communities with regard to attitudes toward engagement with foreign law, the legitimacy of litigation before non-Jewish tribunals, and so on (Ashkenaz and Provence, for example, took a more permissive approach, while northern Africa was more restrictive). Pre-modern Canon and Shari'a law grappled with the related aspects of engagement with the outer legal universe, leading to rifts between inward-looking, "originalist," "textualist," or otherwise strict interpretive approaches and more cosmopolitan, adaptive interpretive schools.

The wealth of knowledge and degree of theoretical sophistication found in this body of pre-modern opinions, essentially a *terra incognita* for today's scholars of comparative constitutionalism, can add a new angle to contemporary debates about engagement with the constitutive laws of others. In particular, exploring pre-modern religion law's encounters with other legal systems can help us to develop a deeper understanding of the considerations and driving forces—principled, necessity-based, and/or ideology-driven—behind a legal system's selective engagement with foreign law and the "outer world" more generally. Such exploration may also help to generate some doctrinal and jurisprudential ingenuity in addressing the challenge of global constitutionalism. In the following pages, I explore elements of early engagement with the constitutive laws of others along these two lines.

In the first part of the chapter, I look at various doctrinal innovations in pre-modern religion law, particularly Jewish law, in respect of engagement with the laws of others. The examples considered in this part illustrate how selective encounters with the outer legal world, constitutional and otherwise, may be driven by a community survival instinct developed in response to powerful canonization and convergence pressures. In the second part of the chapter, I look at some of the earthly motivations for change to religion law's treatment of external sources and practices. Similar motivations, I argue, may be at play in debates about the status of foreign sources in contemporary constitutional law, a theme which is elaborated on further in the following chapter. Illustrations are drawn from various religion-infused settings, near and far. These diverse examples are not meant to provide an exhaustive survey of all or even most areas where religion law may enrich or shed new light on conversations in contemporary comparative constitutional studies, a task that would easily fill several thick volumes. Rather, the goal of this chapter is more modest. Taken as a whole, the examples explored here suggest that the history of engagement with the constitutive laws of others is much longer and thicker than that of the current constitutional convergence trend. Any new arguments in comparative constitutional law that ignore religion law's rich interpretive legacy may therefore run the risk of being too thin and ahistorical to be considered truly novel. Moreover, these examples illustrate that alongside inquisitiveness per se, instrumentalist factors— from community survival to political economy—matter a great deal in explaining purportedly principled, doctrinal debates over convergence, resistance, and selective engagement (to paraphrase Vicki Jackson's terminology) with the constitutive laws of others, past and present.

I conclude by suggesting that the near-exclusive focus on the present in comparative constitutional studies obscures the fact that some of the core conundrums the field is facing are not new. In fact, even a cursory look at pre- and early-modern thought suggests that there is much to appreciate and to learn from early attempts to theorize about what today would be classified as key issues in comparative public law. These early insights are particularly enlightening with respect to tensions between general practice and community tradition.

Surviving the laws of others

Much has been written over the last decade about the migration of constitutional ideas across legal systems, the rise of "constitutionalism beyond the state," or "transnational constitutionalism" and the formation of an Esperanto-like "generic" form of constitutional law (at least in relation to rights and liberties).[1] "Hidden" inspiration, where ideas are borrowed from the constitutional law of others without formal reference, is arguably even more prevalent. As expected, these trends have not gone unnoticed. Domestic responses have ranged from full endorsement to outright resistance. In the United States, for instance, a lively debate has arisen over the legitimacy of judicial recourse to foreign or comparative law and in the EU member states, nationalist opposition groups have voiced grave concerns about the threat to national sovereignty posed by the pan-European constitutional project.[2]

---

[1] See, e.g., Wen-Chen Chang and Jiunn-rong Yeh, "The Emergence of Transnational Constitutionalism: Its Features, Challenges and Solutions," *Penn State International Law Review* 27 (2008): 89–124; Neil Walker, "Taking Constitutionalism beyond the State," *Political Studies* 56 (2008): 519–43; Sujit Choudhry, "Migration as a Metaphor in Comparative Constitutional Law," in Sujit Choudhry, ed., *The Migration of Constitutional Ideas* (Cambridge University Press, 2006), 1–36; David Law, "Generic Constitutional Law," *Minnesota Law Review* 89 (2005): 652–742; Mark Tushnet, "The Emerging Transnational Constitution," *Loyola of Los Angeles Law Review* 37 (2003): 239–70; Christopher McRudden, "Common Law of Human Rights?: Transnational Judicial Conversations on Constitutional Rights," *Oxford Journal of Legal Studies* 20 (2000): 499–532.

[2] See, e.g., Vicki Jackson, *Constitutional Engagement in a Transnational Era* (Oxford University Press, 2010); Jeremy Waldron, "The Supreme Court, 2004 Term-Comment: Foreign Law and the Modern Jus Gentium," *Harvard Law Review* 119 (2005): 129–47.

Meanwhile, anti-globalization activists oppose what they term the "new constitutionalism"—the largely pernicious spread of a set of quasi-constitutional supranational treaties and institutions that place global economic governance beyond democratic reach and promote uneven development by privileging transnational corporations at the expense of the world's economic hinterlands.[3]

All these phenomena are portrayed in the comparative constitutional law literature as a manifestation of newness, as something that scholars of the laws of nations have never previously encountered. Granted, some of the specifics at play are indeed new, most notably the rise of a new transnational constitutional order and judicial class, and the corresponding decrease in the autonomy of "Westphalian" constitutionalism.[4] But at least one central aspect of these developments— namely, the fundamental tension between forces of legal convergence and enduring patterns of divergence—is not novel.

At the most basic level, the idea of acknowledging the legitimacy and integrity of the constitutive laws of others has a long history. The Hellenic World (c. 600 BCE) is considered the first era where experiments with constitutionalism took place. Solon is often credited with most of this constitutional ingenuity, as is Persia's Cyrus the Great, who is believed to have introduced the practice of tolerating religious minorities (c. 540 BCE). Plato compared the laws of the Greek city-states, and on the basis of this comparison constructed what he deemed the ideal constitution. Aristotle, in *Politics*, likewise compared the constitutions of various city-states, and introduced a distinction between a polity's substantive constitution and its formal one. However, evidence of the concrete nature of constitutionalism in that era is sparse and possibly unreliable.

The earliest clear evidence of a concept that is significant for contemporary debates comes from Ptolemaic (Hellenic) Egypt (c. 300–30 BCE), where an official policy of legal diversity was introduced.

---

[3] See, e.g., Stephen Gill, "New Constitutionalism, Democratisation and Global Political Economy," *Pacifica Review* 10 (1998) 23–38; David Schneiderman, *Constitutionalizing Economic Globalization: Investment Rules and Democracy's Promise* (Cambridge University Press, 2008).

[4] As is well known, the Treaty of Westphalia (1648) divided Europe into separate, secular territories under the authority of sovereigns. The treaty recognized that heads of state control internal affairs and have the right to defend territorial boundaries. It was preceded by the Treaty of Augsburg (1555), which established the principle that sovereigns could decide the religion of citizens within their territory.

Egyptian local law, or "the law of the land" (*nomoi tes choras*), applied to the indigenous population, whereas the Greek *nomoi* applied to Hellenic immigrants. In addition, royal decrees allowed the prosperous Jewish community of Alexandria to follow the "Law of Moses" in certain matters. The Roman Empire took a more assimilationist approach, but developed a distinction between *jus civile*, applicable to Romans, and *jus gentium*, the law of nations. Under the latter, the *praetor peregrinus* of the Roman Republic engaged in legal comparisons and adjustments to foreign circumstances to settle disputes to which non-citizens were party.

Similarly, the Charter of Medina—drafted by the Prophet Muhammad (*c.* 622 CE), who was generally considered to have established the first Islamic state—formed an alliance between several local tribes (pagan at the time) and Muslim emigrants from Mecca. Importantly, the Charter distinguished between wars in which all members of the polity were to partake and Muslim wars from which non-Muslims were exempt. The idea of multiple legal identities in the pre-modern world reached its peak with the Moorish reign in al-Andalus (8th to 15th century) and the Ottoman Empire's *millet* system that allowed recognized religious communities to rule themselves under their own laws in matters of personal status and religious identity. In short, many polities throughout history have acknowledged and considered the foundational laws of others.

Perhaps more importantly, several major waves of legal standardization throughout history—most notably the expansion of canon law that swept medieval Europe in the 11th and 12th centuries—have been religion-driven. Canon law is internal ecclesiastical law that governs the Roman Catholic Church, the Eastern Orthodox churches, and the Anglican Communion of churches. It deals mainly with matters of faith, morals, and discipline, although these areas have been generously interpreted by church authorities to encompass numerous material aspects of life. The way in which canon law is legislated, interpreted, and at times adjudicated varies widely among the three bodies of churches it governs. In all three traditions, however, a canon was initially a rule adopted by a central council or religious authority and then imposed over a vast territory by regional and local agents who were organized in a hierarchical structure of authority. Canon law's ontological and epistemological structure, modes of adjudication, and application therefore resemble modern law in many respects. Over the years, the study of canon law became a major scholarly discipline and, through a continual process of precedent accumulation, elaboration, and interpretation, it was refined into an internally consistent code.[5] Noted medievalists have argued that the structure of the medieval church and the medieval state (e.g. tensions between central and local government) influenced the development of modern constitutional thought and institutions.[6] Moreover, prominent legal historians now suggest that the initial streamlining and unification of religious law under what is known as canon law, and the expansion of its territorial applicability throughout much of medieval Europe, planted the seeds of modern law, with its hierarchical structure and unified, central authority.[7]

Before this process of codification occurred, and until the 11th century, most law was customary, and very little of it was in writing. In many respects, this was a golden age of practical (or applied) comparative legal studies, as legal systems did not enjoy complete hegemony, did not stress exclusivity, and were for the most part fairly tolerant of other legal systems.[8] The migration of legal ideas was a routine, ordinary occurrence. There were no problems of legislative sovereignty as there was typically no single legislative center;[9] no professional judiciary, no professional class of lawyers, and no distinct "science" of law existed. As Harold Berman notes, there was "no independent, integrated, developing body of legal principles and procedures clearly differentiated from other processes of social organization and consciously articulated by a corps of persons specifically trained for that task."[10] De facto legal pluralism was an everyday reality. As John Morrall writes: "It was common to find many different codes of customary law in force in the same kingdom, town or village, even in the same house, if the ninth century bishop Agobard of Lyons is to

---

[5] Robert Ekelund et al., *Sacred Trust: The Medieval Church as an Economic Firm* (Oxford University Press, 1996), 63; John Gilchrist, *The Church and Economic Activity in the Middle Ages* (St. Martin's Press, 1969), 12–13. See generally, John Coughlin, *Canon Law* (Oxford University Press, 2011).

[6] See Brian Tierney, *Religion, Law, and the Growth of Constitutional Thought, 1150–1650* (Cambridge University Press, 1982).

[7] See Harold Berman, *Law and Revolution: The Formation of the Western Legal Tradition* (Harvard University Press, 1983).

[8] See Brian Tamanaha, "Understanding Legal Pluralism: Past to Present, Local to Global," *Sydney Law Review* 30 (2008): 375–411.

[9] Maurizio Lupoi, *The Origins of the European Legal Order* (Cambridge University Press, 2000), 429–36.

[10] Berman, *Law and Revolution* (n 7), 50.

be believed when he says, 'It often happened that five men were present or sitting together, and not one of them had the same law as another.'"[11]

But in the late 11th and early 12th centuries a wave of legalism spread throughout Europe. The main driving force behind this sudden transformation was the assertion of papal supremacy over the entire Western church and the push toward independence of the church from secular control. This change, known as the Papal Revolution, was marked by a formal declaration by Pope Gregory VII in 1075. The immediate trigger was the so-called "investiture controversy" between the papacy and the Holy Roman Empire over authority to appoint church officials in the hinterlands, but the dispute quickly turned into a battle over the legal consolidation and control of Europe. Neither monarchs nor civil authorities were willing to accede to the declaration without a fight, and bloody wars took place throughout Europe between the Holy Roman Emperor's party (led by Henry IV) and the papal party, with the latter eventually triumphing (Henry IV famously "walked to Canossa" in 1077 en route) toward the end of the 12th century. Canon law, and with it modern law, was born.

As Berman notes, from that moment on, the "folk law" of the peoples of Europe disappeared almost completely and was replaced by sophisticated legal systems, first for the church and then for secular political orders—canon law, urban law, royal law, mercantile law, and feudal and manorial law. The unification process stretched across the reign of over 40 popes, from Leo IX (1049–54) to Boniface VIII (1295–1303).[12] During this period, any non–church-controlled authority had to submit to the Church's complete spiritual and earthly dominance. During the reign of Pope Gregory VII (1073–85) the rationale given for this was that the Church is responsible for the world's salvation, and temporal power is subordinate to spiritual power.[13] In 1204, Pope Innocent III issued a decree that explicitly asserted the *plenitudo ecclesiasticae potesatis*, that is, the absolute and full power of the pope over all churches and the entire clergy. Innocent IV canonists extended this doctrine to declare the pope to be the vicar of

---

[11] John Morrall, *Political Thought in Medieval Times* (Harper & Row, 1962), 17; a similar quote from a different edition of Morrall's book is cited in Tamanaha, "Understanding Legal Pluralism" (n 8), 378.

[12] Luisa Giuriato, "Succession Rules of the Latin Church," in Mario Ferrero and Ronald Wintrobe, eds., *The Political Economy of Theocracy* (Palgrave Macmillan, 2009), 149.

[13] Giuriato, "Succession Rules of the Latin Church" (n 12).

Christ himself, the judge of all people, with power higher than and beyond any other spiritual or temporal authority.[14] Studies of concrete legal practices—for example, Marianne Constable's account of the English "mixed-jury" doctrine from the Middle Ages to the 19th century—also reveal the disappearance of "law as practice" and the replacement of law rooted in the actual practices and customs of communities with law determined by officials.[15]

Because it was more or less universally applied, internally coherent, and cumulative, the church's canon law, which was administered by ecclesiastical courts overseen by bishops, enjoyed an advantage over its possible competitors. Ecclesiastical courts claimed jurisdiction over a wide array of subject matter, including matrimonial and testamentary matters, civil and criminal matters involving clerics and church property, and issues that the church considered crucial, such as heresy, blasphemy, sorcery, usury, defamation, fornication, homosexuality, adultery, violation of oaths, and perjury (effectively giving them jurisdiction over much of the contract law of the day), and injury to and assault on clerics or religious places.[16] As Berman notes, "as far as canon law was concerned, any case involving any of these matters could be instituted by filing a complaint in the court of the appropriate archdeacon or bishop, and an appeal could be taken by the losing party to the court of the appropriate archbishop and thence to the court of the pope in Rome."[17]

This wave of consolidation is echoed in today's constitutional landscape, in which states struggle to protect their distinct identity amidst a move to a more general global law. This brings us to one of the most important questions in today's converging constitutional universe: how are national constitutional traditions to protect their distinct identities against the sweeping waves of consolidation? Several of the current approaches to this issue have framed it in dichotomous terms, claiming that the two main available options are full authorization of judicial recourse to foreign law, or outright rejection of it. On the one hand, countries ranging from Argentina (1994) to the United Kingdom (1998) to Brazil (2004) have explicitly incorporated provisions of

---

[14] Giuriato, "Succession Rules of the Latin Church" (n 12).

[15] Marianne Constable, *The Law of the Other: The Mixed Jury and Changing Conceptions of Citizenship, Law, and Knowledge* (University of Chicago Press, 1994).

[16] Berman, *Law and Revolution* (n 7), 261.

[17] Berman, *Law and Revolution* (n 7).

international and supranational human rights covenants into their domestic laws. Other countries have made recourse to foreign law a constitutional imperative. Section 39(1) of the Constitution of South Africa provides that "[w]hen interpreting the Bill of Rights, a court, tribunal or forum…may consider foreign law," and reference to foreign law has been interpreted by prominent South African Constitutional Court judges not as a merely optional jurisprudential route but as an integral part of any open-ended constitutional inquiry.

On the other hand, several jurisdictions have taken proactive measures against engagement with certain sets of foreign laws. In the United States, as discussed in Chapter 3, the "American Laws for American Courts" model legislation advocated by extreme nationalist activists calls for "law-fare" throughout the country in an effort to prevent courts from taking foreign and international law into account, and in particular against the incorporation or enforcement by courts of any provisions of Islamic Shari'a law. Several states have passed or attempted to pass laws or constitutional amendments to that effect.

In a different setting, the Holy See reformed its legal system so that with effect from January 1, 2009, Italian laws no longer automatically apply to the Vatican state, thereby reversing the Lateran Pacts of 1929. Instead, pertinent Italian laws will be examined by Vatican clerics to determine their compatibility with canon law and Catholic moral principles. A senior Vatican canon lawyer, Monsignor José María Serrano Ruiz, has gone on record stating that Italian laws are too numerous and too unstable, and that they too often conflict with the moral teachings of the Catholic Church—to take one example, in March 2012 Italy's Constitutional Court recognized the right of same-sex couples to have a "family life." While such extreme approaches are not uncommon, in most cases the reaction to foreign law is neither to embrace it entirely nor to reject it fully but, rather, to engage with it *selectively*.

Pre-modern law provides fascinating examples of "counter-hegemony" survival measures undertaken by religious minorities. These range from variations on mechanisms such as heresy, treason, and sedition to outright rejection and shunning of foreign laws, and in some cases to the adoption of fake identities. An extreme illustration of a survival-driven duality of religious norms is provided by Druze theology. The Druze—of whom there are currently less than two million in total—broke away from Islam in the 10th century. They regard Caliph al-Hakim (11th-century Egypt) as the human incarnation of the divine spirit, and revere Nabi Shu'ayb (Jethro, the non-Jewish father-in-law of Moses) as prophet. Although they share many theological elements with Islam, the Druze do not believe in the Prophet Muhammad as the last of the prophets, do not fast during the month of Ramadan, and do not make a pilgrimage to Mecca. Having lived in a constant minority-religion status in largely Muslim societies, the Druze developed a concept of "presentation" (*takiya*) which allows them to present themselves outwardly (*zahir*) as members of the dominant or ruling religion while inwardly (*batin*) adhering to the unique elements of Druze faith.[18]

At the other end of the spectrum, the Hellenic portrayal of the Scythians—early Iranian nomadic tribes whom Herodotus described as people who avoid foreign customs at all costs—exemplifies outright rejection. Similarly, James Scott argues that "for two thousand years the disparate groups that now reside in Zomia (a mountainous region the size of Europe that consists of portions of several Asian countries) have fled the projects of the organized state societies that surround them—slavery, conscription, taxes, corvée labor, epidemics, and warfare."[19] Among the strategies employed by the people of Zomia to remain free of external interference were physical dispersion in rugged terrain; agricultural practices that enhanced mobility; use of pliable ethnic identities; devotion to prophetic, millenarian leaders; and maintenance of a largely oral culture that allowed them to reinvent their histories and genealogies as they moved between and around states.[20] Contemporary thinkers who oppose any engagement with the constitutive laws of others surely do not think that a Zomia-like way of constitutional life is realistic or desirable.

More nuanced approaches to dealing with the constitutive laws of others—arguably more relevant for today's transnational, seemingly "pluralist" constitutional setting—are also on offer. Jewish law in particular has developed sophisticated legal doctrines to allow Jewish communities, as semi-sovereign entities in exile, to maintain their religious identity for nearly two millennia while engaging selectively

---

[18] See, generally, Nissim Dana, *The Druze in the Middle East: Their Faith, Leadership, Identity and Status* (Sussex Academic Press, 2003).

[19] James Scott, *The Art of Not Being Governed* (Yale University Press, 2009). The boundaries of Zomia are contested, but seem to include the highlands of Laos, Thailand, northern Vietnam, and Burma as well as southwest China, and some suggest also parts of northern India, Nepal, Pakistan, and Afghanistan.

[20] Scott, *The Art of Not Being Governed* (n 19).

with the laws of others. The main thrust of these doctrines is a conceptual distinction between core, underlying, or basic elements of religious identity, and complementary aspects that under less-than-ideal circumstances may be compromised without violating those core pillars of identity.

At the foundational level, the Jewish legal tradition distinguishes between Jewish law (applicable to Jews) and the minimum moral requirements for the laws of all mankind.[21] Judaism recognizes 613 commandments (*Mitzvot*) that Jews must follow. However, Judaism also postulates a corpus of universal law that is binding upon humanity. According to the Jewish law tradition, before the theophany at Mount Sinai, the Noachide code governed all humanity; after God gave the Jews their own legal system, the Noachide code (which was perceived as arising from an alliance between God and Noah—the ancestor of humanity after the Flood) was to serve as the pillar of the laws of non-Jews. The Noachide code (Latin: *praecepta Noachidarum*; Hebrew: *Mitsvot B'nei Noah*), sometimes referred to as the "Seven Laws of Noah," includes six universal prohibitions—idolatry, blasphemy, bloodshed (i.e. homicide), illicit sexual relations, theft, and consumption of a limb torn from a living animal[22]—and a seventh positive commandment, *dinin*, which requires the establishment of courts and perhaps also the adoption of a civil legal code (broadly understood as a general obligation to institute a legal order allowing a regulated, fair, and honest social life).[23] These Noachide commandments are perceived as universal, and adherence to them as a minimum requirement for any moral human society.

Other intriguing distinctions abound. As noted Jewish law scholar Menachem Elon observes, there is an interdependence between Halakha's ritual commandments and its civil aspects. As Halakha has crystallized, it has recognized the:

---

[21] See Suzanne Last Stone, "Sinaitic and Noahide Law: Legal Pluralism in Jewish Law," *Cardozo Law Review* 12 (1991): 1157–214.

[22] Even the dietary rule has its basic dignity rationale: whereas mankind may be carnivorous, humans must separate themselves from wild animals, which tear their meat from living animals.

[23] The reference text is in the Babylonian Talmud treatise *Sanhedrin*, 56a: "Our Rabbis taught: seven precepts were the sons of Noah commanded: to establish courts of justice; to refrain from blasphemy; idolatry; adultery; bloodshed; robbery; and eating flesh cut from a living animal."

essential and fundamental distinction between *issura* [ritual law] and *mamona* [civil or "nonreligious" law], the latter generally corresponding to most of what is included in the *corpus juris* of contemporary legal systems. This basic distinction offer[s] greater flexibility and an extraordinary potential for development to the civil part of Halakha, that part which is most affected by, and subject to changes in economic and social life.[24]

Additionally, the Talmud added another distinction, this one between biblical commandments or halakhic requirements that are biblically mandated (*mitzvot d'oraita*, Aramaic for "directives by an ultimate authority" or "commandments of the Law") and rabbinic injunctions (*mitzvot d'rabbanan*, Aramaic for "directives by our rabbis"). And in the post-Talmudic literature, a further distinction emerged between a rule (*halakha*) and a custom (*min'hag*, also referred to in Ashkenaz as *takanat ha'kahal* or the "common practice").

Dating back to the 3rd century CE, the *dina de-malkhuta dina* doctrine (Aramaic for "the law of the kingdom is the law") is the halakhic principle which states that, with certain important caveats, the general law of the country where Jews reside is binding upon them, and, in certain cases, is to be preferred to Jewish law.[25] The historical context that brought sage Shmuel to introduce the *dina de-malkhuta dina* doctrine are typical of the near-permanently diasporic Jewish existence and of the Jewish people's systemic need to respond and adjust to the law of the land where they reside. The conquest of Babylon from the Parthians (226 CE) by Ardashir I, founder of the Sassanid Empire, brought an end to a period of tranquility for the Jews in Babylonia. Having lost their political and religious autonomy, they had to adapt to the powerful and centralized rule of the Sassanids. In 241, Shapur I, son of Ardashir, succeeded to the throne and granted the minorities under his rule, including the Jews, cultural and religious autonomy. Samuel, the Jews' leader at that time, imbued Babylonian Jewry with the notion that they ought to reconcile their community with the political context within which they were living. He then convinced the community to recognize the new Sassanid kingdom as a legitimate regime

[24] Menachem Elon, "The Legal Systems of Jewish Law," *NYU Journal of International Law and Politics* 17 (1985): 221–43, 227.

[25] An authoritative source on the doctrine and its origins, evolution, and application is Shmuel Shilo, *Dina D'Malkhuta Dina* (1974) [Hebrew]. Elements of it may be found in Shmuel Shilo, "Equity as a Bridge between Jewish and Secular Law," *Cardozo Law Review* 12 (1991): 737–51.

possessing decent and equitable laws which Jews, since they were to pay the taxes the regime imposed, were bound to obey. Over the centuries, *dina de-malkhuta dina* evolved into a fully fledged doctrine governing the relationship of Jewish law and "gentile" law from the Jewish communities' perspective.

As the doctrine evolved, a set of interpretive principles emerged detailing precisely which aspects of the "kingdom's law" were to be observed. These made clear that a law of the kingdom, if it is to be respected, must, among other requirements, derive from a legitimate or recognized authority, apply equally to all citizens, and not infringe upon any core religious prohibition (the previously mentioned *issura*). The last of these requirements underscores that any law of the kingdom respected under *dina de-malkhuta dina* will be civil or "nonreligious" law; for example, the king's right to collect taxes, recognized in the Talmud, was also recognized by all halakhic authorities in the post-Talmudic period. Around the time of the aforementioned *Shulkhan Arukh*, an earlier restriction of *dina de-malkhuta dina* that limited its application to ancient law was relaxed. This interpretive move allowed communities in late-medieval and early-modern times to adjust to the sweeping changes made to the legal systems around them as new nonreligious political entities began to form.

A "principled pragmatism" approach has also been developed with respect to the closely related yet separate challenge of litigation before non-Jewish courts ("*erka'ot shel goyim*").[26] The principled aspect of this approach emerged from the fact that the ban on litigation in foreign courts was considered a core prohibition. The prohibition was even stricter at times and places (e.g. 12th-century Spain) where Jewish communities enjoyed jurisdictional autonomy in personal-status laws, and often also in commerce and criminal law. As we know, however, parties will engage in forum shopping whenever possible, and for much of the time the Jewish community was no exception. Voluntary litigation in "gentile" courts was quite common in medieval Ashkenaz

---

[26] The *dina de-malkhuta dina* doctrine is closely related to yet separate from the issue of non-Jewish courts ("*erka'ot shel goyim*") and attitudes toward litigation before them, what to do with community members who choose to litigate before them, the validity and legitimacy of them, and their verdicts or writs, etc. Whereas the *dina de-malkhuta dina* doctrine shares some core elements of what are today labeled "conflict of laws," the issue of litigation before gentile courts and the legitimacy of their verdicts is closer in nature to matters of "forum shopping," "full faith and credit," and other inter-jurisdictional problems of law, enforcement, and coordination.

(Germany), Italy, France, and Provence, where Jews enjoyed little jurisdictional autonomy. As the reality of Jewish–gentile relationships within a Muslim or Christian context became permanent, a reappraisal of the Talmudic attitudes and rules became necessary. As a result, a nexus of exemptions (e.g. a "mutual consent" rule, a "salvation from the hands of gentiles" rule) was developed to ensure that the Jewish community's use of gentile courts was made "kosher."

The Talmudic position on the moral codes of others is quite clear. Leviticus (18:3) states that "You shall not copy the practices of the land of Egypt where you dwelt, or the land of Canaan to which I am leading you; nor shall you follow their laws" ("*u'vekhukoteihem lo telekhu*"; literally: "and their constitutions you shall not walk/follow"). And Leviticus (20:23) states (in the context of immoral sexual behavior): "You shall not follow the practices of the nations [*khukot ha'goy*; literally: "the constitutions of the gentiles"] that I am driving out before you. For it is because they did all these things that I abhorred them." The early Mishna extends the concept of *khukot ha'goy* to include forbidden practices not listed in Leviticus and ranging from idolatrous or immoral associations to superstitious and magical practices termed "the ways of the Amorites" ("*darkhei ha'emori*").

Prominent figures of 16th- and 17th-century legal thought—most notably Hugo Grotius and John Selden—drew on these distinctions to support their views about natural law, the boundaries of religious toleration and the faith of others, core tenets of belief that may not be compromised and precepts that are amenable to some flexibility, and the relations of civil and ecclesiastical authority more generally. In 1613, to pick an example, Grotius (then acting in the role of legal counselor of the Netherlands) wrote an edict (*Decretum pro pace ecclesiarum*) advocating a policy of toleration where only the basic tenets necessary for underpinning civil order (e.g. the existence of God and His providence) ought to be enforced with differences in obscure theological doctrines left to private conscience and out of state control. The Israelite example—often referred to as *respublica hebraeorum*, the "republic of the Hebrews"—was deployed to defend Erastianism (state control of religious affairs) and toleration (core tenets are to be enforced; malleable precepts may be subjected to discretion and interpretation). Applying these rationales to religious divisions of his time, Grotius suggested that the core truths of Christianity held in common by Catholics, Calvinists, Lutherans, and Arminians, were "fundamentally more important compared to the peripheral points on which they felt they differed."[27]

Distinctions between foundational and supplementary values in religion law remain relevant to contemporary debates in comparative constitutional jurisprudence. One intuitively thinks of distinctions between *jus cogens*-like norms in constitutional law (decisive principles or norms from which no derogation is permitted) and other, softer norms, where expressions of particular constitutional identities or deference to local traditions may be legitimate. Likewise, such distinctions feature centrally in the constitutional jurisprudence of religion-laden settings, where the question of what religious precepts are to be protected by the state preoccupy the constitutional domain.

Fast forwarding to today, consider the constitutional interpretation of "Islamic provisions" in predominantly Muslim countries. In 1980, Egypt amended Article 2 of its constitution (originally adopted in 1971) to introduce Shari'a as "the" (instead of "a") primary source of legislation; this provision was reproduced in the 2012 constitution introduced by the since-ousted Muslim Brotherhood regime, and again in the 2014 constitution.[28] Egypt's courts have thus been grappling for over 30 years with the contested status and role of Shari'a as a potentially authoritative source of laws. To address this question in a moderate way, Egypt's Supreme Constitutional Court (SCC) developed an innovative matrix of religious directives—the first of its kind used by a non-religious tribunal. This model warrants that the state must obey any unambiguous scriptural rule that scholars have found in the Qur'an or a trustworthy *hadith*; however, the state is not obliged to follow secondary interpretations or principles that have been extrapolated

---

[27] See "Editorial: Grotius and the Natural Law Tradition," *Literature of Liberty: A Review of Contemporary Liberal Thought* 1:4 (1978).

[28] The constitution introduced in December 2012 by President Mohamed Morsi (of the Freedom and Justice Party founded by the Muslim Brotherhood) not only reproduced Article 2 (principles of Islamic Shari'a are "the" source of legislation), but also introduced Article 219, which uses technical terms from the Islamic legal tradition to define what is actually meant by "the principles of the Islamic Shari'a" as stated in Article 2, most likely in direct reaction to the modernist jurisprudential trend described later. The constitution also guaranteed (Article 4) that al-Ahzar, the great institution of higher Islamic learning in Cairo, would be consulted on matters of Islamic law; Article 11 stated that the state is to "protect ethics and morality and public order"; and Article 44 prohibited the insulting of prophets, such that it may be interpreted as prohibiting blasphemy. While Article 2 is maintained by the post-Morsi 2014 constitution, most other "Islamic morality" provisions have been removed from that constitution by the 50-member drafting panel. The 2014 draft constitution was overwhelmingly approved in a referendum in January 2014.

from scriptural rules but which are not the only logical understanding capable of being ascribed to them.[29] The distinction between putatively undisputed, universally binding principles of Shari'a and flexible applications of those principles stands at the heart of the Court's Islamic review.[30] Legislation that contravenes a strict, unalterable principle recognized as such by all interpretive schools is declared unconstitutional and void, while at the same time *ijtihad* (reasoning or external interpretation) is permitted in cases of textual lacunae, or where the pertinent rules are vague, open-ended, or subject to various acceptable interpretations. The Egyptian SCC's two-tier hierarchy of Shari'a norms has allowed it (along with the Supreme Administrative Court) to issue moderate or liberalizing rulings on contested matters such as the wearing of religious attire in the public school system, the scope of Islamic banking restrictions, Islamic divorce procedures, and female genital mutilation.[31] The common rationale in all these rulings is essentially that since there is no consensus within religious authorities on the centrality of the practice, the state is not obliged to follow it in order to remain sufficiently "Islamic."

Similar distinctions exist in other Islam-infused jurisprudential settings, ranging from Tunisia to Indonesia. A two-tier conceptual matrix similar to that deployed by the Egyptian Constitutional Court allowed Habib Bourguiba, the first president and great modernizer of Tunisia, to adopt the Personal Status Code in 1956; this was arguably the most liberal personal-status legislation adopted by a country that is constitutionally committed to the teachings of Islam. The same interpretive flexibility led to further modernizing revisions of the Code in 1993.[32] Kuwait's Constitutional Court ruled in a landmark 2009 case that women lawmakers do not have to wear the hijab while in parliament.

---

[29] Clark Lombardi, *State Law as Islamic Law in Modern Egypt: The Incorporation of the Shari'a into Egyptian Constitutional Law* (Brill, 2006), 48–100.

[30] Clark Lombardi, "Islamic Law as a Source of Constitutional Law in Egypt: The Constitutionalization of the Sharia in a Modern Arab State," *Columbia Journal of Transnational Law* 37 (1998): 81–123; Nathan Brown, "Islamic Constitutionalism in Theory and Practice," in Eugene Cotran and Adel Omar Sherif, eds., *Democracy, the Rule of Law and Islam* (Springer, 1999).

[31] For a prime example, see *Wassel v. Minister of Education* (the niqab [veil] case), Case No. 8 of the 17th Judicial Year (May 18, 1996) [Egypt]; a translation into English is available at *American University International Law Review* 21:3 (2006): 437–60.

[32] See Amira Mashhour, "Islamic Law and Gender Equality—Could There Be a Common Ground? A Study of Divorce and Polygamy in Shari'a Law and Contemporary Legislation in Tunisia and Egypt," *Human Rights Quarterly* 27 (2005): 562–96.

As Shari'a law is not unified in its approach to the headscarf, the Court reasoned, one cannot fairly conclude that wearing the hijab is the only possible interpretation of the "compliance with Islam" clause in a 2005 law that allows women to vote and run for parliament.[33] Likewise, in a landmark ruling that struck down the proposed establishment of an "Islamic morality" (*hisba*) police in the North-West Frontier Province (NWFP), the Supreme Court of Pakistan ruled that "Islamic jurists are unanimous on the point that except for *sallat* [prayer] and *zakat* [alms] no other religious obligation stipulated by Islam can be enforced by the state."[34] Much like its Egyptian counterpart, the Court suggested that there is no consensus within Islamic jurisprudence that state enforcement of religious values is warranted.

India's rich constitutional jurisprudence of religion provides a different illustration of the conceptual distinction between *essential* elements of religion and *supplementary* or *voluntary* aspects of it. Article 25 of India's constitution (1950) protects "Freedom of conscience and free profession, practice and propagation of religion." Through numerous rulings over the years, the Supreme Court of India has developed a sophisticated interpretive framework to delimit the scope of religious practice protected under Article 25. In a nutshell, it provides that the constitutional protection of religious practice extends only to religious practices considered "essential" or "integral" to a particular religion. In the Court's words: "protection under Article 25 extends a guarantee for rituals and observances, ceremonies and modes of worship which are *integral* parts of religion and as to what really constitutes an essential part of religion or religious practice has to be decided by the courts with reference to the doctrine of a particular religion or practices regarded as parts of religion."[35]

In *Acharya Jagdishwaranand v. Commissioner of Police, Calcutta* (1984), the Supreme Court of India held that the performance in public places of tandava dance (a symbolic dance involving skulls, firearms, spears, and tridents) was not an "essential" practice for the Anand Margis spiritual movement.[36] In *T. V. Narayana v. Venkata Subbamma* (1996), the court upheld a law abolishing "the hereditary right to appointment

[33] *Ministry of Islamic Affairs v. Rola Dashti and Aseel al-Awadhi*, Constitutional Court of Kuwait, Decision of Oct. 28, 2009 [Kuwait].

[34] Reference 2/2005 In Re: NWFP Hisba Bill, P.L.D. 2005 S.C. 873 [Pakistan].

[35] *N. Adithyan v. Travancore Devaswom Board* AIR 2002 SC 106 [India].

[36] *Acharya Jagdishwaranand v. Commissioner of Police, Calcutta* AIR 1984 SC 51 [India].

as an *archaka*" (will execute) as this right was not an essential aspect of the Hindu religion.[37] Questions have also arisen as to whether cow sacrifice by Muslims on Bakr-Id (Eid al-Adha) day is an essential practice in Islam. As is well known, veneration for the cow exists among most Hindu groups and, in the Indian context, this is sometimes pitted against the ritualistic animal sacrifice associated with Muslim festivals such as Bakr-Id. In all of its rulings on the matter, the Court has held that the pertinent Islamic precepts say that cows are merely one type of animal that may be sacrificed, so that their sacrifice is not an essential practice.[38] In its most recent decision on the matter, the Supreme Court reiterated that a total prohibition on the slaughter of the progeny of cows does not violate Article 25 of the constitution, as the sacrifice of cows per se is not essential to Islam.[39]

At the same time, the Supreme Court of India also ruled, in the landmark case of *Bijoe Emmanuel v. State of Kerala* (1986), that Jehovah's Witness students may be exempt from singing the national anthem at school, since compelling them to join in would violate their "genuine, conscientious religious objection" to doing so.[40] Lower courts have taken note of the Supreme Court of India's two-tier matrix for accommodating religion. Having carefully examined scholarly opinion and detailed evidence, the Punjab High Court agreed in the high-profile case of *Gurleen Kaur v. State of Punjab & Haryana* (2009) that a Sikh school's decision to deny admission to students who had shorn off their hair and plucked their eyebrows deserved constitutional protection, since having uncut hair is an essential requirement of Sikhism. The court stressed in reaching its decision that "retaining hair unshorn is an essential component of the Sikh religion ... Maintaining hair unshorn is a part of the religious consciousness of the Sikh faith."[41]

A similar distinction between mandatory and commendable practices informs the approach adopted by the Supreme Court of Malaysia (now renamed the Federal Court of Malaysia) to evaluating whether constitutional protection ought to be assigned to a religious practice. That Malaysian court has interpreted "the right to practice religion" as

---

[37] *T. V. Narayana v. Venkata Subbamma* AIR 1996 SC 1807 [India].

[38] See, e.g., *Mohd. Hanif Qureshi v. State of Bihar* AIR 1958 SC 731 [India]; *State of West Bengal v. Ashutosh Lahiri* AIR 1995 SC 464 [India].

[39] *State of Gujarat v. Mirzapur Moti Kureshi Kassab Jamat* (2005) 8 SCC 534 [India].

[40] *Bijoe Emmanuel v. State of Kerala* AIR 1987 SC 748 [India].

[41] *Gurleen Kaur v. State of Punjab* (High Court of Punjab and Haryana), decision released on May 30, 2009 [India].

the right to perform "essential and mandatory practices to that religion." In the leading case on the matter (*Kamaruddin v. Public Service Commission Malaysia*, 1994), the Court applied the "mandatory practice test" to determine that the wearing of *purdah* (generally meaning a regime of female seclusion from public observation, in this case referring to a veil-like head and neck cover) by a Muslim woman while she is working in the public service may be restricted by law in the name of the public interest since it is a non-mandatory practice within Islam.[42]

In 2006, the Federal Court of Malaysia upheld the constitutionality of the School Regulation Act (1997), which prohibited the wearing of the turban (*serban*) as part of the school uniform, since "th[is] 'practice' was of little significance from the point of view of the religion of Islam."[43] (Interestingly, the circumstances of this case were nearly identical to those in the British Law Lords' frequently referenced decision in *Shabina Begum*, 2006).[44] The court made clear that if the practice in question is compulsory or "an integral part" of the religion, courts should give more weight to it but, if it is not, they should assign it less weight: "In the Islamic context, the classification made by jurists on the 'hukum' (meaning or command) regarding a particular practice will be of assistance. Prohibition of a practice which is 'wajib' (mandatory) should definitely be viewed more seriously than the prohibition of what is 'sunat' (commendable)." Wearing the turban, the court held, does not belong to the first category of practices. In support of this two-tier matrix for classifying religious practices, the court referenced landmark Indian cases articulating the "integral part of religion" test.[45]

Might similar "two-tier" hierarchies of rules—hierarchies that distinguish foundational, unambiguous constitutional values from malleable, supplementary preferences—prove helpful in avoiding the rigid dichotomy between full endorsement and outright rejection of foreign law? Might a similar logic be drawn upon to facilitate a given country's

---

[42] *Kamaruddin v. Public Services Commission Malaysia* [1994] 3 MLJ 61 [Malaysia].

[43] *Meor Atiqulrahman Ishak et al. v. Fatimah Sihi et al.*, 4 CLJ 1 (2006) [Malaysia]. See Jaclyn L. Neo, "Religious Dress in Schools: The *Serban* Controversy in Malaysia," *International and Comparative Law Quarterly* 55 (2006): 671–88.

[44] *R (on the application of Shabina Begum) v. Headteacher and Governors of Denbigh High School* [2006] UKHL 15 [United Kingdom].

[45] Among the Supreme Court of India decisions cited were: *The Commissioner, Hindu Religious Endowments, Madras v. Sri Lakshmindra Thirtha Swamiar* AIR 1954 SC 282; *Sardar Syedna Taher Saifuddin Saheb v. State of Bombay* AIR 1962 SC 853; *Javed v. State of Haryana* AIR 2003 SC 3057.

efforts to maintain its constitutional identity while at the same time incorporating transnational constitutional values that are not deemed threatening? The pre- and early-modern world of religion law might help us to answer these questions, since it offers ample illustrations of the frictions that arise from states' inevitable engagement with the constitutive laws of others and of the potential responses to those frictions. As I hope to have shown, pre- and early-modern religion law, as it has struggled for survival amid pressure from rival legal systems provides a vivid illustration of how creative jurisprudential concepts and distinctions can help us move beyond prevalent yet overly simplistic love–hate attitudes toward the constitutive laws of others.

The social and political context of external engagements

Necessity may well be "the mother of invention," as the proverb attributed to Plato (*Republic*) goes. However, doctrinal attitudes toward engagement with the constitutive laws of others may be informed not just by pure necessity or survival instincts but also by earthly, even instrumentalist, considerations. That interpretation matters a great deal in constitutional law is not news; examples are plentiful. Interpretation has likewise been a cornerstone of religion law. Everyone who follows Jewish law, for instance, is familiar with the long interpretive journey undergone by the Jewish dietary prohibition against eating meat and dairy together, from the Torah verses that tell us not to "boil a young goat (*g'di*) in its mother's milk" to today's complex labyrinth of rules concerning kosher foods.[46] However difficult it is to amend a venerable constitution that has acquired a "larger than life" status, sacred texts are outright impossible to amend (and are seldom replaced with others). Therefore, doctrinal adjustments made via interpretation seem even more crucial to religion than they are to constitutional law. It is hardly surprising, then, that fierce interpretive struggles have come to

---

[46] *Exodus* 23:19; *Exodus* 34:26; *Deuteronomy* 14:21. The prominent 11th-century Talmudic commentator Rabbi Shlomo Yitzhaki (Rashi) suggested that *g'di* must refer to a broader category of kosher mammal offspring, e.g. calves and lamb. Other Talmudic sources suggested that because it was difficult to distinguish between domesticated kosher animals and other meats, there should be a generic prohibition of dairy and any kosher animal meat except fish. The rest is history, as the saying goes.

dominate the translation of sacred directives into practical guidelines for private and public life. In fact, one could argue that the main reason the domain of religion has seen so many internal interpretive struggles over the centuries is precisely that sacred texts—while often relatively easy to interpret or distort—are impossible to amend.

When a novel legal question presents itself, a religious authority, much like a constitutional judge, may look to draw inferences from verdicts handed down in analogous situations within the corpus of the religion's sacred texts and canonical secondary sources; or he may opt to incorporate external solutions that are compatible with the religion's core values.[47] Both routes involve a fair amount of result-driven "cherry-picking." Religious interpreters throughout history, much like some of today's philosopher-king constitutional court judges, often relied on discerning readings of sacred texts to advance their worldviews and preferences. The entire domain of religious law, one could argue, offers the most spectacular example of the living-tree approach to interpretation. And there are striking parallels—largely, alas, under-explored and under-theorized—between the interpretation of sacred texts and of constitutional texts.[48] Abstract as they may be, these parallels may shed light on the forces that drive the purportedly principled debate concerning the importance of interaction with foreign law.

Like most constitutional provisions, the wording of almost all religious imperatives is open-ended and subject to various interpretations.[49] Driven by an instinct to remain relevant and to increase or maintain their support base, and by a need to find plausible ways to address widening gaps between traditional interpretations and changing realities, framers and interpreters of religious law have long taken into account social and economic factors rather than limiting themselves strictly to principled theological discourse. Indeed, the history of religious interpretation is filled with examples of such internal adjustment and adaptation to exogenous changes.

---

[47] See Shilo, "Equity as a Bridge between Jewish and Secular Law" (n 25); Jeffrey Roth, "Crossing the Bridge to Secular Law: Three Models of Incorporation," *Cardozo Law Review* 12 (1991): 753–64.

[48] An exception to this trend is found in Thomas Grey, "The Constitution as Scripture," *Stanford Law Review* 37 (1984): 1–25; Sanford Levinson, "Divided Loyalties: The Problem of 'Dual Sovereignty' and Constitutional Faith," *Touro Law Review* 29 (2013), available at: http://digitalcommons.tourolaw.edu/lawreview/vol29/iss2/3.

[49] Interestingly, not all religious traditions follow a logic similar to the common law's *stare decisis*, a fact that also makes the interpretative field even more open and potentially contested.

Jewish law, in particular, has been conducive to ingenuity and change driven by social and economic needs. It has evolved mainly through a living-tree—"a tree of life," as the Book of Proverbs puts it—approach to interpretation. The best interpretive minds throughout the last two thousand years of the Jewish tradition—Maimonides being one pertinent example—spent most of their intellectual energy debating possible changes to the law that were meant to respond to variance in geographic conditions among communities or to changing social and economic conditions. The Talmud, Mishnah, and other halakhic literature feature rich legal casuistry aimed at demonstrating how certain interpretations and practices that reflect social change or economic necessity are not, in fact, in opposition to pertinent religious rules, despite appearances to the contrary.[50]

As Menachem Elon observes, an enormous mass of materials, comprising hundreds of thousands of legal opinions and responses covering all areas of Jewish law, came into being "against the background of, and as a result of, the application of Jewish law to practical, day-to-day life."[51] Furthermore, the areas of law that preoccupied the Jewish community and its leadership were those in which significant social and economic change occurred. Because many religious directives were based on the experience of simple agrarian societies or otherwise pre-modern markets, adaptation to modern states and markets was inevitable.[52] As Elon explains: "The Halakhic authorities and the lay leadership were required to respond to these changes and supply new solutions."[53] In many instances, adaptation involved separating a precept's *telos* (in the Aristotelian sense of "purpose" or "goal") from the concrete narrative or context within which it exists in the sacred texts. In this way, the talented interpretive minds were able to assign new meanings to old verses.

Although domestic circumstances are not the only reason for variance among legal systems, they do play a role. For example, even though it is normally forbidden for a Jew to instruct a non-Jew to work on the Sabbath, Jewish communities in very cold climates (e.g. Poland

---

[50] See Suzanne Last Stone, "On the Interplay of Rules, Cases, and Concepts in Rabbinic Legal Literature: Another Look at the Aggadot on Honi the Circle-Drawer," *Diné Israel* 24 (2007): 125–56.

[51] Elon, "The Legal Systems of Jewish Law" (n 24), 231.

[52] See Suzanne Last Stone, "Religion and State: Models of Separation within Jewish Law," *International Journal of Constitutional Law* 6 (2008): 631–61.

[53] Elon, "The Legal Systems of Jewish Law" (n 24), 232.

and Russia) permitted Jews to ask a non-Jew to heat their homes on that day. Similarly, the daily afternoon prayer and the evening prayer were combined into one afternoon praying session in Jewish communities in northern Germany because darkness fell in the early afternoon during winter, so that attendance at the separate evening prayer was minimal. And while Maimonides, who lived in Muslim Spain and later Egypt, ruled that a married woman who failed to carry out her wifely duties might be physically chastised by a Jewish court, Jewish communities in Christian Europe were horrified at the very thought of it.[54] To take yet another example, the attitude of Jewish communities in medieval Ashkenaz (today's Germany) toward commercial litigation before "gentile" tribunals was quite lenient compared to the strict rejection of the practice by Jewish communities in Northern Africa. A plausible explanation for this variance may be that non-Jewish tribunals in Ashkenaz, unlike Muslim communities in northern Africa, which viewed Jewish litigation in Muslim courts as an act of conversion or acceptance of Muslim supremacy, viewed such litigation in considerably more casual terms.[55]

Countless other interpretive innovations came into being in the same way. One of the International Monetary Fund's mantras is that a precondition for economic development is the existence of predictable laws governing the marketplace and a legal regime that protects capital formation and ensures property rights. Noted institutional economists have built a career from this and related ideas concerning the significance of credible commitments to economic growth.

Some two thousand years ago, Hillel the Elder, a famous Jewish religious leader and scholar who lived in Jerusalem during the politically tumultuous time of King Herod the Great, introduced the revolutionary *pruzbul*, an institution that, notwithstanding the Jewish law concerning cancellation of debts in the sabbatical year, ensured the repayment of loans. The motive for introducing the *pruzbul* was the "repair of the world" (*tikkun olam*), that is, the repair of social and economic order; it both protected the creditor against the loss of his property and protected the needy against being refused loans of money for fear of loss. Other similar ingenuity ensued, such as the ceremonial

---

[54] Louis Jacobs, *A Tree of Life: Diversity, Flexibility, and Creativity in Jewish Law* (2nd edn, Littman Library of Jewish Civilization, 2000), 117.

[55] See Gideon Libson, *Jewish and Islamic Law: A Comparative Study of Custom during the Geonic Period* (Harvard University Press, 2003).

sale to a non-Jew of *chametz* (bread, grains, and other leavened products) before Passover and the legal fiction of *eruv chatzerot*—"mixed
ownership of courtyards/domains"—which applies on the Jewish Sabbath only and designates an entire area as its residents' common
"home" so that Jews who observe the traditional rules concerning
Shabbat may carry children and belongings anywhere within the
jointly held property without transgressing the prohibition against
carrying a burden across a property line on the Sabbath. Or, in modern
times, the invention of the Shabbat elevator (*ma'alit shel Shabbat*)—an
elevator that is programmed to go up and down and stop at every floor
by itself so that it can be used without violating the rules of the Jewish
Sabbath.

Jewish law is by no means unique here. Shari'a, for example, renders
impermissible the practice of usury or charging interest (*riba*). This is
based on a moral objection to "unjust enrichment," or moneymaking
without actual work. It is also meant to discourage borrowing, which is
feared to be addictive and irresponsible. The classical approach to *riba*
defines it as any increase over the nominal value of a sum lent. In the
religious schools of interpretation this view is the most popular and, as
such, acts as a considerable pressure on governments attempting to
Islamize their state or to align their banking practices with the tenets of
Islam. An Islamic government that followed the classical approach
would have to rid its banking practices of interest in any form. However, economic exchange is quite limited without interest-yielding
credit. In pre-modern times this gave birth to the "double sell"—a
practice whereby a loan is awarded alongside the transfer of another
object to the borrower, with the agreement that the nominal value of
the loan plus a grossly inflated price for the accompanying object (so
that the portion of the price above the object's fair value serves as de
facto interest) will be paid back to the lender.

In modern times a flexible, pragmatic, form-over-substance
approach to Islamic banking has been developed, with countless
innovations in place that formally circumvent the prohibition on *riba*
while ignoring the substantive moral message of the prohibition.[56]
Several major banks in the Muslim world even employ clerics whose
job is to ensure compliance of banking products with pertinent religious directives. Beyond this, some modern interpreters have suggested

[56] See, e.g., Mahmoud A. El-Gamal, "Interest and the Paradox of Contemporary Islamic
Finance," *Fordham International Law Journal* 27 (2004): 108–49.

that whereas interest would be prohibited in an ideal world, the use of it as a temporary measure promotes the greater good and may be justified on the ground of necessity. Some even argue that money and interest are modern concepts outside the scope of the *riba* prohibition, and that interest on money-lending is therefore permissible.

Outside influence on doctrinal transformation may also take a broader "law and society" direction. As the renowned Talmudic scholar Marcus Jastrow notes, modern research into Talmudic literature has proven that there was a "marvelous familiarity of the rabbis with the events, institutions, and views of life of the world outside and around their own peculiar civilization."[57] And so, as the context within which Jewish law operated changed over time, so too did the strictness with which the concept (discussed earlier) of *khukot ha'goy* was interpreted. At times when Jewish religious identity did not face major threats, a lenient approach was adopted. In the 12th century, for instance, Rabbi Eliezer of Metz (France) laid down a firm rule that the concept of *khukot ha'goy* only applies to the *religious* practices of gentiles, and that the mere fact that gentiles may engage in a certain practice does not in itself mean the practice is forbidden. On the other hand, in the face of credible emancipation threats and the rise of Reform Judaism in 19th-century Europe, the *khukot ha'goy* principle was invoked against the use of an organ in the synagogue, against adopting gentile names, against hunting animals for sport, against not growing a beard, and even against the wearing of a tie.[58]

Similar retorts against engagement with the laws of others are detectable in earlier times. Uriel Simonsohn's comparative study of Christian and Jewish legal behavior under early Muslim rule (focusing on the late 7th to early 11th centuries in the region between Iraq and present-day Tunisia) exposes considerable fluidity among different communities. Simonsohn shows how a disregard for religious affiliations threatened to undermine the position of traditional religious elites; and how, in response, they acted vigorously to reinforce communal boundaries, censuring recourse to external judicial institutions and even threatening transgressors with excommunication.[59] Resemblance to certain inward-looking positions within contemporary

---

[57] Marcus Jastraw, *Dictionary*, preface, p. xiii; cited in Jacobs, *A Tree of Life* (n 54), 80.

[58] See Jacobs, *A Tree of Life* (n 54), 88–9.

[59] Uriel Simonsohn, *A Common Justice: The Legal Allegiances of Christians and Jews under Early Islam* (University of Pennsylvania Press, 2011).

debates on the legitimacy of reference to the constitutive laws of others is not coincidental.

A similar primary/secondary norm duality may be identified in the jurisprudence of religious tribunals in present-day Israel. As Daphna Hacker shows, Israeli rabbinical courts diverge far more in divorce disputes than in inheritance conflicts.[60] While in the former the rabbinical courts fight ardently to preserve their authority vis-à-vis the secular legal system (efforts that often include blatant violations of gender equality standards), they take a considerably more pragmatic position in the context of inheritance conflicts (including higher regard for gender equality standards). These findings correspond with Ayelet Shachar's distinction between the demarcating (identity-oriented) and distributive aspects of a religious tradition.[61] Whereas the former aspect helps to maintain a group's membership boundaries vis-à-vis the larger society (i.e. helps to define the group and its members as such), the latter is more inwardly directed, as it shapes and allocates rights, duties, and ultimately powers among group members. The distinction between these two functions parallels the distinction between two legal aspects of divorce: the change made to personal status (the demarcating function) and the determination of property relations between spouses (the distributive function). While often intermingled in practice, personal status and property relations are legally two distinct subjects.

A clear illustration of broader societal influence on doctrinal change within Jewish law is the so-called "Maimonidean Controversy." This erupted in early 13th-century Spain and Provence following the dissemination of Maimonides' *Guide for the Perplexed* (*Moreh Nevokhim*)— widely regarded as the pinnacle and summary of the philosophical and halakhic tradition of the Golden Age of the Jews in Muslim Spain.[62] The book was originally written in Arabic (1170–80), and was translated into Hebrew in 1204. The controversy involved the Maimonidean idea that God is omnipresent and incorporeal, and that any other

---

[60] Daphna Hacker, "Religious Tribunals in Democratic States: Lessons from the Israeli Rabbinical Courts," *Journal of Law and Religion* 27 (2012): 59–81. See also, Michael Peletz, *Islamic Modern: Religious Courts and Cultural Politics in Malaysia* (Princeton University Press, 2002).

[61] Ayelet Shachar, *Multicultural Jurisdictions: Cultural Differences and Women's Rights* (Cambridge University Press, 2001).

[62] See "The Maimonidean Controversy," in Eliezer Schweid, *The Classic Jewish Philosophers: From Saadia through the Renaissance* (Brill, 2008), 301–25.

view is heretic. At the heart of the controversy, however, was Maimonides' call for a substance-over-form interpretive approach to sacred precepts, and his notion that intellectual–philosophical idealism, not worship for the sake of worship, should be the main motivation for religious learning, indeed for leading a Torah-based life generally. It followed, under this reasoning, that general (as in non-Jewish) modes of philosophical inquiry, including methods of reasoning, comparison, analogy, and contrast, were acceptable thinking tools in interpreting the Torah.

As one would expect, Maimonides' radical ideas were not endorsed by the entire rabbinical establishment of the time. While they were well received by the generally liberal and cosmopolitan Sepharadic Jewry (centered in today's Catalonia under Muslim rule), they were uncompromisingly rejected by the orthodox and largely "textualist" Ashkenazic Jewry of Provence. A main accusation against Maimonides was that his views undermined fundamental beliefs by formally endorsing them on the one hand but effectively subverting them through external interpretation that amounted to their negation. (One may think here of similar claims made in the very different context discussed in the next chapter, of contemporary debates in the United States concerning engagement with foreign constitutional law and interpretive approaches). Maimonides' official embrace of the Jewish law traditional doctrine was not in line with his more philosophical views, which ultimately were "a cover for denial, or for insecure belief riddled with doubts."[63] So deep were the differences that some of the Ashkenazic rabbis were repeatedly denounced by Sepharadic Jewish leaders as being insular zealots and narrow-minded "fools and lunatics with clogged minds who are devoted to superstitious nonsense and immersed in the fetid waters of unilluminated caves."[64] Rabbi Solomon of Montpellier (Provence) emerged as the leader of the anti-Maimonidean movement, pronouncing a sentence of excommunication on Maimonides' works, and later (in 1233) encouraging the Dominican Church leaders of Montpelier to publicly burn them. A bitter doctrinal

[63] See Schweid, "The Maimonidean Controversy" (n 62), 306. A well-known critical account of the Maimonidean views, and of later Enlightenment Judaism more generally, is Leo Strauss, *Philosophy and Law: Contributions to the Understanding of Maimonides and His Predecessors* (SUNY Press, 1995).

[64] David Berger, "Judaism and General Culture in Medieval and Early Modern Times," in Jacob J. Schacter, ed., *Judaism's Encounter with Other Cultures: Rejection or Integration?* (Jason Aronson Inc., 1997), 57–141, 118.

war erupted, threatening to split the Jewish people. Ultimately, the Maimonidean ideas prevailed, but only after tremendous interpretive and political maneuvering, stretching over much of the 13th century, helped to mitigate the inter-communal tensions.

The different social context within which each of these communities lived mattered a great deal. In al-Andalus, the parts of the Iberian Peninsula governed by the Muslim Moors from the 8th century to the 15th century, various dynasties of caliphs and emirs competed for political and military control. Islam was a key marker of collective identity. However, over prolonged periods a so-called Muslim-Jewish *convivencia* (coexistence) is said to have existed in al-Andalus. Although for much of its history al-Andalus existed in conflict with Christian kingdoms to the north, within al-Andalus Muslims and Jews collaborated relatively peacefully (by medieval European standards) for centuries. Why? Unlike Jews in Christian Europe (including Provence), who were mostly isolated from the rest of the population in deplored professions such as money-lending, those in al-Andalus were well integrated into the Islamic marketplace, which was marked by a substantial degree of interdenominational cooperation. The Jews there lived as Dhimmis (protected non-Muslims living in a land governed by Muslims) and were granted limited religious and cultural autonomy, as well as jurisdictional autonomy in matters pertaining to their faith. This brought about an unprecedented cultural revival within the Jewish community, alongside increased cross-fertilization between Jewish and Muslim poets, commentators, and philosophers. In return, the Jews paid a special annual poll tax (*jizya*) to their protective rulers. This tax, higher than the tax Muslims had to pay, was at times one of the most important sources of income for the kingdom. At the same time, in several city-kingdoms (e.g. Córdoba and Toledo) translation programs were established under which Jews would translate Arabic books into Romanic languages, mainly Latin, and Greek and Hebrew texts into Arabic. In this way, many major works of Greek science and philosophy were translated into Arabic, and many accomplishments of the Moorish Empire in mathematics, medicine, botany, geography, astronomy, poetry, and philosophy were disseminated throughout the Christian world, contributing to the revival of these texts in the early Renaissance era.

In this context, Maimonides' outward-looking ideas, steeped in the philosophy and scientific insights of the time, reflected the general intellectual ambiance within which he worked. What is more, it was critically important for the minority Jewish communities in both Spain and Provence not to feel inferior to their respective host societies, be it with respect to cosmopolitanism in Spain or religious devotion in Provence. As scholars of medieval Jewry note, in Spain the resulting imitation "was cultural and intellectual"; in Ashkenaz, "given the different complexion of both majority and minority culture, it was a competition in religious devotion."[65] In the view of Rabbi Moses ben Nahman of Girondi (Nahmanides—the leading medieval Jewish scholar of the immediate post-Maimonides generation), Maimonides satisfied a major need among the Jews of Muslim Spain: their immersion in the general culture of their environment brought about perplexity, but Maimonides responded to this confusion by arguing that philosophical inquiry and self-questioning, not blind following and obedience, are the basis for religious belief.[66] This example demonstrates how a change to religion's approach to engagement with its surroundings, as in constitutional law, cannot be fully understood in isolation from the social and political context within which it evolves.

Many other intra-religious rifts throughout history revolved, at least ostensibly, around different attitudes toward external culture, laws, and moral principles, and they often do today. Recent divisions within the Anglican Church were spurred by claims by conservatives, such as Peter Akinola, Anglican primate of the Church of Nigeria (2000–10), that the church was unwarranted in its openness to foreign, overly liberal, and supposedly inauthentic influences.[67] In addition, the split has been characterized as one between two hemispheres, the "global south" and the "global north," with the church leadership traditionally coming from the latter camp, although the majority of church followers now come from the former. Although Akinola and others drew on ideology (a literal interpretation of the Bible) to support their position, they also accused the Church of England of attempting to maintain its colonial-era powers over worshippers worldwide, and inappropriately inculcating "northern" liberalism in the more traditional South.

Two millennia earlier, the struggle between "authentic," "Hellenized," and later "Romanized" Judaism fuelled theological and political

---

[65] Berger, "Judaism and General Culture in Medieval and Early Modern Times" (n 64), 121.

[66] Schweid, The Classic Jewish Philosophers (n 62), 304.

[67] See Evan F. Kuehn, "Instruments of Faith and Unity in Canon Law: The Church of Nigeria Constitutional Revision of 2005," Ecclesiastical Law Journal 10 (2008): 161–73.

rifts in Judea, eventually leading to religious sectarianism among the Jews (e.g. the divisions between the Pharisees, Sadducees, and Essenes), the birth of Christianity in Judea, and the Roman invasion of the land by Titus.[68] This took place in the politically charged context of the Hasmonean Kingdom (*c.* 164–63 BCE), amid dwindling Hellenic dominance in the region and, later, the struggle between the Hasmonean dynasty and King Herod the Great, a Roman client-ruler who advanced an amalgam of Judaic and Roman culture. So prevalent was foreign influence over the region that even prominent leaders of the Hasmonean Kingdom who formed an autonomous Jewish state in ancient Israel on an anti-Hellenic platform went by Hellenized or Romanized names such as Hyrcanus, Aristobulus, Alexander Jannaeus, and Salome Alexandra (Hebrew: *Shlomtzion*)—the last of these the final leader of an independent Jewish state prior to the establishment of the State of Israel in 1948. Their successors later accused Herod the Great of being an inauthentic Jew, causing Jews to pejoratively refer to him as "the Idumean"—*Ha'Edomi* (his father was an Idumean who converted to Judaism). To date, the high Hebrew word for those who live a supposedly inauthentic life that is overly influenced by foreign culture is *Mityavnim*, literally meaning "those who live like the Greeks."

These and other similar examples highlight the conceptual affinity between the rejection of external sources by those who follow "originalist" or otherwise inward-looking interpretive approaches in constitutional and in religion law. Originalists in both religious and constitutional enterprises take the text to reflect the authentic and inerrant word of the pertinent authority. They therefore downplay the inevitable fluidity of interpretive practice and consciously seek to block its use. Explicit reference to external sources is perceived as bordering on the sinful. The text, they argue, has the ultimate authority by virtue of being *original*—the actual words of the source that brought it into being. It should be read only as a record of the views of those who drafted it, with no implied invitation to subsequent

---

[68] The political science and sociology of religion literature on this period is meagre at best. The main primary sources are Flavius Josephus's *The Jewish War* (published *c.* 75 CE) and *Antiquities of the Jews* (published *c.* 94 CE). For more recent socio-religious accounts, see Richard Horsley, *Scribes, Visionaries, and the Politics of Second Temple Judea* (Westminster John Knox Press, 2007); Anthony Saldarini, *Pharisees, Scribes, and Sadducees in Palestinian Society* (Michael Glazier Inc., 1988); J. W. Lightley, *Jewish Sects and Parties in the Time of Jesus* (Epworth Press, 1925); and Julius Wellhausen, *The Pharisees and the Sadducees: An Examination of Internal Jewish History* (Mercer University Press, 2001 [1874]).

interpreters to make their own judgments about the ideals reflected in it. This original–intent principle is seemingly more purist and authentic than any other interpretive practice; the interpreter is regarded as a guardian of the faith whose task is to convey the original textual meaning to future generations.

Manifestations of originalism in the Judaic tradition of interpreting religious directives are rare. Two exceptions are the ancient Sadducees and the "textualist" or "literalist" Kara'ites—a small movement that emerged in the 9th century that resents rabbinic Judaism's emphasis on oral law and tradition and enshrines the written Hebrew Bible (Torah, Nevi'im, K'tuvim, Hebrew acronym *Tanach*) as the sole constitutive religious authority. After the destruction of the Second Temple in Jerusalem (70 CE), Rabbinic Judaism turned almost exclusively to normative, evolving, living-tree Judaism, based on the Torah and its many written and oral interpretations throughout the centuries.

A possible explanation for the thin originalist tradition in Jewish law as compared to other major religions may be the "Diaspora thesis." According to this theory, because Jews were stateless for two millennia and were spread across Europe and northern Africa, adaptive law and flexible interpretation were necessary to sustain religion. Interestingly, an emphasis on flexible or "purposive" interpretation has emerged in the theology of several other historically stateless, and at times persecuted, religious groups whose members were spread across many countries, for example the Ismaili Muslims, the Circassians, and the Assyrians.

In contrast, fundamentalist approaches to interpreting the New Testament are quite common in North American Christianity. Likewise, the Salafist (or Wahhabist) movement in Islam insists that only the Prophet himself and the two generations that followed should be relied on for spiritual guidance. Other somewhat less rigid but distinctly orthodox interpretive schools exist within virtually all of the world's religions. Unlike in the religious domain, originalism or textualism in constitutional interpretation, while it does exist, is far less common outside the United States. In any event, all these manifestations of originalism take a doctrinal position that sharply differentiates them from other interpretive approaches. In virtually all interpretive contexts, calls against looking outside emerged as an alternative to what those making them perceived as an inauthentic interpretative approach that renders community boundaries overly porous. Although debates on these matters are disguised as being purely interpretive, they often reflect sociopolitical divisions at least as much as they reflect ideational or jurisprudential factors.

Virtually all originalist voices, whether in the "textualist" or "original intent" camp, claim to have a monopoly over the authentic reading of the original text, the meaning of it, or the original intentions of its framers; "non-originalist" interpretive schools, they argue, have drifted away from the authentic meaning of the text, and in doing so have inevitably incorporated extra-textual influences. Reference to foreign sources in interpreting a community's sacred, constitutive texts is thus perceived to have no legitimate grounding (how any contemporary interpretation of an old text may be free of such exogenous influences remains unclear, and is a contested issue). Fundamentalist sects of various sorts (e.g. "Torah-true" Naturei Karta Jews, hardcore Christian Reconstructionists, or the Shining Path radical Maoist guerillas in Peru) believe that their cause has grave, even near-cosmic importance. All of them, some admittedly more than others, see themselves as protecting not only a distinctive doctrine but also a vital principle and a way of life and of salvation. Some prefer to remain insular in their purist beliefs. Others locate their *raison d'être* in the proactive advancement of their cause against the grain of a hostile, loosely defined "system" or "outer world." Radical originalists are, by and large, critical of moral "contamination" in the wider culture. They tend to dismiss what they regard as relativism and to advance instead a rigid set of worldviews and beliefs based on unbending, simplistic dichotomies of good and bad, pure and corrupt, right and wrong, and just and unjust. Alternative interpretations of constitutive texts are viewed as inauthentic, theologically diluted, interest-driven, and often over-infused with considerations external to the faith's sovereign virtue.

Textualists often claim that doctrines said to be orally revealed and passed on are likely "to be invented by the priests, rabbis, *qadis*, or judges who claim to be transmitting them," and that "to admit oral tradition as a separate source is to grant additional power to its institutional guardians and transmitters."[69] Fundamentalist schools therefore erect a conceptual "wall of virtue" that protects their identity not only against other religions, but also against what they deem irrelevant, nominal, contaminated, or even threatening versions of their own

---

[69] Grey, "The Constitution as Scripture" (n 48).

faith or cause. All uphold a sharp inward–outward distinction, whereby a limited number of texts, interpreters, and interpretive methods are sacred, with other possible sources or interpretations dismissed as external, a-contextual, misguided, and interest-driven rather than principled. Reference to these latter sources is immoral and deviant. Therein we see the affinity, in religion as well as in constitutionalism, between originalism and the tendency to despise close engagement with the constitutive laws of others; and conversely, between the "living tree" interpretive approach and the tendency to engage more closely with, and assign some moral authority to, foreign laws.

In summary, there are striking parallels between attitudes toward encounters with foreign law in constitutional law and in religion law. A combination of community survival instincts, theological innovation, and instrumentalist considerations guided engagement with the constitutive laws of others in much of the religion-laden, pre-modern world. We will see various configurations and constellations of this "trinity" of need, inquisitiveness, and politics reappear in the modern history of comparative constitutional law—the focus of the next chapter.

Conclusion

When scientists search for life on other planets, they look for worlds that feature a set of preconditions understood as being conducive to sustainable life (water, oxygen, livable climate, etc.). Comparative constitutionalists, by contrast, need not look any further than the nearest library. Pre-modern *religion law* (not religion) is in several important respects a mirror universe of constitutional law.

Constitutional law and religion law are often portrayed as diametrically opposed domains. But they have much more in common than first meets the eye. Both are revered symbolic systems that reflect ideals, aspirations, and principles that are larger than ordinary life. In both there appears to have been a trade-off between interpretation and amendment whereby the harder it is to alter the text, the greater the likelihood of interpretive wars over the text's true meaning. The challenge of when and how to engage with the laws of others—a challenge that comparative constitutional law has been grappling with over the last several decades—is something that religion law has been wrestling with for centuries, perhaps millennia. Moreover, support for originalist, purposive, and living-tree interpretive schools is evident in both spheres. And neither domain is a purely reverent one. Constitutionalism and religion may both be forums of principle, but they are also domains of political strife, in which various stakeholders, interests, and worldviews fight for recognition, influence, and other gains. They operate within particular social, political, and economic contexts and cannot be fully understood outside those contexts. In particular, both domains feature sophisticated, and in many respects comparable, legacies of engagement with the laws of others and of translating morally elevated yet open-ended texts into guidelines for public life.

Despite these striking similarities, there is a persisting tendency in comparative constitutional law to study the constitutional present while overlooking pertinent histories, near and far.[70] This avoidance among constitutional scholars reflects a somewhat thin scholarly culture, and perhaps also a missed opportunity to break the traditional confines of the case law method as the dominant mode of inquiry in constitutional law. Alongside other new horizons of comparative inquiry discussed elsewhere in this book, religion law provides what appears to be a most fertile terrain for placing contemporary debates in (comparative) constitutional law in a broader, richer, and more sophisticated context.

More specifically, few authors have paid close attention to the potential value of legal concepts developed within religion law to the challenge of encounters with foreign law. Even fewer have drawn analogies between the effect of extra-doctrinal factors on interpretation in the two domains. Given the exceptional richness of the interpretive wars that have occurred in religion law through the ages, the thin reference to it by contemporary comparativists and constitutional theorists is intellectually sinful. A cross-disciplinary analysis seems all the more warranted as dilemmas of rejection of or interaction with foreign law increasingly become as relevant to contemporary constitutional law as they have long been to religion law.

---

[70] Undoubtedly, scholars of religion law are no more universalists than their constitutional counterparts, and, more often than not, tend to exemplify particularism—but they at least readily admit to their parochial inclinations.

3

Engaging the Constitutive
Laws of Others

Necessities, Ideas, Interests

"It may be stated that the peculiar nature of political knowledge, as
contrasted by the 'exact sciences', arises out of the inseparability ... of
knowledge from interest and motivation."

Karl Mannheim (*Ideology and Utopia*, 1936)

The Age of Discovery—an era of extensive overseas explorations that
began in the 15th century and continued to the 17th century—was
driven in part by scientific curiosity and a genuine desire to probe the
new world. At the same time, it also served the evolving trade interests
of European superpowers and their quest to dominate the high seas.
The space explorations of the 1960s and 1970s were driven by a
scientific thirst to explore our extraterrestrial surroundings, but were
given added impetus by international politics and the drive to achieve
technological supremacy and global dominance at the height of the
Cold War. Interest in the constitutive laws of others has been driven by
a similar combination of intellectual curiosity and a compatible ideological outlook, political cause, or instrumentalist agenda that calls for
comparative ventures.

The influence of the 20th century's dramatic political transformations on comparative constitutionalism is self-evident. It is widely
accepted that the prevalence of human rights in the international law
and constitutional law of the past half-century is attributable largely to
the international community's disgust with the horrors of World War II.
Similarly, the distinct liberal tilt toward Western comparative constitutional discourse began as a direct reaction to the existential fear of
Bolshevik totalitarianism and "big brother" government. The sophisticated debates in comparative constitutional design and, indeed, the

rise of the entire field of constitutional engineering, are intimately related to broad processes of decolonization, new state formation, and what Samuel Huntington famously labeled the third wave of democratization. The list of examples goes on, and the take-home message is clear: large-scale political processes and other "extra-constitutional" factors had a considerable impact on the direction that comparative constitutional inquiry took throughout much of the 20th century. But the history of comparative constitutional inquiry began well before the 20th century, and the dialogue between *pre-20th-century* comparative constitutional inquiry and the outer political world is equally telling.

What may be learned by looking into the rich history of engagement with the constitutive laws of others? What has driven comparative constitutional journeys through the ages? Why have certain communities or thinkers at certain times and places embarked on them, while others have rejected them? As we have seen in Chapter 2, selective openness toward (or rejection of) the constitutive laws of others may be determined by a host of instrumentalist factors alongside principled considerations or intellectual curiosity per se. In this chapter, I explore how the interplay between highbrow scholarly inquisitiveness and ideological or instrumentalist agendas influenced many of comparative constitutional inquiry's epistemological and methodological leaps in early-modern times. To that end, I consider a few examples of these compounds of theoretical innovation and earthly motivation in the context of comparative constitutional inquiry.

Many political and legal thinkers—some well known (e.g. Francis Bacon or Gottfried Wilhelm Leibniz), others not (e.g. Gottfried Achenwall)—contributed to the birth of what is now termed comparative public law. A detailed intellectual history of this field, from the first attempts to study the constitutive laws of others in a methodical fashion in mid-16th-century Europe to the formation of the academic discipline as we now know it in the early 21st century, lies beyond the scope of this work. Instead, each of the past six centuries is represented by a pre-eminent figure or an epistemological transformation whose approach to comparative study exemplifies the main intellectual and political challenges of its time. I begin by examining in some detail the epistemological matrix underlying the public law comparisons of four early luminaries whose approaches to comparative work highlight the key scholarly and political struggles of their time: Jean Bodin (16th century), John Selden (17th century), Montesquieu (18th century), and

Simón Bolívar (19th century), all of whom were concerned with settings troubled by political instability and calls for transformation. Bodin's *Six livres de la république* (*Six Books of the Commonwealth*, 1576), Selden's *De Iure Naturali et Gentium Juxta Desciplinam Ebraeorum* (*On Natural Law and Nations, according to the Teaching of the Jews*, 1640), and Montesquieu's *Lettres persanes* (*Persian Letters*, 1721) and *De l'esprit des lois* (*The Spirit of the Laws*, 1748) are all masterpieces (some acknowledged as such more than others) of early comparative public law scholarship. Simón Bolívar, in particular, was not only the great liberator of Spanish South America and an important figure in the framing of a host of independence constitutions in Latin America, but also one of the first political leaders of the early-modern era to devote considerable thought to the uneasy reconciliation of foreign constitutional ideals with local realities. His comparative constitutional excursions—in particular his rhetorical and instrumentalist invocation and repudiation of comparative constitutional ideas—demonstrate the role of political conviction in inducing engagement with the constitutive laws of others.

I close the chapter with a brief account of the continental divide, to borrow Seymour Martin Lipset's metaphor, between the current controversy in the United States over reference to the constitutional jurisprudence of other countries, and the Canadian antidote—confident reception and meaningful contribution to comparative constitutional inquiry. Three forces—the inevitability of encounters with foreign legal materials in an age of globalization, the tremendous brainpower of the American legal academia, and above all the deep political divide in the contemporary United States—have converged to generate an intense public debate about the status of comparative constitutional law in a polity that sees its own constitution as a revered marker of national collective identity. This is a prime illustration of how, as in the early-modern world, necessity, inquisitiveness, and political persuasion come together to shape contemporary attitudes toward comparative constitutional law. The stark contrast with Canada's open dialogue with comparative constitutionalism further suggests that the variance across time and space in attitudes toward the constitutive laws of others cannot be understood solely by intra-constitutional factors.

I conclude by suggesting that, despite the considerable epistemological and methodological differences that exist among the various threads of comparative constitutional thought I address in this chapter, a thumbnail account of some of the field's intellectual leaps indicates that they are driven by a combination of necessity, a drive for intellectual innovation, and a political agenda or ideological outlook that calls for and feeds into the comparative inquiry. In some instances, systemic factors or scholarly inquisitiveness has led the way, with a concrete ideological agenda providing added impetus. In others, comparative constitutional inquiry has been more directly driven by ideological conviction and political interests, writ large or small. Either way, epistemological leaps with respect to engagement with the constitutive laws of others cannot be understood in isolation from the broader political context within which they evolved.

Bodin, Selden, and other pioneers

Montesquieu is often identified as the founding father of comparative public law. But traces of scholarly interest in the constitutive laws of others can be found at least 200 years prior to the publication of Montesquieu's seminal work. Thomas More's *Utopia* (1516) depicts a fictional island society and its religious, social, and political customs; it describes a web of pagan, divine, and civil laws that governs the community. It is widely understood to be a self-reflecting comment that engages in a critical dialogue with the political and theological real world of 16th-century England. As early as the mid-16th century, French jurists, in particular Jean Bodin, began to deploy methods of what today would be called comparative public law, or at least a historical variant of it, as they questioned the relevance of Roman law as the legal lingua franca of the time.[1] The political setting was highly charged: the French Wars of Religion between Catholics and Huguenots are said to have cost the lives of hundreds of thousands of people, perhaps as many as two million; the St. Bartholomew's Day massacre alone (August 24, 1572) resulted in the death of thousands of people including many Huguenot aristocrats and community leaders. Huguenots disfavored Roman law due to its perceived conceptual affinity with canon law and the Catholic Church. Radical Catholic factions began to seriously question the authority of the monarchy and

---

[1] Julian Franklin, *Jean Bodin and the Sixteenth Century Revolution in the Methodology of Law and History* (Greenwood Press, 1963). Other French "early comparitivists" of that period are Éguinaire-François Baron, François Baudouin, and François Hotman.

called for an expanded governance role for the Roman Catholic Church. The royalist–statist project was in dire need of a new line of jurisprudential thought that would help to transform Roman law into French law, and to develop legal concepts such as national sovereignty and jurisdiction in order to establish and justify the king's ultimate authority over the land.

In 1567, François Hotman—one of the most avid Huguenot advocates of developing an authentic French law to replace the Justinian Code—wrote in his treatise *Anti-tribonianus* (1567): "The learned men of every age have observed... that the laws should be accommodated to the form and condition of the commonwealth, not the commonwealth to the laws... consequently, the laws of one monarchy are often useless to the another, just as medicines are not all suitable to all men whatsoever without consideration of their sex, their age, and nationality... [T]his principle being posited," continues Hotman, "we may judge whether the books of Justinian are of any special value for the state of France."[2] Enter the comparative public law revolution of mid-16th-century France.[3]

Jean Bodin (1530–96), an erudite political philosopher of moderate Catholic upbringing who advanced a vision of the king's indivisible sovereignty, was arguably the chief figure in the intellectual quest to challenge the authority of Roman law through a comparative public law inquiry. Unlike Huguenot thinkers of his time (e.g. François Hotman, Theodore Beza), Bodin's objection to a blanket acceptance of Roman law was not driven by opposition to Roman-Catholicism per se, but by his support for the monarch's undisputed legal authority over France. Bodin studied Roman law at the University of Toulouse before moving to Angers and later immersing himself in the intellectual legal circle of the royal court in Paris. In 1566, he published *Methodus ad facilem historiarum cognitionem* (*Method for the Easy Comprehension of History*), which included "a very self-conscious effort to apply a

---

[2] François Hotman, *Anti-tribonianus*, 139–41, cited in Franklin, *Jean Bodin and the Sixteenth Century Revolution* (n 1), 46–7.

[3] Hotman's major work was *Francogallia* (1573), in which he argued that the ancient French political tradition warranted some limits and constraints on the monarch's power. Hotman's message is that royal power is not equivalent to tyrannical power. He supports his argument with some comparative reference to the laws of other nations.

comparative method to public law."[4] Bodin forcefully states the book's premise at the outset: "I shall not mention the absurdity of wishing to draw conclusions about universal law from the laws of Rome ... [T]he only way to arrange the laws and govern the state ... is to collect all the laws of all or the most famous commonwealths, to compare them and derive the best variety."[5] The lengthy (over 130 pages) Chapter 6 of *Methodus*, titled "The Types of Government in States," engages in comparative analysis of what we would call today the constitutional foundations or basic rules of government. Bodin compares the laws of ancient empires, medieval polities, and the kingdoms, grand duchies, and city-states of his time on a variety of public law matters such as citizenship, municipal law, taxation, jurisdiction, and sovereignty.[6] The underlying logic of the work can be summed up in two propositions: (i) the legal organization of a polity may be taken as an indicator of that polity's political organization; and (ii) knowledge about various legal systems throughout history is essential for assessing the quality of present laws, as well as for effectively designing tomorrow's. At the most abstract level, Bodin attempted to achieve legal renewal and political self-betterment through the identification of a "best practice" arrangement for political organization—a classic invocation of the "concept building through multiple description" mode of inquiry, as discussed in Chapter 6. This legal and political transformation was to be promoted through a comparative inquiry into the constitutive laws of others, including what we would describe today as their constitutional law, and perhaps even their constitutional identity.[7]

Bodin's initial foray into comparative public law involved an examination of French law, Roman law, canon law, and the legal systems of ancient Egypt and Athens. His work was emulated by Huguenot thinkers of his time, most notably Theodore Beza, who in an attempt to show that monarchy is not equivalent to absolutism included in *De jure magistratuum* (*The Right of Magistrates*, 1574) references to early forms of social contract and provisional (i.e. non-absolutist) monarchical

---

[4] See Donald Kelley, "Civil Science in the Renaissance: Jurisprudence in the French Manner," *History of European Ideas* 2 (1981): 261–76, 270.

[5] Bodin, *Methodus* 107b; cited in Franklin, *Jean Bodin and the Sixteenth Century Revolution* (n 1), 69–70.

[6] See Jean Bodin, *Method for the Easy Comprehension of History* (W.W. Norton, 1945), 153–290.

[7] See George Huppert, *The Idea of Perfect History: Historical Erudition and Historical Philosophy in Renaissance France* (University of Illinois Press, 1970).

authority in Rome, Athens, Sparta, England, Poland, Venice, Spain, and France as well as by the Israelites.[8] But the period's magisterial comparative public law project only reached its zenith with the publication in 1576 of Jean Bodin's *Six livres de la république* (*The Six Books of the Commonwealth*, 1576)—a comprehensive work that in retrospect may be considered the first real study of comparative public law in the early-modern era. As in his earlier work, Bodin's overarching project was to break the jurisprudential exclusivity of Roman law and to reconstruct juristic science "through a comparison and synthesis of all the juridical experience of the most famous states."[9] The normative stand was clear: royalist-absolutism and strong legal statehood are a remedy for sectarian divisions and other external, non-statist influences. Bodin attempted to release the concepts of sovereignty, dominion, and jurisdiction from the sole grip of Roman law, and thereby to support the king's exclusive control of his kingdom (*rex imperator in regno sue*, "the king himself is emperor in his kingdom"). To that end, he examined the formulation of these legal concepts across time and space in order to find out how various polities understood and defined their legal and political sovereignty.

Bodin is "arguably the greatest theorist of non-democratic constitutional restraints, that is of constitutional restraints freely adopted by a powerful monarch power."[10] His comparative work led him to contemplate intriguing ideas about the utility of constitutional restraints on the king's powers. Constitutionally entrenched parliamentary immunity, for example, while it may appear to be a concession on behalf of the king, in practice may allow for more effective monitoring and oversight of policy implementation in the hinterlands. Bodin suggested that, given the difficulty of monitoring the king's numerous agents, allowing open complaints by representatives in the Estates General (the legislative assembly in pre-revolution France) with no threat of punishment may help to expose gaps in the enforcement of and compliance with royal policies that would otherwise have been impossible to trace. Legal exemption from liability for accusations made in parliament would encourage disclosure of "the robberies and extortions

---

[8] See Scott Gordon, *Controlling the State: Constitutionalism from Ancient Athens to Today* (Harvard University Press, 1999), 124.

[9] Franklin, *Jean Bodin and the Sixteenth Century Revolution* (n 1).

[10] Stephen Holmes, "Constitutions and Constitutionalism," in Michel Rosenfeld and András Sajó, eds., *The Oxford Handbook of Comparative Constitutional Law* (Oxford University Press, 2012), 193.

committed in the prince's name, whereof he knoweth nothing."[11] This is an early precursor of the "fire alarm" logic of regulatory oversight (as we would call it today), stunningly identified and recommended by Bodin more than four centuries ago.[12]

The scope of Bodin's comparative research (recall, this is the 16th century) is beyond impressive. Notably, his research is not confined to the "usual suspect" legal systems of his time. In addition to probing into the formulation of sovereignty in French law, Roman law, canon law, and ancient Egyptian and Greek law, *Six livres* includes careful reference to ancient civilizations such as those of the Assyrians, Phoenicians, and Persians, as well as to the laws of 16th-century Russia, Poland, and Scandinavia. Perhaps the most far-reaching innovation in Bodin's work is the comparative dimension of his work. Under the "aristocratic state" category, to pick one example, "there is a concise presentation of all available data as to the size, composition, and status of the ruling organs for Pharsalia, Sparta, Epidaurus, Thebes, Rhodes, Genoa, Geneva, Zurich, Basel, Berne, Lucerne, Fribourg, Venice, Rhagusa, Lucca, the German Empire, and then finally the political system of Nuremburg considered as representative of Augsburg, Worms, and other independent German cities."[13]

The argument at the foreground of this is that the laws of a polity should not be imposed on it from the outside or applied to it in a mechanical, insensitive fashion (think the anti-Roman law project). Indeed, argues Bodin, "the wise governor of a people should fully understand its humor and its nature before expecting anything from an

---

[11] Jean Bodin, *The Six Books of the Commonwealth*, book 3, chapter 7; cited in Holmes, "Constitutions and Constitutionalism" (n 10), 194.

[12] Over four centuries after Bodin, scholars drew on a similar rationale to develop theories of delegation and effective political control of administrative agencies. Institutional economists, for example, suggested in the 1980s that judicial review may constitute an efficient "fire alarm" mechanism for monitoring the bureaucracy. Legislators routinely delegate discretion over public policy programs to bureaucrats, but must try to ensure that these bureaucrats implement the programs as they were intended. Investments in measures that enhance judicial independence may accordingly be interpreted as efforts by executive branch leaders to avoid the high costs of constant central supervision of bureaucratic agencies (or a "police patrol" mechanism). Adopting a decentralized "fire alarm" monitoring model would allow those who feel they have been treated unfairly to sue through the courts. See Mathew McCubbins and Thomas Schwartz, "Congressional Oversight Overlooked: Police Patrols Versus Fire Alarms," *American Journal of Political Science* 28 (1984): 165–79; Mathew McCubbins et al., "Administrative Procedures as Instruments of Political Control," *Journal of Law, Economics and Organization* 3 (1987): 243–77.

[13] Franklin, *Jean Bodin and the Sixteenth Century Revolution* (n 1), 76.

alteration of the state or of the laws. For one of the most important and perhaps the principal foundation of the commonwealths is the adaptation of the state to the nature of the citizens, and the edicts and ordinances to the nature of the places, the persons, and the times."[14]

The organizing principle of the comparative inquiry resembles, as mentioned earlier, what we may call "concept formation through multiple descriptions" of the same constitutional phenomena across countries. Along with this came substantive, systematic comparison of the advantages and disadvantages of the different types of constitutional arrangement and forms of government. The outcome, writes a prominent scholar of the French Renaissance, "is a comprehensive system of comparative constitutional law, which is a major step in the beginning... of comparative jurisprudence."[15] In short, comparative public law as a systematic inquiry into the constitutive laws of others is certainly not a 20th-century invention. It was born in mid-16th-century France, and Jean Bodin may legitimately be considered among its founding fathers. As is evident, this pioneering comparative foray cannot be understood independent of the political context within which it emerged. In fact, the entire comparative exercise was driven by a perspicuous political agenda.

The rapidly expanding intellectual and geographical horizons of early to mid-17th-century Europe stirred interest among the leading thinkers of the time in the laws of other nations. A variety of theoretical threads emerged. Francis Bacon, the famous philosopher, jurist, and statesman, and a key figure in the scientific revolution of the early-modern age, suggested in 1623 that a system of national law as the object of scholarly judgment cannot at the same time provide the standard of judgment. Advocating a scientific (or unbiased) approach to the study of law, he argued that lawyers should free themselves from the bonds of their own national systems in order to evaluate objectively its merits and drawbacks.[16] In his opinion, comparative assessment driven by a cosmopolitan outlook is not merely a normatively preferable option, but an analytically superior one. The only scientific way to assess a given legal system is by an international or exogenous standard. (Even liberal constitutionalists in the United States, let alone conservative nationalists, would find Bacon's argument about the necessity

[14] Franklin, *Jean Bodin and the Sixteenth Century Revolution* (n 1), 78.
[15] Franklin, *Jean Bodin and the Sixteenth Century Revolution* (n 1), 77.
[16] Francis Bacon, *De dignitate et augmentis scientiarum* (1623).

of a cosmopolitan baseline for legal comparison difficult to accept).
A related thread of comparative thought was driven by an early
encyclopedist impulse. In 1667, Gottfried Wilhelm Leibniz proposed,
but never completed, a comprehensive catalogue—*theatrum legale
mundi*—that would have collated and classified the laws and customs
of all peoples, times, and places as the ultimate tool for comparative
legal research.[17] A third thread of comparative thought at the time was
driven by a quest to formulate what today would be labeled as international public law. The Age of Discovery, and in particular the Dutch
Golden Age of the mid-17th century, laid the foundations of modern
international trade, colonialism, and exploitation of foreign lands, and
the evolving political and economic interests of European superpowers
of the time intensified their quest to dominate the high seas. A need for
some form of supranational law emerged. The work of Dutch thinker
Hugo Grotius, most notably his classic *On the Law of War and Peace*
(1625), compared various systems of national law in an attempt to lay
down the basics of an international legal framework. German Samuel
von Pufendorf's *Two Books of the Elements of Universal Jurisprudence*
(1661) and *On the Law of Nature and of Nations* (1672) famously followed
this line of inquiry.

Whereas modern constitutional theory often disregards religion law,
these major 17th-century scholars of the "laws of nations" were fascinated by Jewish law's distinction between general norms applicable
to humanity and Jewish law applicable to Jews alone. Their interest in
Jewish law was influenced in part by the "Hebrew revival" in political
thought in the late 16th century and early 17th century, which made
respectable a hitherto unknown (to Christian Europe) or disreputable
legal tradition. These thinkers—all working at the intersection of what
would today be designated as international law, public law, and legal
theory—devoted considerable time to studying the Noachide precepts
of the Talmudic tradition and the possibility of its restoration as a
baseline of moral obligations for all mankind.[18]

---

[17] See Frederick Pollock, "The History of Comparative Jurisprudence," *Journal of the
Society of Comparative Legislation* 5 (1903): 74–89, 83.

[18] On the significant impact of Jewish sources, biblical and rabbinical, on European
political thought in the 17th and 18th centuries, see Eric Nelson, *The Hebrew Republic: Jewish
Sources and the Transformation of European Political Thought* (Harvard University Press, 2010).
Earlier accounts pointed to the possible influence of Jewish sources on the development of
international law. See, e.g., Shabtai Rosenne, "The Influence of Judaism on the Development of International Law," *Netherlands International Law Review* 5 (1958): 119–49. The

An unsung pioneer of comparative public law scholarship of that era was John Selden (1584–1654). Known for his contributions as a political theorist and British parliamentarian as well as to the international law of the sea, Selden's immense comparative scholarship on the constitutive laws of others, most notably on Jewish law, has remained largely unexplored. His meticulous work on Jewish law and the Noachide precepts as a template for universal law—in particular his magnum opus *De Iure Naturali et Gentium Juxta Desciplinam Ebraeorum* (*On Natural Law and Nations, according to the Teaching of the Jews*, 1640)— makes him the first "full-time" legal comparativist of the modern era. Considered to be one of the most erudite people of his time, Selden was described by notable luminaries as "the glory of the English nation" (Hugo Grotius), "Monarch in letters" (Ben Jonson), and "the chief of learned men reputed in this land" (John Milton).[19] Selden devoted half his adult life to the study of foreign law and international law. For roughly 25 years, from the late 1620s to the early 1650s, he meticulously studied the foundational principles of the Jewish legal tradition as a potential source for a basic set of universal legal norms applicable to all mankind.

Selden's interest in the subject was first reflected in *De Successionibus in Bona Defunctorum* (*On the Law of Inheritance*, 1631), in which he probed extensively into the Jewish law of inheritance. In 1644, he published *De Anno Civili* (*On the Civil Year*)—a treatise on the Jewish calendar that pays close attention to the doctrines and practices of the Karaites (as explained earlier, a small literalist sect within Judaism). In 1646, he published *Uxor Ebraica seu De Nuptiis et Divortiis Veterum Ebaeorum* (*On the Jewish Law of Marriage and Divorce*) before turning to his trilogy on Jewish courts—which focuses particularly on the chief Second Temple rabbinical tribunal (the Sanhedrin)—*De Synhedriis Veterum Ebraeorum* (with the first part of the trilogy appearing in 1650, the second in 1653, and the third in 1655, a year after Selden's death). But Selden's most monumental work on Jewish law was *De Iure Naturali et Gentium Juxta Desciplinam Ebraeorum* (*On Natural Law and Nations, according to the Teaching of the Jews*, 1640), in which he invokes

---

"Golden Age" of Jewish thought's influence on legal thinkers came to an end with the early 18th-century writings of French jurist Jean Barbeyrac, who questioned the coherence, authority, and relevance of rabbinic sources.

[19] See Jason Rosenblatt, *Renaissance England's Chief Rabbi: John Selden* (Oxford University Press, 2006). See also, G. J. Toomer, *John Selden: A Life in Scholarship* (Oxford University Press, 2009).

the Noachide precepts as a template for a universal code of morality. As with most jurists of his time, Selden suggests that law requires an authority to prescribe it, and that, therefore, reason cannot be the sole source of law. At the same time, he allows that God has imprinted certain moral rules in the minds of all men, and this, he suggests, is where the Noachide precepts become relevant.[20] (To appease his Christian audience and church establishment, Selden concludes *De Iure Naturali* with a disclaimer, stating that his high regard for Jewish teachings on natural law should not be taken as an endorsement of those teachings over Christian ethics).[21] Selden contrasts "natural law," which he takes to be law that is common to all mankind, with the "law of nations" that he defines as the laws and customs that are observed by many peoples but are not universal, that is, not followed by all peoples at all times. In the context of Jewish law, natural law refers to the Noachide precepts as incumbent upon all sons of Noah.[22] Selden regarded this core message as useful in developing a basis or a minimum standard for enlightened legal systems applicable to all people at all times.

To illustrate the universal–particular duality within Jewish law, Selden examines rules of proselytism, powers of the monarch, marriage and divorce, excommunication, charity and economic law, capital punishment, war and peace, the concluding of treaties, and more. Having outlined the existence and nature of the duality in the preface to *De Iure Naturali*, Selden uses the body of the work to explore each of the seven Noachide precepts. He goes on to praise the existence of the Noachide precepts within Jewish law as a strong example of the coexistence of universal and particular law. Nearly four centuries later, the duality between Jewish law as an emblem of the particular, and the Noachide precepts within the Jewish legal tradition as an emblem of the universal, still offers an intriguing conceptual framework for analyzing the tension between national constitutional identity and supranational constitutional norms.

The motives for Selden's immense comparative endeavors are not entirely clear. His work on the international law of the sea (e.g. *Mare Clausm* (*The Closed Sea*), 1635) was clearly driven by a national interest

---

[20] See *The Cambridge History of English and American Literature* (Putnam, 1907–21), Vol. VII (edited by A. W. Ward and A. R. Waller), "Cavalier and Puritan."

[21] Toomer, *John Selden: A Life in Scholarship* (n 19), 493.

[22] Toomer, *John Selden: A Life in Scholarship* (n 19), 492.

to control the waters around the British Isles. In a direct response to Hugo Grotius's *Mare Liberum* (*The Free Sea*, 1609) in which Grotius argued in line with Dutch international trade interests that the sea was international territory and all nations were free to use it for seafaring trade, Selden argued that countries have jurisdiction over the sea close to their shores. With respect to his devotion to the study of Jewish law and the Hebrew Republic, some scholars have pointed to his genuine learnedness and unbounded intellectual curiosity.[23] Others have suggested that Selden's work was driven by his own political career and agenda;[24] in particular, his commitment to upholding the "holy commonwealth," his support for Erastianism (state endorsement and control of religion), and his desire to understand the relations between secular law and sacred sources and ideals.[25] And there is a clear universal outlook (by 17th-century standards) in Selden's work. As Jason Rosenblatt notes, "Selden's discovery in the Talmud and in Maimonides' *Mishneh Torah* of shared moral rules in the natural, pre-civil state of humankind provides a basis for relationships among human beings anywhere in the world."[26] One thing is undisputed: unlike major luminaries of his time who referred to the laws of others in passing and whose interest in the subject was incidental to their interest in the philosophical foundations of scientific inquiry (Leibniz), or in what today would be designated as customary international law (e.g. Hugo Grotius and Samuel von Pufendorf), Selden was genuinely interested in the law of others as *the* subject of his inquiry.

In all his writings on the subject, Selden regarded the Talmud, and the Jewish legal tradition more generally, as a system of law, distinguishing him from many of his "age of intolerance" contemporaries who approached Jewish law with ignorance, suspicion, and derision. As G. J. Toomer notes in his remarkable intellectual biography of Selden, "Jewish law presented itself to him as a fourth self-contained system [in addition to English, Roman, and canon law], with its own

---

[23] Toomer, *John Selden: A Life in Scholarship* (n 19).

[24] Paul Christianson, *Discourse on History, Law and Governance in the Public Career of John Selden 1610–1635* (University of Toronto Press, 1996).

[25] Reid Barbour, *John Selden: Measures of the Holy Commonwealth in Seventeenth-Century England* (University of Toronto Press, 2003). See also, Eric Nelson, "The Religious Origins of Religious Toleration," *The Templeton Lecture on Religion and World Affairs* (Foreign Policy Research Institute, 2010), 14–17; Selden would "describe Erastus as 'another Copernicus'" Nelson notes.

[26] Rosenblatt, *Renaissance England's Chief Rabbi* (n 19), [back cover outline].

canonical texts and expository corpus, its own courts, and its own jurisprudents. His usual appellation for these authoritative rabbis of the Talmud and the commentaries thereon is the honorific 'Magistri', a word also used for the authorities in Roman law... [W]e find in *De Iure Naturali* an eloquent advocacy of the value of this Jewish tradition, which he consistently calls a *legal* tradition."[27]

While he was certainly not a "halakhist" per se, Selden exhibited tremendous empathy toward his research subject. The few scholars who studied his careful treatment of Jewish law praise his respect for major medieval rabbinical luminaries such as Shlomo Yitzchaki (known by his acronym Rashi), Ibn Ezra, David Kimkhi (known by his acronym Radak), and Maimonides.[28] Maimonides' magnum opus *Mishneh Torah* (*Restatement of the Jewish Oral Law*, c. 1170–80)—widely considered one of the two most significant commentaries on Jewish law as a coherent legal tradition (the other being Rabbi Yosef Caro's 16th-century *Shulkhan Arukh* (*Code of Jewish Law*), a codification of *Halakha*)—served as Selden's main gateway to the Talmud. Throughout his explorations of Jewish law, and in particular of the existence of the Noachide precepts within Jewish law as an effective illustration of the coexistence of universal and particular law, Selden compares the Talmudic literature to Roman law as well as to norms in French, Spanish, English, and canon law, and regularly points out similarities and differences between them.[29] Selden's work, most notably *De Iure Naturali et Gentium*, is thus a genuine and truly impressive study of comparative public law, published roughly a century prior to Montesquieu's work.

Montesquieu as a comparativist

Problems of governance, mainly tensions between central and local government, continued to pose challenges to 17th-century constitutional thought. As noted medievalist Brian Tierney observes, thinkers

---

[27] Toomer, *John Selden: A Life in Scholarship* (n 19), 441–2.

[28] See, e.g., Rosenblatt, *Renaissance England's Chief Rabbi* (n 19). For a critique of Selden's qualifications as a true "inside" scholar of Jewish law, see Isaac Herzog, "John Selden and Jewish Law," *Journal of Comparative Legislation and International Law* 13 (1931): 236–45.

[29] On Selden's comparative methods, see Toomer, *John Selden: A Life in Scholarship* (n 19), 818–21.

of the time "had to reconcile as best they could the claims of court and country, kings and nobles, emperor and princes, pope and bishops, general assembly and local presbytery."[30] The challenge grew greater with the gradual decline of church hegemony and the rise of the secular state. The Protestant Reformation of the 16th and early 17th centuries, with its emphasis on breaking down the invidious political structures of the Catholic Church, is often thought of as the birth of the secular age.[31] However, it was not until a few decades later that the changing intellectual landscape of Europe brought about a change in the method and substance of comparative constitutional inquiry. In the mid-17th century, Baruch Spinoza and other rationalists started to raise persuasive arguments against theology-induced politics. Because of a confluence of more concrete political, economic, societal, and technological factors—all widely documented by historians of Western civilization—republican ideas and modern nationalism started to gain momentum in Europe and among European settlers in the New World. Consequently, the unified theological–political pact of the Middle Ages began to implode. The theory of divine right (the ruler's authority as an extension of God's will) was abandoned in England during the Glorious Revolution of 1688–89, and certain political freedoms and constitutional limitations on the monarch's power and authority were introduced at around the same time.

Along with these grand transformations, there emerged interest in the systematic study of constitutions across polities. This is manifested in Montesquieu's satirical take in *Lettres persanes* (*Persian Letters*, 1721) on the laws and government of Louis XVI's France, which he considers through the "outsider" observations of two fictitious Persian merchants, Usbec and Rica, and a few years later in Jonathan Swift's travel odyssey *Gulliver's Travels* (1726), which considers the laws and government of Gulliver's imagined destinations. On the more empirical side, a lesser known author, German Gottfried Achenwall of the University of Göttingen published *Staatsverfassung der Europäischen Reiche im Grundrisse* (*Constitution of the Present Leading European States*, 1749). In this pioneering yet largely unknown book, Achenwall provided a

[30] See Brian Tierney, *Religion, Law, and the Growth of Constitutional Thought, 1150–1650* (Cambridge University Press, 1982), 105–6.

[31] For a thorough account of the decline of religion and the rise of secularism in Western culture from the Protestant Reformation onward, see Charles Taylor, *A Secular Age* (Belknap Press of Harvard University Press, 2007).

comprehensive view of the constitutional structure of various European countries (Spain, Portugal, France, Great Britain, the Netherlands, Russia, Denmark, and Sweden), described their social, legal, and political order, examined the material condition of their agriculture, industries, and commerce, and backed his analysis with descriptive statistical analysis and illustrations (Achenwall is considered one of the founders of modern statistics).

While these are all important early beginnings, the publication of Montesquieu's monumental *De l'esprit des lois* (*The Spirit of the Laws*, 1748) is indisputably a—if not the—defining moment in the history of comparative public law. Montesquieu's foundational strategy of unearthing links between law and society across cultures has inspired an impressive tradition of comparative scholarship. It has also led to a curiously different genealogy in the social sciences scholarship than in legal scholarship. Thus, Montesquieu's comparative socio-legal work may be used as a benchmark against which we can assess the epistemology, methodology, and thematic framework of later generations of comparative public law scholarship.

Montesquieu's contribution as forerunner, if not founder, of modern sociology and anthropology was acknowledged by pioneers of these disciplines, from Auguste Comte to Émile Durkheim and E. E. Evans-Pritchard. Later sociological giants such as Max Weber, A. R. Radcliffe-Brown, Raymond Aron, and Louis Althusser have all emphasized the scientific nature of Montesquieu's scholarship. Likewise, Montesquieu may be considered the first grandmaster of comparative public law. His attempt, tentative as it was, to draw upon comparative research to trace causal links between a polity's material, demographic, and cultural characteristics and the nature and organization of that polity's legal and political institutions was a major leap forward in the evolution of comparative law as a method, discipline, and science.

At the outset of *The Spirit of the Laws*, Montesquieu defines laws as "the necessary relations deriving from the nature of things,"[32] and states that the purpose of the work is to "examine all these relations."[33] With this monumental task before him, he analyzes and classifies the different types of laws and governments, describing how they connect

---

[32] Charles-Louis de Secondat, Baron de Montesquieu, *The Spirit of the Laws* (Cambridge University Press, 1989 [1748]), 3.
[33] Montesquieu, *The Spirit of the Laws* (n 32), 9.

to, and are affected by, a range of factors. And he has an explicit political agenda: he argues that out of the different types of government he examines—monarchy, republic, and despotism—monarchy is to be preferred.

In the book's first part, Montesquieu describes these three basic forms of government in topological form and with reference to Aristotle's *Politeia*. His approach entails the use of an extensive taxonomy—a classification of laws and governments according to their distinguishing characteristics. He sets out several types of laws: invariable law (the laws of God and the physical world) and variable laws (the laws of human creation); moral, civil, and political laws; and finally natural laws (which derive from the human constitution) and positive laws (of human creation). Man is similarly classified into states: man in the "state of nature" (a timid, solitary creature) is fundamentally different from "man in society" (man after the introduction of property and inequality, which created a state of war that laws can remedy by providing man with liberty). He also outlines the three types of government societal man can form: republics (in which all or part of the people rule, with two subclasses of democracy and aristocracy); monarchies (in which one alone governs by fixed and established laws); and despotisms (in which one alone governs according to his own will and without fixed laws).

The Spirit of the Laws is full of distinctions and sub-distinctions. The most important aspect of its theme of separation is Montesquieu's argument in favor of a separation of powers. The most successful government is the one which provides the highest degree of political liberty (security). This is best achieved when the legislative, executive, and judicial branches operate independently: "When legislative power is united with executive power in a single person or in a single body of the magistry," he explains, "there is no liberty, because one can fear that the same monarch or senate that makes tyrannical laws will execute them tyrannically."[34] Montesquieu argues that this separation of powers can only occur in a monarchy because the constitution of a monarchy demands that countervailing powers exist to check the power of the prince. Such divisions of power do not exist in either republics or despotisms, Montesquieu suggests, because of the fundamentally egalitarian nature (though they are egalitarian in different

---

[34] Montesquieu, *The Spirit of the Laws* (n 32), 157.

ways) of those governments. For these reasons, monarchy must be considered the best form of government.

Having identified the three types of government, Montesquieu connects each of them to a principle, which functions as both a goal and an animating force. In monarchies, the principle is honor; in republics, it is civic virtue; and in despotism it is fear. The structure of the government and its principle is connected to the type of laws it should have if it is to function effectively. Montesquieu then outlines the manner in which laws in each type of government should and do govern areas of social interaction: education; inheritance; civil and criminal laws; sumptuary laws; luxury; the condition of women; defense; religion; and commerce. In a typical descriptive/prescriptive paragraph he suggests that:

Laws should be so specific to the people for whom they are made, that it is a great coincidence if those of one nation can suit another. They should be relative to the physical qualities of the country; to its frozen, burning, or temperate climate; to the quality, location, and size of the territory; to the mode of livelihood of the people, farmers, hunters, of pastoralists; they should relate to the degree of liberty which the constitution can admit, to the religion of the inhabitants, to their inclinations, to their wealth, to their numbers, to their commerce, to their mores, to their manners....[35]

Following his exploration of the nature of government, Montesquieu turns to the second theme of his work: not only do laws affect a wide variety of issues, but laws are themselves affected and dictated by various environmental, societal, and cultural factors. The second part of *The Spirit of the Laws* deals with the effect of material factors, such as climate and soil quality, on the structure of human societies, their traditions, and their organizations. The book's third part focuses on the significance of social and economic factors, such as trade and commerce, demographic conditions, and religiosity, to the traditions and laws of various societies and their political institutions. The last section of the book illustrates the arguments put forth in the second and third parts by comparing the laws of ancient Rome and medieval feudal society, mainly in France. It is here that Montesquieu's

[35] Montesquieu, *The Spirit of the Laws* (n 32), 8.

comparative mastery and theory of the mutual cause and effect relationship between law and society are best exemplified.

Montesquieu's arguments in *The Spirit of the Laws* are supported by
hundreds of comparative examples, which are cast in an inductive form
of argumentation. "History and our laws would have said . . . 'we shall
testify for you'," he exclaims.[36] The book features 667 citations, 204 of
which are drawn from ancient Rome (primarily Tacitus, Livy, and
Denis of Halicarbassus). Remarkably for its time, no less than 213 of the
book's citations, approximately one-third, refer to the non-European
world. Of these, the vast majority (165) concern Asia, primarily China,
Turkey and Persia, India, and Japan. Sources on the Americas are cited
18 times while sources on Africa are cited merely eight times. Asian
"despotism" in particular provides Montesquieu with a useful antithesis
of Europe.[37] The "great princes of the east" and their laws serve as
cautionary tales against laws which are too severe, the corruption of
monarchy, and other perils of despotism,[38] whereas Native North
American, West Indies, and African "savagery" help Montesquieu to
demonstrate principles of natural law. The government of England, a
constitutional monarchy, figures prominently in *The Spirit of the Laws* as
an ideal regime type, one that is in accordance with the nature of the
country, and the "one government in modern Europe that made
freedom the aim of its constitution and policies."[39]

Montesquieu's methodology in *The Spirit of the Laws* is not unprob-
lematic. A rather crude taxonomy informs his genuine quest to determine causal links between pertinent factors (in *Persian Letters*
Montesquieu demonstrates another purpose of comparative inquiry:
self-reflection through analogy and contrast). His choice of comparative examples is biased: he cites either situations in which a government
or law succeeded because it followed the approach he advocates, or
situations where a government or law failed, presumably because the
Montesquieu formula was not applied. This normatively driven selection of supposedly prototypical cases highlights the dual nature of *The
Spirit of the Laws* as both descriptive (comparative examples illustrate the
taxonomy of regime types and their characteristics) and prescriptive

---

[36] Montesquieu, *The Spirit of the Laws* (n 32), 659.
[37] Robert Launay, "Montesquieu: The Specter of Despotism and the Origins of Comparative Law," in Annelise Riles, ed., *Rethinking the Masters of Comparative Law* (Hart
Publishing, 2001), 28–9.
[38] Montesquieu, *The Spirit of the Laws* (n 32), 20.
[39] Judith Shklar, *Montesquieu* (Oxford University Press, 1987), 85.

(particular examples are brought to further Montesquieu's own arguments for effective means of governance). His information-gathering
methods are best described as "armchair" constitutional ethnography:
his analysis of non-European societies is haphazard, and relies exclusively on secondary sources, primarily travel literature, Jesuit missionary
propaganda, and biased reports by French and Dutch merchants.[40]
And, like many authors after him, Montesquieu was quite willing to
overlook the attitudes of the authors he cited when they did not suit his
purpose.[41]

Notwithstanding these deficiencies, Montesquieu is clearly one of
the founders of comparative law. Few authors before him (and, alas,
too few after him) have drawn so knowledgably and extensively
on comparative law materials as the illustrative backbone of their
socio-legal work. Although Montesquieu's comparative scholarship is
primarily taxonomic, at the same time it treats law as an indicator,
cause, and outcome of society's development. It is descriptive, prescriptive, and explanatory. One could hardly ask for more from the first
comprehensive, widely recognized, and deeply influential work in
comparative public law.

The impact of Montesquieu's comparative thought on 19th-century
socio-legal studies was tremendous. In his Latin dissertation on *Montesquieu's Contribution to the Rise of Social Science*, Emile Durkheim
suggests that "[I]t was he, who, in *The Spirit of the Laws*, laid down
the principles of the new science of sociology."[42] Akin to Montesquieu, prominent late 19th-century socio-legal thinkers—Maine,
Morgan, and Durkheim—all draw on comparative examples, analogies, and dissimilarities between the laws and societal institutions of
different polities to illustrate and substantiate their arguments. As was
common among social thinkers in the 18th and 19th centuries, a
Eurocentrist perception of the world, alongside a genuine fascination
with the life of "others" and the ultimate uniformity of human experience, shaped these scholars' picture of the legal (and constitutional)
universe. A central theme in their work is the historical development
of law; more precisely, they consider the various factors which influence the formation and evolution of laws and, in turn, how laws

---

[40] Launay, "Montesquieu: The Specter of Despotism" (n 37), 30.
[41] Launay, "Montesquieu: The Specter of Despotism" (n 37), 31.
[42] Émile Durkheim, *Montesquieu and Rousseau: Forerunners of Sociology* (University of
Michigan Press, 1960 [1892, 1918]), 1.

influence society. Maine, Morgan, and Durkheim all understand that the mores and ethos of a society have a central effect on its legal organization. At the same time, they appreciate that law is also an important indicator of societal and political development.

There are at least three features which distinguish these 19th-century evolutionary theorists from Montesquieu. First, the work of Maine, Morgan, and Durkheim is more methodologically rigorous. While they may still be considered "armchair anthropologists," their collection and analysis of data is more systematic and less biased than that of Montesquieu. The evolutionary theorists put more emphasis on the need to control their comparisons, as well as on the basic principles of inference-oriented case selection. A second and related difference is that their more scientific (or empirical) orientation leads them to debunk earlier philosophical notions about pre-societal man, the state of nature, and natural law. As Tom Pangle argues, Montesquieu accepts a type of natural law to which he believes laws and governments should conform regardless of whether doing so actually produces good effects. So, although comparative illustrations form the backbone of Montesquieu's argument, the historical record is not the sole means by which he deems a law or government to be just or effective. Unlike Montesquieu, the 19th-century thinkers treat law as being purely man-made:[43] variance in legal development, for Maine or Durkheim, reflects nothing more than variance in social progress. A third difference, and probably the most important one, is the attempt by the 19th-century thinkers to build a coherent theory of social and legal change. The "uniform development thesis" and its emphasis on organic societal change goes beyond Montesquieu's taxonomy to offer a parsimonious explanation—not merely a description—of the evolutionary dynamic of social and legal transformation.[44] Montesquieu's despotic Asian polities lack the necessary conditions to develop into successful republics. Unlike Montesquieu's static depiction of fundamentally different types of legal and governmental systems, evolutionists argue that all societies progress through a uniform series of developmental stages;

---

[43] Thomas L. Pangle, *Montesquieu's Philosophy of Liberalism* (University of Chicago Press, 1973).

[44] Similar arguments in the broader context of economic and political development have been advanced by S. N. Eisenstadt and Talcott Parsons. Maine's evolutionary thesis of the development of law is echoed by structural functionalist legal sociologists such as Niklas Luhmann and his theory of the evolution of law as a function of the increasing complexity and contingency of modern societies.

different societies may be at differing stages of social or legal development, but all are essentially on the same trajectory.

In summary, by the end of the 19th century, comparative legal studies, constitutional and otherwise, began to produce a considerable body of intellectual insights, sporadic and tentative though they might have been. This led to the emergence of the disciplinary divide between law and the social sciences, the former with its embedded tilt in favor of rules, formalism, court decisions, and vocational training; the latter with its focus on human behavior, political institutions, and social organization across time and space. The result of this stark disciplinary divide was that by the time Max Weber published the landmark comparative work (*Economy and Society*, 1914) in which he attempts to explain the ascendancy of the West by drawing causal links between law and social and economic development across societies, it was widely recognized as a work in comparative legal sociology, not in comparative (public) law.

Bolívar and other 19th-century innovators

Early experiments with democratic governance took place in 18th-century Sweden (the Age of Liberty), and are manifested in the Corsican Constitution (1765), which was inspired by the writings of Jean-Jacques Rousseau. This set the stage for the adoption of the US Constitution in 1789, the Polish Constitution in 1791, the post-revolution constitutions in France, the Spanish Constitution of Cádiz (1812), the Constitution of Norway in 1814, and a host of independence constitutions adopted in Latin America from the 1810s to the 1830s. Inevitably, this era was a heyday of constitutional innovation, from the powerful ideas of America's Founding Fathers in the late 18th century to the innovative thought of Henri-Benjamin Constant in the early 19th century (e.g. Constant's distinction between ancient liberty and modern liberty, or his notion of constitutional monarchy in which royal power was conceptualized as that of a moderating authority, balancing and restraining the excesses of the three classic powers).[45]

---

[45] See, generally, Stephen Holmes, *Benjamin Constant and the Making of Modern Liberalism* (Yale University Press, 1984); K. Steven Vincent, *Benjamin Constant and the Birth of French Liberalism* (Palgrave, 2011); Helena Rosenblatt, ed., *The Cambridge Companion to Constant* (Cambridge University Press, 2009).

The political background and significance of these ideas are readily evident. The *Federalist Papers* is arguably the single most influential work of constitutional theory to date. Constant's ideas were contemplated and eventually applied in Portugal (1822), Brazil (1824), France (the Charter of 1830, which essentially removed the king's power to instigate legislation), and Sardinia (1848, preceding the constitution of Italy, 1861).

Perhaps the best illustration of the proximity of scholarly ideas and political agendas in comparative constitutional thought is provided by the constitutional preaching of Simón Bolívar, the great liberator of Spanish South America, and probably the first political leader to openly draw lessons from comparative constitutional law while at the same time expressing serious reservations about whether it was wise to allow the constitutional law of other states to shape domestic law. The leadership vacuum that followed the collapse of Spanish colonial reign in Latin America resulted in decades of political and social instability, with over 100 different constitutions being drafted in the region throughout the 19th century, starting with the first constitution of Venezuela in 1811.[46] From the outset of the independence era, a great divide emerged between those who believed that the new political and constitutional order should incorporate liberal ideas about individual liberty and regional autonomy borrowed from the American and French revolutions, as well as from British constitutional thought of the time, and those, Bolívar among them, who admired foreign constitutional ideals but preferred a localized, contextual, and nuanced application of these ideals to the newly liberated continent.[47] Initially, the first school of thought prevailed. However, the sudden shift away from despotic colonialism to weak and overly decentralized political institutions quickly led to political anarchy. The collapse of the first Venezuelan constitution, which emphasized individual liberties and regional autonomy, is "exhibit A" of this trend. Calls for a centralized government with a stronger executive branch and a more limited democratic input soon followed.

[46] Roberto Gargarella, "Towards a Typology of Latin American Constitutionalism, 1810–60," *Latin American Research Review* 39 (2004): 141–53, 141.

[47] Gabriel Negretto and José Antonio Aguilar-Rivera, "Rethinking the Legacy of the Liberal State in Latin America," *Journal of Latin American Studies* 32 (2000): 361–97, 365.

Enter Bolivarian constitutional thought.[48] In a series of grand constitutional schemes from the mid-1810s to the mid-1820s (in particular the Constitution of Gran Colombia of 1821, and the Constitution of Bolivia of 1826), Bolívar laid out his plans for a constitutional order that would purportedly balance tyranny and anarchy through the rejection of federalism in favor of representative republicanism, the granting of strong and at times perpetual powers to the executive of the central authority alongside the imposition of constitutional constraints on presidential powers, and the selective introduction of limitations on the right to vote that are grounded in supposedly meritocratic considerations. This last measure was particularly novel. Bolívar lamented the failures of the Venezuelan constitution, which in his view granted "power without training in citizenship";[49] however, unlike other thinkers of his time who wished to limit the right to vote based on wealth, land ownership, ethnicity, or race, Bolívar suggested that limitations on participation should be based on how well versed and interested a person is in the pressing political issues of the time.

Selective reference to examples from overseas was an essential aspect of Bolívar's development of a suitable constitutional platform for Latin America. On the one hand, Bolívar—an erudite and widely traveled leader—venerated British, French, and American constitutional thought; and, on the other, he frequently cautioned against the blanket transplantation of grand foreign ideas that were unsuitable to the social conditions in Latin America. Arguably the best illustration of Bolívar's ambivalence toward comparative constitutional wisdom is his famous Angostura Address (February 15, 1819) given on the occasion of the gathering of the Congress of Angostura (today's Ciudad Bolívar), Venezuela's second legislative congress.[50] "Passing from ancient to modern times," he states, "we find England and France arousing the admiration of all nations and offering eloquent lessons on every aspect of government."[51] He continues:

[48] On contemporary manifestations of Bolivarian centrist constitutional thought, see Phoebe King, "Neo-Bolivarian Constitutional Design: Comparing the 1999 Venezuelan, 2008 Ecuadorian, and 2009 Bolivian Constitutions," in Denis J. Galligan and Mila Versteeg, eds., *Social and Political Foundations of Constitutions* (Cambridge University Press, 2013), 366–96.

[49] David Bushnell, *El Libertador: Writings of Simón Bolívar* (Oxford University Press, 2003), 6; John Lynch, *Simón Bolívar: A Life* (Yale University Press, 2006), 201.

[50] The Venezuelan Constitution of 1819 was officially adopted in Angostura on August 15, but it was quickly made obsolete by the creation of Gran Colombia (of which Venezuela was part) in December 1819.

[51] Simón Bolívar, "The Angostura Address" (Feb. 15, 1819), in Bushnell, *El Libertador* (n 49), 41.

Let us not forget the lessons of experience; let the schools of Greece, Rome, France, England, and America instruct us in the difficult science of creating and preserving nations with laws that are appropriate, just, legitimate, and above all practical...Rome and Great Britain are the two outstanding nations of ancient and modern times; both were born to rule and be free; both were formed not with brilliant modes of freedom but on solid foundations. Therefore, Representatives, I suggest that you study the British constitution, which is the one that seems destined to bring the greatest good to the peoples who adopt it. However, for all its perfection, I am far from recommending servile imitation of it. When I speak of the British government, I refer only to its republican features.[52]

With respect to federalism, Bolívar has this to say:

I should say that however successful this form of government proved for North America, it never entered my mind to compare the situation and nature of two states as diametrically different as English America and Spanish America. Would not it be difficult to apply to Spain England's political, civil and religious Charter of Liberties? Well, it is even more difficult to adapt the laws of North America to Venezuela.[53]

Referring directly to Montesquieu's main thesis, Bolívar continues:

Do we not read in the *Spirit of the Laws* that [laws] must be suitable for the country for which they are written? That it is an astonishing coincidence for the laws of one nation to be applicable to another? That they must take into account the physical aspect of the country, its climate, the nature of its terrain, its location, size and the way of life of its people? That they must reflect the degree of freedom that the constitution can support, the religion of the inhabitants as well as their inclinations, their standard of living, their number, their commerce, their customs and their character? This then is the code we should consult, not the one written for Washington![54]

A similar "compare and contrast" approach characterizes Bolívar's later constitutional thought. In his famous May 1826 address to the Bolivian Congress (the constituent body that adopted the Bolivian Constitution

---

[52] Bushnell, *El Libertador* (n 49), 42.
[53] Bushnell, *El Libertador* (n 49), 37.
[54] Bushnell, *El Libertador* (n 49).

of 1826), Bolívar advocates a strong presidency featuring a lifetime appointment and the power to choose a successor. To support his centrist ideas, he invokes the rather dictatorial French Consulate Constitution ("Constitution of the Year VIII," 1799) that effectively assigned all authority to Napoleon Bonaparte. Bolívar also selectively invokes American constitutional ideals and practices that he sees as advancing his cause:

In the government of the United States, the practice of appointing the secretary of state to succeed the president has been observed in recent years. Nothing is as beneficial in a republic as this procedure. It has the advantage of placing at the head of government a person who is experienced in managing the state. From the moment he enters office he is prepared, and he is endowed with the aura of popular approval and consummate experience. I have borrowed this idea and established it as law.[55]

To drive his centrist views home, Bolívar emphasizes the anarchy of post-revolution France, and refers to the appointment for life of Alexandre Pétion as president of Haiti (1816), a move that he believed had brought stability to a nation plagued by political and social upheaval since the 1791 revolution. In his complementary proposal to establish a fourth branch of power—this new branch was to serve as an apex public service commission that would define the requirements for becoming an elector and put forward candidates for public positions—Bolívar freely borrows from the Napoleonic constitutions of the years VIII and X, the Constitution of Cádiz, and the 1823 Peruvian Constitution.[56]

In short, Bolívar's oratorical and instrumentalist invocation and repudiation of comparative constitutional ideas provides a prime example of how the discipline may be, and often is, driven by political conviction just as it is driven by intellectual vision. It similarly illustrates the inevitability of reference to the constitutive laws of others. Methodologically, Bolívar craftily uses the technique of negative "borrowing." In the end, notes Roberto Gargarella, a leading scholar of Latin American constitutionalism, "there seemed to be too little room for

---

[55] Simón Bolívar, "Address to the Constituent Congress of Bolivia" (May 25, 1826), in Bushnell, El Libertador (n 49), 59.

[56] Roberto Gargarella, Latin American Constitutionalism, 1810–2010: The Engine Room of the Constitution (Oxford University Press, 2013), 67.

defending fully local ideals or institutions; it was actually very difficult to propose political institutions without taking into account proposals and institutions originated beyond the national borders."[57] Powerful words, which may well serve as a parable for today's charged debates in North America, to which I turn next.

Two present-day primers: Canada and the United States

The profound effect of the 20th century's political transformations on constitutional thought, comparative and otherwise, is readily evident. The voluminous literature on comparative constitutional design is a direct by-product of and response to large-scale de-colonization and democratization that have taken place in Latin America, Southern Europe, Africa, and Asia over the past half-century. The work of comparative constitutional grandmasters such as Boris Mirkine-Guetzevitch, Carl Friedrich, or Joseph Weiler may not be understood separately from Europe's tumultuous political history—from the two World Wars and the Weimar Republic as an experimental interlude, to totalitarianism behind the Iron Curtain, or the trans-nationalist vision of the European Union that has transformed Europe's political and constitutional landscape since the Treaty of Rome of 1957. However, it is the North American "natural experiment" that provides a textbook illustration of how ideological outlooks and political interests interact with theoretical innovation to shape comparative constitutional law. No two neighboring democratic countries in the world sport such a stark difference in their attitudes toward comparative constitutional law than Canada and the United States. (To paraphrase George Bernard Shaw, they are two countries separated by a common—here, comparative constitutional—language). As much as the quasi-natural "North American experiment" reflects differences in constitutional law and legacy, the dissimilarity also mirrors differences in national meta-narratives and in self-perceptions of what it means to be an American or a Canadian vis-à-vis the rest of the world.

Arguably the most significant development in 20th-century comparative constitutionalism is the global spread of constitutional courts,

[57] Gargarella, *Latin American Constitutionalism, 1810–2010* (n 56), 68.

judicial review, and bills of rights as the centerpieces of the comparative constitutional universe. No single country's constitutional scene exemplifies this transformation more vividly than Canada's, which provides a paradigmatic illustration of everything that comparative constitutionalism over the past century stands for and has been preoccupied with. Canada entered the 20th century as a living exemplar of deferential, British-style constitutional tradition; it emerged out of that century with a robust constitutional culture, featuring active judicial review, an acclaimed constitutional bill of rights (the Charter of Rights and Freedoms), a pervasive rights discourse, and, as we have seen in Chapter 1, one of the most frequently cited peak courts in the world. This is a stunning change considering that it was not until the late 1940s that appeals to the Judicial Committee of the Privy Council were abolished and the Supreme Court of Canada became the top court of the land. Furthermore, as part of its 1982 constitutional revolution, constitutional innovations such as a commitment to bilingualism, multiculturalism, indigenous peoples' rights, proportionality (via the Charter's section 1—the "limitation clause"), and majority rule (via section 33—the "override clause") were introduced, and later analyzed and emulated abroad. Landmark rulings such as the *Quebec Secession Reference* (1998) have been commonly invoked in comparative constitutional design discourse;[58] other Supreme of Canada decisions (e.g. *R. v. Oakes*, 1986) now feature in many textbooks on comparative constitutional law.[59] In short, constitutional thought in its entire variety is now one of Canada's main intellectual exports.

The astounding comparative turn in Canadian constitutionalism may be traced back to the adoption of the Canadian Charter of Rights and Freedoms in 1982, and the set of innovative constitutional protections and mechanisms it establishes. The introduction of "weak-form" judicial review mechanisms such as section 33 cannot be explained without taking into account the concrete circumstances that brought about the 1982 constitutional overhaul as well as Canada's Westminster parliamentary tradition. But a fuller understanding of how Canada has emerged from a humble former British colony into the comparative constitutional powerhouse that it currently is requires a broader look at the social and ideational transformation—specifically the profound

---

[58] *Reference re Secession of Quebec*, [1998] 2 SCR 217 [Canada].
[59] *R v. Oakes*, [1986] 1 SCR 103 [Canada].

multicultural and cosmopolitan shift in the national meta-narrative—
that Canada has witnessed for more than half a century.

It is well known to students of Canadian politics that the Quebec
question has dominated modern-day Canadian politics. The "Quiet
Revolution" and the emergence of cultural nationalism and secession-
ist sentiments in Quebec in the early 1960s triggered a series of attempts
to amend the constitution in order to address Quebec's claims. As a
result, over a period of 25 years from the mid-1960s and the early
1990s, Canada was in a continuous state of constitutional flux. During
that period alone, it witnessed five major attempts at a constitutional
overhaul in which all but one—the "patriation round" of 1982—
failed. No other established democracy has ever been through so
many grandiose attempts at constitutional reform during such a short
period. The challenge of acknowledging difference and recognizing
linguistic, religious, and cultural diversity within a framework of
national unity stood at the heart of all these attempts.

Until the 1960s, preferred immigrants from the British Isles were
highly sought after; others were "non-preferred" or excluded. In 1967,
Canada's immigration policy became distinctly more universal with the
introduction of criteria such as educational attainment, language com-
petency, and employment potential, with ethnicity and race ceasing to
serve as key determinants of admission.[60] By 1977, immigrants from
Asia, Latin America, and Africa made up over 50 percent of annual
flows. As a result, since that time the demographics of the Canadian
body politic have transformed in an unprecedented way. When compared with other countries such as the United States, the United
Kingdom, France, Germany, and Italy, Canada has the highest percentage of foreign-born residents as a percentage of the overall
population—according to the 2011 national census, over 20 percent
of Canada's population is foreign born. In Toronto (Canada's largest
city and the 4th largest urban center in North America), over 48
percent of the population is foreign born. Relative openness to the
world therefore becomes an essential part of public life.

In parallel, an official policy of multiculturalism was introduced in
Canada in the early 1970s. "In the face of this [country's] cultural

---

[60] Triadafilos Triadafilopoulos, "Dismantling White Canada: Race, Rights, and the
Origins of the Points System," in Triadafilos Triadafilopoulos, ed., *Wanted and Welcome?
Policies for Highly Skilled Immigrants in Comparative Perspective* (Springer, 2013), 15–37, 16.

plurality there can be no official Canadian culture or cultures,"[61] stated the 1972 Special Joint Committee of the Senate and House of Commons on the Constitution of Canada. Instead, a new vision was crafted of a "pluralistic mosaic," promoting "equal respect for the many origins, creeds and cultures" that form Canadian society.[62] That vision was given constitutional recognition in 1982; section 27 of the Canadian Charter of Rights and Freedoms states that the entire Charter is to be "interpreted in a manner consistent with the preservation and enhancement of the multicultural heritage of Canadians." The adoption of the Canadian Multiculturalism Act (1988) further reflects a concerted focus by federal institutions to build awareness of multiculturalism and promote inclusiveness and accommodation of diversity.[63]

The scholarly reaction was immediate. Canadian political science has undergone a considerable "comparative turn."[64] Charles Taylor, Will Kymlicka, James Tully, and other Canadian philosophers are often considered among the most prominent theorists of multiculturalism, citizenship, and the constitutional accommodation of difference. Unlike in Canada's neighbor to the south, the practice of foreign citations by the Supreme Court has never been seriously contested within Canada's legal academia, let alone in the popular media or the broader political sphere. Justice Claire L'Heureux-Dubé of the Supreme Court of Canada (1987–2002) emerged as an international champion of inter-jurisdictional constitutional cross-fertilization. A younger generation of productive scholars, including my colleague Kent Roach, my former colleague Sujit Choudhry, and this author have since found Canada to be a setting conducive for the comparative study of constitutional law and courts. Whereas cosmopolitanism faces some internal opposition, the country's openness toward the foreign and different—an attitude that is neatly captured by the Canada as a "cultural mosaic" metaphor—remains distinct, certainly when compared to the intoxicating debates in the United States. It is against this

---

[61] *Special Joint Committee of the Senate and House of Commons on the Constitution of Canada* (1972); cited in Ayelet Shachar, "Interpretation Sections (27 & 28) of the Canadian Charter," in Errol Mendes and Stéphane Beaulac, eds., *Canadian Charter of Rights and Freedoms / Charte canadienne des droits et libertés* (5th edn, LexisNexis, 2013), 147–90.

[62] Shachar, "Interpretation Sections (27 & 28) of the Canadian Charter" (n 61).

[63] See Howard Kislowicz, "Freedom of Religion and Canada's Commitments to Multiculturalism," *National Journal of Constitutional Law* 31 (2012): 1–23.

[64] See Linda White et al., eds., *The Comparative Turn in Canadian Political Science* (UBC Press, 2008).

profound shift in Canada's national meta-narrative and self-perception of the country's place and role in the world—not merely constitutional transformation per se—that Canada's endorsement of and considerable contributions to comparative constitutionalism should be understood.

Another effective contemporary illustration of how politics and ideological outlooks shape attitudes toward comparative constitutional inquiry is the controversy surrounding reference to foreign law by American courts. For more than a decade, tens of books, hundreds of academic articles, and countless lectures by the nation's top legal scholars addressed the matter. Outspoken US Supreme Court Justices Scalia, Breyer, Ginsburg, and others referred to it extensively and media talking heads of all political persuasions devoted many hours to the subject. And politicians, political animals as they are, were quick to jump on the bandwagon. Unlike most of the examples discussed in this chapter, the trigger for this particular episode in the history of comparative constitutional law is familiar to many. The frenzy started when in several rulings, most notably *Lawrence v. Texas* (2003) and *Roper v. Simmons* (2005), the US Supreme Court's majority cited foreign judgments to support their decisions.[65] This modest reference to foreign law—a common practice in many other jurisdictions—brought about an overwhelming reaction and heated debate over the appropriateness and legitimacy of judicial reference to foreign laws in general, and to the constitutional laws of other nations in particular.[66] One of the main

---

[65] *Lawrence v. Texas*, 539 U.S. 558 (2003); *Roper v. Simmons*, 543 U.S. 551 (2005). In *Atkins v. Virginia*, 536 U.S. 304 (2002), the majority opinion referred in a footnote to an amicus brief by the European Union. The reference supported a factual statement that: "within the world community, the imposition of the death penalty for crimes committed by mentally retarded offenders is overwhelmingly disapproved." In his opinion in *Lawrence v. Texas* (overturning the 1986 decision in *Bowers v. Hardwick* criminalizing homosexual intercourse between consenting adults), Justice Kennedy stated that: "[T]o the extent *Bowers* relied on values we share with wider civilization, it should be noted that the reasoning and holding in *Bowers* have been rejected elsewhere. The European Court of Human Rights has followed not *Bowers* but its own decision in *Dudgeon v. United Kingdom*...Other nations, too, have taken action consistent with an affirmation of the protected right of homosexual adults to engage in intimate, consensual conduct."

[66] See Norman Dorsen, "The Relevance of Foreign Legal Materials in U.S. Constitutional Cases: A Conversation between Justice Antonin Scalia and Justice Stephen Breyer," *International Journal of Constitutional Law* 3 (2005): 519–41; Richard Posner, "No Thanks, We Already Have Our Own Laws," *Legal Affairs* (July–Aug. 2004); Vicki Jackson, "Yes Please, I'd Love to Talk with You," *Legal Affairs* (July–Aug. 2004). See also Martha Minow, "The Controversial Status of International and Comparative Law in the United States," *Harvard International Law Journal Online* (Aug. 27, 2010).

aims of comparative constitutional law—self-reflection through comparative reference—was put on public trial.

The more conservative members of the current Court—Chief Justice Roberts and Justices Alito, Scalia, and Thomas—oppose the citation of foreign law in constitutional cases. By contrast, the Court's more liberal wing tends to be more open toward the practice. Justice Ginsburg has been one of the more outspoken representatives of that camp. In a 2009 speech at Ohio State University, she stated: "I frankly don't understand all the brouhaha lately from Congress and even from some of my colleagues about referring to foreign law." Reference to a foreign ruling, she said, is not binding and thus does not encroach upon the Court's or the US Constitution's sovereignty, "Why shouldn't we look to the wisdom of a judge from abroad with at least as much ease as we would read a law review article written by a professor?"[67]

Of the several arguments advanced by those opposed to constitutional borrowing, of whom Justice Antonin Scalia is the best known, the one that carries the most weight in America's debate is that such borrowing leads to "social progressiveness by stealth." Because the rights jurisprudence of most other leading democracies is more progressive than that of the United States, the argument goes, reference to these countries' rulings advances, almost by definition, a more progressive line of interpretation. Indeed, all pertinent arguments against borrowing reflect a view of American constitutionalism as unique, exceptional, and particular—a shining city upon a hill to draw on a familiar image—whereas the main arguments for the practice are neatly aligned with a universal and cosmopolitan view of constitutionalism and of human experience more generally. Republicans and other right-wingers tend to resent borrowing; Democrats, liberals, and progressives tend to support it. Unsurprisingly, then, the political split in the US Supreme Court is closely aligned with the justices' positions on foreign reference. Most or all of the five judges who voted against a recount in the *Bush v. Gore* courtroom battle over the fate of the American presidency (thereby paving George W. Bush's way to the White House) reject reference to foreign judgments. Most or all of the justices who voted for a recount tend to support, either tacitly or explicitly, reference to foreign judgments.

---

[67] Adam Liptak, "Ginsburg Shares Views on Influence of Foreign Law on Her Court, and Vice Versa," *New York Times*, Apr. 11, 2009.

Those who oppose reference to foreign jurisprudence make what seem to be at least five additional arguments, that for the sake of simplicity may be encapsulated as follows: (i) the constitution constitutes the nation, and so reference to foreign rulings infringes on a nation's constitutional sovereignty; (ii) as a matter of principle, constitutional change is better accomplished through amendment and legislation, not through other means such as flexible interpretation or reference to foreign sources; (iii) foreign court judges have not been appointed or confirmed by the president and Congress and so bear no accountability to or authority from the American people; (iv) there are serious methodological problems with referencing foreign cases, for example problems of "cherry-picking" favorable cases, out-of-context analysis, and selective designation of relevant sources (designating certain countries but not others as legitimate sources from which to borrow); and (v) the onus of proof in this debate should be on those who advocate reference to foreign rulings because historically the practice has been not to refer to such rulings.

Much like other ostensibly principled interpretive debates in the United States and elsewhere, the debate over reference to foreign law in the United States is portrayed as analytical but is mainly political. It cannot be understood separately from the deep culture wars that have characterized the American polity for decades and are omnipresent in the American public sphere, from Yale Law School to Wyoming's ranches, from PBS to Fox News, and from the *New Yorker* to the *Christian Science Monitor*. Suffice it to recount the argument voiced by those affiliated with the Republican Party that Justice Elena Kagan (former Dean of Harvard Law School) was not a suitable nominee for the Supreme Court because of her support of foreign reference.[68] When asked about her approach to foreign reference in her 2010 confirmation hearings before the US Senate Committee on the Judiciary, Kagan said: "I'm in favor of good ideas . . . wherever you can get them; . . . foreign decisions do not rank as precedent, [but] they could be informative in much the same way as one might gain knowledge or insight from reading a law review article."[69] By comparison, in his confirmation hearing a few years earlier, Justice Alito, a Bush

[68] One of the points raised against Kagan is that during her deanship she invited Aharon Barak—a noted proponent of foreign referencing—to visit Harvard.

[69] *Confirmation Hearing on the Nomination of Elena Kagan to be Associate Justice of the Supreme Court of the United States Before the S. Comm. on the Judiciary*, 111th Cong., 2d Sess. (2010).

nominee, stated: "I think the framers would be stunned by the idea that
the Bill of Rights is to be interpreted by taking a poll of the countries of
the world."[70] Equally political was the right-wing objection to President Obama's choice of Harold Koh (former Dean of Yale Law
School) to serve as Legal Adviser to the Department of State. Koh
has been an outspoken advocate of the view that tenets of international
law and foreign legal precedent may be drawn upon to inform
the deliberative process of judicial decision-making in the United
States. Koh's position on foreign sources was described by Republican
opponents as "transnational progressivism" and a "most perilous" stand
that amounted to a "threat to democracy."[71]

A similar enmity toward foreign law is evident at the state level. In
virtually all instances it has been driven by right-wing activists and
politicians. As of 2013, over 40 bills of various types and scope have
been introduced in the United States against the incorporation or
enforcement of any provisions of religious law, and in some cases
against the legitimacy of Islamic Shari'a law and/or international and
foreign law in general. The Arizona legislation against the enforcement
of foreign law (2011), to pick one example, is explicit in stating that: "A
court, arbitrator, administrative agency or other adjudicative, mediation or enforcement authority shall not enforce a foreign law if doing
so would violate a right guaranteed by the Constitution of this state or
of the United States or conflict with the laws of the United States or of
this state."[72] The contested Oklahoma "Save Our State" Amendment
suggests that when exercising their judicial authority, the courts "shall
uphold and adhere to the law as provided in the United States Constitution, the Oklahoma Constitution, the United States Code, federal
regulations promulgated pursuant thereto, established common law,
the Oklahoma Statutes and rules promulgated pursuant thereto, and if
necessary the law of another state of the United States provided the law
of the other state does not include Sharia Law, in making judicial
decisions. The courts shall not look to the legal precepts of other
nations or cultures. Specifically, the courts shall not consider

[70] *Confirmation Hearing on the Nomination of Samuel Alito to be Associate Justice of the Supreme Court of the United States Before the S. Comm. on the Judiciary*, 109th Cong., 2d Sess. (2006).
[71] See, e.g., Meghan Clyne, "Obama's Most Perilous Legal Pick," *New York Post* (Mar. 23, 2009). For an exposition of Koh's views, see Harold H. Koh, "International Law as Part of Our Law," *American Journal of International Law* 98 (2004): 43–57.
[72] Amendment to the Arizona Revised Statutes §12-3103: Prohibited Enforcement of Foreign Law (signed into law Apr. 12, 2011).

international or Sharia Law."[73] This amendment was approved by 70 percent of Oklahoma voters in a November 2010 referendum, but was eventually declared unconstitutional by a federal court in August 2013 on the ground that its targeting of Shari'a law violated the Establishment Clause of the US Constitution.[74]

The legislative crusade against foreign law continues in several Republican-led states. The current trend is well captured by the American Laws for American Court (ALAC) framework.[75] Instead of banning the use of all foreign law, the ALAC framework calls for prohibiting the use of "[any] law, legal code or system that would not grant the parties affected by the ruling or decision the same fundamental liberties, rights, and privileges granted under the U.S. and [State] Constitutions, including but not limited to due process, freedom of religion, speech, or press, and any right of privacy or marriage as specifically defined by the constitution of this state."[76] As of 2013, the ALAC proposal has been enacted in Kansas (2012) and Oklahoma (2013), and seriously considered in several other states. Somewhat narrower variants of it have been adopted in Arizona, Louisiana, and Tennessee.

The strong correlation between support for anti-foreign law measures and a political right agenda is indisputable. Politicians who advocate legal limits on the use of foreign law tend to support gun rights and unrestricted corporate speech, and are more likely to object to initiatives such as public health care or amnesty for undocumented

---

[73] Oklahoma State Question 755 (2010).

[74] See *Muneer Awad et al. v. Paul Ziriax et al.* (Case No. CIV-10-1186-M; decision released Aug. 15, 2013). A temporary restraining order and later preliminary injunction against the amendment were issued within days following the vote. The US Court of Appeals for the 10th Circuit upheld that injunction in 2012, citing the state's failure to identify a "compelling interest based on an actual problem." In making the injunction permanent, Judge Vicki Miles-LaGrange ruled that "It is abundantly clear that the primary purpose of the amendment was to specifically target and outlaw Sharia law" and to act as a pre-emptive strike against it. "While the public has an interest in the will of the voters being carried out, the court finds that the public has a more profound and long-term interest in upholding an individual's constitutional rights," Judge Miles-LaGrange concluded.

[75] In other words, the ALAC proposal advocates barring any foreign law or jurisprudence that does not meet the standards set by American rights and liberties. For an accessible and illuminating discussion of this and other similar-in-nature measures, see Eugene Volokh, "Foreign Law in American Courts," *Oklahoma Law Review* 66 (2014): 219–43.

[76] Importantly, the ALAC proposal excludes claims brought by "a corporation, partnership . . . or other legal entity that contracts to subject itself to foreign law in a jurisdiction other than this state or the United States."

immigrants. In fact, in 2010 the State of Arizona—under Republican governorship since January 2009, and one of the leaders in anti-foreign law legislation—passed what many regard as a particularly harsh piece of anti-immigrant legislation (S.B. 1070, 2010). In any event, the ideological and political foundations of (dis)engagement with the constitutive laws of others have never been so evident as they are in the debate concerning the status of foreign law in the contemporary United States. This is, as Mark Tushnet astutely observed, an episode in America's culture wars.[77]

The controversy over the role of comparative constitutional law is closely tied to debates over constitutional interpretation (e.g. "originalism" versus a "living tree" approach). With very few exceptions, originalism is not considered a mainstream interpretive method in any long-standing constitutional democracy other than the United States. As Jack Balkin explains (in an essay "addressed to scholars outside the United States"), "American originalism is primarily a nationalist idea. It arises from distinctive features of American cultural memory—namely, that in popular imagination the American nation was created by Americans themselves through a self-conscious act of political revolution, and that the American nation, people, and constitution came into being more or less simultaneously through this initial act of self-creation."[78] This notion is reflected in another closely related perception—the near-sacred status of the US Constitution, and the genuine sense that when it comes to constitutional law, there is little the United States—the founding father of it all—can learn from others. As Sanford Levinson eloquently observes, the US Constitution is the nation's most revered text and has evolved into a pillar of American "civil religion."[79] In an article published in 1937, Max Lerner described the US Constitution as America's "totem and its fetish."[80] "In fact," wrote Lerner, "the very habits of mind begotten by an authoritarian Bible and a religion of submission to higher power have been carried

[77] Mark Tushnet, "Referring to Foreign Law in Constitutional Interpretation: An Episode in the Culture Wars," *University of Baltimore Law Review* 35 (2006): 299–312.

[78] See also Jack Balkin, "Why Are Americans Originalist?" in Richard Nobles and David Schiff, eds., *Law, Society and Community: Socio-Legal Essays in Honour of Roger Cotterrell* (Ashgate Publishing, 2014), 309–326.

[79] Sanford Levinson, *Constitutional Faith* (Princeton University Press, 1988).

[80] Max Lerner, "Constitutions and Courts as Symbols," *Yale Law Journal* 46 (1937): 1290–319.

over to an authoritarian Constitution and a philosophy of submission to 'higher law;' and a country like America, in which its early tradition had prohibited a state church, ends by getting a state church after all, although in a secular form."[81]

Similarly, noted scholar of Christian thought Jaroslav Pelikan suggests that "with the reduction in the private authority of the Christian Scripture, and especially in its public authority, American Scripture has been called upon to fill some of the gap."[82] And so, the discussion that began in Chapter 2 with a consideration of religion law's selective engagement with the constitutive laws of others concludes here with the story of a religion-like constitutional order that endeavors to uphold its uniqueness while maintaining its relevance and status in the world of new constitutionalism.

Conclusion

The thumbnail history of epistemological leaps in comparative public law offered in this chapter carries two substantive take-home messages: (i) consideration of past engagements with the constitutive laws of others may prove helpful for understanding the present and possibly the future of such engagements; and (ii) necessity, intellectual inquisitiveness, and political drive have all played a significant role in triggering comparative constitutional endeavors through the ages.

What drives comparative constitutional engagements? The history of encounters with, reactions to, and studies of the constitutive laws of others suggests that three main factors are at play: (i) *necessity*—the systemic need for extra-large political entities, from the Roman Empire to the European Union, to govern their multinational and legally diverse territory effectively, or a knee-jerk survival instinct of minority groups who are striving to maintain their core identity by opening up to the laws of others on secondary, non-core issues; (ii) *inquisitiveness*—intellectual curiosity and a quest to explore the unknown, trace a general logic of matters, or attempt better to understand one's own constitutional setting through comparison, analogy, and contrast with other comparable settings; and (iii) *politics*—comparative engagement as a means of promoting a concrete political agenda and worldview, an

---

[81] Lerner, "Constitutions and Courts as Symbols" (n 80), 1294–5.

[82] Jaroslav Pelikan, *Interpreting the Bible and the Constitution* (Yale University Press, 2004).

ideological outlook, or a certain conception of the good society, the advancement of which may be aided (or inhibited) in some way by an assessment of the laws of others.

These three factors may overlap and intersect, yet they remain analytically distinguishable. They have appeared in different combinations in different periods, and have many historical variants, sometimes in conjunction with other factors that have also been present at various times and places. Significantly for the purpose of this discussion, these three motivations illuminate the importance of understanding comparative constitutional law in a broader, interdisciplinary framework rather than merely focusing on doctrinal analysis, as is often the case with the typical mainstream legal approach. Elements of all three of these forces are evident in virtually all the epistemological leaps I discuss in this chapter.[83] In certain contexts (think diasporic Judaism), necessity played a key role. In others (think John Selden) intellectual curiosity did the heavy lifting. And in others again (think Jean Bodin, Simón Bolívar, or the controversy over foreign citation in the United States), a concrete political agenda was driving the enterprise.

Other recent epistemological shifts in comparative constitutionalism continue to reflect a combination of need, intellect, and politics. The rise of "proportionality analysis" as the lingua franca of comparative constitutional jurisprudence is inseparable from the rise of an all-encompassing vision of rights and the ever-increasing reliance on constitutional law and courts to settle some of the most fundamental political quandaries and moral predicaments a polity can face. A supposedly apolitical, quasi-scientific method for adjudicating clashes of rights or competing moral claims that do not have ready-made answers within the confines of the law has emerged. Its development required great intellect; the need for it is obvious; and its political tilt toward moderate solutions and mainstream thought is clear. The dramatic increase in scholarly attention to constitutional law in predominantly Muslim countries or to the legitimacy of state surveillance measures may not be understood in isolation from the political events of the late 1990s and early 2000s, most notably the rise of Islamic fundamentalism, the cataclysmic events of 9/11, and the "Arab Spring"

---

[83] In other contexts as well, we find multiple threads and competing visions interacting in dynamic ways to shape the conceptual boundaries and developments of a given legal arena. For a classic exposition, see Rogers M. Smith, *Civic Ideals: Conflicting Visions of Citizenship in U.S. History* (Yale University Press, 1999).

and its aftermath. The political project of a unified Europe and the corresponding eminence of the pan-European rights regime have generated renewed interest in comparative constitutional inquiry among European jurists.[84] Concepts such as "constitutional pluralism" or the "margin of appreciation" quickly evolved to aid the reconciliation of centripetal forces of constitutional convergence with persisting centrifugal forces of constitutional divergence, and to help make sense of the multiplicity of constitutional authority and traditions in Europe.[85] In short, necessity, inquisitiveness, and politics, writ small or large, are the basic elements that epistemological leaps in comparative constitutionalism are made of.

[84] See Armin von Bogdandy, "National Legal Scholarship in the European Legal Area—A Manifesto," *International Journal of Constitutional Law* 10 (2012): 614–26.

[85] See Nico Krisch, *Beyond Constitutionalism: The Pluralist Structure of Postnational Law* (Oxford University Press, 2010).

4

From Comparative Constitutional Law to Comparative Constitutional Studies

"If constitutional law begins to ask what people actually do under a particular constitution, and not merely what battle of words they engage in for the settlement of conflicts among them, the constitutional lawyer becomes a political scientist (one hopes)."

Carl Friedrich (*Constitutional Government and Democracy: Theory and Practice in Europe and America*, 1941)

Eighty years ago, John H. Wigmore, author of the seminal *Panorama of the World's Legal Systems*, characterized the comparative law journals of his time as offering an abundance of valuable materials on the customary laws of the Lagos and Bantus, on the principles of inheritance in "Mohammedan law," on the early sources of "Romanian law," and on the principles of marriage law in China and in South Africa, but almost nothing in the way of comparison and contrast of the ideas in different systems or elucidation of their correspondence or divergence. Since the time of Henry Maine, stressed Wigmore, anthropologists and sociologists have made great progress in the field of comparative social studies, but jurists have not been nearly so productive in the field of comparative law.[1] There is no doubt that comparative constitutional law has enjoyed a certain renaissance since the mid-1980s. However, despite the field's many scholarly advances, too little has changed since Wigmore's days with respect to comparative (constitutional) law's

---

[1] John H. Wigmore, "Jotting on Comparative Legal Ideas and Institutions," *Tulane Law Review* 6 (1932): 49–50.

ambivalent stance toward the social sciences, a stance marked by admiration on the one hand, resentment and exclusion on the other.

In particular, a simple yet powerful insight is often overlooked: constitutions neither originate nor operate in a vacuum. Their import cannot be meaningfully described or explained independent of the social, political, and economic forces, both domestic and international, that shape them. Indeed, the rise and fall of constitutional orders—the average lifespan of written constitutions since 1789 is 19 years—are important manifestations of this idea.[2] Culture, economics, institutional structures, power, and strategy are as significant to understanding the constitutional universe as jurisprudential and prescriptive analyses.[3] Any attempt to portray the constitutional domain as predominantly legal, rather than imbued in the social or political arena, is destined to yield thin, ahistorical, and overly doctrinal or formalistic accounts of the origins, nature, and consequences of constitutional law. From Montesquieu and Weber to Douglass North and Robert Dahl, prominent social thinkers who have engaged in a systematic study of constitutional law and institutions across polities and through the ages have accepted this plain (and possibly inconvenient) truth.[4]

By their very nature, legal institutions—for example, property rights regimes, labor law, or electoral rules—produce differential distributive effects: they privilege some groups, interests, worldviews, and policy preferences over others. This effect is accentuated when it comes to constitutions. After all, the *raison d'être* of a constitution is to create, legitimize, allocate, and check power. Given their entrenched or "higher law" status, they provide an ideal platform for "locking in" certain worldviews, policy preferences, and institutional structures, and for disadvantaging, limiting, or precluding the consideration of others.

---

[2] Zachary Elkins, Tom Ginsburg, and James Melton, *The Endurance of National Constitutions* (Cambridge University Press, 2009).

[3] Interestingly, none of Ronald Dworkin's six passionately argued books on constitutionalism cites any empirical work on the origins and consequences of constitutionalization and judicial review. See Mark Graber, "Constitutional Politics and Constitutional Theory: A Misunderstood and Neglected Relationship," *Law and Social Inquiry* 27 (2002): 309–38. For a European perspective on the challenge of doctrinalism, see Armin von Bogdandy, "The Past and Promise of Doctrinal Constructivism: A Strategy for Responding to the Challenges facing Constitutional Scholarship in Europe," *International Journal of Constitutional Law* 7 (2009): 364–400.

[4] Thinking about law as reflective of broader forces, rationales, and interests is certainly not foreign to legal scholarship. Legal Realism and Critical Legal Studies have been two important strands within American legal academia that do so. The influential branch of Law and Economics and certain threads within Law and Society and Legal History are others.

Constitution drafting, like constitutional interpretation, does not occur out of thin air. Power will be differentially allocated at the drafting table, and the likelihood of political, economic, and judicial stakeholders voluntarily conceding power, prestige, or privilege during this process is not high.

Nonetheless, much (though certainly not all) of the contemporary literature even in the relatively interdisciplinary North American legal academia, let alone in the considerably more doctrinal European and Latin American ones, is focused on questions of case law and jurisprudence. The canonical discourse rarely entails discussion of other crucial issues, such as the real-life impact of constitutional jurisprudence and its efficacy in planting the seeds of social change; how constitutions reflect and shape nationhood and identity;[5] how constitutions construct, not merely constrain, politics (e.g. by framing the goals and interests people believe they can pursue in politics);[6] the actors and factors involved in demanding or bringing about constitutional transformation; the place of constitutionalism, national and transnational, in the emerging global economic order;[7] and the ever-increasing judicialization of politics worldwide, and its impact on the legitimacy of the courts and the quality of democratic governance more generally.[8]

The narrowing down of comparative constitutionalism to court-centric analyses or interpretive methods is neither inevitable nor grounded in the modern history of the field. It is common knowledge that major political philosophers, from Aristotle to Jean-Jacques Rousseau and Henri-Benjamin Constant, were keenly interested in elements of comparative constitutionalism as a foundation of good government.[9] The German term *Staatswissenschaft* (the science of the state, or political science)—understood as early as the mid-18th century as the accumulation of historical, economic, social, and legal knowledge

---

[5] See, e.g., Gary J. Jacobsohn, *Constitutional Identity* (Harvard University Press, 2010); Michel Rosenfeld, *The Identity of the Constitutional Subject: Selfhood, Citizenship, Culture, and Community* (Routledge, 2009).

[6] See, generally, Mark Tushnet, *Why the Constitution Matters* (Yale University Press, 2010); Mark Graber, *A New Introduction to American Constitutionalism* (Oxford University Press, 2013), 212–49.

[7] See Stephen Gill and Claire Cutler, eds., *New Constitutionalism and World Order* (Cambridge University Press, 2014).

[8] Ran Hirschl, "The Judicialization of Mega-Politics and the Rise of Political Courts," *Annual Review of Political Science* 11 (2008): 93–118.

[9] E.g. Jean-Jacques Rousseau, *The Constitution of Corsica* (1765); Henri-Benjamin Constant, *The Liberty of Ancients Compared with the Moderns* (1816).

necessary to governance, statecraft, or statesmanship—included integral references to constitutional structure and institutions. But even as
recently as the late 19th and early 20th centuries, prior to the present
disciplinary divide, American scholars of comparative constitutionalism
saw the constitutional domain as an extension of, not separate from, the
political domain. In 1884, William W. Crane and Bernard Moses
published *Politics: An Introduction to the Study of Comparative Constitutional Law*—perhaps the first book in North America devoted to the
study of comparative constitutionalism as a distinct phenomenon.[10]
A given nation's constitution, Crane and Moses suggested, was a
reflection of that nation's political realm, specifically the people's will
and the nation's enduring values and legacy. The book includes chapters on the "bicameral system of legislature" and "distribution of
powers" alongside an explicitly political analysis in a chapter on "the
conditions and tendency of normal political growth," several chapters
on actual constitutional actors (e.g. "the makers of constitutional law,"
"the makers of administrative law," and "political parties"), and three
chapters on "the tendency of power" in the United States and several
European federations.

Another work that approaches comparative constitutional law as the
study of formal political institutions is John William Burgess's seminal
two-volume book *Political Science and Comparative Constitutional Law*,
published in 1893.[11] (Burgess had published earlier articles on comparative constitutionalism, all with a political science orientation, dating back to 1886).[12] Burgess was a professor of political science and law
at Columbia University, and is considered one of the founding fathers
of the discipline of political science in the United States.[13] His book is
devoted to a systematic comparison of the constitutional formation of
branches of government and formal political institutions in the United
States, Imperial Germany, the United Kingdom, and France, with
passing references to numerous other polities.

---

[10] William W. Crane and Bernard Moses, *Politics: An Introduction to the Study of Comparative
Constitutional Law* (G. P. Putnam's Sons, 1884).

[11] John W. Burgess, *Political Science and Comparative Constitutional Law* (Ginn & Co., 1893).

[12] See, e.g., John W. Burgess, "Von Holst's Public Law of the United States," *Political
Science Quarterly* 1 (1886): 612–35; John W. Burgess, "Laband's Public Law of the German
Empire," *Political Science Quarterly* 3 (1888): 123–35.

[13] Among his many other contributions, in 1886 Burgess founded *Political Science Quarterly*, the oldest political science journal in the United States.

Burgess regards the comparative approach as the book's major asset. "If my book has any peculiarity," he wrote, "it is in its method. It is a comparative study. It is an attempt to apply the method, which has been found so productive in the domain of Natural Science, to Political Science and Jurisprudence."[14] He asserts that although he is not the first to apply such an approach to the study of comparative constitutional law, "in the French, American and British literatures, it is . . . relatively new. Boutmy, Bryce [see discussion later in this section, R.H], Dicey [ditto, R.H.], Moses and Wilson, have indeed already broken the ground, but the field is capable of a much wider, and also more minute, cultivation."[15] Burgess goes on to suggest that his approach is systematic, not encyclopedic, and justifies his case selection by explaining that the American, British, French, and German constitutions govern the most important states of the world, and that "these constitutions represent substantially all species of constitutions which have as yet been developed. If any general principles of public law are to be derived from a comparison . . . surely they will be more trustworthy if we exclude the less perfect systems from the generalization, disregard the less important states, and pass by those species which are not typical."[16] Even as early in the life of the field as the late 19th century, political scientists studying comparative constitutionalism were concerned with principles of case selection and research design.

For Burgess, the drafting of constitutions was inherently a political, rather than legal, process. Placing his treatise under the heading of political science rather than constitutional law, Burgess declares that "[t]he formation of a constitution seldom proceeds according to the existing forms of law. Historical and revolutionary forces are the more prominent and important factors in the work . . . These cannot be dealt with through juristic methods."[17] His book exemplifies the idea that, as Dick Howard observes, the study of comparative constitutional

---

[14] Burgess, *Political Science and Comparative Constitutional Law* (n 11), Vol. I, vi; cited in A. E. Dick Howard, "A Traveler from an Antique Land: The Modern Renaissance of Comparative Constitutionalism," *Virginia Journal of International Law* 50 (2009): 3–41.

[15] Burgess, *Political Science and Comparative Constitutional Law* (n 11), Vol. I, vi.

[16] Burgess, *Political Science and Comparative Constitutional Law* (n 11), 90–1.

[17] Burgess, *Political Science and Comparative Constitutional Law* (n 11), 90; cited in Howard, "A Traveler from an Antique Land" (n 14), 8.

law, in the scholarship of the late 19th and early 20th centuries, was perceived as an extension of comparative politics.[18]

A comparable epistemological approach characterized late 19th- and early 20th-century comparative constitutional scholarship in Europe. The seminal writings of Georg Jellinek, James Bryce, and A. V. Dicey illustrate this point. Jellinek—a prominent German scholar of public law who spent his academic career in Vienna, Basel, and Heidelberg— engages in comparative constitutional inquiry in his works on the basic laws of states (e.g. *The Theory of the Unifications of States*, 1882; *General Theory of the State*, 1900), and most notably in his *The Declaration of the Rights of Man and of Citizens: A Contribution to Modern Constitutional History* (1895), in which he argues for a universal theory of rights, as opposed to the culturally and nationally specific accounts of rights that were prevalent at the time. In particular, Jellinek suggests that Anglo-American and other comparative insights, and not merely the writings of Jean-Jacques Rousseau, influenced the framers of the French revolutionary declaration of 1789.

Likewise, James Bryce—prolific legal scholar at Oxford and British ambassador to the United States from 1907 to 1913—conceived of comparative constitutional studies as a subcategory of comparative politics. Bryce's *The American Commonwealth* (1888) thoroughly examines the government institutions of the United States from the point of view of a historian and constitutional lawyer, and in his late work *Modern Democracies* (1921) he engages in a thorough discussion of what later became one of the classic themes of the constitutional design literature—the merits and drawbacks of parliamentarism and presidentialism.[19] A similarly holistic approach to constitutional law as an element of the political system was taken by other influential scholars in interwar Europe, notably Boris Mirkine-Guetzévitch—director of the Paris Institute of Comparative Law in the interwar period and initiator of comparative constitutional law scholarship in France—and Hugo Preuss, a public law scholar and chief drafter of the Weimar Constitution.[20]

---

[18] Howard, "A Traveler from an Antique Land" (n 14).

[19] The most prominent exponent of this line of inquiry is Juan Linz. See, e.g., Juan Linz and Alfred Stepan, eds., *The Breakdown of Democratic Regimes* (Johns Hopkins University Press, 1978); Juan Linz and Arturo Valenzuela, *The Failure of Presidential Democracy: Comparative Perspectives* (Johns Hopkins University Press, 1994).

[20] See, e.g., Mirkine-Guetzévitch's *Les Constitutions de l'Europe nouvelle* (Librairie Delagrave, 1928); *Le droit constitutionnel international* (Sirey, 1933); and later *Les Constitutions Européennes* (Presses Universitaires de France, 1951).

Newly published lectures on comparative constitutionalism by the renowned scholar of British constitutionalism at the turn of the 20th century A. V. Dicey, suggest that even the often formalist Dicey thought it was "more profitable to compare the conceptions or ideas which underlie political arrangements" than just to compare institutions or laws.[21] In these lectures (written between 1895 and 1908), Dicey compares elements of constitutionalism in the British Commonwealth with the situation in France, the United States, and Prussia, and addresses topics such as representative government, separation of powers, varieties of constitutions and regime types, and given polities' "constitutional spirit." Dicey describes his comparative method as "the elucidating of existing institutions or laws and in our case of the English constitution by comparison with analogous institutions or laws which have existed in other times or which now exist in other lands" as well as with institutions that have not had "an actual historical life" but have been "constructed by the fancy of philosophers or poets."[22]

In short, the epistemological difference between the comparative constitutionalism of the early 20th century and that of the 21st century is substantial. Prior to the current era, which is marked by law school dominance, the ever-expanding political salience of constitutional courts, and a preoccupation, for scholars and activists, with rights claims—all of which have led to a considerable "juridification" of the comparative study of constitutions—great works in the field took a considerably broader perspective according to which constitutions are basic instruments of government, and the study of comparative constitutionalism and that of comparative government are adjoined. Formalist and descriptive as many of these works were, they rested on a common treatment of the constitutional domain as subsumed in the political one.

As we saw earlier, the tectonic shifts of the first half of the 20th century—most notably World War I, the collapse of the Weimer Republic, and World War II and its aftermath, particularly the rise of totalitarianism and Communism—brought about a new conceptual and normative approach to comparative constitutional inquiry. Within political science, Carl Friedrich—a German-born American citizen and a prominent scholar of comparative constitutional government who

[21] A. V. Dicey, "Introduction," in *Comparative Constitutionalism* (J. W. F. Allison, ed., Oxford University Press, 2013), 6.

[22] Dicey, "Introduction" (n 21).

taught at Harvard for half a century and served, inter alia, as president of both the American and International Political Science Associations— began in the 1940s to conceptualize the constitutionalization of the modern state in a way that resembles today's "historical institutional-ism" approach, which situates law and courts within a broader, more normative, and more interactive "law and politics" conception of constitutionalism.[23] The essence of Friedrich's approach is perhaps best captured in the epigraph to this chapter, which is drawn from one of his seminal books, *Constitutional Government and Democracy*.[24] Friedrich—described as the "the great academic exponent of German liberalism"—may also be credited with introducing a normative (lib-eral, democratic, pluralist) tenor to comparative constitutional studies, exemplified by the strong anti-totalitarian impulse of his comparative constitutional work.

Meanwhile, in the 1960s and 1970s, trends of post-colonialism and democratization brought about a burst of scholarly interest in a new field of inquiry: comparative constitutional design (or constitutional engineering). The premise underlying this field is that desirable social and political outcomes can be achieved through optimal institutional planning and careful, painstaking implementation. The various approaches to constitutional design share in common a belief that constitutional provisions, institutions, and arrangements can and should be optimized to induce, support, or allow social and political change. By idealist accounts, constitutions evolve organically and are said to reflect the people's authentic will or the polity's enduring values— whereas constitutional design advocates a second-order, pragmatic vision of constitution-making as a response to concrete problems and challenges.

In democratic settings, the purported goals of such design may be the enhancement of the political system's legitimacy and democratic cre-dentials (e.g. participation and representation), increased accountability and transparency, or the balancing of the principle of majority rule with the idea that democracy may have more to it than just adherence to that principle. In transitional settings—most commonly post-conflict situations or situations requiring transition from an authoritarian

[23] See Jonathan O'Neill, "Carl J. Friedrich's Legacy: Understanding Constitutionalism as a Political System," *The European Legacy* 14 (2009): 283–300.
[24] Carl J. Friedrich, *Constitutional Government and Democracy: Theory and Practice in Europe and America* (Little, Brown & Co., 1941).

regime—constitutional design is aimed at building trust and ensuring effective transition while maintaining incentives for major stakeholders to stick to the transitional pact and accomplish its stated goals. The literature on constitutional design of this kind, which is often referred to as "consociationalism" (or "accommodation-centered" constitutionalism), emphasizes the significance of joint-governance institutions, mutual veto points, power-sharing mechanisms, and the like.[25] In its more strategic, "centripetal" (or "integrationist") guise, this brand of scholarship advocates the adoption of institutions that would make the political process more attractive to recalcitrant stakeholders, encourage moderation, and defuse causes of strife by providing incentives to vote across group lines.[26] All of that said, the role of constitutional design in the actual stabilization and tranquilization of conflict or post-conflict settings where they are most needed is very much an open question.[27]

Another prolific line of inquiry debates the supposed merits and drawbacks of various political governance meta-structures—presidentialism, parliamentarianism, and their variations such as semi-presidentialism or uni/bi-cameral parliamentarism—designed to facilitate a successful transition to and consolidation of democracy. Constitutions, it is supposed, may be engineered to accomplish these goals. More recent work has shown that regardless of the particular regime type, astute constitutional design may facilitate democratization by lowering the costs of upholding the democratic bargain (e.g. by allowing outgoing authoritarians a role in the new democratic order or by providing international incentives for collaboration among rival factions at the domestic level), or by elevating the costs of a slide back to authoritarianism.[28] In particular, strategic constitution-making is evident in the area of executive term limits and their evasion.[29] Attempts to tinker

---

[25] Arend Lijphart, *Democracy in Plural Societies: A Comparative Exploration* (Yale University Press, 1977); Arend Lijphart, "Constitutional Design for Divided Societies," *Journal of Democracy* 15 (2004): 96–109.

[26] Donald Horowitz, *Ethnic Groups in Conflict* (University of California Press, 1985).

[27] See, e.g., Tom Ginsburg, Zachary Elkins, and Justin Blount, "Does the Process of Constitution-Making Matter?," *Annual Review of Law and Social Science* 5 (2009): 201–23, 223.

[28] See, e.g., Susan Alberts, Chris Warshaw, and Barry Weingast, "Democratization and Countermajoritarian Institutions: Power and Constitutional Design in Self-Enforcing Democracy," in Tom Ginsburg, ed., *Comparative Constitutional Design* (Cambridge University Press, 2012), 69–100.

[29] Tom Ginsburg, Zachary Elkins, and James Melton, "Do Executive Term-Limits Cause Constitutional Crises?" in Ginsburg, *Comparative Constitutional Design* (n 28), 350–79.

with constitutionally imposed term limits have taken place in dozens of countries, ranging from Algeria to Venezuela and Colombia, and from Russia to Honduras and Uganda although, on the whole, term limits have proven effective in the vast majority of cases.[30]

In any event, as with many other theoretical developments in comparative constitutional studies, social scientists have taken the lead. Virtually all the grandmasters of 20th-century constitutional design literature—Arend Lijphart, Donald Horowitz, Juan Linz, Alfred Stepan, Giovanni Sartori, and Guillermo O'Donnell, to mention a few—are political scientists by education or by vocation. The same generally holds true with respect to the literature on the transition to and consolidation of democracy that followed waves of democratization in Latin America, Asia, and most notably Southern, Central, and Eastern Europe; many of the prominent authors in this area (e.g. Samuel Huntington, Jon Elster, Stephen Holmes, Adam Przeworski, or Andrew Arato) are political scientists, or hold joint appointments in law schools but are not doctrinal lawyers.

Meanwhile, institutional economists and political scientists have developed theories of constitutional transformation that treat constitutions and judicial review as mechanisms to mitigate systemic collective-action concerns such as commitment, enforcement, and information problems. One such theory, which derives directly from Max Weber's work (and has been advanced by Nobel Prize Laureate Douglass North, among others), sees the development of constitutions and independent judiciaries as an efficient institutional answer to the problem of "credible commitments."[31] The constitutional entrenchment of limitations on a given regime's ability to behave unpredictably (e.g. property rights, independent judicial monitoring of legislative and executive branches) is seen as an effective way of increasing that regime's credibility vis-à-vis potential lenders and investors.

The broader premise that decision-makers tend to be risk-averse under conditions of systemic uncertainty is a textbook example of how core concepts and discoveries by social scientists may be fruitfully applied to the study of comparative constitutional law. This premise

---

[30] Ginsburg, Elkins, and Melton, "Do Executive Term-Limits Cause Constitutional Crises?" (n 29), 374.

[31] Barry Weingast, "Constitutions as Governance Structures: The Political Foundations of Secure Markets," *Journal of Institutional and Theoretical Economics* 149 (1993): 286–311; Barry Weingast, "The Political Foundations of Democracy and the Rule of Law," *American Political Science Review* 91 (1997): 245–63.

has been advanced in a wide array of non-legal scholarship, from John Rawls's discussion of the "principles of justice" agreed upon behind a veil of ignorance,[32] to Marshall Sahlins's paradigm-shifting explanation for the lack of food accumulation or storage among hunter-gatherer societies,[33] to Tversky and Kahneman's seminal work on the psychology of choice under conditions of uncertainty.[34] The entire conceptualization of constitutions as pre-commitments or as predictability-enhancing instruments is based on a similar understanding of human nature and behavior.[35] It has also been applied to help to understand other aspects of the constitutional domain, such as variance in high court independence (as it reflects the competitiveness of a polity's electoral market or the time horizons of its governing politicians)[36] and the strategic incorporation of international human rights covenants into domestic law.[37]

Taking the notion of constitutions as political institutions even further, more recent political science scholarship, both quantitative and qualitative, attempts to move beyond the traditional focus on constitutionalization as emanating from broad public or organic pressures in order to identify the concrete political conditions that are conducive to constitutional reform and the expansion of judicial power more generally. This new direction in comparative constitutional studies emphasizes specific "supply-side" factors such as the nature of the political market and the changing interests and incentives of pertinent political stakeholders as key determinants of constitutionalization and

[32] John Rawls, *A Theory of Justice* (Harvard University Press, 1971).

[33] Marshall D. Sahlins, *Stone Age Economics* (Routledge, 1972). In a nutshell, a perception—prevalent among early hunter-gatherer societies—that there were unlimited resources and a corresponding, pervasive belief in a "giving environment" may render accumulation of resources, and by extension savings or insurance, unnecessary.

[34] Amos Tversky and Daniel Kahneman, "The Framing of Decisions and the Psychology of Choice," *Science* 211 (1981): 453–8.

[35] See, e.g., Douglass North and Barry Weingast, "Constitutions and Commitment: The Evolution of Institutions Governing Public Choice in Seventeenth Century England," *Journal of Economic History* 29 (1989): 803–32; Torsten Persson and Guido Tabellini, *The Economic Effects of Constitutions* (MIT Press, 2005).

[36] William Landes and Richard Posner, "The Independent Judiciary in an Interest Group Perspective," *Journal of Law and Economics* 18 (1975): 875–901; J. Mark Ramseyer, "The Puzzling (In)dependence of Courts: A Comparative Approach," *Journal of Legal Studies* 23: 721–47; Matthew Stephenson, "'When the Devil Turns...': The Political Foundations of Independent Judicial Review," *Journal of Legal Studies* 32 (2003): 59–89.

[37] Andrew Moravcsik, "The Origins of Human Rights Regimes," *International Organization* 54 (2000): 217–52; Tom Ginsburg, "Locking in Democracy: Constitutions, Commitment, and International Law," *Journal of International Law and Politics* 38 (2006): 707–59.

judicial empowerment.[38] The time horizons of power-holders, and any perceived threats to them, are key factors here. It is the arrival of credible political competition, or a new constellation of power, that makes those who operate in an insecure political environment, whether politicians, parties, or social groups, see the utility of constitutional protection and powerful courts. Those that have better control over and affinity with the constitutional arena in a given polity are more likely to resort to it as a power-preserving measure when present or prospective transformations in the political system threaten their own political status, worldviews, and policy preferences. In short, constitutionalization is often not merely, or even mainly, a form of Ulysses-like self-binding against one's own desires, but rather a self-interested binding of other credibly threatening actors who advance rival worldviews and policy preferences.[39]

The main assertions of this strategic-realist approach to constitutionalization—most notably the assertion that the degree of political uncertainty facing politicians, whether because they are on the decline or because they are insecure in their newly acquired power, is an important predictor of whether a constitutional court will be established (and with what review competencies)—have been supported in a variety of studies ranging from formal modeling or large-N statistical analyses to detailed comparative studies of constitutionalization.[40]

---

[38] Tom Ginsburg, *Judicial Review in New Democracies: Constitutional Courts in Asian Cases* (Cambridge University Press, 2003); Ran Hirschl, *Towards Juristocracy: The Origins and Consequences of the New Constitutionalism* (Harvard University Press, 2004).

[39] For an overview, see Ran Hirschl, "The Strategic Foundations of Constitutions," in Denis J. Galligan and Mila Versteeg, eds., *Social and Political Foundations of Constitutions* (Cambridge University Press, 2013), 157–81. Scholars who have engaged in this type of study have drawn on the logic of insurance against political threat to explain the variance in choice of constitutional institutions between different periods in the late 19th-century United States, between two Argentine provinces, among several polities in Eastern Europe, among post-authoritarian Asian countries (South Korea, Mongolia, and Taiwan), among three new democracies in Southern Europe (Greece, Spain, and Portugal), and between two periods in 20th-century Mexican politics, one characterized by an uncontested single-party rule (and therefore involving little or no judicial review), the other by a considerably more competitive electoral market (leading to various expansions of constitutional law and judicial review competencies). Conversely, little or no judicial empowerment has taken place in countries such as Japan or Singapore where a single political force has most controlled the political system for over 50 years. The same logic may explain why the ANC, now the undisputed ruling party in South Africa, has become considerably less keen on judicial activism than it was during the tumultuous transition of the early 1990s.

[40] Tom Ginsburg and Mila Versteeg, "Why Do Countries Adopt Constitutional Review?" *Journal of Law, Economics and Organization* 30 (2014): 587–622.

Even when it comes to court-centric scholarship, social scientists have made great contributions, often as part of an attempt to analyze constitutional courts and their jurisprudence as integral elements of a larger political setting. The first steps in this direction were Robert Dahl's conceptualization of the US Supreme Court as a mainly political, rather than juridical, institution and later Robert McCloskey's detailed accounts of the US Supreme Court's interactions with the political sphere.[41] Martin Shapiro's *Courts: A Comparative and Political Analysis* was the first thorough application of Robert Dahl's theory of courts as political institutions to the study of comparative public law.[42] Meanwhile, in the mid-1960s political scientists such as Glendon Schubert and Walter Murphy laid down the basis for the empirical study of judicial behavior.[43]

Unfortunately, very little of this scholarship has found its way into comparative constitutional law course syllabi. The proliferation of constitutional courts, judicial review, and constitutional rights jurisprudence worldwide, indeed the rise of human rights discourse more generally, has turned the comparative study of constitutionalism into a predominantly legalistic enterprise that is heavily influenced by the prevalent case law method of instruction. Twenty years ago Mark Tushnet astutely noted that the most basic characteristic of constitutional scholarship in the United States is that it is "oriented to Supreme Court decisions."[44] Today, much of comparative constitutional law scholarship follows suit in its court-centric focus. Two dozen court rulings from South Africa, Germany, Canada, and the European Court of Human Rights alongside a more traditional set of landmark rulings from the United States and Britain and an occasional tribute to India or Australia, now form an unofficial canon of "global constitutionalism" that informs comparative constitutional law syllabi throughout much of the English-speaking world.

---

[41] Robert Dahl, "Decision-making in a Democracy: The Supreme Court as a National Policymaker," *Journal of Public Law* 6 (1957): 279–95; Robert McCloskey, *The American Supreme Court* (1st edn, University of Chicago Press, 1960). Four additional editions of this seminal book have appeared over the years, the 5th and most recent edition was published in 2010.

[42] Martin Shapiro, *Courts: A Comparative and Political Analysis* (University of Chicago Press, 1981).

[43] Glendon Schubert, *Judicial Decision-Making* (Free Press, 1963); Walter Murphy, *Elements of Judicial Strategy* (University of Chicago Press, 1964).

[44] Mark Tushnet, "Justification in Constitutional Adjudication: A Comment on Constitutional Interpretation," *Texas Law Review* 72 (1994): 1707–30, 1709.

Proof of the law school's "appropriation" of contemporary comparative constitutional studies can be found by looking at the main disciplinary affiliation of the contributors to three recently published comprehensive handbooks on the subject. Of the 72 contributors to the definitive *Oxford Handbook of Comparative Constitutional Law*—a landmark scholarly accomplishment in many respects—64 (or 89 percent) are affiliated with law faculties, courts, or legal institutions; 8 (or 11 percent) are affiliated with social science or humanities disciplines.[45] Although many contributors refer to pertinent political science literature, themes, and insights, relatively few of them depart from a law-, court-, or jurisprudence-centric approach to explore other actors and processes in the constitutional domain. The *Routledge Handbook on Constitutional Law*—another authoritative volume edited by major comparative constitutionalism scholars—addresses distinctly interdisciplinary topics such as "international relations and international law," "constitutions and legitimacy over time," or "multicultural societies and migration" alongside many more traditional constitutional law themes.[46] At the same time, here too 64 (or 89 percent) of the 72 contributors are affiliated with law schools and legal institutions, whereas eight (or 11 percent) are affiliated with social science departments or public policy institutions. The picture is only slightly different in *Comparative Constitutional Law*—a third definitive "state of the field" volume.[47] Of the 37 contributors there, law is the main disciplinary affiliation of 28 (or 76 percent); while 9 (24 percent) are mainly affiliated with social science disciplines. Similarly, the number of legal academics that can be counted among the authors of the *International Journal of Constitutional Law* (I-CON)—published under the auspices of Oxford University Press, and arguably the leading journal in the field—far exceeds the number of political scientists. Among the journals most cited by I-CON authors as of 2013 are the *Harvard Law Review*, *Yale Law Journal*, *Modern Law Review*, *European Journal of International Law*, and *American Journal of Comparative Law*.[48] By contrast,

---

[45] Michel Rosenfeld and András Sajó, eds., *The Oxford Handbook of Comparative Constitutional Law* (Oxford University Press, 2012).

[46] Mark Tushnet, Thomas Fleiner, and Cheryl Saunders, *The Routledge Handbook on Constitutional Law* (Routledge, 2013).

[47] Tom Ginsburg and Rosalind Dixon, eds., *Comparative Constitutional Law* (Edward Elgar, 2011).

[48] Statistical analysis of citation patterns, on file with author. A similar pattern is evident with respect to citations of I-CON articles. Among the journals that most frequently cite

only thin, sporadic reference is made to comparative public law studies published in leading political science or law and society journals. A similar pattern is detectable in the *European Constitutional Law Review* (launched in 2005), the *Indian Journal of Constitutional Law* (launched in 2007), and *Global Constitutionalism* (launched in 2011).

The recent dominance of law schools in the field of comparative constitutionalism is also reflected in the number of articles published on the subject in leading American political science journals and law reviews. Up until the mid-20th century, considerably more articles on comparative constitutionalism were published in political science journals than in legal periodicals. The last half-century has, however, seen a reversal of this trend. To provide a snapshot of this shift, from 1990 to 2010 alone, a total of 33 articles that included significant comparative constitutional components were published in the *Columbia Law Review*, *Harvard Law Review*, and the *Yale Law Journal*; during the same period of time, merely six articles on comparative constitutionalism were published in the *American Political Science Review*, *American Journal of Political Science*, and the *Political Science Quarterly*. None of the 12 articles on judicial and constitutional politics that was published over the four-year period between January 2010 and December 2013 in the *American Political Science Review* (5) and in the *American Journal of Political Science* (7), dealt with comparative aspects per se; all focused on the United States. As David Fontana notes, there was a surge during the 1950s and 1960s in law review articles on comparative public law, most of them "about exporting American constitutional ideas to the rest of the world."[49] Over the past three decades there has been another sharp increase in the number of articles on the subject published in leading law reviews and a corresponding decline in the number published in top political science journals.

Predictably, then, in contemporary comparative constitutional law, constitutional jurisprudence is considered the central component of the constitutional universe, and the main subject of inquiry. Debates about comparative constitutional doctrine and interpretive methods dominate the terrain. Other key actors and elements of the constitutional

---

I-CON articles as of 2013 are the *European Constitutional Law Review*, *European Law Journal*, *European Journal of International Law*, as well as the *Stanford Law Review*, *NYU Law Review*, and *Cornell Law Review*.

[49] David Fontana, "The Rise and Fall of Comparative Constitutional Law in the Postwar Era," *Yale Journal of International Law* 36 (2011): 1–53, 22.

domain—the constitutional text in its entirety; constitutional litigants and the legal profession; constitutional development and history; the extent to which constitutions actually shape or alter behavior; and the institutional, ideological, and political sphere with which the constitutional order constantly interacts—are not taken to be part of what scholars of comparative constitutional law "do."

Why look to the social sciences?

There are many reasons why the social sciences ought to be incorporated into the comparative study of constitutions, but in the interest of brevity I will here focus on five core rationales: (i) the social sciences offer well-developed and tested theories of judicial behavior and decision-making patterns; (ii) the social sciences can help to explain how and why constitutions, constitutional courts, and judicial review emerge, change, and occasionally fall apart; (iii) constitutional design—one of the more prolific areas of comparative constitutional inquiry in the last half-century—has at least as much to do with social and political inquiry as it has with any form of constitutional theory or jurisprudential principles; (iv) the social sciences can facilitate the study of the actual effects of constitutions beyond the courtroom; and (v) the social sciences offer a well-thought-out methodological matrix that may bolster comparative constitutional law's ability to engage in general theory building. I briefly discuss each in turn.

(i) Theories of judicial behavior

Whereas law professors, by and large, believe that "legal doctrine still matters, and commit themselves to this belief, both in their pedagogy and scholarship,"[50] an overwhelming body of evidence suggests that extrajudicial factors play a key role in constitutional court decision-making patterns. Constitutional courts and judges may speak the language of legal doctrine but, consciously or not, their actual decision-making patterns are correlated with policy preferences and ideological and attitudinal tilts, and appear to reflect strategic considerations vis-à-vis political surroundings, panel compositions, their professional

---

[50] Anthony Niblett and Albert H. Yoon, "Judicial Disharmony: A Study of Dissent" (University of Toronto, Faculty of Law Working Paper 2014; on file with author).

peers, and the public as a whole.[51] This can be explained by reference to the costs that judges as individuals or courts as institutions may incur as a result of adverse reactions to unwelcome decisions, or to the various benefits they may acquire through rendering welcome ones.[52] A wide array of empirically grounded studies suggests that harsh political responses to unwelcome activism or interventions on the part of the courts, or even the credible threat of such a response, can have a chilling effect on judicial decision-making patterns. Variations on the same logic have been used compellingly to explain judicial behavior in countries as varied as Argentina, Brazil, Germany, Pakistan, Canada, Russia, South Korea, Taiwan, Georgia, Ukraine, Kyrgyzstan, and Mexico.[53] Other works point to judges' relations with their epistemic communities of reference (the network of jurists), or their concern with the court's legacy, reputation, and public stature, both domestically and internationally, as important determinants of judicial behavior, particularly in politically significant cases.

Meticulous empirical studies conducted by economists and psychologists provide conclusive evidence that judges are interested in their own reputation, chances of promotion, and salary matters, and that even experienced judges' decision-making can be affected by legally irrelevant extraneous factors, so much so that they may be more favorable to parole applicants early in the day and after their food breaks.[54] Recent studies of the federal judiciary in the United States

---

[51] A well-known exposition of the so-called "attitudinal" model of judicial behavior in the US context is Harold J. Spaeth, *The Supreme Court and the Attitudinal Model Revisited* (Cambridge University Press, 2002).

[52] For an overview of this approach, see Lee Epstein and Tonja Jacobi, "The Strategic Analysis of Judicial Decisions," *Annual Review of Law and Social Science* 6 (2010): 341–58.

[53] See, e.g., Jeffrey Staton, *Judicial Power and Strategic Communication in Mexico* (Cambridge University Press, 2010); Gretchen Helmke, *Courts Under Constraints: Judges, Generals, and Presidents in Argentina* (Cambridge University Press, 2005); Alexei Trochev, *Judging Russia: The Role of the Constitutional Court in Russian Politics 1990–2006* (Cambridge University Press, 2008); Diana Kapiszewski, "Tactical Balancing: High Court Decision Making on Politically Crucial Cases," *Law and Society Review* 45 (2011): 471–506; Wen-Chen Chang, "Strategic Judicial Responses in Politically Charged Cases: East Asian Experiences," *International Journal of Constitutional Law* 8 (2010): 885–910.

[54] Shai Danziger, Jonathan Levav, and Liora Avniam-Pesso, "Extraneous Factors in Judicial Decisions," *Proceedings of the National Academy of Science of the United States* 108 (2011): 6889–92. For an accessible survey of this body of research, see Lee Epstein and Jack Knight, "Reconsidering Judicial Preferences," *Annual Review of Political Science* 16 (2013): 11–31. See also J. Mark Ramseyer and Eric Rasmusen, "Why are Japanese Judges So Conservative in Politically Charged Cases?," *American Political Science Review* 95 (2001): 331–43.

find that judges behave as "any other economic actors: as self-interested individuals motivated by both the pecuniary and non-pecuniary aspects of their work."[55] While not all of these discoveries are equally germane to explaining constitutional courts and judges, it is safe to say that insights from political science, social psychology, behavioral economics, and network and organizational theory have never been more relevant to the study of comparative constitutional law even if one accepts the view that constitutional courts and their output form the constitutional universe's center of gravity.

The limits of doctrinal, intra-legal analysis—of settling for the insular study of judicial reasoning without taking into account the socio-political context within which a given court is operating or a given judgment is rendered—are most obvious in cases where the politics of jurisprudence is evident to the naked eye. Examples are many. In 2008, the then explicitly pro-Kemalist Turkish Constitutional Court invoked a never-before-used doctrine imported from the constitutional jurisprudence of India and Germany to declare unconstitutional a constitutional amendment initiated by the AKP-led government that had been intended to revise Turkey's militant secularist outlook.[56] In the 2009 Lisbon Treaty decision, arguably one of the most significant political rulings in its history, the German Federal Constitutional Court took a decidedly fuzzy stance, such that the judgment may easily be interpreted as suggesting both firm German constitutional sovereignty vis-à-vis the emerging European constitutional order and full subjection of the former to the latter.[57] When the thick smoke of legal rhetoric fades away, the main beneficiary of this vagueness remains the court itself, now firmly established as the sole and exclusive decision-making authority over which set of norms should prevail in any given context.[58] Citing late 19th-century British election law and rules of evidence, the Supreme Court of Uganda legitimized the results of that country's 2006 presidential election (won by Yoweri Museveni, ruler of Uganda since 1986) despite having acknowledged massive problems with the electoral process and violations of key constitutional

---

[55] See Lee Epstein et al., *The Behavior of Federal Judges: A Theoretical and Empirical Study of Rational Choice* (Harvard University Press, 2012).

[56] TCC Decision 116/2008 (Unconstitutional Constitutional Amendment Case), June 5, 2008; legal reasoning released on Oct. 22, 2008 [Turkey].

[57] Lisbon Treaty Case, BVerfG, 2 BvE/08 (June 30, 2009) [Germany].

[58] For further analysis see Daniel Halberstam and Christoph Möllers, "The German Constitutional Court Says 'Ja Zu Deutschland!'," *German Law Journal* 10 (2009) 1241–58.

principles.[59] Having lost the 2010 presidential elections to the current president of the Philippines, President Benigno Aquino III, and a month before her term expired, then-president Gloria Macapagal Arroyo appointed Renato Corona Chief Justice of the Philippines Supreme Court. This apparent violation of a constitutional prohibition on last-minute (so-called "midnight") appointments required a timely and helpful decision from the Supreme Court, a ruling that the pro-Arroyo court happily delivered in order to ensure that Corona was allowed to take office (he was later impeached by President Aquino through a senate hearing).[60] And in Egypt, the Supreme Constitutional Court has become the main ally of the country's military apparatus and secularist–statist elites in their attempt to preserve their privileged position in Egypt's political system. In 2012, to pick one glaring example, the Court ordered the dissolution of the Muslim Brotherhood-dominated parliament after finding that one-third of its members were elected illegally.[61] All these landmark rulings, and numerous others like them, are filled with judicial recourse to constitutional doctrines.

And one more example, just to drive the message home: in 2000, the Supreme Court of Pakistan, including then-Justice Iftikhar Chaudhry, unanimously rubber-stamped (based on the doctrine of "state necessity" and the principle of *salus populi suprema lex*) then-President Musharraf's 1999 coup d'état and ousting of Prime Minister Nawaz Sharif.[62] In July 2009 (Musharraf was already in exile in London at the time), the same Supreme Court of Pakistan that rubber-stamped Musharraf's military rule a few years earlier, now led by Chief Justice Chaudhry (who, it should be noted, also sat on the Court in that earlier case), declared unconstitutional the state of emergency imposed by former President Pervez Musharraf in late 2007.[63] Consequently, the Court declared unconstitutional (this time based on principles of judicial independence and *ultra vires*) Musharraf's 2007 ousting of Chaudhry.

---

[59] Election Petition 1/2006, *Rtd. Col. Dr. Kizza Besigye v. Electoral Commission, Yoweri Kaguta Museveni* [2007] UGSC 24 [Uganda].

[60] G.R. 191200, *Arturo M. De Castro v. Judicial and Bar Council, et al.* (Mar. 17, 2010) [Philippines].

[61] The law governing the parliamentary elections was ruled unconstitutional as it breached the principle of equality since it allowed party members to contest one-third of seats set aside for independent candidates.

[62] *Syed Zafar Ali Shah v. Pervez Musharraf*, P.L.D. 2000 S.C. 869 [Pakistan].

[63] Constitution Petition 9/2009 *Sindh High Court Bar Association v. Federation of Pakistan*, P.L.D. 2009 S.C. 789 [Pakistan].

The bottom line seems to be this: while a military coup d'état against an elected government is constitutional based on a state emergency doctrine, the ousting of a judge based on that very same doctrine is apparently not. Translation: constitutional ideas and doctrines are many; their selective deployment in politically charged cases is often strategic.

In summary, there is a persisting resistance among constitutional courts and judges (and to a large extent among legal scholars who study and teach constitutional law as a fully autonomous enterprise) to accept the notion that constitutional law is a species of politics and that courts are a part of the social and political system in which they are embedded.[64] Undoubtedly, the problem is often mutual. Although more methodologically rigorous, much of the potentially relevant work in political science fails to take the role of legal reasoning seriously, often treating it as merely post-hoc rationalization.[65] This doctrinal separation of law and politics is problematic, especially when it comes to constitutional law in politically turbulent settings. The rulings discussed here illustrate the demonstrably strategic basis of judicial behavior in politically charged cases. The strained, improvised, and all-too-obvious attempts by the courts to conceal these extrajudicial motives by drawing on seldom-invoked constitutional doctrines and interpretive manipulations make these rulings textbook examples of why social science research is essential for fully understanding constitutional jurisprudence.

(ii) Why the rise of constitutionalism and judicial review?

Stories begin at the beginning. Without one, plot climaxes—spectacular, joyous, or tragic—make little sense. Likewise, constitutions do not fall from the sky but are created or transformed in response to societal needs, political interests, or normative persuasions. Their foundations as either authentic expressions of the people's will, abstract mission statements, effective mechanisms for solving complex coordination problems, or strategic instruments of power are an integral element of any comparative constitutional narrative.

[64] The seminal and most influential study to establish this point remains Robert A. Dahl, "Decision-Making in a Democracy: The Supreme Court as a National Policymaker," *Journal of Public Law* 4 (1957): 279–95.
[65] See, e.g., Barry Friedman, "Taking Law Seriously," *Perspectives on Politics* 4 (2006): 261–76.

There is a certain degree of fuzziness in the conventional story of how and why constitutions emerge and change, in particular with respect to the origins of the astounding global convergence toward constitutionalism and judicial review over the past few decades. An interdisciplinary approach, with a healthy dose of social science research, can help to rectify this. The large-scale convergence toward constitutional supremacy is typically portrayed as stemming from modern democracies' post-WWII acceptance of and commitment to the notion that democracy means more than mere adherence to the principle of majority rule. Not least, the canonical view goes, this convergence reflects every "mature democracy's" (in Ronald Dworkin's terms) subscription to the view that democracy must protect itself against the tyranny of majority rule through constitutionalization and judicial review, most notably by way of checks on government action and an entrenched, self-binding protection of the rights of vulnerable groups and individuals.[66] According to this common account, liberal constitutionalism is both normatively superior to its alternatives and the most effective way to prevent despotism, advance democratic politics, and protect basic rights and freedoms. The morally elevated status of these values—the fact that they are seen by many political leaders, institutions, and voters to reflect a just ideological platform—is the main factor explaining the spread of constitutionalism in the past half-century.

To the extent that concrete societal factors matter in this story, it is often in the context of supposedly authentic, bottom-up calls for a liberalizing constitutional change. During such "constitutional moments," massive popular mobilization—often accompanied by international cheering by rights advocates, Western media, and democracy supporters—leads to mounting pressure on a despotic regime to relinquish power, democratize politics, and protect individual rights through constitutional reform.[67] Accordingly, a given polity's constitution is often taken to be the most genuine reflection of its popular will, worldviews, and aspirations. Constitutional courts that are said to be removed from the pressures of partisan politics, and whose judges

---

[66] Ronald Dworkin, *A Bill of Rights for Britain* (University of Michigan Press, 1990); Lorraine Weinrib, "The Postwar Paradigm and American Exceptionalism," in Sujit Choudhry, ed., *The Migration of Constitutional Ideas* (Cambridge University Press, 2006), 83–113.

[67] For a classic exposition, see Bruce Ackerman, *We the People: Foundations* (Belknap Press, 1993).

are neutral, apolitical adjudicators, are responsible for translating the constitutional provisions into practical guidelines for public life in a way that, to paraphrase Ronald Dworkin, takes rights "seriously" and reflects the polity's "enduring values." The combination of popular participation, the liberating capacity of rights, and the centrality of courts and rights litigation has become a cornerstone of the canonical "feel good" ethos informing the rise of constitutionalism.

While appealing from a normative standpoint, this prevalent idea-tional account of what constitutions are, what they do, and how they come about poses several nontrivial challenges from an empirical standpoint. Notably, rights-based explanations often tell a broad, at times vague, demand-side causal story that is difficult to operationalize. The analytical distinction between the force of ideas per se and the instrumental interests of actors and agents that adhere to and advance those ideas is quite nebulous. There is no doubt that ideas do shape (or delimit) behavior to some extent. Rights ideology is a key component of post-WWII constitutional discourse and one of the reasons why constitutions are adopted.[68] However, these insights do not independently explain the tremendous variance in institutional design, forms of constitutional review, scope of judicial activism, and above all the precise timing of constitutionalization. And whereas a commitment to certain ideas or values may well explain the substantive content of constitutional documents, that content may also reflect transnational diffusion and imitation trends;[69] populist accounts resplendent with myths about the liberalizing power of rights and the Herculean cap-acities of judges;[70] "window dressing" by governments whose democratic or human rights records are questionable;[71] the overarching effect of international covenants and supranational rights regimes;[72]

---

[68] See, generally, Mauro Cappaletti, *The Judicial Process in Comparative Perspective* (Oxford University Press, 1989).

[69] Zachary Elkins, "Diffusion and the Constitutionalization of Europe," *Comparative Political Studies* 43 (2010): 969–99; Benedikt Goderis and Mila Versteeg, "The Transnational Origins of Constitutions: Evidence from a Global Data Set on Constitutional Rights" (2013) (unpublished paper on file with author).

[70] See, famously, Stuart Scheingold, *The Politics of Rights: Lawyers, Public Policy, and Political Change* (University of Michigan Press, 2004).

[71] See, e.g., David Law and Mila Versteeg, "Sham Constitutions," *California Law Review* 101 (2013): 863–952.

[72] See, e.g., Zachary Elkins, Tom Ginsburg, and Beth Simmons, "Getting to Rights: Treaty Ratification, Constitutional Convergence, and Human Rights Practice," *Harvard International Law Journal* 54 (2013): 61–95.

or some combination of these and other factors.[73] As ideologically appealing or normatively superior as liberal constitutionalism may be, the variance within the substantive (i.e. not merely textual) global constitutional domain is simply too large for the ideational story to be the sole explanatory factor.

Canada adopted a constitutionally entrenched bill of rights in 1982, Hong Kong did the same in 1991, and Jamaica followed in 2011. Australia and the United Kingdom, by contrast, remain without a constitutional bill of rights to date. What accounts for these considerable variations in the nature, scope, and timing of constitutional reforms? Surely there are more concrete factors at play in each of these settings than those accounted for by the generic rights-based ideational storyline. The variable status of constitutional courts further demonstrates this point. In some settings (e.g. Colombia), powerful constitutional courts have emerged, whereas in other substantively similar settings (e.g. Ecuador), such courts have been repeatedly criticized, tinkered with, or simply dissolved and replaced with a more compliant body. In yet other settings (e.g. Hungary) dramatic fluctuations in the independence of constitutional courts occurred over a short period of time, often following considerable change in the political arena. The ideational narrative alone cannot account for these differences.

Supporters of historically disenfranchised groups, advocates of women's or minority rights, lawyers concerned with the rights of the accused, and a host of other social movements and ideational agents have supported the constitutionalization of rights for much of the past half-century, and in most countries were doing so long before it was formalized. And yet, the establishment of constitutional review in Israel happened between 1992 and 1995, not a decade earlier or later. The adoption of the Canadian Charter took place in 1982, not in 1972 or in 1992. At best, then, ideational factors may provide a broad, fuzzy, pro-constitutionalization environment, within which key political actors operate. An explanation of why the Canadian Charter was adopted in 1982, however, or of why Israel embarked on its constitutional revolution precisely when it did, must be far more concrete.

Furthermore, rights-based explanations tend to posit a somewhat romantic notion of constitutionalization as reflecting massive political

---

[73] For a survey, see David Law and Mila Versteeg, "The Evolution and Ideology of Global Constitutionalism," *California Law Review* 99 (2011): 1163–258.

mobilization and genuine popular will. The reality, however, is that the vast majority of constitutional revolutions in the last few decades were culminations of elite bargains, or otherwise do not fit this "bottom-up" narrative. Indeed, as Denis Galligan demonstrates, the notion of substantive popular participation in constitutionalization processes is largely fictitious.[74] Instead, constitutional revolutions are either negotiated among rival parties during times of political transition (as in South Africa), promoted by external actors (as was the case in Afghanistan in 2004 and Iraq in 2005, and over half a century earlier in Japan and Korea), seized by influential stakeholders (e.g. the constitutional transformation in Egypt following the toppling of President Mubarak in 2011 and later President Morsi in 2013), or initiated in the first place by political elites whose interests do not necessary reflect the popular will (e.g. the continuous attempt by "Eurocentric" politicians, bureaucrats, and jurists to create an "ever-closer union" in Europe by the adoption of an EU constitution). In other words, popular will and other forms of bottom-up pressure may be a pro-constitutionalization factor, but they are certainly not a necessary, let alone sufficient condition for reform to actually take place.

In fact, quite a few constitutions simply do not reflect the prevalent worldview in their respective polity.[75] In a new empirical study, Mila Versteeg finds that the link between nations' specific constitutional choices and their citizens' values has generally been weak, at times even non-existent.[76] For example, India, Turkey, and the United States are consistently cited as three of the most religious polities in the world in the sense that members of these polities are among the most likely to define themselves by their religious affiliation, attend religious services, or resort to religion for guidance in their everyday lives. Yet the constitutions of these countries advance, by and large, secular visions of politics that do not reflect this characteristic.[77]

[74] Denis J. Galligan, "The People, the Constitution, and the Idea of Representation," in Galligan and Versteeg, *Social and Political Foundations of Constitutions* (n 40), 134–56. See also Denis J. Galligan, "The Sovereignty Deficit of Modern Constitutions," *Oxford Journal of Legal Studies* 33 (2013): 703–32.

[75] See, generally, Gary J. Jacobsohn, "The Disharmonic Constitution," in Stephen Macedo and Jeffrey Tulis, eds., *The Limits of Constitutional Democracy* (Princeton University Press, 2010), 47–65.

[76] Mila Versteeg, "Unpopular Constitutionalism," *Indiana Law Journal* 89 (2014): 1133–90.

[77] See Gary J. Jacobsohn, *Constitutional Identity* (Harvard University Press, 2010).

Furthermore, if genuine long-term ideational processes are indeed significant to the promotion of constitutionalization, how are we to explain the fact that constitutional orders frequently get changed or abolished? As mentioned previously, empirical studies of the lifespan of constitutions worldwide report that only half of all constitutions last more than nine years, with an overall average of 19 years.[78] Such frequent change in constitutional order must reflect either a rapidly changing ideological platform or, more likely, changes in the concrete conditions and constellations of power within which constitutions emerge, function, and ultimately, die.

It is therefore hardly surprising that against the prevalent ideational canon, a "strategic-realist" approach to constitutionalization has emerged.[79] It identifies a set of concrete political vectors, interests, and incentives that affect the introduction of new constitutional orders and, consequently, the interplay between political and constitutional actors and institutions. In a nutshell, the take-home message of those advocating the strategic-realist approach is that the quest to increase benefits or lower risks and costs—most notably by enhancing regime legitimacy and stature, promoting centralization and fostering nation-building, or locking in a certain set of contested worldviews and policy preferences—is a major determinant of constitutionalization. While this does not provide a complete explanation for all instances of constitutionalization, it marks an important theoretical and empirical departure from both formalist legal analyses and overly idealistic normative accounts, as well as from political scientists' and economists' traditional emphasis on functionalist, systemic needs-based explanations of how constitutions emerge and what they do. More than any other extant theory, the strategic-realist approach rests on genuinely comparative, empirically grounded findings, and provides a plausible explanation for the considerable variance worldwide in the scope, nature, and timing of constitutionalization. It illustrates that social science research into the concrete driving forces behind constitutionalization and judicial empowerment trends is essential for bridging the inexplicable gap between normative constitutional theory and real-life constitutional politics.

---

[78] Elkins et al., *The Endurance of National Constitutions* (n 2).
[79] See, generally, Ran Hirschl, "The Strategic Foundations of Constitutions," in Galligan and Versteeg, *Social and Political Foundations of Constitutions* (n 40), 157–81.

(iii) Constitutional design as political science

From "neo-institutionalism" to constitutional design, tracing the complex interrelations between institutional factors and societal or cultural factors in explaining policy and political outcomes has occupied political science scholarship for generations.[80] As suggested earlier, virtually all grandmasters of comparative constitutional design over the last half-century were political thinkers. And the same holds true with respect to the closely related fields of democratization, where Samuel Huntington's work is considered a must-read, or in democratic theory more generally, where prominent political scientists such as Robert Dahl and later Ian Shapiro have led the way. Symbolically, the first three recipients of the Swedish Johan Skytte Prize in Political Science—dubbed the Nobel Prize of that discipline—were Robert Dahl, Juan Linz, and Arend Lijphart, three of the most significant contributors to the "institutional versus societal factors" debate.

But constitutional design as an intellectual enterprise has at least as much to do with social and political inquiry as with legal or constitutional inquiry for substantive reasons, not merely by virtue of the training or affiliation of its main contributors over the years. The significance of politics and society to constitutional design seems intuitive. The root causes of ethnic, religious, or linguistic strife (or alternatively of inter-ethnic or inter-faith collaboration) in any given setting are not constitutional or juridical but social, economic, and political.[81] Simply put, there cannot be an effective constitutional design for a failed state such as Somalia, a new political entity such as South Sudan, or a deeply divided country such as Belgium, without a profound understanding of each of these polities' pertinent societal and political perimeters. Just as no urban planning or economic policy-making exercise would be credible without a careful examination of the concrete setting that it purports to address, no dependable constitutional engineering exercise for any given polity can proceed

---

[80] "New institutionalism" is a theoretical branch within political science that advances a sociological view of institutions and how they emerge, interact with, and affect society. It views institutions in a distinctly more "political" way—as reflecting and affecting power relations—than the view of institutions advanced by economics or by law.

[81] For a substantiation of this point, see, e.g., David Laitin, *Hegemony and Culture: Politics and Change among the Yoruba* (University of Chicago Press, 1986); Ashutosh Varshney, *Ethnic Conflict and Civic Life: Hindus and Muslims in India* (Yale University Press, 2002); Steven Wilkinson, *Votes and Violence: Electoral Competition and Ethnic Riots in India* (Cambridge University Press, 2006).

without close attention to that polity's history, demographics, economics, and politics.

And the need for more political science in the comparative study of constitutions further intensifies when we take into account the far-reaching political effects of entrenched constitutional design choices. Examples are many. Sanford Levinson, one of the United States' most prominent constitutional thinkers, has persuasively advanced the argument that what he labels "hard-wired" and dated features of the US Constitution helped to make America not only undemocratic but indeed ungovernable, fostering the politics of extremism and undermining the spirit of compromise.[82] As Levinson points out, entrenched institutional features such as the electoral system and Electoral College (four US Presidents have been elected after receiving less votes than one of their opponents), the Senate (two senators for each state, California with nearly 40 million people or Wyoming with a little over half a million), and even the lack of a mandatory retirement age for Supreme Court justices or the two months' difference between presidential elections in late November and Inauguration Day on January 20, have all had distorting, even undemocratic effects on how the United States—the supposed leader of the democratic world—is governed. Either way, the challenge of constitutional obsoleteness and the distorted policy outcomes it yields seem particularly pressing; it is clear that a constitutional order adopted in the late 18th century is no longer entirely suitable for a 21st-century powerhouse democracy with a population of over 300 million, let alone for addressing new-age challenges such as the megacity and the environment.

Here, too, expanding the horizons to incorporate a comparative angle may prove illuminating. Even a cursory look overseas indicates that, for all its constitutional shortcomings, the United States does not have a monopoly over inadequate, démodé constitutional design that impedes effective government and that may yield derisory political outcomes. Italy's regional variation and understandable fear of a strong executive (think Mussolini) brought about a post-WWII constitutional system with a distinctly weak executive. The electoral threshold is low, small parties abound, and the prime minister needs a majority in both

[82] See Sanford Levinson, *Our Undemocratic Constitution: Where the Constitution Goes Wrong (and How We the People Can Correct It)* (Oxford University Press, 2006); Sanford Levinson, *Framed: America's 51 Constitutions and the Crisis of Governance* (Oxford University Press, 2012).

the House of Deputies and the Senate to govern.[83] Forming a government, and then keeping it together and ensuring its active functioning, depend on the cooperation of a multitude of groups, often with diverging interests. If a small party falls out with its coalition partners, it can bring down the government. The result: since its political reconstruction in 1946, Italy has had no less than 62 separate coalition governments, each lasting a little over a year on average.[84] That is a stunning figure for one of Europe's major polities, even without taking into account the colorful personality of some of Italy's heads of state over that period (Silvio Berlusconi served as head of state three times since 2001).

In Canada, the House of Commons has been prorogued three times since 2008 (most recently for two months in 2013) to save the serving government from harsh parliamentary scrutiny. A similar "kosher but fishy" maneuver was used in Ontario (Canada's most populous province) in 2012–13 to save a serving government from collapse. According to the Constitution Act 1867, the Senate (upper house) is an entirely nominated body (i.e. not democratically elected). For historical reasons, provincial representation in the Senate is disproportional. According to the amending formula adopted as part of the 1982 Constitution Act, to fundamentally transform the Senate, the unanimous consent of all ten provinces, the federal government, and the House of Commons is required. And there is more.

Canada's smallest province, Prince Edward Island (population of less than 140,000) has a constitutionally guaranteed representation of four House of Commons seats, that is, one parliament member per less than 35,000 residents.[85] Ontario (population 13 million) has 106 guaranteed House of Commons seats, that is, one parliament member per approximately 125,000 residents. In other words, an average Ontarian is about 3.5 times less represented than an average resident of PEI.[86] Furthermore, within Ontario itself, electoral districts (ridings) vary in

[83] "Why Is It So Hard to Form a Government in Italy?," *The Economist* (Apr. 24, 2013), <http://www.economist.com/blogs/economist-explains/2013/04/economist-explains-8>.

[84] "Why Is It So Hard to Form a Government in Italy?" (n 83).

[85] The constitutional source for this anomaly is section 51a of the Constitution Act, 1867, which establishes a "Senate floor" rule whereby "no province shall have fewer members in the House of Commons than in the Senate."

[86] According to the Fair Representation Act passed in 2011, the number of members of parliament is set to increase from 308 to 338; the number of Ontario seats is set to increase to 121 in the next Canadian federal election, so that there will be one seat for every 107,000 Ontarians, still three times the ratio as in PEI.

population from less than 65,000 (e.g. in the largely rural Kenora riding) to over 150,000 (e.g. Vaughn) per riding.

And in the hotly contested 2013 general elections in Malaysia, the populist-ethnic PKR party (led by Anwar Ibrahim) received the majority of the popular vote (approximately 5.6 million votes or 50.9 percent), whereas the establishment BN party, headed by PM Najib Razak, garnered approximately 5.25 million votes or 47.3 percent of the popular vote. Nonetheless, as a result of Malaysia's rather odd electoral system, the BN managed to secure 133 seats (60 percent) in the 222-seat parliament, with only 89 seats won by the PKR.

In short, the political effects of constitutional design, even in stable democracies let alone in more tumultuous settings, are significant to say the least. And as I suggested earlier, the origins of the deep cleavages that require constitutional engineering to mitigate them often have little to do with public law per se. Whether the focus of comparative constitutional design is on academic scholarship in its own right or on a practical level of global good-doing, it must closely engage the social sciences to remain a viable intellectual enterprise.

(iv) The actual effects of jurisprudence: social rights as a parable

The study of constitutional jurisprudence seems limited, absent study of its actual capacity to induce real, on-the-ground change, either independently or in association with other factors.

Here, too, social science research may prove useful for assessing constitutional law's impact at both the macro and micro levels. Without doubt, the sweeping worldwide convergence toward constitutional rights and judicial review has brought about tremendous advances—real and symbolic—in the legal protection and public awareness of basic rights and liberties. The entire procedural justice domain, in particular criminal due process and the rights of accused, has undergone a tectonic shift in the past few decades that may be attributed to a large extent to judicial activism and rights jurisprudence that extends from the "Warren Court" era to the more recent jurisprudence of the European Court of Human Rights. And these shifts have certainly entrenched in the public mind the notion that there is far more to democracy than mere adherence to the majority-rule principle. Indeed, the effects of the elimination of formal, de jure discrimination against historically disenfranchised groups have been nothing short of transformative. This observation is reinforced by the rich ethnographic literature within the law and society scholarship on "soft law" and the "everyday life" or "on the ground" effects of rights, in particular with respect to litigation-oriented activism by equality-seeking groups.[87]

That said, the sort of simple and sweeping claims often heard in the popular media about the supposedly unequivocally positive effects of the constitutionalization of rights ought to be taken with a grain of salt. First, even a cursory look at relevant data suggests that the supposed correlation between courts and judicial review as independent variables and democracy as a dependent one may not be nearly as organic and natural as it has been portrayed by proponents of the canonical view. Sweden, Finland, Norway, and Denmark—four of the most developed and prosperous nations on Earth—have long adhered to social democracy while being less than enthusiastic (to put it mildly) about the American notion of rights and judicial review. Norway, for example, deferred giving human rights explicit constitutional protection until 1994. In Finland, substantive judicial review of legislation was explicitly forbidden prior to 2000, while in Denmark and Sweden nontechnical judicial review has seldom been practiced. The Danish Supreme Court has set aside legislation only once (the *Tvind Case* from 1999) in the past 160 years, and the Danish Constitution is silent on the issue. The picture is similar in Sweden. In the Nordic region, then, a combination of well-established, *ex ante* parliamentary preview and restrained *ex post* judicial review has proven effective in mitigating the counter-majoritarian difficulty embedded in excessive judicial review and in ensuring an alternative, non-juristocratic way of protecting rights.[88] And this has hardly come at the expense of civil liberties in these countries. In all of the international human rights watchdog reports—those of Amnesty International, Human Rights Watch, and their various counterparts—the sections on alleged human rights violations in each of the Scandinavian countries are slim to non-existent. The status of individual freedoms in the Netherlands—one of the European countries that, until recently, had stringently opposed the idea and practice of judicial review—has certainly not been lower than in the United States, which has had more than two centuries' use of a

---

[87] See, e.g., Michael McCann, *Rights at Work: Pay Equity Reform and the Politics of Legal Mobilization* (University of Chicago Press, 1994).

[88] See Ran Hirschl, "The Nordic Counter-Narrative: Democracy, Human Development and Judicial Review," *International Journal of Constitutional Law* 9 (2011): 449–69.

widely celebrated Bill of Rights and two centuries of active judicial review. As Robert Dahl skeptically observed 25 years ago: "No one has shown that countries such as the Netherlands or New Zealand, which lack judicial review, or Norway and Sweden, where it is exercised rarely and in highly restrained fashion, or Switzerland where it can be applied only to cantonal legislation, are less democratic than the United States, nor, I think could one reasonably do so."[89]

The Human Development Index (HDI) produced by the United Nations Development Programme (UNDP) is a widely recognized metric that combines standardized measures of life expectancy, literacy, educational attainment, and GDP per capita for countries worldwide. HDI is used to rank countries by level of "human development" on a scale of 0 to 1 (based on a complicated yet reliable formula). The most recent Human Development Report (2013) ranks Norway at the top with a score of 0.955, followed by Australia, the United States, the Netherlands, Germany, New Zealand, Ireland, Sweden, Switzerland, Japan, Canada, South Korea, Hong Kong, Iceland, and Denmark (0.901). With the exceptions of Japan (where there is humble constitutionalism and limited judicial review) and the United States (where there is extravagant constitutionalism and great judicial visibility), none of the world's most populated countries is among the world leaders in terms of human development. Mexico, Nigeria, Brazil, Indonesia, Bangladesh, and Pakistan, not to mention India and China, have made strides but still do not excel in terms of HDI. In addition to moderate population size and stable electoral processes, the winning formula in terms of HDI appears to include the existence of a developed market economy and centralized planning that cherishes public investment in science, education, and health care. A large middle class and a well-developed civil society—precisely what the Nordic countries exemplify—are key societal factors. And what is the net impact of each country's approach to the constitutional status of rights and judicial review? Quite negligible, frankly.

Data on the legal profession—another area of inquiry that is often ignored in constitutional law scholarship—shows the relation, or lack thereof, between the size and nature of a country's legal profession and its level of democracy. As of 2011, Israel leads the world in number of attorneys relative to population size, with 585 lawyers per 100,000

---

[89] Robert Dahl, *Democracy and Its Critics* (Yale University Press, 1989), 189.

residents. To pick two other examples, Sweden has 45 lawyers per 100,000 people, and Scotland a modest five lawyers per 100,000 people. Israel is certainly not the most democratic of these three polities judged by most conventional parameters. Similarly, Ireland (a stable democracy), as of 2011, has seven judges per 100,000 residents, whereas Russia (the reader is free to label the Putin regime as she sees fit) has 3.5 times as many (24) per 100,000 people. These figures may lead one to several possible conclusions: either courts and lawyers are not an essential building block of a democratic polity, or more democracy equals less courts (or vice versa), or—barring those possibilities—there is no readily apparent correlation between the number of lawyers and judges in a polity and its level of democracy. At any rate, no plausible reading of the data supports the "more courts equal more democracy" argument.

Perhaps more important for our discussion, the simple distinction between de jure discrimination that may be addressed by courts and de facto social and economic gaps that are widening but not justiciable is often blurred in "pure" legal analysis. Empirical sociologists and democratic theorists alike argue that the de facto "political constitution" is more significant than the formal one in shaping the common good and the overall human condition.[90] A considerable body of research in comparative politics, sociology, and public policy suggests that there are important extrajudicial factors that explain the cross-jurisdictional variance in the actual realization of constitutional rights and in the implementation of landmark court rulings pertaining to those rights.[91]

The comparative constitutional discourse on social rights provides one illustration of the puzzling disconnect between the study of rights and the study of realities in comparative constitutional law. Of the world's approximately 195 written constitutions, roughly three-quarters make reference to a right to education, and nearly half to a right to health care. Most written constitutions also include a generic protection of "the right to life" or of "human dignity" and several key regional and international human rights regimes protect a variety of subsistence rights. Interestingly, some courts (e.g. the Supreme Court

---

[90] See, e.g., Dahl, *Democracy and Its Critics* (n 89); and more generally, Robert Putnam, *Making Democracy Work: Civic Traditions in Modern Italy* (Princeton University Press, 1993).

[91] See, e.g., Donald Horowitz, *The Courts and Social Policy* (Brookings Institution Press, 1977); Gerald Rosenberg, *The Hollow Hope: Can Courts Bring About Social Change?* (University of Chicago Press, 1991); Charles Epp, *The Rights Revolution Lawyers, Activists, and Supreme Courts in Comparative Perspective* (University of Chicago Press, 1998).

of India) have interpreted the right to life such that it imposes positive obligations on the state to provide material necessities to the impoverished, while others (e.g. the Supreme Court of Canada) have consistently held that such rights do not entail a right to subsistence, often notwithstanding the near identical wording of the relevant constitutional provisions: Article 21 of the Constitution of India ("No person shall be deprived of his life or personal liberty except according to procedure established by law"), for instance, is very similar to section 7 of the Canadian Charter of Rights and Freedoms ("Everyone has the right to life, liberty and security of the person and the right not to be deprived thereof except in accordance with the principles of fundamental justice"). What explains the differing approaches courts take to these rights, or the fact that the social rights jurisprudence of certain constitutional courts (e.g. those of South Africa or Colombia) has undergone dramatic transformation even though the pertinent constitutional text has remained unchanged?

In Canada, to dwell on that example a bit longer, an inexplicable gap exists between the polity's long-standing commitment to a relatively generous version of the Keynesian welfare state model and the outright exclusion of subsistence social rights from the purview of rights provisions. During national and provincial election campaigns, Canadians consistently refer to health care as the public policy issue about which they care the most. Moreover, the existence of a viable, publicly funded health-care system is repeatedly cited by Canadians as one of the most important and distinctive markers of Canadian collective identity, and as a crucial difference between their own country and their neighbor to the south. The Canada Health Act enjoys near-sacred status in public discourse, as was reiterated by the overwhelming public reaction to the landmark Supreme Court of Canada ruling in *Chaoulli v. Quebec (Attorney General)* concerning the provision of private health-care services in Quebec.[92] And not too far behind health care on the list of public priorities are issues such as education, child care, welfare benefits, and affordable housing—all of which fall under the umbrella of subsistence rights. Yet, subsistence social rights are not protected by

---

[92] *Chaoulli v. Quebec (AG)*, [2005] 1 SCR 791 [Canada]. The court ruled that limits on the delivery of private health care in Quebec violated Quebec's Charter of Human Rights and Freedoms. Three of the judges also ruled that the limits on private health care violated section 7 of the Charter of Rights and Freedoms. The decision could have significant ramifications on health-care policy in Canada and may be interpreted as paving the way for a "two-tier" health-care system.

the Charter and have been altogether excluded from its purview by Supreme Court of Canada jurisprudence. According to former Chief Justice Lamer in *R v. Prosper*, "it would be a very big step for this court to interpret the Charter in a manner which imposes a positive constitutional obligation on governments."[93] By a 5:4 decision, the Court held in *Gosselin v. Quebec (Attorney General)*[94] that the "right to security of the person" does not guarantee an adequate level of social assistance by the state. In her majority opinion, Chief Justice McLachlin stated that section 7 restricts the state's ability to deprive people of their right to life, liberty, and security of the person but does not place any positive obligations on the state. And it was not until its ruling in *Health Services v. British Columbia* in 2007, after 20 years of a neo-liberal approach to the matter, that the Court recognized that the right to collective bargaining is protected by the Charter.[95] In other words, it would appear that it is the "political constitution," not the legal one, that protects social and economic rights in Canada.

And the list of apparent oddities does not end here. In South Africa—until recently a poster child of supposedly progressive constitutional protection of social and economic rights following the adoption of a new, liberal constitution in 1995—the Gini coefficient (which represents equality/inequality in the income distribution of a nation's residents) has actually gone up from 0.566 (1995) to 0.631 (2009), with a staggering 0.674 in 2006. Likewise, the actual provision of education, health care, and housing varies dramatically across the world even when pertinent constitutional protection factors are held to be equal. For example, the impressive improvements in alleviating poverty in Brazil since former president Lula took office in 2003 have been achieved without any constitutional reform and with a constitutional jurisprudence no more progressive than that in the pre-Lula years.[96]

---

[93] [1994] 3 SCR 236 [Canada], para. 31.

[94] [2002] 4 SCR 429 [Canada].

[95] *Health Services and Support-Facilities Subsector Bargaining Assn v. British Columbia*, [2007] 2 SCR 391 [Canada].

[96] In fact, some research has suggested that Brazilian social rights jurisprudence has actually hindered the realization of these rights by siphoning government funds away from pro-poor initiatives in order to satisfy court-ordered pharmaceutical provision that disproportionately benefits the middle and upper classes; see Virgilio Afonso da Silva and Fernanda Vargas Terrazas, "Claiming the Right to Health in Brazilian Courts: The Exclusion of the Already Excluded?," *Law and Social Inquiry* 36 (2011): 825–53; Octávio Luiz Motta Ferraz, "Harming the Poor through Social Rights Litigation: Lessons from Brazil," *Texas Law Review* 89 (2010): 1643–68. For an alternative view, see Mariana Mota Prado, "The Debatable Role of Courts

What might explain this? Might it be that, unlike the constitutional sphere, government policy—shaped by political factors—matters a great deal when it comes to the realization of socioeconomic rights? We need to ask: which countries have fared better or worse than others in the actual provision of welfare rights, and why? How much of the variance is explained by differences within the constitutional domain versus other factors such as a given society's political market or ideational outlook, its state capacity, its history of welfare provision, and its international political economy concerns? These key "how and why" questions cannot be answered simply by looking at constitutional provisions, social rights jurisprudence, and a few landmark rulings.

Nonetheless, much of comparative constitutional law scholarship on the subject focuses almost exclusively on a few landmark rulings from South Africa, Colombia, or India as supposed indicators of the new and more generous approach toward social rights in those countries, and of how jurisprudence should look in other, closer-to-home polities. Almost no attention has been paid by constitutional scholars to factors that may explain the variance in judicial interpretation of socioeconomic rights provisions or the divergence in the actual distributive consequences of social rights regimes. In the world of comparative social rights jurisprudence, there are no macroeconomic doctrines, fiscal realities, political interests, legacies of welfare provision, elections, or patterns of executive–judiciary relations. Very few studies have been devoted to the actual potential of constitutional courts in different settings to advance pro-poor, redistributive policies.[97] In order truly to understand the status of social rights, a thicker, more holistic approach is required, one that goes beyond idealist normative accounts or insular case law discourse to understand social rights as part of a larger matrix of public policy, economics, and politics, constitutional and otherwise.[98] A close look at the vast political economy literature on

---

in Brazil's Health Care System: Does Litigation Harm or Help?" *Journal of Law, Medicine and Ethics* 41 (2013): 124–37.

[97] For a commendable exception, see Daniel Brinks and Varun Gauri, *Law's Majestic Equality? The Distributive Impact of Litigating Social and Economic Rights* (The World Bank Development Research Group, 2012).

[98] Ran Hirschl and Evan Rosevear, "Constitutional Law Meets Comparative Politics: Socio-Economic Rights and Political Realities," in Tom Campbell et al., eds., *The Legal Protection of Human Rights: Sceptical Essays* (Oxford University Press, 2011), 207–28; Avi Ben-Bassat and Momi Dahan, "Social Rights in the Constitution and in Practice," *Journal of Comparative Economics* 36 (2008): 103–19.

the welfare state and its varieties would be a natural starting point.[99]
Either way, collaboration, dialogue, mutual awareness, and cross-reference
between comparative constitutional law and comparative politics are
essential to yielding a complete account of social rights in theory and
in practice.

(v) Comparative constitutional law's amorphous methodological matrix

A fifth reason to take a close look at the social sciences is that comparative constitutional law's methodological matrix is fuzzy and
amorphous at best. In contrast, the social sciences, despite (or perhaps
because of) having bitter debates about approaches and methods, have
developed a rich and sophisticated framework for guiding serious
comparative work.[100] A more in-depth look at social science methods
could suggest a toolkit of methodological considerations that should be
addressed in the conduct of comparative constitutional inquiry, thus
effectively supporting various types of comparative constitutional studies, qualitative and quantitative, inference-oriented or hermeneutic. It
may also disperse some of the mist (from the standpoint of the legal
academia) surrounding basic concepts such as participant observation,
content analysis, selection bias, interaction effects, statistical significance, spurious correlation, or intervening variables.

There is no a priori analytical reason why the study of comparative
constitutional law could not engage in a more explanation-oriented
mode of scholarship.[101] Using comparative research to explain variance
among legal phenomena across polities was the main objective of
legal sociology's founding fathers. Explanation, as opposed to mere

---

[99] For an overview of this vast body of literature, see Torben Iversen, "Capitalism and
Democracy," *Oxford Handbook of Political Economy* (Oxford University Press, 2006), 601–23.

[100] On the possibility of a unified logic of causality in the shadow of this plurality, see John
Gering, *Social Science Methodology: A Unified Framework* (Cambridge University Press, 2012);
Gary King et al., *Designing Social Inquiry: Scientific Inference in Qualitative Research* (Princeton
University Press, 1994); John Gering, "Causation: A Unified Framework for the Social
Sciences," *Journal of Theoretical Politics* 17 (2005): 163–98; Henry Brady and David Collier,
eds., *Rethinking Social Inquiry: Diverse Tools, Shared Standards* (Rowman & Littlefield, 2004);
Alexander L. George and Andrew Bennett, *Case Studies and Theory Development in the Social
Sciences* (MIT Press, 2005); Lee Epstein and Gary King, "The Rules of Inference," *Chicago
Law Review* 69 (2002): 1–93; Judea Pearl, *Causality: Models, Reasoning, and Inference* (Cam-
bridge University Press, 2009).

[101] For a discussion of the possibility of pursuing explanatory accounts in pure legal and
constitutional theory, see Nicholas Aroney, "Explanatory Power, Theory Formation, and
Constitutional Interpretation: Some Preliminaries," *Australian Journal of Legal Philosophy* 38
(2013): 1–31, in particular 24–9.

description or taxonomy, has long been a main objective of evolutionary and functionalist approaches to legal transformation. Deriving explanations from comparisons across jurisdictions, time, or institutions is common in subfields of legal scholarship such as law and development, law and economics, and the emerging trend toward empirical legal scholarship. Moreover, the judge's main skills are assessing evidence, weighing probabilities for conviction or acquittal purposes, and ultimately rendering a verdict. This is, in essence, a causality-oriented exercise.

To be perfectly clear: there is little doubt that the high-quality comparative public law scholarship produced over the past two decades has contributed tremendously not only to the mapping and classification of the world of new constitutionalism, but also to the creation of conceptual frameworks for studying comparative law more generally. Indeed, we must not underestimate the importance of concept formation through "multiple description" of the same phenomenon in various settings. We acquire a far more complex, nuanced, and sophisticated understanding of what, for example, solids or mammals are by studying the variance and commonality among exemplars within their respective categories.[102] Comparative constitutional inquiries' embedded cosmopolitanism and genuine curiosity about the constitutive laws of others is therefore a major methodological asset. Nonetheless, a key distinguishing mark of scientific inquiry is making valid inferences that go beyond the particular observations collected. Because of its traditional lack of attention to principles of research design, controlled comparison, case selection, and hypothesis testing, comparative constitutional law scholarship, its development in recent years notwithstanding, often fails to engage in theory-building of this type.

In fact, precisely because the concern with the a-systematic "cherry-picking" of "friendly" examples (often raised by opponents of comparative inquiry) may not be easily dismissed, scholars who wish to engage in valuable comparative work ought to pay close attention to social science research methods, and the philosophy of comparative social inquiry more broadly. The response to the cherry-picking

---

[102] Indeed, it is well known that Charles Darwin's expedition to the Galapagos Islands on the *Beagle* (1832–36) was initially driven by a modest attempt to collect and identify new species of plants and animals unknown to scholars in 19th-century Europe. Darwin's various findings also served as the basis for his *Origin of Species*—and the development of one of the most influential theories of the modern era.

concern is not to abandon comparative work; rather, it is to engage in comparative work while being mindful of key methodological considerations. (I devote the next two chapters to a detailed elaboration of these considerations, and how they may be addressed and put to work for the benefit of general theory-building in comparative constitutional inquiry).

An often cited hurdle to generalizable theory in comparative constitutional law is the difficulty of stepping outside the institutional, political, and doctrinal context. Without attention to contextual details, it is argued, important nuances and idiosyncrasies are easily lost.[103] Avid contextualists, culturalists, and postmodernists go as far as suggesting that no purportedly "naturalistic" or "scientific" methods of analysis may be applied to the study of law to begin with, much like they may not be applied to the study of a given literary or theological text. It may indeed be a daunting task to "[u]nderstan[d] what someone wrote or thought in a different culture long ago, or what his social practices meant to him."[104] And more generally, even if we ignore the time issue, law remains an essentially man-made textual enterprise and thus, contextualists maintain, only a deep hermeneutic interpretation of a concrete legal text and what it meant to its authors and audiences can unveil its true meaning. That interpretation, in turn, will inevitably bear the intellectual fingerprints of its interpreter and of what Heidegger famously termed the "fore-structure of understanding." In short, the contextualist argument goes, full generalizability in comparative constitutional law is very difficult and perhaps even outright impossible to achieve. What is more, given the contextualized nature of the enterprise, it may not be a suitable goal to begin with.

There is, no doubt, justification for this concern, which I explore in greater detail in Chapter 5. While an argument that one must master a certain medieval Tuscan dialect to be able to grasp and appreciate the depth of Dante's *Divine Comedy* or of Machiavelli's *The Prince* seems extreme, variance among world literatures remains significant. Likewise, convergence processes notwithstanding, there no doubt remains significant variance in the constitutional history, law, and jurisprudence of countries worldwide. But this does not mean that

---

[103]   This is, in a nutshell, the argument advanced in Mark Tushnet, "Interpreting Constitutions Comparatively: Some Cautionary Notes, with Reference to Affirmative Action," *Connecticut Law Review* 36 (2004): 649–63.

[104]   See Ronald Dworkin, *Law's Empire* (Harvard University Press, 1986), 422 fn 15.

serious comparative work can be of no benefit. Even social anthropology—arguably the most contextual and hermeneutic discipline in the social sciences—attempts to produce generalizable insights regarding human development and behavior that are based on, but ultimately transcend, detailed ethnographies. A favorite example is Richard Lee's meticulous ethnographic work on patterns of food-gathering and consumption among the !Kung San in the Kalahari.[105] Lee's work led to the expansion of the homo-economicus thesis to the least likely of settings, and ultimately to a paradigm shift in our understanding of the economic and political organization of hunter-gatherer societies. Likewise, the intriguing Sapir–Whorf hypothesis, which suggests that language structures affect thought and cognition, originally emanated from Edward Sapir's ethnographic work on the Inuit languages of northern Canada and Benjamin Lee Whorf's work on the Hopi Native American language.[106] In other words, even the most in-depth, single-case-study works may, and in fact often do, carry theoretical insights that travel well beyond the specific setting studied.

Outside this, context is surely more significant to a study of the transition from childhood to adolescence in early 20th-century New Guinea (Margaret Mead), patterns of reciprocity in remote Melanesian islands (Bronisław Malinowski), or magic rituals among the Nuer of southern Sudan (E. E. Evans-Pritchard)—to name but three ethnographic classics—than it is to studies of popular phenomena such as mass media, air traffic, professional sports, scientific discoveries, or modern constitutionalism. In other words, the more universal and widespread certain norms (e.g. constitutional supremacy), practices (e.g. proportionality analysis), and concepts (e.g. "human dignity") become, the less convincing or significant the contextualist concern may become. It may thus be argued, for example, that while each individual language or dialect is in many respects unique or idiosyncratic, what makes a great scientific discovery is the development and substantiation of a core common element or general linguistic principle that applies to many or all languages (e.g. Chomsky's theory of generative grammar or universal structure of languages). As Margaret Mead once said: "Always remember that you are absolutely unique, just like everyone else."

---

[105] See, e.g., Richard B. Lee, *The !Kung San: Men, Women, and Work in a Foraging Society* (Cambridge University Press, 1979).

[106] See, e.g., Benjamin Lee Whorf, "Some Verbal Categories of Hopi," *Language* 14 (1938): 275–86.

Conclusion

In this chapter I developed the case for greater incorporation of social science insights into the systematic study of constitutions across time and space, emphasizing the field's focus on comparative government prior to its extensive "juridification" over the past several decades, as well as the essential contribution of theory and evidence from contemporary comparative politics to the understanding of the origins of constitutions and judicial review, the prospects of constitutional design, patterns of constitutional court behavior, and the effect of constitutional structures beyond the courtroom.

Comparative constitutional law professors will continue to hold a professional advantage in their ability to identify, dissect, and scrutinize the work of courts, or to critically assess the persuasive power of a given judicial opinion. No one is better positioned than comparative constitutional law professors to evaluate constitutional texts, trace patterns of convergence alongside persisting divergence in constitutional jurisprudence across polities, or advance the research on how constitutional courts interact with the broader, transnational legal environment within which an increasing number of them operate.[107] But theorizing about the constitutional domain as part of the outer world requires more than that. Many of the tools necessary to engage in the systematic study of constitutionalism across polities can be found in the social sciences in general, and political science in particular. Maintaining the disciplinary divide between comparative constitutional law and other closely related disciplines that study the same set of phenomena does not stand up to scrutiny. It artificially limits the scope, depth, and breadth of the questions we can address, the choice of methods we make, and the kind of accounts we can offer.[108]

---

[107] A recent commendable illustration for such work is Wojciech Sadurski, *Constitutionalism and the Enlargement of Europe* (Oxford University Press, 2012).

[108] Here I concur with Armin von Bogdandy's call for "pluralisation" of disciplinary identities. In defending such trends in the context of the largely formalistic European legal academia, von Bogdandy argues that "empirical, theoretical, and critical examination of the law but also essayistic speculation, are needed for a vibrant discipline. Such scholarship cannot limit itself to doctrinal terminology but needs to employ research interests, concepts, theories, and methods from other disciplines and must be linked to larger cultural debates. This pluralization has a transforming character: It follows that scholarship is no longer shaped by a single, so-called 'legal method.' This new approach will in turn transform the disciplinary identity, i.e. what it means to be a scholar and what one is expected to do in order to become

The need for scholars of comparative government to understand the constitutional vocabulary of the polities they study is as urgent as it has ever been. Politics pursued through constitutional law has its own vernacular, and is distinct from politics pursued through electoral campaigns, diplomacy, or war.[109] As the political significance of constitutional law and courts increases and the extensive judicialization of politics and policy-making continues, there is now hardly any major moral dilemma or political controversy that, to paraphrase Alexis de Tocqueville, does not sooner or later become a judicial one. Any aspiring legislators, policymakers, and social activists must master the art of making good *constitutional* arguments. The ability to grasp modes of legal reasoning, and to appreciate constitutional histories and interpretive legacies that are deeper than any particular constitutional court ruling, is essential to comparative constitutional inquiry, whether practical or theoretical.

At the same time, the study of comparative constitutional law must open up to the social sciences. The constitutional universe is wider than the text itself or the traces of it that appear in high court jurisprudence. There is much more to comparative constitutional inquiry than interpretive methods or judicial reasoning, fascinating as these facets of the field are. The time has come to go beyond selective accounts of specific provisions, inward-looking jurisprudential debates, or detailed analyses of a handful highly regarded court rulings (comparative constitutional *law*) toward a more holistic approach to the study of constitutions across polities (comparative constitutional *studies*) that appreciates the tremendous descriptive depth and explanatory potential of the social sciences with respect to the constitutional universe. The intellectual foundations of such an approach are already in place; indeed, a close look at the "cosmology" of comparative constitutional studies as reflected in the seminal works of many of its grandmasters, past and present, indicates that comparative constitutionalism as an area of inquiry is at its best when it crosses disciplinary boundaries with respect to both substance and method.

one." See Armin von Bogdandy, "National Legal Scholarship in the European Legal Area—A Manifesto," *International Journal of Constitutional Law* 10 (2012): 614–26, 624.

[109] Mark Graber, *A New Introduction to American Constitutionalism* (Oxford University Press, 2013), 71–86.

5

How Universal is Comparative Constitutional Law?

"All cases are unique and very similar to others."

T. S. Eliot (*The Cocktail Party*)

In this chapter and the next, I attempt to disperse some of the mist surrounding comparative constitutional studies' epistemological and methodological matrix. To that end, I draw attention to core questions concerning the current state of that matrix, and outline a series of considerations that should be addressed in the conduct of comparative constitutional inquiry. The discussion proceeds in two main parts. I begin the discussion in this chapter by elucidating some of the existential tensions that have characterized comparative constitutional studies from the dawn of the 20th century onward, focusing on the debate between contextualists and universalists and its implications for core methodological considerations such as case selection and research design. I will revisit this debate again in the next chapter by contrasting the approach taken by legal academics and political scientists to the same sets of comparative constitutional phenomena. Whereas some core distinctions of comparative inquiry (e.g. the distinction between contextualism and universalism) have crossed disciplinary boundaries, others (e.g. the distinction between a focus on formal rules and a focus on behavioral patterns) have been neatly demarcated along disciplinary lines.

In the second part of this chapter, I address what I term the "World Series" syndrome of comparative constitutional law: the pretense that insights based on the constitutional experience of a small set of "usual suspect" settings—all prosperous, stable constitutional democracies of the "global north"—are truly representative of the wide variety of constitutional experiences worldwide, and constitute a "gold standard" for understanding and assessing it. The question here is this: how truly "comparative" or generalizable is a body of knowledge that seldom draws on or refers to the constitutional experience, law, and institutions of the global south? What are we to make of supposedly universal insights that are constructed by focusing mainly (and often solely) on a very small fraction of the world's constitutions? My aim is to unpack and evaluate the various claims raised by proponents of this "global south" critique of comparative constitutional law, and to assess the relevance of these claims to the epistemological and methodological challenges of comparative constitutional inquiry.

A key concern is the very definition of the term *comparative*. As we have seen, in the field of comparative constitutional law (and comparative law more generally) the term "comparative" is often used indiscriminately to describe what, in fact, are several different types of scholarship: (i) freestanding, single-country studies—often quite detailed and "ethnographic" in nature—that are characterized as comparative by virtue of dealing with a country other than the author's own (as any observer is immersed in their own (constitutional) culture, studying another constitutional system involves at least an implicit comparison with one's own); (ii) genealogies and taxonomic labeling of legal systems; (iii) surveys of foreign law aimed at finding the "best" or most suitable rule across cultures; (iv) references to the laws or court rulings of other countries aimed at engendering self-reflection through analogy and contrast; (v) concept formation through multiple descriptions of the same constitutional phenomena across countries; (vi) normative or philosophical contemplation of abstract concepts such as "constitutional identity," "transnational/supranational/global constitutional order," etc.; (vii) careful "small-N" analysis of one or more case studies aimed at illustrating causal arguments that may be applicable beyond the studied cases; and (viii) "large-N" studies that draw upon multivariate statistical analyses of a large number of observations, measurements, data sets, etc. in order to determine correlations among pertinent variables. These last two purport to draw upon controlled comparison and inference-oriented case-selection principles in order to assess change, explain dynamics, and make inferences about cause and effect. With a few notable exceptions, the study of comparative constitutional law by legal academics has focused on a small set of supposedly representative court rulings, while generally lagging in its adherence to the inference-oriented case-selection and research-design standards employed by social scientists who engage in "small-N," "large-N," or "multi-method" research on constitutional law and courts.

Granted, this conceptual fuzziness around the term "comparative" is not unique to comparative law; it is quite prevalent in other "comparative" disciplines, from comparative literature to comparative religion.[1] Some comparative disciplines (comparative psychology is a good example) are more methodologically rigorous than comparative law, although even in these disciplines there is some ambiguity as to what qualifies as truly *comparative* work.[2]

A few existential tensions

Since its birth, comparative law has struggled with questions of identity: whether it is a method of inquiry or a substantive discipline, whether and how to move beyond descriptive accounts of the laws of others toward explanatory accounts that suggest why, how, and when laws change or evolve, and how to account for the dynamic between increasing global convergence and the enduring divergence of the world's legal systems. Unsurprisingly, the field of comparative law has excelled in self-reflection and, often, self-lamentation.[3] Most of

[1] E.g. a sample issue of *Comparative Literature* (a leading journal in that field) featured articles such as: David Quint, "The Genealogy of the Novel from the *Odyssey* to *Don Quijote*," *Comparative Literature* 59 (2007): 23–32—a genealogical study; Ilya Kliger, "Anamorphic Realism: Veridictory Plots in Balzac, Dostoevsky, and Henry James," *Comparative Literature* 59 (2007): 294–315—"concept formation" through multiple description; and Vivasvan Soni, "Trials and Tragedies: The Literature of Unhappiness: A Model for Reading Narratives of Suffering," *Comparative Literature* 59 (2007): 119–39—an attempt to develop an explanatory model.

[2] A sample issue of the *Journal of Comparative Psychology* (a leading journal in that field) features articles with a variety of "comparative" elements to them, such as: Anna Wilkinson et al., "Spatial Learning and Memory in the Tortoise (*Geochelone carbonaria*)," *Journal of Comaprative Psychology* 121 (2007): 412–18; Jan Langbein et al., "Learning to Learn During Visual Discrimination in Group Housed Dwarf Goats (*Capra hircus*)," *Journal of Comparative Psychology* 121 (2007): 447–56; Anthony Wright and Jeffrey Katz, "Generalization Hypothesis of Abstract-Concept Learning: Learning Strategies and Related Issues in Rhesus Monkeys (*Macaca mulatta*), Capuchin Monkeys (*Cebus apella*), and Pigeons (*Columba livia*)," *Journal of Comparative Psychology* 121 (2007): 387–97; or Carole Parron and Joël Fagot, "Comparison of Grouping Abilities in Humans (*Homo sapiens*) and Baboons (*Papio papio*) with the Ebbinghaus Illusion," *Journal of Comparative Psychology* 121 (2007): 405–11.

[3] A few notable examples are: James Gordley, "Is Comparative Law a Distinct Discipline?," *American Journal of Comparative Law* 46 (1998): 607–15; John Reitz, "How to Do Comparative Law," *American Journal of Comparative Law* 46 (1998): 617–36; George Fletcher, "Comparative Law as a Subversive Discipline," *American Journal of Comparative Law* 46 (1998):

the writings that have contributed to this are abundant with sophisticated analysis and highbrow jargon but ultimately do not feature a
particularly attractive substance-to-ink ratio. They do, however, reflect
the intellectual cul-de-sac in which traditional, encyclopedic, taxo-
nomic-style, or legal families-based comparative law is stuck. A recent
article went as far as to suggest that comparative law is not, and never
will be, a distinctive academic discipline.[4]

The objective of the landmark congress held in Paris in July 1900 by
the Société Française de Législation Comparée was "to seek to provide
the science of comparative law with the precise model and the settled
direction it requires if it is to develop."[5] Over a century later, that
direction remains very much unsettled. Although intellectual interest
in the laws and legal institutions of other countries has been growing
steadily in recent years, surprisingly little has changed with respect to
the basic epistemology and methodology of comparative law. We still
find that much of the canonical contemporary comparative law scholarship replicates the formalistic and largely descriptive or taxonomic
approach to comparative legal scholarship carried out a century ago,
although there is a growing body of critical work from within the
discipline.[6] All too often, knowledge is still pursued and presented as it
was back in the 1920s and 1930s by scholars like John Wigmore,
Roscoe Pound, Walther Hug, and Herman Kantorowicz.[7] Today,

683–700; Geoffrey Samuel, "Comparative Law and Jurisprudence," *International and Comparative Law Quarterly* 47 (1998): 817–36; James Gordley, "Comparative Legal Research: Its
Function in the Development of Harmonized Law," *American Journal of Comparative Law* 43
(1995): 555–67; Pierre Legrand, "Comparative Legal Studies and the Matter of Authenticity,"
Journal of Comparative Law 1 (2006): 365–460.

[4] Stephen Smith, "Comparative Legal Scholarship as Ordinary Legal Scholarship," *Journal
of Comparative Law* 5 (2011): 331–56.

[5] Georges Picot and Fernand Daguin, "Circulaire," in *Congrès International de Droit
Comparé, Procèc-Vebaux des Sèances et Documents*, vol. 1 (LGDJ, 1905), 7–8.

[6] See, e.g., Günter Frankenberg, "Critical Comparisons: Re-thinking Comparative Law,"
Harvard International Law Journal 26 (1985): 411–55; Annelise Riles, ed., *Rethinking the Masters
of Comparative Law* (Hart Publishing, 2001); Pierre Legrand and Roderick Munday, eds.,
Comparative Law: Traditions and Transitions (Cambridge University Press, 2003); Peer Zum-
bansen, "Comparative Law's Coming of Age? Twenty Years after *Critical Comparisons*,"
German Law Journal 6 (2005): 1073–84; Ugo Mattei, "Comparative Law and Critical Legal
Studies," in Mathias Reimann and Reinhard Zimmermann, eds., *The Oxford Handbook of
Comparative Law* (Oxford University Press, 2006), 815–36.

[7] See, e.g., John H. Wigmore, *Panorama of the World's Legal Systems* (West, 1928); Roscoe
Pound, "The Revival of Comparative Law," *Tulane Law Review* 5 (1930): 1–16; Walther
Hug, "The History of Comparative Law," *Harvard Law Review* 45 (1932): 1027–70; Herman
Kantorowicz, "Some Rationalism about Realism," *Yale Law Journal* 43 (1934): 1240–53.

the distinctions between foreign and comparative law remain unclear to many, as do the distinctions between description, taxonomy, and explanation. Much comparative legal literature is still pursued through a traditional case law approach or learned classifications of legal "traditions," "origins," and the like.[8] Over 150 years after its inception, tracing genealogies and the classification of legal systems is still a main organizing principle of virtually all leading textbooks on comparative law.

It is not uncommon to encounter in comparative law journals articles that engage in a predominantly encyclopedic pursuit of knowledge, without much attention to theoretical innovation per se. (Clearly, many articles, certainly those published in the discipline's leading journals, do not fit that description). Some of these pieces are single-country studies characterized as comparative only because they deal with a country other than the author's own. Others subscribe to Konrad Zweigert and Hein Kötz's description of the essence of the comparative inquiry as the comparing of "one's own home system" to a "foreign system of law."[9] While very informative and certainly helpful in developing a better understanding of one's own or of other legal systems, these works seldom amount to an inherently holistic and naturalistic, "thick description" of the sort advocated in social or legal anthropology.[10] The still-prevalent thread of taxonomic scholarship results in multi-tome legal genealogies that resemble 19th-century expositions of newly discovered flora and fauna, some of which focus on pseudo-exotic settings.[11] Other works are preoccupied with a quest to find the evolution of a given legal concept, or to determine the most efficient rule in order to suggest a "best practice" in a given area.[12]

---

[8] A paradigmatic example of this type of comparative scholarship is H. Patrick Glenn's classic and authoritative, now in its 4th edition, *Legal Traditions of the World: Sustainable Diversity in Law* (Oxford University Press, 2010).

[9] Konrad Zweigert and Hein Kötz, *An Introduction to Comparative Law* (3rd edn, Oxford University Press, 1998), 32.

[10] See Clifford Geertz, "Thick Description: Toward an Interpretive Theory of Culture," and "Deep Play: Notes on the Balinese Cockfight," in *The Interpretation of Culture* (Basic Books, 1973).

[11] An example of this type of comparative scholarship is John H. Barton et al., *Law in Radically Different Cultures* (West, 1983).

[12] An illustration of this way of thinking about comparative law is provided in Bernhard Grossfeld, *Core Questions of Comparative Law* (Carolina Academic Press, 2005).

At the heart of comparative constitutional law's blurred epistemo-logical and methodological matrix is the tension between universalism and particularism. This may take the form of fundamental disagreements among US Supreme Court justices about the status of foreign law as a valid point of reference for interpreting the US Constitution,[13] but is more vividly reflected in the different approaches to comparative con-stitutional scholarship taken by those favoring expansive "country stud-ies" or other forms of *idiographic* knowledge (the prevalent mode of comparative constitutional law scholarship to date) and those who seek to produce more generalizable conclusions or other forms of *nomothetic*, presumably objective and transportable knowledge.

The debate between "universalists," who emphasize the common elements of legal systems across time and place, and "particularists" (or "culturalists") who emphasize the unique and idiosyncratic nature of any given legal system, has long characterized comparative law. This divide is clearly illustrated by the debate concerning "legal transplants." Universalists such as Alan Watson contend that inter-country pollin-ation, borrowing, or migration of legal ideas has been a key element of legal change throughout history regardless of the concrete political, social, or cultural context in the "receiving" legal order.[14] Watson challenges the Montesquieuian view that law is a local phenomenon linked to the living conditions of a given society. Against this, Watson argues that in most cases legal rules are not peculiarly reflective of the particular society in which they operate. Legal borrowing (or "trans-plants" of rules, institutions, or doctrines) occurs primarily because existing law in a given polity is not in touch or in concert with current social or economic needs. As systemic needs evolve, critical gaps in existing laws call for completion, more often than not through bor-rowing. (This pattern reappears in different historical moments, as elucidated in Chapters 1 to 3).

On the other hand, "culturalists" (e.g. Pierre Legrand, David Nelken, Csaba Varga) take a position that is not qualitatively different than that expressed in Friedrich Nietzsche's famous maxim (*Notebooks*, 1886) "there are no facts, only interpretations." These interpretations,

---

[13] See, e.g., Antonin Scalia and Stephen Breyer, "A Conversation between Justices," *International Journal of Constitutional Law* 3 (2005): 519–41. See also the discussion in Chapters 1 and 3.

[14] See, e.g., Alan Watson, *Legal Transplants: An Approach to Comparative Law* (Scottish Academic Press, 1974).

in turn, depend on "culture"—understood by Legrand as "the frame-work of intangibles within which an interpretive community operates, which has normative force for the community . . . and which, over the *longue durée*, determines the identity of a community as community."[15] The culturalist–relativist position suggests that since law is a complex cultural and linguistic construct, a given polity's laws are inevitably reflective of that polity's shared history, culture, and aspirations.[16] Legal rules in any given polity reflect its cultural habitus, that is, its distinctive mode of understanding reality (the "legal mentalité" that defines the frame of perception and understanding of a legal community, accord-ing to Legrand), as well as its shared, deeply embedded historical experience. Thus, "importation" of legal constructs may occur in a superficial or technical form, but is not in any substantive way reflective of the receiving polity's authentic legal evolution. With respect to comparison, the meaning of the culturalist–relativist position is that neutral or objective comparison is virtually impossible; inevitably, similarity and difference are dependent on the observer's subjective standpoint or perspective and thus cannot be measured on an absolute scale. The role of the comparativist is thus not to draw general con-clusions about law across time and space, but to focus on understanding the deep contextual structure of a given legal culture, to decipher its "legal mentalité" and how that mentality is embedded in a specific context.

(The reader may think here of similar divisions in very different domains: think international corporate headquarters with a good grasp of the big picture versus small-town branch managers with an intimate acquaintance of individual customers. Similarly, recent baseball movies such as *Moneyball* (starring Brad Pitt) and *Trouble with the Curve* (starring Clint Eastwood) focus on the tension in professional sports scouting between sophisticated statistical analyses or predictive models, which are supposedly unaffected by clichés, common biases, and predisposi-tions, and "old fashioned" scouts who lack this element of objectivity but bring to the table a deep understanding of the game, years of on-the-ground experience, and a "gut feeling" about certain players' talents and promises).

---

[15] Pierre Legrand, *Fragments on Law-as-Culture* (Kluwer, 1999), 27.

[16] See, e.g., Pierre Legrand, "European Legal Systems Are Not Converging," *International and Comparative Law Quarterly* 45 (1996): 52–81.

In the social and human sciences, the debate over epistemology and methods has been largely aligned along the positivism/relativism divide, with each camp developing its own research agendas, methods, acceptable types of evidence, and explanatory goals. The issues and claims informing this debate are complex and many. The hierarchy implied by the alignment of the positivist and nomothetic approaches, and its implied suggestion that contextual research is only useful insofar as it generates testable hypotheses, is one of the main bones of contention in contemporary social science. Ultimately, however, the trade-off seems to be between breadth and depth, with an accompanying claim by relativists that unlike in the core sciences, key determinants of human behavior or social processes are non-quantifiable, measurable, or even observable to begin with, and so the dependence of positivist research on actual observations makes it an inherently limited approach for studying politics and society. While certain branches of the human sciences (e.g. social psychology) express a clear preference for positivism and scientific, inference-oriented experiments, other disciplines (e.g. social anthropology) have remained committed to relativist, contextual, mostly qualitative scholarship. (This is not meant to suggest in any way that social anthropology lacks scientific rigor. Quite the contrary. In fact, Franz Boas, whose work spawned modern anthropology, is well known for applying the scientific method to the study of human cultures and societies, and for his rejection of the formulation of grand theories based on anecdotal and often unrepresentative knowledge). The epistemological and methodological matrix of some social sciences, most notably political science and sociology, have in effect been split into a quantitative hemisphere and a qualitative one.

In normative constitutional theory that addresses comparative matters, the tension between particularism and universalism is reflected in the different visions of the current "meta-constitutional" structure. At the contextual end stand *constitutional sovereigntists* who see the national demos as the ultimate constitutional sovereign; suggest that domestic constitutional traditions and institutions are unique and inherently more authentic than any external legal (or constitutional) order; and portray global law as lacking in legitimacy and moral authority, as suffering from chronic democracy deficit, and as imposing a certain set of moral values and policy preferences on national states.

At the universal end, stand *global constitutionalists* who stress the significance of universal values (e.g. human dignity or the right to be free of torture or inhuman treatment), and the importance of supra-national legal norms and quasi-constitutional regimes that commit and in effect subordinate national constitutional orders to an overarching cosmopolitan legal framework. When domestic constitutional orders "go astray" or become overly insular, transnational rights regimes may and often do function as a welcome force of progressive humanism. Some universalists have gone as far as suggesting that a given country's very constitutional legitimacy depends not only on the democratic quality of, and approach to rights in, its domestic constitutional prac-tices, but also on "how the national constitution is integrated into and relates to the wider legal and political world."[17] Proponents of this position emphasize what they see as the taming power of such a regime and its human-rights-oriented aspirational and ideational commit-ments, while significantly downplaying if not altogether overlooking the non-trivial economic and political interests in promoting supra-national legal and constitutional orders that often increase standardiza-tion yet weaken democratic voice and national fiscal autonomy.

The multi-layered, fragmented structure of the emerging pan-European constitutional framework has given rise to a third camp—constitutional pluralists. Building on the German Federal Constitutional Court's articulation of dual (EU and German) constitutional authority in its famous Maastricht Case decision (1993), proponents of this view describe a reality of, and provide normative justification for, a post-national, multi-focal constitutional order (at least with respect to the distribution of constitutional authority in Europe) in which there is no single legal center or hierarchy, and "where there is a plurality of institutional normative orders, each with its functioning constitution."[18]

---

[17] Mattias Kumm, "Constitutionalism and the Cosmopolitan State," *Indiana Journal of Global Legal Studies* 20 (2013): 605–28. Kumm argues, in a nutshell, that "the drawing of state boundaries and the pursuit of national policies generate justice-sensitive externalities that national law, no matter how democratic, cannot claim legitimate authority to assess." Whatever one might think of Kumm's substantive argument, it is fair to say that he is unlikely to be elected governor of Texas on this sort of platform.

[18] Neil MacCormick, *Questioning Sovereignty: Law, State, and Nation in the European Commonwealth* (Oxford University Press, 1999), 104. See, generally, Nico Krisch, *Beyond Constitutionalism: The Pluralist Structure of Postnational Law* (Oxford University Press, 2010). For a recent variant on this position, see Vlad Perju, "Cosmopolitanism in Constitutional Law," *Cardozo Law Review* 35 (2013): 711–68. For critiques of "constitutional pluralism," see J. H. H. Weiler, "Prologue: Global and Pluralist Constitutionalism: Some Doubts," in Gráinne de Búrca and J. H. H. Weiler, eds., *The World of European Constitutionalism* (Cam-bridge University Press, 2011), 8–18; Martin Loughlin, "Constitutional Pluralism: An

In comparative constitutional jurisprudence, the debate between universalists and particularists has taken a somewhat different direction, focusing on the tension between supranational norms (e.g. gender equality or reproductive freedoms) and local traditions (e.g. Ireland or Poland's Catholic heritage). An effective illustration is the heated debate concerning the legitimacy of voluntary judicial reference to foreign sources (discussed in detail in Chapter 1), where proponents of the practice stress the *jus cogens*-like nature of certain constitutional norms and the universality of the human condition more generally, while its opponents stress the incompatibility of some such "external" norms with a given nation's unique constitutional identity and heritage.

The tension between local traditions and purportedly general values commonly manifests itself in legal battles concerning the cultural defense in criminal law or dilemmas of reasonable accommodation under a multicultural constitutional framework. It is vividly evident in the jurisprudence of trans- or supranational quasi-constitutional entities such as the European Court of Human Rights (ECtHR) and the Court of Justice of the European Union. In 2009, to pick one example, the ECtHR overruled Bosnia and Herzegovina's consociational power-sharing arrangements in the case of *Sejdić and Finci v. Bosnia*, finding in favor of two applicants (one Roma, the other Jewish) who challenged the provision of the Bosnian Constitution restricting certain political offices to members of the three "constituent peoples" (Bosniaks, Croats, and Serbs) to the exclusion of "Others."[19] The ECtHR held that the constitutional restrictions on "Others" standing for office violated the European Convention's prohibition on discrimination in Article 14. In so doing, the Court assigned greater weight to general principles of equality than to a highly politicized and

---

Oxymoron?," *Global Constitutionalism* 3 (2014): 9–30. Hybrids of global trends and local values and traditions have emerged outside the European context. A good example is the idea of "Confucian constitutionalism" in Asia. See, e.g., Tom Ginsburg, "Confucian Constitutionalism: Emergence of Constitutional Review in Korea and Taiwan," *Law and Social Inquiry* 27 (2002): 763–99; Chaihark Hahm, "Conceptualizing Korean Constitutionalism: Foreign Transplant or Indigenous Tradition?," *Journal of Korean Law* 1 (2001): 151–96; Chaihark Hahm, "Ritual and Constitutionalism: Disputing the Ruler's Legitimacy in a Confucian Polity," *American Journal of Comparative Law* 57 (2009): 135–203; Ngoc Son Bui, "Beyond Judicial Review: The Proposal of the Constitutional Academy," *Chinese Journal of Comparative Law* (2013): 1–35.

[19] *Sejdić and Finci v. Bosnia and Herzegovina*, Application Nos. 27996/06 and 34836/06 (ECtHR, Grand Chamber, judgment of Dec. 22, 2009) [Council of Europe].

contextualized multiethnic power-sharing pact that was reached following the vicious Bosnian war of 1992–95.[20]

In *Lautsi v. Italy* (2011)—to pick another ruling that vividly illustrates the tension between cosmopolitan theory and local traditions in comparative constitutional jurisprudence—the Grand Chamber of the ECtHR rejected the human rights claim of a Finnish-born mother residing in Italy who objected to the display of religious symbols (crucifixes) in her sons' public school.[21] Rather than requiring state schools to observe confessional neutrality, the Court upheld the right of Italy to display the crucifix, an identity-laden symbol of the country's majority community, in the classrooms of public schools.[22] Using the margin-of-appreciation concept, Europe's highest human rights court held that it is up to each signatory state to determine whether to perpetuate this (majority) tradition. The crucifix was taken to be so central to Italian collective identity that it was up to Italians themselves to decide on its status. Unlike the ECtHR ruling *Sejdić and Finci v. Bosnia* that gave priority to universal principles over local arrangements, the ECtHR's ruling in *Lautsi v. Italy* gave precedent to the particular over the universal, in part by ruling that in the EU context there was no "universal" line on the matter.

Interestingly, the Grand Chamber's hearing of the *Lautsi* case provided a stage for a poetical climax in the tension between universalism and particularism in comparative constitutional jurisprudence: Professor Joseph Weiler's pro bono intervention on behalf of eight European governments that opposed a ban on the display of crucifixes in Italian

---

[20] For a passionate critique of the ruling, see Christopher McCrudden and Brendan O'Leary, *Courts and Consociations* (Oxford University Press, 2013).

[21] *Lautsi and Others v. Italy*, Application No. 30814/06 (ECtHR, Grand Chamber, judgment of Mar. 18, 2011) [Council of Europe].

[22] In an earlier decision in this case, the Italian Consiglio di Stato interpreted the crucifix as a religious symbol when it is affixed in a place of worship, but in a non-religious context like a school. It was defined as an almost universal symbol (from the perspective of the majority) capable of reflecting various meanings and serving various purposes, including "values which are important for civil society, in particular the values which underpin our constitutional order, the foundation of our civil life. In that sense the crucifix can perform—even in a 'secular' perspective distinct from the religious perspective specific to it—a highly education symbolic function, irrespective of the religious professed by the pupils" (*Lautsi*, 2011, para. 16). No less revealing, the Italian administrative court ruled that: "it is easy to identify in the constant central core of Christian faith, despite the inquisition, despite anti-Semitism, despite the crusades, the principles of human dignity, toleration, and freedom, including religious freedom, and therefore, in the last analysis, the foundations of the secular State" (quoted in *Lautsi*, 2009, para. 30).

classrooms. Weiler is one of the greatest comparativists of our generation—a prominent academic, president of the European University Institute (EUI) in Florence, editor-in-chief of the *International Journal of Constitutional Law* and the *European Journal of International Law*, and one of the founding fathers of the study of the emerging pan-European constitutional order. His versatile work in comparative public law best captures the intellectual zeitgeist of, and the tensions embedded in, the age of global constitutionalism.

Arguing skillfully before a transnational constitutional tribunal that he deeply respects and has studied thoroughly, Weiler eloquently maintained that no consensus exists throughout Europe with respect to the accommodation of religious symbols in the public sphere. In France, a strict policy of secularism (laïcité) has long been in place; in Poland and Malta, Catholicism has been a part of the collective identity; in Scandinavia, the Evangelical Lutheran Church is the "state church"; in England, the monarch is "Supreme Governor" of the Church of England and "Defender of the Faith"; and the national flags of quite a few European countries, from Sweden to Switzerland and from Greece to Georgia, feature a Christian cross. In the face of such multiplicity, Weiler suggested, the ECtHR ought to avoid imposing a one-rule-fits-all policy on all Council of Europe member states (with their combined 800 million strong population), and ought instead to defer to local values and traditions. In short, the default in no-consensus situations should be a preference for national constitutional sovereignty.

Either way, neither contextualists nor universalists have a monopoly over the "right" or "correct" approach to comparative constitutional inquiry. Proponents of universalism tend to overemphasize cross-national similarities, while advocates of contextualism tend to over-emphasize differences. Although they reach diametrically opposed conclusions, both sides seem to overstate their case. Neither side's arguments work equally well across the board. From an empirical standpoint, there are areas of constitutional law (e.g. basic rights) where contextualist concerns may be less powerful (and hence comparisons are more beneficial) as opposed to other areas (say, polity-specific aspirational goals or organic features of a constitution) where idiosyncrasies and contingencies may have more of a bite. Nevertheless, due to broad economic, technological, and cultural convergence processes; the dramatically improved availability of comparative constitutional jurisprudence; and the growing number of constitutional "engineers" ready to hop on a plane to any of the four corners of the world to provide expert advice as to how to draft a constitution—jurisprudential cross-fertilization and the globalization of certain aspects of constitutional law more generally seem inevitable.[23] However idiosyncratic or rooted in local traditions and practices a given polity's constitutional law may be, it is unavoidably more exposed to such global influences.[24] As Vicki Jackson suggests, jurists, scholars, and policymakers must accept that constitutional law, in the United States and elsewhere, now operates in an increasingly transnational legal environment of international treaties and supranational human rights, trade, and monetary regimes.[25] The outcome of this new reality is what may be poetically described as "difference in similarity," or alternatively, "similarity within difference."

Clearly, an old water well and the concept of infidelity are hardly comparable. But a duck and a stork are. To restate my University of Toronto colleague Catherine Valcke's powerful point, comparability requires unity *and* plurality.[26] Plurality is essential as there is not much sense in comparing things that are perfectly identical; little would be gained by such a comparison. Likewise, there is hardly any utility in comparing things that share little or nothing in common (e.g. a shiitake mushroom and a sewing machine) other than some highly abstract or random attributes (e.g. both are objects, words, or things that begin with the letter S). Contrary to the old saying, apples and oranges share enough in common yet are sufficiently different from each other to be fruitfully (think about it . . .) compared.[27] By contrast, the analytical or theoretical yield of comparing two mid-size broccoli florets (too

---

[23] Mark Tushnet, "The Inevitable Globalization of Constitutional Law," *Virginia Journal of International Law* 49 (2009): 985–1006.

[24] Greater exposure does not necessarily translate into acceptance. It may engender instead a "reactive" response *against* such influences, as we have seen in Chapter 2. Originalism in American constitutional law is arguably a contemporary example of this pattern at work. Even a reactive pattern is not simply an expression of a pure unalloyed culture, so much as the result of a cross-fertilization that has already occurred. On the pattern of "reactive culturalism," see Ayelet Shachar, *Multicultural Jurisdictions: Cultural Differences and Women's Rights* (Cambridge University Press, 2001), 35–44.

[25] See, generally, Vicki Jackson, *Constitutional Engagement in a Transnational Era* (Oxford University Press, 2010).

[26] Catherine Valcke, "Comparative Law as Comparative Jurisprudence—The Comparability of Legal Systems," *American Journal of Comparative Law* 52 (2004): 713–40, 720–1.

[27] Valcke, "Comparative Law as Comparative Jurisprudence" (n 26). For an actual chemical comparison of apples and oranges (they turn out to be quite similar), see Scott Sandford, "Apples and Oranges—A Comparison," *Annals of Improbable Research* 1 (1995).

similar), or a broccoli floret and a manual transmission gearbox (too different) is not likely to be high.

It is undisputed that a considerable convergence of constitutional structures, institutions, texts, and interpretive methods has taken place over the past few decades. At the same time, few constitutional norms are truly universal.[28] The increased constitutional similarity alongside patterns of persisting divergence opens up new comparative horizons. To follow the metaphor, it presents us with an orchard filled with ripe apples and oranges, different yet similar and, most importantly, perfectly suitable for comparison. With the exception of uber-totalitarian North Korea and a small handful of other outlier polities, there is copious similarity alongside sufficient degrees of difference in the world of new constitutionalism to allow for some productive comparison, at least in theory. As I shall argue in Chapter 6, the sensibility and rationality of such comparisons boil down to the concrete perimeters of any given comparison, the scope and nature of the substantive claim they purport to advance, and whether the case-selection criteria deployed is properly tailored to suit the theoretical or empirical question a given comparative study is set to address.

The "World Series" syndrome and the "global south" critique

Turning to the literature as it stands, one is compelled to ask how truly "comparative" a field is when its canon draws principally on the constitutional experience of half a dozen (on a good day) politically stable, economically prosperous, liberal democracies? Is this (or should it be) a concern? Should it qualify or limit the applicability of canonical scholarship, perhaps even requiring an "epistemic break" within comparative legal studies, in order to provide "equal discursive dignity to non-European-American traditions"?[29] Or does it merely point to the relativism of lessons that are purportedly universal?

---

[28] See Zachary Elkins, Tom Ginsburg, and Beth Simmons, "Getting to Rights: Treaty Ratification, Constitutional Convergence, and Human Rights Practice," *Harvard International Law Journal* 54 (2013): 61–95.

[29] Upendra Baxi, "The Colonial Heritage," in Pierre Legrand and Roderick Munday, eds., *Comparative Legal Studies: Traditions and Transition* (Cambridge University Press, 2003),

As any North American sports fan knows, the finals of Major League Baseball is called "The World Series." This is a rather pretentious and presumptuous title. The league includes 30 teams, 29 of which are based in the United States, with the remaining team (the Toronto Blue Jays) based in Canada. The vast majority of players come from either the United States or one of a handful of Central American nations. Odd, then, that this final is called, of all possible titles, the *World* Series. Informing this choice of title is an attitude that—to borrow from a famous charity song—"We are the World."

This "World Series" syndrome is certainly not limited to baseball. How many comparative accounts of constitutional law in Cameroon, Paraguay, or the Gambia can the readers of this book recall seeing of late? Chances are, not many. This, in a nutshell, is the essential question posed by the "global south" critique of comparative constitutional law's intellectual foundations: how universal, representative, or generalizable are the lessons of a body of knowledge that seldom draws on or refers to constitutional experience, law, and institutions in over 95 percent of the constitutional universe (at present comprising of approximately 200 national constitutions, hundreds of sub-national unit constitutions, and several supranational quasi-constitutional regimes, not to mention a large number of past constitutions, thousands of constitutional amendments, and hundreds of thousands of constitutional court rulings)? From this, other questions follow. Does the selective "northern" (or "western") emphasis in comparative constitutional law qualify or limit the applicability or value of canonical scholarship in the field? (Answer: it hinges on the concrete question being asked). Might it be that the focus on the constitutional "north" betrays not only certain epistemological and methodological choices, but also a normative preference for some concrete set of values the constitutional north is perceived to uphold? (Answer: yes, certainly!) In the following pages I unpack these issues. I begin by presenting the core contentions of the global south critique, before turning to assess some of its methodological implications for comparative constitutional studies.

50; cited in Robert Blitt, "The Bottom Up Journey of 'Defamation of Religion' from Muslim States to the United Nations: A Case Study of the Migration of Anti-Constitutional Ideas," *Studies in Law, Politics and Society* 56 (2011): 121–211.

(i) The "global south" critique

The divide between the global north and the global south is commonly linked to the global socioeconomic and political divide, a divide once commonly expressed in the slightly pejorative terminology of "first world" versus "third world" and now often expressed in terms of the "developed world" versus the "developing world." The global north as a geopolitical reference point is taken to include North America, most of Europe, and parts of Oceania (Australia, New Zealand) and East Asia (Japan), whereas the global south habitually refers to Africa, Latin America, and much of Asia and the Middle East. Although there are no formal definitions of the "north" and "south," the understanding is that countries in the global north generally sport higher levels of democracy, government capacity and accountability, economic development, and human development (e.g. as measured by United Nations Development Programme (UNDP) human development indices). Membership in several global organizations reflects this divide: the countries in the global north are commonly classified by the International Monetary Fund (IMF) as having an "advanced" economy, rather than a "developing" economy as in much of the south. All nations in the G7 are located in the global north; of the 34 members (as of early 2014) of the Organisation for Economic Co-operation and Development (OECD), only four (Chile, Israel, Mexico, Turkey) are not located in regions associated with the global north.

In international political economy literature, the acronym BRICS is often used to refer to an association of five major emerging nations (Brazil, Russia, India, China, and South Africa) that are newly industrialized, fast-growing, and very large in scale both population-wise (over 3 billion people combined) and economically (a combined nominal GDP of over $17 trillion per annum). The BRICS countries and their smaller counterparts—think Singapore, Hong Kong, and Taiwan—are increasingly difficult to place on a dichotomous north/south matrix of socioeconomic and political development. But these fuzzy north/south boundaries notwithstanding, there is no doubt that there remain considerable differences between Switzerland and Swaziland in terms of key socioeconomic, political, and human development parameters.

Thus, a common argument raised in debates about global justice is that inequality between life opportunities in the global north and in the global south is increasing, and that the wealthy northern nations do not do enough to deal with problems such as "Third World" debt, global climate change, mass forced relocation, natural disaster relief, ethnic cleansing, the AIDS epidemic, or extreme poverty. Those who put forward the global south critique commonly point to the underrepresentation, marginalization, or exclusion of the south and the corresponding apathy, disregard, and paternalism demonstrated by the north, with these latter tendencies perhaps informed by the legacies of colonialism, imperialism, racism, Eurocentrism, and fear of the "Other."[30]

The privileging of the global north and the view that it upholds the most advanced and most desirable set of values and practices is as common in comparative legal and constitutional inquiry as it is in economic or political development circles. As David Trubek and Mark Galanter argued in 1974 in their pivotal "Scholars in self-estrangement" essay, the set of ideas known as "law and development" is built on the questionable assumption that American law, and Western law more generally, can be exported abroad to catalyze legal and economic development.[31] The field, they argue, is more an adjunct to development policy organizations than an autonomous academic enterprise. Law and development initiatives, they claim, often amount to little more than the transplanting of legal concepts from the global north into the global south. Others have argued that "law and development" evolved, at least in part, in the context of the Cold War and in alignment with the Western interest in promoting a certain breed of political and economic order in the developing world.[32]

---

[30] There is also a growing body of scholarship within international law that raises some similar concerns and traces the genealogy of the field as both constituting and constituted by the history of colonialism, imperialism, and the inequalities that followed. See, e.g., Antony Anghie, *Imperialism, Sovereignty, and the Making of International Law* (Cambridge University Press, 2004); Anne Orford, ed., *International Law and its Others* (Cambridge University Press, 2006); Brado Fassbender and Anne Peters, eds., *The Oxford Handbook of the History of International Law* (Oxford University Press, 2012).

[31] David Trubek and Mark Galanter, "Scholars in Self-estrangement: Some Reflections in the Crisis in Law and Development Studies," *Wisconsin Law Review* 4 (1974): 1062–104. See also Kevin Davis and Michael Trebilcock, "The Relationship between Law and Development: Optimists versus Skeptics," *American Journal of Comparative Law* 56 (2008): 895–946; Brian Tamanaha, "The Lessons of Law-and-Development Studies," *American Journal of International Law* 89 (1995): 470–86; Brian Tamanaha, "The Primacy of Society and the Failure of Law and Development," *Cornell International Law Journal* 44 (2011): 209–48.

[32] See Jedidiah Kroncke, "Law and Development as Anti-comparative Law," *Vanderbilt Transnational Law Journal* 45 (2012): 477–555. See also, Jedidiah Kroncke, "An Early Tragedy of Comparative Constitutionalism: Frank Goodnow and the Chinese Republic," *Pacific Rim Law and Policy Journal* 21 (2012): 533–90.

A similar epistemic vision also informs the comparative constitutional economics literature. As is well known, Max Weber suggested that from a legal standpoint, the West had a key advantage in the early development in European societies of formal–rational legal systems alongside rational systems of political authority. The resulting constellation of formal and rational structures and norms provided fertile ground for the development of capitalism. In a similar fashion, Douglass North and Robert Thomas argued that efficient economic organization is the key to growth; the development of a rational economic organization in Western Europe accounts for the rise of the West, suggesting that the lack of such organization may be responsible for backwardness in other parts of the world.[33] "Efficient organization," they argue, "entails the establishment of institutional arrangements and property rights that create an incentive to channel individual economic effort into activities that bring the private rate of return close to the social rate of return ... [I]f a society does not grow, it is because no incentives are provided for economic initiative."[34] The West's rationality and efficiency have led it to adopt legal mechanisms that enhance investors' trust, most notably the constitutional protection of property rights, which in turn has led to economic growth in various historical contexts.

Along roughly similar lines, it may be argued that while the "constitutional design" literature has been traditionally focused on fostering values such as "democracy" or "stability" in deeply divided, post-conflict, or post-authoritarian polities, the vast majority of which happen to be in the global south, it has seldom taken the widening socioeconomic gaps, growing anti-immigrant sentiment, or deep democratic deficits within North America or Europe as challenges that may be remedied through constitutional "engineering" promoted by external actors (as occurred in Afghanistan in 2004 and Iraq in 2005, and to a large extent half a century earlier in Japan). This literature, too, rests on an assumed exportability of key Western constitutional concepts and ideals to troubled and often idiosyncratic settings.

The concept of "human rights" has also drawn its fair share of criticism by advocates of a distinct global south version of human

---

[33] Douglass North and Robert Thomas, *The Rise of the Western World: A New Economic History* (Cambridge University Press, 1973).

[34] North and Thomas, *The Rise of the Western World* (n 33), 2–3.

rights.[35] The traditional account of human rights outlines three categories or generations of rights: civil and political rights; economic,
social, and cultural rights; and collective rights. However, Upendra
Baxi, among others, challenges this conceptualization, arguing that it
presents human rights in a Western-centric manner. Baxi suggests
instead that human rights are the product of real, on-the-ground
human struggles against suffering and that they should therefore be
viewed as consisting of two generations: modern and contemporary.[36]
The modern era of human rights was characterized by the use of
international law to perpetuate human suffering through colonialism
and other hegemonic practices. During that era, only a small subset of
human beings was considered worthy of international law's protection,
with others deemed to be mere heathens and barbarians.[37] The contemporary era is characterized by a more individual-focused and universal conception of human rights. The categorization of human rights,
argues Baxi, should be based not on a sterile "functionality" but rather
on the political context in which they emerged and developed. Moreover, human rights discourse should first and foremost be interpreted
and used to further the interests of the worst-off.

   Christine Schwöbel forcefully argues that global constitutionalism
discourse (which she conceptualizes as part of international law theory),
and perhaps canonical international law theory more broadly, is marred
by significant omissions and biases "caused by investment in a particular
kind of political practice and thought, namely the unquestioned
extrapolation of liberal democratic precepts, poorly suited for global
constitutional purposes."[38] The theory of global constitutionalism, she
argues, falsely assumes universality, is heavily premised upon Western
conceptions and structures of law, and fails to account for local constitutional realities. Schwöbel advocates a more organic approach to
global constitutionalism (again, understood as part of international
law) that would take account of local needs and ideas, treat global

[35]   See, e.g., Upendra Baxi, *The Future of Human Rights* (3rd edn, Oxford University Press,
2012); William Twining, "Human Rights, Southern Voices: Francis Deng, Abdullahi
An-Na'im, Yash Ghai, Upendra Baxi," *Review of Constitutional Studies* 11 (2005): 203–79;
Samuel Moyn, *The Last Utopia: Human Rights in History* (Harvard University Press, 2010).

[36]   See Twining, "Human Rights, Southern Voices" (n 35), 258–74.

[37]   A particularly (in)famous example of this pattern at work is found in James Lorimer, *The
Institutes of the Law of Nations: A Treatise of the Jural Relations of Separate Political Communities*
(William Blackwood and Sons, 1883).

[38]   Christine E. J. Schwöbel, "Organic Global Constitutionalism," *Leiden Journal of International Law* 23 (2010): 529–53, 529.

constitutionalism as an inescapably political domain, and void it of fixed, quasi-universal, one-size-fits-all content.

Similarly, James Tully has advanced a vision of constitutional democracy as an "empire of uniformity"—a modern form of imperialism that sanctifies impartiality and sameness, disregards genuine cultural diversity, and assumes an embedded right, perhaps even a duty, to convert everyone to its values and perspective.[39] According to Tully, constitutional democracy sees itself as a force of reason against what it portrays as irrational, different (as in the "Other"), "ethnic," "radical," and everything else that does not subscribe to the mainstream liberal vision of the modern. The global spread of constitutional democracy, Tully argues, is not always voluntary, and often follows what in earlier days was perceived as a "right of the self-proclaimed civilized imperial powers to extend colonial and international modern constitutional regimes around the world correlated with a 'sacred duty to civilize' the indigenous peoples under their rule."[40]

Writing within the field of comparative law, authors such as Werner Menski suggest that a close look at some global south polities (in his discussion, India), may show that due to their colonial legal heritage and long history of ethnic and religious diversity, these countries' legal frameworks, in particular personal status laws, are better equipped for dealing creatively with today's dilemmas of multiculturalism and diversity than most Western countries that adhere to stricter legal uniformity. Yet, Menski writes, "non-Western legal systems and concepts have been systematically belittled over the past centuries"; although there has been an increased awareness of legal systems beyond Europe, the rethinking "remains shackled by 'white' colonial presuppositions."[41]

With respect to comparative constitutional law per se, the northern selection bias seems even more engrained. The constitutional experiences of entire regions—from sub-Saharan Africa to Central America and Eurasia—remain largely a *terra incognita*, understudied and generally overlooked. While there are widespread scholarly accounts of constitutional matters in a handful of "usual suspect" settings that are mainly of the Western, liberal-democratic breed, the constitutional

---

[39] See James Tully, *Strange Multiplicity: Constitutionalism in an Age of Diversity* (Cambridge University Press, 1995); James Tully, "Modern Constitutional Democracy and Imperialism," *Osgoode Hall Law Review* 46 (2008): 461–93.

[40] James Tully, "Modern Constitutional Democracy and Imperialism" (n 39), 484.

[41] Werner Menski, "Beyond Europe," in Esin Örücü and David Nelken, eds., *Comparative Law: A Handbook* (Hart Publishing, 2007), 191–216, 191.

experience, law, and institutions elsewhere—say, in Indonesia (population 250 million), Pakistan (185 million), Nigeria (160 million), Bangladesh (155 million), Mexico (120 million), the Philippines (100 million), or Vietnam (90 million)—is seldom even referred to, let alone thoroughly studied, in mainstream European or North American comparative constitutional scholarship. How many comparative accounts of constitutional law in Russia (the most populous country in Europe and Eurasia) or Brazil (population 200 million, the second most populous country in the Americas, and the host nation of the 2014 World Cup and the 2016 Summer Olympics) immediately come to readers' minds, let alone countries like Botswana (the most prosperous economy in Africa) or Kazakhstan (larger in size than the entirety of Western Europe)? Very few, I would guess. The unfortunate yet inevitable result of this is that purportedly universal insights concerning constitutions and constitutionalism are based, more often than not, on a handful of frequently studied and not always representative settings or cases.

A small number of recent monographs and edited collections attempt to address this substantive gap, mainly by focusing on constitutionalism and judicial review from a regional perspective, for instance by looking at constitutionalism in Asia, in Latin America, or in Africa.[42] However, very few of the leading "state of the discipline" collections contain substantial analysis of the north/south gap as such, although some do feature chapters that address the gap indirectly by analyzing constitutions outside the global north and beyond the beaten track.[43] The "Methodologies" chapter of the *Oxford Handbook of Comparative Constitutional Law* (2012) alludes to challenges in comparative constitutional inquiry that contribute to the bias in favor of countries in the global north (e.g. language and legal education), although this point is

---

[42] See, e.g., Albert Chen, ed., *Constitutionalism in Asia in the Early Twenty-first Century* (Cambridge University Press, 2014); Tom Ginsburg and Rosalind Dixon, eds., *Comparative Constitutional Law in Asia* (Edward Elgar, 2014); Roberto Gargarella, *Latin American Constitutionalism* (Oxford University Press, 2013); "Symposium: The Changing Landscape of Asian Constitutionalism," *International Journal of Constitutional Law* 8 (2010): 766–976; and "Perspectives on African Constitutionalism," *International Journal of Constitutional Law* 11 (2013): 382–446.

[43] See, e.g., the chapters on "Islam and the Constitutional Order" and "Constitutionalism in Illiberal Polities," in *The Oxford Handbook of Comparative Constitutional Law* (Oxford University Press, 2012), and chapters on "Federalism, Devolution and Secession: From Classic to Post-conflict Federalism" and "Socio-economic Rights" in *Research Handbook on Comparative Constitutional Law* (Edward Elgar, 2011).

not made explicitly. The introductory essay in another major collection, the *Research Handbook on Comparative Constitutional Law* (2011), acknowledges the need for a broader empirical base: "It is probably the case," the editors state, "that 90% of comparative work in the English language covers the same ten countries, for which materials are easily accessible in English."[44] Leading constitutional comparativists agree. Sujit Choudhry observes that "[f]or nearly two decades," comparative constitutional law has been "oriented around a standard and relatively limited set of cases: South Africa, Israel, Germany, Canada, the United Kingdom, New Zealand, the United States, and to a lesser extent, India."[45] In his chapter in the *Research Handbook* on anti-terrorism laws, Kent Roach notes that "[c]omparative constitutional law scholarship needs to expand its horizons by examining countries beyond the usual Anglo-American axis,"[46] arguing that while India and Israel have provided fertile ground for anti-terrorism scholars, Arab states' responses to terrorism are still seldom covered in the literature. Similarly, in the introduction to his important book on the rise of judicial review in Asian democracies, Tom Ginsburg describes his attempt to expand the theoretical and empirical basis of comparative constitutional law outside its past "core areas" of the United States and Europe and notes that "[s]tudies of non-western countries have been less frequent" than studies of Western countries.[47]

Likewise, Cheryl Saunders, a prominent Australian scholar of comparative constitutional law, notes that "one [assumption] which seems obvious enough to need little justification, is that the discipline does not presently [take full account of the global experience]. Much of the discourse of comparative constitutional law," she explains, "focuses on the established constitutional systems of North America and Europe and a few outrider states with similar arrangements, based on similar assumptions."[48]

---

[44] Rosalind Dixon and Tom Ginsburg, "Introduction," in *Research Handbook on Comparative Constitutional Law* (n 43), 13.

[45] See Sujit Choudhry, "Bridging Comparative Politics and Comparative Constitutional Law: Constitutional Design in Divided Societies," in Sujit Choudhry, ed., *Constitutional Design for Divided Societies: Integration or Accommodation?* (Oxford University Press, 2008), 3–31, 8.

[46] Kent Roach, "Comparative Constitutional Law and the Challenges of Terrorism Law," in *Research Handbook on Comparative Constitutional Law* (n 43), 545.

[47] Tom Ginsburg, *Judicial Review in New Democracies: Constitutional Courts in Asian Cases* (Cambridge University Press, 2003), 15.

[48] Cheryl Saunders, "Towards a Global Constitutional Gene Pool," *National Taiwan University Law Review* 4 (2009): 1–38, 3.

Prescriptively, Saunders laments that "[o]ne consequence of the concentration on North America and Europe is that constitutional law and practice in other regions, where the majority of states is located, is not factored into mainstream comparative constitutional law and is, in effect, marginalised." She explains that "[m]arginalisation may take a variety of forms: overlooking the constitutional experience of particular states and regions; assuming their effective similarity with western constitutional systems; reserving them for specialist study by those with anthropological or sociological interests and skills."[49]

As we saw in Chapter 1, voluntary judicial reference to foreign sources tends to center on jurisprudence from a handful of constitutional peak courts. Even those outside the "club" of heavily cited courts, such as constitutional judges from Pakistan to Colombia to Uganda, cite northern jurisprudence much more often than comparable southern jurisprudence. In addition to the conceptual marginalization effect that such one-way traffic of constitutional ideas may have, overlooking constitutional experience in certain regions may also lead to the mischaracterization of certain constitutional developments in the global constitutional north as novel or groundbreaking when in fact they have already occurred in one of the many constitutional settings in the global constitutional south. In his review of David Dyzenhaus's edited collection *The Unity of Public Law* (2004), for instance, Upendra Baxi makes the following point:

The statement by David Dyzenhaus that *Baker* [a major Supreme Court of Canada ruling] "establishes for the first time in the common law world a general duty for administrative decision-makers to give reasons for their decisions and . . . imposes a reasonable standard for the criterion of evaluating the legality of exercises of official discretion" is plainly and surprisingly wrong. The Indian Supreme Court has already, and reiteratively, further with multiplier impacts in South public law jurisprudence, performed this feat ever since 1950! So has the Botswana Supreme Court in the *Unity Dow* (1992) decision. It is simply pointless to multiply instances of the global south public law juridical creativity. Surely, notions framing a "unity of public law," and oriented to a fashioning of a new *jus cosmopoliticum, at least* ought to take more fully into account the creative jurisprudence of the Commonwealth of Coloured Peoples![50]

---

[49] Saunders, "Towards a Global Constitutional Gene Pool" (n 48).
[50] Upendra Baxi, "Review of David Dyzenhaus, ed., *The Unity of Public Law*," *Law and Politics Book Review* 14 (2004): 799–804, 804.

From a methodological point of view, an exclusive focus on the global constitutional north may likewise lead to the entrenchment of misconceptions and false generalizations. Countless books and articles are devoted each year to the study of religion in the West, often with an eye to American constitutional law on religion or the accommodation of religious difference (or lack thereof) in the supposedly neutral European public sphere. The reality, however, is that even if we leave aside claims à la Charles Taylor that Western secularism has never really banished religion, as of 2014 approximately half of the world's population, perhaps more, lives in polities that do not subscribe to the Franco-American doctrine of strict structural and substantive separation of religion and state, and where religion continues to play a key role in political and constitutional life. Of this population, approximately one billion people now live in polities in which religion is strongly entrenched. In the past four decades, for instance, at least 30 of the world's predominantly Muslim polities, from Mauritania to Oman to Pakistan, have declared Shari'a (Islamic law) "a" or "the" source of legislation, meaning that all legislation must comply with principles of Islam. As recent developments in Tunisia and Egypt indicate, this type of constitutionalism is not likely to vanish following the so-called Arab Spring. In several other countries precepts of Islam have been incorporated into the constitution, penal code, and personal status laws of sub-national units, most notably in 12 Nigerian states, Pakistan's North-West Frontier Province, Indonesia's Aceh, to varying degrees in two Malaysian states, and to an increasing extent in Russia's Chechnya and Dagestan. In half a dozen Indian states, to highlight another example, harsh restrictions on conversion from Hinduism have been introduced into law by the Hindu nationalist Bharatiya Janata Party (BJP). A further billion people, perhaps more, live in countries such as Thailand where religious affiliation is a pillar of collective identity, or in countries such as Israel or Sri Lanka, where a single religion is granted preferential status.[51] Despite all this, little is known about the "other models" of governing relations between the state and religion. With

---

[51] On the resurgence of religion in world politics, see, e.g., John Micklethwait and Adrian Wooldridge, *God Is Back* (Penguin Books, 2009); Gabriel Almond et al., *Strong Religion: The Rise of Fundamentalisms around the World* (University of Chicago Press, 2003); Peter Berger, ed., *The Desecularization of the World: Resurgent Religion and World Politics* (Eerdmans, 1999); Hent de Vries and Lawrence Sullivan, eds., *Political Theologies: Public Religions in a Post-Secular World* (Fordham University Press, 2006). See, generally, Charles Taylor, *A Secular Age* (Belknap Press of Harvard University Press, 2007).

few exceptions, the world of constitutional law and religion that lies beyond the separation-of-religion-and-state paradigm has remained a "black hole" of sorts, a whole slice of the comparative constitutional law universe that is seldom explored or theorized.

Perhaps the most systematic articulation of the global south critique in comparative constitutional law is that offered by Daniel Bonilla Maldonado in his 2013 edited collection on the constitutional jurisprudence of the Supreme Court of India, the South African Constitutional Court, and the Constitutional Court of Colombia.[52] The book as a whole is a study of judicial activism outside the better known contexts of the United States and Western Europe. It compares three high-capacity courts operating in distinct political contexts but with similar problems. It shows how courts in developing countries are wrestling with newer topics like socioeconomic rights and indigenous rights. Further, it raises interesting normative questions about the judicial role. It is ultimately unclear to what extent there is a distinctive constitutional jurisprudence of the global south and, if there is, to what extent these three highly touted and sometimes West-gazing courts actually represent it—but, nonetheless, the book raises important research questions and epistemological challenges.

As a backdrop to this collection, Maldonado describes comparative constitutional law as a field that excludes the legal communities of countries outside the United States and Europe. He begins with the noncontroversial claim that there is a grammar of modern constitutionalism that circumscribes how we talk about the field, originating in European Enlightenment philosophers and currently dominated by a handful of courts and contemporary Anglo-American philosophers. The effect of this is that contributions from scholars and courts in global south countries are excluded from canonical constitutional scholarship, or at least ranked very low in its hierarchy. A main reason for this, Maldonado argues, is that those countries' legal systems are seen as merely derivative of European common or civil law systems, even where European-derived law is mixed with native legal orders. It is assumed that global south legal systems are less effective than those in the north, and that this contributes to the legal and economic underdevelopment of global south countries. Study of these systems is

[52] Daniel Bonilla Maldonado, "Introduction: Towards a Constitutionalism of the Global South," in D. B. Maldonado, ed., *Constitutionalism of the Global South: The Activist Tribunals of India, South Africa and Colombia* (Cambridge University Press, 2013), 1–37.

therefore often limited to describing their failures and prescribing improvements.

Maldonado then describes how the peak courts in India, South Africa, and Colombia have dealt with both issues that are important to all liberal democracies and with issues that have special significance in the global south. Despite their differences, India, South Africa, and Colombia share key traits: they are all diverse, unequal societies with a history of political violence and of attempts to consolidate democracy. They also each have a constitution that entrenches a panoply of rights and checks and balances, but that is juxtaposed with a weak political system, a largely impoverished population, and widespread discrimination. For Maldonado, because these challenges are all common in the global south, recounting how these courts have grappled with them is an important step in bringing the south properly into comparative constitutional law.

All told, the importance of the piercing global south critique to the understanding of the field's contemporary epistemological and methodological matrix is obvious. Indeed, it is surprising that it has not received due scholarly attention to date. More than anything else, the global south critique questions the genuineness of the "comparative" in comparative constitutional law, and poses a serious challenge to the universality and general applicability of the field's main insights. At the same time, the global south critique may plausibly be understood as advancing a number of different arguments, closely related yet dissimilar, not all of which appear to pose an equally strong or valid challenge to the comparative constitutional canon. Some unbundling of what exactly is claimed, and on what theoretical and empirical grounds, may be helpful.

(ii) Unraveling the "global south" critique

The global south critique poses at least two major challenges to contemporary comparative constitutional inquiry: (i) it highlights the obvious methodological problem with generalizing from a small and consistently unrepresentative sample, and of presenting these false generalizations as common knowledge and universal truth; and (ii) it underlines the prioritization in comparative constitutional scholarship of concepts such as liberal rights and freedoms or limits on government action, and the corresponding neglect of concepts particularly relevant to the global south, such as the realization of human development, progressive notions of distributive justice, and the enhancement of state capacity via the constitutional domain. The critique also emphasizes the stark imbalance in reporting and media attention. For example, during the same week in March–April 2013 that the US Supreme Court began hearing arguments concerning gay marriage, the Supreme Court of India released a landmark decision on the copyright of cancer and HIV/Aids drugs that may well be the most important ruling ever made by a court in the area of public health and the eradication of poverty more generally.[53] The former development preoccupied virtually all mainstream media outlets in the West even though at least a dozen Western countries, including Canada, Spain, and Portugal, had already legalized and confirmed the constitutionality of gay marriage. The Indian ruling, by contrast, despite its obvious significance, was reported in far fewer international media outlets, and even then only in a cursory fashion.

Having said that, the global south critique has analytical challenges of its own. One difficulty is over-inclusiveness, that is, the idea that the global south may reasonably be taken to refer to over 160 polities which demonstrate tremendous constitutional variance. Ultimately, it is unclear whether there is a single, unified character of the constitutional south that holds this category together, or whether it is merely useful as a rhetorical alternative—south as "non-north"—to the self-professed constitutional mainstream. In other words, the multiplicity of constitutional experiences in the global south casts doubt on whether the term refers to a single, coherent alternative to the liberal-democratic model of constitutionalism, which itself is multi-varied and nonuniform.

Consider the heterogeneity within merely one subject matter in one corner of the global constitutional south: the comparative constitutional law of religion in Asia. Asia—the birth place of many faith traditions—is not only the most populous continent, but also the most religiously diverse. Hundreds of millions follow Islam, Christianity, Hinduism, and Buddhism. Crude estimates suggest that followers of Islam account for approximately 28 percent of Asia's population (with Islam the majority religion in 26 of the 48 Asian countries); 24 percent follow Hinduism (the vast majority of them in India and Nepal); 18 percent follow varieties of Buddhism (which is the majority religion in eight countries); and the remaining 30 percent follow

---

[53] *Novartis v. Union of India and Others*, Civil Appeal No. 2706–2716 of 2013 (decision released on Apr. 1, 2013) [India].

another religion.[54] The various post-colonial legacies influencing Asia—British in India and Pakistan, French in Vietnam, Spanish in the Philippines, Portuguese in Macao and East Timor, and Dutch in Indonesia—alongside postwar (as in Japan) and post-Soviet (in the six Asian nations that were once part of the USSR) reconstruction, add another layer of complexity. It is hardly surprising that when it comes to the constitutional law of religion, Asia has it all. It sports the entire array of "religion and state" models, from India's secularism to Iran's constitutional theocracy, and from North Korea's atheism to the transplantation of the American constitutional ideas of "free exercise" and "(dis)establishment" in the predominantly Catholic Philippines.

In fact, it is hard to think of a single pertinent factor that is common to Oman (an Islamic sultanate), Laos (which features a mix of communist atheism and Buddhism), and East Timor (a predominantly Catholic new democracy) other than the classification of all three as Asian countries. This multiplicity and lack of a substantive common denominator defies attempts to identify a common "Asian" approach to constitutional law and religion, and calls into question the intellectual merit of concepts such as "Asian values" when dealing with law and religion on that continent. The lesson to be applied to the considerably broader area of the global south is obvious: given the tremendous diversity of constitutional experiences in the global south, it is difficult to see what holds this category together from an analytical standpoint other than its being contrasted with and offering a purported alternative to the north. More than anything else, the global constitutional south is essentially the global constitutional "non-north."

A second difficulty plaguing the global south concept in comparative constitutional inquiry is that it is not entirely clear what exactly is meant by the "south." At the simplest of levels, the "south" may refer to constitutional settings in the southern hemisphere. But when we move away from that basic criterion, things get considerably blurrier. The "south" may mean "non-canonical," "peripheral," "underrepresented," "marginalized," or "excluded"—that is, it may refer to constitutional settings that are not commonly analyzed or referred to in mainstream comparative constitutional law. However, by that "southness by underrepresentation" definition it is not clear why Finland or Norway are not commonly taken to be members of the constitutional

---

[54] John Esposito et al., *Religions of Asia Today* (Oxford University Press, 2011).

south, for there seem to be many more accounts of Indian or South African constitutional law in comparative perspective than of Finnish or Norwegian law. Similarly, it might seem appealing to define the constitutional south in terms of the socioeconomic distinction between the global "haves" and "have-nots," but this too is problematic. Latvia is a member of the EU which, according to the Human Development Report 2013, belongs to the group of very high human development countries. Does it truly belong to the global constitutional north? Can countries traverse these divides over time? Argentina, for instance, may have appeared more closely aligned with the north in the early 20th century than at the dawn of 21st century. Is the deeply divided Belgium, a Western country at the heart of Europe, nevertheless closer in some respects to countries struggling with similar existential dilemmas in the global constitutional south? Furthermore, if by "global south" we mean countries characterized by lesser economic development, countries such as Brazil, India, Indonesia, and South Africa—all members of the G20—are hardly authentic representatives of the global south. Perhaps "south" is meant in a linguistic sense; that is, perhaps it refers to places where English—the *lingua franca* of the global constitutional conversation—is not the language in which constitutional matters are conducted, or where constitutional matters are not conducted in *any* of the world's major languages. But does this mean that Israel or Sweden are members of the global south? Another interpretation is that the south consists of countries that were subject to colonialism and imperialism in a way that has significantly affected their constitutional domain and practice. On this account, however, it is not clear why Canada (which gained its independence from Britain in 1867 but did not cut its formal constitutional ties with the British parliament until 1982) and New Zealand (which remained a British Dominion for many years, has no single date of official independence, and abolished appeals to the Privy Council only in 2004) are not considered members of the global constitutional south, whereas Brazil (which gained its independence from Portugal in 1822, i.e. 45 years prior to Canada's independence) is. In short, when taken on its own, none of these understandings of what is actually meant by the "global south" yields a consistently sensible selection of constitutional settings.

A third difficulty with the generic global south critique is its tendency to rely on a group of supposedly "alternative" constitutional settings—most notably India and South Africa—that are anything but underrepresented in the literature. Can anyone make a serious claim that the Constitutional Court of South Africa has been understudied compared to, say, the constitutional court of Austria or Greece? Likewise, it has not been established, nor do I think it will be, that the methods of interpretation used by the South African Constitutional Court or the jurisprudential outcomes it commonly produces are substantively different than those of apex courts elsewhere, nor has it been shown that any substantive difference that does exist is attributable to South Africa's constitutional "south-ness." It may well be the case that the truest representatives of the constitutional global south are not its most studied members, but rather its silent majority, namely Guatemala, Fiji, Vietnam, Angola, and other countries that are seldom referred to in comparative constitutional studies, whose prominent jurists rarely go on lecture tours in the world's top law schools, and whose jurisprudence is almost never referenced by courts overseas or listed in syllabi for courses on comparative constitutionalism.

A common and intuitively plausible claim is that because the socioeconomic gaps in the global south are often considerably wider than those in the north, and because state capacity is, by and large, lower in the south, constitutional courts in these countries will be more inclined to intervene on behalf of the poor, or to support the constitutional recognition and progressive realization of social and economic rights. Anecdotal evidence on this matter seems to cut both ways. As we have seen in Chapter 1, a comparison that supports this proposition is a comparison between the generous interpretation of Article 21 of the Indian Constitution with respect to social and economic rights, and the restrictive interpretation of the nearly identical section 7 of the Canadian Charter of Rights and Freedoms with respect to such rights. It is plausible that the visible socioeconomic gaps in India, and the inability of the country's political sphere to close them, have something to do with the Supreme Court of India's willingness to extend relatively generous protection to socioeconomic rights. However, let us then compare Mexico and Colombia. The socioeconomic gaps in these two countries are roughly similar, and both of them would be considered as belonging to the global south—yet, there has been nearly no jurisprudence on socioeconomic rights in Mexico, and an explosion of progressive jurisprudence on such rights in Colombia. In other words, it appears that factors that are not directly related to the common characterization of these countries as members of the constitutional south account for the considerable differences in their socioeconomic rights jurisprudence.[55] The experience in South Africa also supports this idea. South Africa's constitutional jurisprudence on social and economic rights was very modest prior to the country's transition to a new constitutional order in 1995. Drawing on a new constitutional framework, the newly established South Africa Constitutional Court turned itself, in the first decade of its existence, into one of the most innovative and progressive tribunals in the world with respect to the adjudication of social and economic rights. In recent years, the Court's progressiveness on this front has declined considerably. Through all of these transformations, South Africa's "southness" remained virtually unchanged. In short, the net independent explanatory contribution of the global south factor is unclear, and at any rate may vary from one comparative setting or period to another.

As a normative and critical set of arguments that calls for greater inclusion of those once excluded settings and demands consistency in the invocation of "difference in similarity" or "similarity in difference" principles, values, and voices, the global south critique is powerful. From a methodological perspective, the invocation of the experience of the "constitutional south" is substantively useful to our understanding of a certain area of constitutionalism mainly where there is substantive difference, such that a focus on the "south" factor qualitatively expands the variance of observations on a given constitutional phenomenon, or where observations on the constitutional front (dependent variable) are similar to those witnessed in "canonical" settings despite considerable differences in key background factors (independent variables). When invoked in one of these contexts, the idea of the global south has a "black swan" effect in the sense that it debunks or at least raises doubts about the validity of an "all swans are white" generalization (no pun intended), and is useful to that extent. Where such substantive difference does not exist, however, and what is being looked at is yet another white swan just like all the others (although located elsewhere), the invocation of a "southern" example—fascinating as it may seem—adds little to theory-building as such. If we approach the global south with this in mind—which would be arguably a more analytically robust and methodologically

---

[55] For further elaboration on variance in economic and social rights constitutional provisions worldwide, see Courtney Jung, Ran Hirschl, and Evan Rosevear, "Economic and Social Rights in National Constitutions," *American Journal of Comparative Law* 62 (2014): 1043–1093.

astute approach to the idea—a given constitutional setting may belong to the global south in one context or comparative dimension but not in another, or may be relevant for some studies but not others. As we shall see in the following chapter, a similar set of considerations applies to any astute deployment of case-selection and research-design principles, whether drawing on "north" or "south" constitutional settings.

An intuitive solution to the fluidity of categories such as "the global constitutional south" is the use of problem-driven, inference-oriented controlled comparisons, whether of the small-N or large-N breed. Here, the constitutional experience of a particular country, or indeed of the global constitutional south category in itself, could be treated as relevant or irrelevant to any concrete question a given comparative study purports to address. This sort of approach would ensure that there is a rational, analytically robust connection between the research questions being asked and the observations about the global constitutional south being used to address them. Somewhat ironically (as we have seen, some global south critics argue in favor of context and qualitative analysis, and against a fallaciously unified narrative in comparative constitutionalism), a large-N research design that is often indifferent to the context and particularities of concrete cases rests on a fundamentally "egalitarian" vision that treats the constitutions of the Gambia and of the United States as two data observations of equal weight.

It may well be the only research design that systematically overcomes the north/south division in comparative constitutional studies. Paradoxically, it can do this by its tendency to ignore context, overlook many pertinent differences among countries, and by applying a unidimensional yet universal "sameness" principle to comparative constitutional analysis. If one's concern is the overrepresentation of a handful of countries at the expense of the rest of the constitutional universe, or the stratification of the world's constitutions through the construction of "platinum club" constitutional orders that are considered "important" and "serious" while other constitutional orders are taken to have considerably less (or even no) moral and theoretical value, then a large-N research design, with its "no constitution is left behind" approach, offers a potential remedy. This, then, brings us to problems of case selection and research design in comparative constitutional studies. I take a closer look at these matters in the next chapter.

6

Case Selection and Research Design in Comparative Constitutional Studies

"I'm investigating things that begin with the letter M."
The Mad Hatter (Lewis Carroll, *Alice in Wonderland*, 1865)

Paul Cézanne's painting, *Pommes et oranges*, reproduced on the cover of this book vividly reminds us that the task of comparison requires close attention to case-selection principles. The admonition "let's not compare apples and oranges" is familiar enough, but how to give it meaning and content in the field of comparative constitutional law has remained remarkably under-explored and under-theorized. A systemic discussion of the relationship between the analytical aims or intellectual goals of the field, and the research design and methods of comparison, is urgently needed. This chapter contributes to this task.

In Chapter 5, I highlighted problems of context, relativism, and systemic selection biases as hindering generalization in comparative constitutional law. In this chapter I address another impediment to theoretical elevation and coherence of comparative constitutional law: the field's ambivalence, if not outright reluctance, with respect to theory-building through causal inference (some may prefer the term "explanation" or "deep understanding"). Despite tremendous scholarly advancements in the comparative study of constitutional law and institutions, explanation-oriented constitutional scholarship—whether based on formal modeling, causal extrapolation, historical narrative, or ethnographies—is not easy to come by. More specifically, comparative constitutional law scholarship often overlooks (or is unaware of) the methodological principles of controlled comparison, research design, and case selection deployed in the human sciences.

Undoubtedly, the constitutional lawyer, the judge, the law professor qua professor, the normative legal theorist, and the social scientist engage in comparison with different ends in mind. A lawyer, for instance, may be forgiven for selectively using comparative evidence in an attempt to enhance her client's case. A judge who wishes to make a good public policy decision may look selectively at other jurisdictions that have been contemplating the same issues. A law professor trying to illustrate to her students the variance across countries with regard to, say, the law of reproductive freedoms would be well advised to survey the state of affairs with respect to the right to have an abortion in a few pertinent polities. The legal philosopher is interested in formulating moral justifications or principles for best practices at the *ought* (rather than the *is*) level, and may thus be forgiven for supporting her insights with a small number of possibly unrepresentative cases. However, a more methodologically astute approach is warranted when there is an attempt to explain or establish causality. A researcher who wishes to advance a causal claim concerning legal institutions and the ways in which they interact with the social and political environment in which they operate must follow basic case-selection principles that support claims of that nature, allow for inductive reasoning and generalization, or are otherwise conducive to causal inference. One cannot move freely from engaging with any given purpose of comparative work to engaging with another without adjusting one's case-selection principles accordingly.

Even within the positivist, evidence-based branch of comparative constitutional studies, the term "comparative" is often used indiscriminately to describe what are in fact several different types of scholarship, ranging from "thick description," single-country "constitutional ethnographies" or taxonomies of constitutional systems to attempts at identifying "best practices" or "most effective" solutions applicable across polities; and from reference to foreign constitutional law aimed at engendering self-reflection through analogy, distinction, and contrast to controlled, inference-oriented comparisons used to assess change, explain dynamics, and make inferences about cause and effect. Even this last category may be pursued by way of a study of several comparable cases, or through a "large-N" statistical analysis of sizeable data sets that purport to encompass the entire constitutional universe. The upshot is that there is no magic bullet or one-size-fits-all research design "formula" for a field as rich and diverse as comparative constitutional studies. What may be said with some confidence is that the choices we make when thinking about which cases or units to compare and at what the level of abstraction must coherently reflect and be informed by the research questions we seek to address.

Thorough investigation of a single case study is quite common in the humanities. The majority of social scientists who study comparative law follow the "small-N" school of research design, case selection, and data analysis. While statistically oriented "large-N" studies have become dominant in American political science and sociology, they are far less common in constitutional studies, both in North America and elsewhere. The "empirical legal studies" movement, which has gained intellectual momentum in American legal academia in the 2000s, has made a concentrated effort to introduce rigorous data collection methods and statistical analyses into legal (and constitutional) scholarship, with some success in the context of comparative constitutional studies. However, with a few notable exceptions, the systematic study of comparative constitutional law has been characterized by a lack of adherence to inference-oriented case-selection and research-design standards. While it has contributed significantly to concept formation and the accumulation of idiographic knowledge, it has, for the most part, fallen short of advancing knowledge through inference-oriented, controlled comparison.

This is a missed opportunity, and a rather curious one considering the field's self-definition as comparative. International conversation among scholars and jurists, aided by new information technologies, has generated a wealth of easily accessible information about the many different constitutional systems around the world. As a result, it is now possible—more comprehensively than ever before—to draw on comparative research in order to engage in thorough understanding, test arguments and hypotheses, or formulate generalizable insights concerning the causal relationships between law and various political, social, or economic phenomena. Common rules of causal inference will help comparativists to make better and fuller use of the impressive corpus of constitutional law-related information that we now possess. A serious dialogue between ideas and evidence, theory and data, can now replace, or at least complement, the detailed classification of laws and legal concepts as the ultimate goal of comparative legal studies, constitutional and otherwise.

The social sciences have always taken diverse approaches to social inquiry. They are characterized by an aspiration to *explain*—rather than merely describe—social (including legal) phenomena through the validation or refutation of propositions about the world. (Here too I use the term "explain" in a broad, inclusive sense to capture a range of research objectives such as the uncovering of general laws, the development of correctives to extant theories, or the advance of a deeper understanding of action in specific contexts). This is true of quantitative, qualitative, behavioralist, and historical-interpretive approaches to social inquiry.[1] Even the social scientists who attempt to illuminate large, complicated, and untidy social phenomena that cannot easily be measured or that resist definitive explanation agree that a good theory must go beyond mere description, classification, or normative justification.

Granted, there is genuine skepticism about much of what passes for comparative work in the social sciences: it is often empirically thin, relying too much on "theory" and reflecting too little knowledge of the cases under consideration. Other "comparative" disciplines—comparative literature, comparative religion, or film studies, for instance—have gravitated over the years toward a more hermeneutic mode of inquiry that emphasizes the unique, exceptional, or idiosyncratic aspect of their research subject. But as we have seen, a concern with context, meaning, and contingencies does not prevent the disciplines of history and social anthropology—both of which often rely on thorough investigation of a single case study—from attempting to advance knowledge that is relevant and illuminating beyond their specific case study.

There is no a priori analytical reason why the study of comparative constitutional law could not engage in a more explanation-oriented mode of scholarship.[2] Using comparative research to explain variance among legal phenomena across polities was the main objective of legal sociology's founding fathers. Explanation, as opposed to mere description or taxonomy, has long been a main objective of evolutionary and functionalist approaches to legal transformation. Deriving explanations from comparisons across jurisdictions, time, or institutions is common in sub-fields of legal scholarship such as law and development, law and economics, certain branches of law and society, and the emerging trend

---

[1] See, e.g., Henry Brady and David Collier, eds., *Rethinking Social Inquiry: Diverse Tools, Shared Standards* (Rowman & Littlefield, 2004); Alexander George and Andrew Bennett, *Case Studies and Theory Development in the Social Sciences* (MIT Press, 2005).

[2] For a discussion of the possibility of pursuing explanatory accounts in pure legal and constitutional theory, see Nicholas Aroney, "Explanatory Power, Theory Formation, and Constitutional Interpretation: Some Preliminaries," *Australian Journal of Legal Philosophy* 38 (2013): 1–31.

toward empirical legal scholarship. Moreover, we value in our judges the skills required for assessing evidence, weighing probabilities for conviction or acquittal purposes, and ultimately rendering a verdict. This causality-oriented exercise is central to legal reasoning.

The vast majority of high-quality comparative public law scholarship produced over the past several decades has contributed tremendously not only to the mapping and classification of the new world of constitutionalism, but also to the creation of conceptual frameworks for studying comparative law more generally. Indeed, we must not underestimate the importance of the "concept formation through multiple description" aspect of comparative inquiry. We acquire a far more complex, nuanced, and sophisticated understanding of what, for example, solids or mammals are by studying the variance and commonality among exemplars within these categories. Nonetheless, a distinguishing mark of scientific inquiry is the presence of inferences about cause and effect (or reason and outcome) that attempt to go beyond the particular observations collected.

Without doubt, a devotion to quasi-scientific, inference-oriented principles of research design is certainly not the only valuable mode of social (let alone legal) inquiry. Any type of academic analysis that advances our knowledge and understanding of the enterprise of public law in a meaningful way—be it qualitative or quantitative, normative or positivist, descriptive or analytical—is potentially of great value. Adhering to inference-oriented principles of research design and case selection is not a requirement, as long as no claim is made that the study is determining causality or developing explanatory knowledge. However, intellectual integrity warrants that a scholar who aspires to establish meaningful causal claims or explanatory theories through comparative inquiry should select her case studies in a theory-minded fashion and follow clearly articulated methodological principles. And, in fact, neither advanced knowledge of the epistemological foundations of social inquiry nor a mastery of complex research methods is necessarily required. Simply following certain basic principles that are commonly used in small-N studies in the social sciences will in many cases be sufficient.

There are several reasons for the limited focus on causality, inference, and explanation in comparative constitutional law. These include traditional doctrinal boundaries; trajectories of academic training; lack of an established tradition of anonymous peer review in most law reviews; and the different epistemologies of social and legal inquiry.

Part of the reaction against social science methods stems from its unfamiliar language. Simple concepts such as "variable" (essentially, a thing that can vary and that is important to the issue being studied) or the distinction between necessary and sufficient conditions—let alone more complex concepts such as selection bias, interaction effects, spurious correlation, and intervening variables—may incite antagonism simply because some legal scholars may not be familiar with them. The traditional "case law" method of instruction commonly drawn upon in legal academia is geared toward studying the legal forest through a detailed examination of some of its individual trees. Aimed at teaching students to "think like lawyers," this method is quite effective at conveying the significance of subtle distinctions between the facts, legal concepts, and language of different cases and judicial opinions. Unfortunately, it does not lend itself to comparative inquiry carried out with a view to establishing broad causal links or exposing extrajudicial factors that may shape legal outcomes.

Another part of the problem appears to be structural. Despite the increasing interest in comparative legal analysis, comparative law remains a niche field. Indeed, in the current atmosphere of cultural and ideological wars within the American polity (reflected, inter alia, in the rather hyperbolic debate over the sporadic reference by the US Supreme Court to the constitutional norms of a handful of other polities as discussed in earlier chapters) anyone who makes serious reference to or studies comparative constitutional law risks being branded a member of a legion of liberals, cosmopolitans, and progressives who are set to destroy America's unique constitutional legacy. A related problem is that studying comparative law requires the mastery of multiple legal systems and languages, as well as proficiency in a more rigorous methodology than is usually found in legal academia that commonly focuses on elaborating disputed legal issues, carefully distinguishing cases and doctrines, refining modes of reasoning, or studying the art of effective client representation. Bar associations do not require knowledge of comparative constitutional law and hiring and tenure committees gloss over it, and at times may be simply unequipped to evaluate it. Moreover, it is time-consuming, resource-intensive, and requires a substantial start-up investment in mastering the language, history, and laws of others polities. But the reward, intellectual, and in our increasingly interconnected world practical too, is well worth the investment.

To be perfectly clear: there is no doubt that the high-quality comparative public law scholarship produced over the past few decades has contributed tremendously not only to the mapping and classification of the world of new constitutionalism, but also to the creation of conceptual frameworks for studying comparative law more generally. In addition, comparative constitutional law's embedded cosmopolitanism and genuine curiosity about the constitutive laws of others is a major methodological asset in itself. Nonetheless, a key distinguishing mark of scientific inquiry is making valid inferences that go beyond the particular observations collected. Because of its traditional lack of attention to principles of research design, controlled comparison, case selection, and hypothesis testing, comparative constitutional scholarship, its development in recent years notwithstanding, appears to be limited in its ability to engage in theory-building of this type.

The discussion advances in three main steps. First, I identify the various meanings, purposes, and modes of comparative inquiry in contemporary comparative constitutional studies. I argue that while the study of comparative constitutional law by legal academics has generated sophisticated taxonomies, concept formations, and valuable normative accounts of comparative constitutional studies, it has, for the most part, fallen short of advancing knowledge through inference-oriented, controlled comparison, as is common in the social sciences.

In the second part of the chapter I discuss a few basic principles of case selection that may be employed in inference-oriented small-N studies in the field of comparative constitutional studies: (i) the "most similar cases" principle; (ii) the "most different cases" principle; (iii) the "prototypical cases" principle; (iv) the "most difficult case" principle; and, (v) the "outlier cases" principle. I subsequently illustrate the successful application of these principles by examining a few recently published and genuinely comparative works dealing with the foundations, practice, and consequences of constitutionalization worldwide. Comparative constitutional scholarship that strives to advance valid *causal* arguments, I argue, should look more like these works.

In the chapter's third part, I explore the emerging world of multivariate, large-N studies of comparative constitutionalism. The era of works that attempt to capture the commonalities of the constitutional universe by drawing on statistical analyses of large data sets, Bayesian probability, and correlation is still in its early days. These studies may suffer from most of the shortcomings of a-contextual science, and may be seen by those who favor historical or cultural explanations as irrelevant and possibly even harmful.[3] But for the intellectually curious observer, large-N studies appear to introduce a novel, refreshing dimension to comparative constitutional studies. One reason for this is that these studies often make a conscious effort to avoid conflating positive ("factual") and normative claims. They also pay close attention to research design, formulation of hypotheses, and data analysis. Perhaps most importantly, by treating constitutional law as a universal phenomenon with multiple manifestations worldwide, these studies signal a departure from the field's traditional overreliance on a handful of frequently discussed examples.

I conclude the extensive discussion of methodological considerations by suggesting that while there are many valuable purposes, approaches, and methods for studying comparative (constitutional) law, the aspiration to make valid causal claims based on comparative research warrants adherence to inference-oriented principles of research design and case selection. Attention to, and reliance on, such considerations and principles may help scholars studying the migration of constitutional ideas to make valuable causal claims as to why, when, and how such migration is likely to occur. It would also facilitate a more substantive scholarly dialogue between law and other related disciplines, and help to lower traditional doctrinal boundaries.

However, because no research method enjoys an a priori advantage over any other without taking into account the scope and nature of the studied phenomenon or the question the research purports to address, attempts to outline an "official" comparative method, or calls for the adoption of a stringent, one-size-fit-all approach to research methods, are not only unrealistic but also unwise. Alternatively, I argue that comparative constitutionalists should settle on a set of four notably more sensible guiding principles: (i) define clearly the study's aim—descriptive, taxonomical, explanatory, and/or normative; (ii) articulate clearly the study's intended level of generalization and applicability, which may range from the most context-specific to the most universal and abstract; (iii) encourage methodological pluralism and analytical eclecticism when appropriate; and (iv) ensure that the research design and methods of comparison reflect the analytical aims or intellectual goals of specific studies, so that a rational, analytically adaptive

---

[3] For the purposes of this chapter, I use the "culturalists" and "contextualists" labels interchangeably, although in other discussions there may be differences between these positions.

connection exists between the research questions and the comparative methods used. In other words, choices as to the appropriate unit and method of analysis should be theoretically informed by the questions sought to be addressed.

Modes of comparative inquiry in constitutional law

As we have seen, in the field of comparative constitutional law there are a variety of modes and methods of inquiry that may be considered "comparative." These various modes and methods reflect different epistemological visions and involve different levels of abstraction.

The first and arguably the most contextual of these modes is the *single-country study*. Single-country studies are characterized as comparative because they concern a country other than the author's or the reader's own, or implicitly contain comparisons to an ideal-type system against which the theoretically significant elements of the studied constitutional system are identified. Such studies are often aimed at developing a deep understanding of other constitutional systems while implicitly developing a better understanding of one's own. Case selection tends to be based on the author's acquaintance with the constitutional system under study or the supposed significance of the country's constitutional legacy to the general understanding of constitutionalism as a system of governance. Because the aim here is not to trace general patterns of causality, but rather to engage in a deep, detailed consideration of a given country's constitutional law and practice, basic methodological considerations pertaining to case selection are often overlooked, and indeed may not be expected to begin with.

In its information-provision guise, this type of scholarship is useful to students of constitutional law, and often contributes to the mapping of the still under-charted terrain of constitutional law worldwide. Great works of this genre provide encyclopedic knowledge alongside thoughtful analyses of the constitutional law of the polity being examined, often serving as an authoritative reference guide to that law.[4] The

---

[4] See, e.g., Donald Kommers and Russell Miller, *The Constitutional Jurisprudence of the Federal Republic of Germany* (3rd edn, Duke University Press, 2012); Stephen Zamora et al., *Mexican Law* (Oxford University Press, 2005).

internal organization of these works often follows classical functional-
ism, and so considers elements of the constitutional system being
studied in terms of the function they fulfill: "the executive," "the
legislature," "the judiciary," "federalism," "rights." Unlike in comparative law generally, taxonomy—classifying a given constitutional
system within the "legal traditions" or "family trees for legal systems"
matrix coined by Rene David and further developed by Zweigert,
Kötz, and others—is not common in this mode comparative constitutional law.[5] This may be because the rise of supranational rights
regimes and the emerging global canon of constitutional law are
increasingly defying traditional common law/civil law distinctions.
Although "legal tradition" still accounts for considerable differences
in modes of constitutional adjudication, reasoning, and foreign
citation sources, legal families cannot explain why constitutional
jurisprudence in Germany, Spain, Israel, Canada, and South Africa
looks increasingly similar.

In its more theory-building guise, the thorough, nuanced analysis of
a carefully selected single constitutional system may yield illuminating
"ethnography-like" accounts of constitutional transformation in given
polities.[6] Ideally, it may also spawn general insights or lessons for other,
similarly situated constitutional settings. Recent examples of well-
executed "constitutional ethnographies" include Mark Tushnet's *The
Constitution of the United States of America: A Contextual Analysis*, Cheryl
Saunders's *The Constitution of Australia: A Contextual Analysis*, Shigenori
Matsui's *The Constitution of Japan: A Contextual Analysis*, as well as other
books published in the same series on the constitutions of France,
Germany, the United Kingdom, China, Indonesia, Malaysia, and

---

[5] The "legal families" approach serves as the organizing principle of most leading text-
books in comparative law. See, e.g., Konrad Zweigert and Hein Kötz, *An Introduction to
Comparative Law* (3rd edn, Oxford University Press, 1998). For further discussion see, e.g.,
Esin Örücü, "Family Trees for Legal Systems: Towards a Contemporary Approach," in Mark
Van Hoecke, ed., *Epistemology and Methodology of Comparative Law* (Hart Publishing, 2004).

[6] Kim Lane Scheppele, "Constitutional Ethnography: An Introduction," *Law and Society
Review* 38 (2004): 389–406. Two effective illustrations of this genre of scholarship in action
are: Heinz Klug, *Constituting Democracy: Law, Globalism, and South Africa's Political Reconstruction* (Cambridge University Press, 2000)—a detailed account of the South African constitutional revolution of the mid-1990s that illustrates the impact of international political
economy pressures on domestic constitution drafting; and Joseph Weiler's seminal work on
the origins and nature of the emerging EU constitutional order, which illustrates the central
role of courts in creating supranational constitutionalism, *The Constitution of Europe: 'Do the
New Clothes Have an Emperor?' and Other Essays on European Integration* (Cambridge University
Press, 1999).

Vietnam.[7] Each of these studies carefully canvasses a single constitu-tional system, explains its form and operation, and provides a critical evaluation of its foundations, evolution, and contemporary challenges. Unique elements in each setting are defined as such by reference to comparative anchors.

Critical reflection by an external observer on a given polity's con-stitutional law and institutions is a subcategory in this genre of com-parative constitutional studies. The study of constitutional system X by a researcher steeped in constitutional background Y, it may be argued, meets the basic requirement of comparative analysis—the existence of at least two targets of observation or points of view—because the observer at least implicitly perceives and describes system X in contrast with system Y. Montesquieu's *Persian Letters* or de Tocqueville's *Dem-ocracy in America* are prime examples of this. Within recent political science studies, Alexei Trochev's detailed account of the Russian Constitutional Court's "difficult childhood" years, and of its jurisdic-tional "wars" with other courts and the political sphere, makes a most valuable contribution to the understanding of how newly established courts in post-transition settings begin to gain traction and authority.[8] Likewise, Lisa Hilbink's meticulous exploration of the culture of formalism and passivity in Chilean courts is a prime illustration of how a carefully crafted constitutional ethnography of a single country can be pursued in a way that contributes to general theory-building.[9]

However, even without such a general contribution or other con-crete payoffs, "one can unapologetically study a foreign legal system simply for its own sake."[10] As Tom Ginsburg argues (in the context of studying Japanese law): "Even if one starts with a more instrumentalist premise, we cannot conceivably know whether any particular legal rule or institution will be of broader theoretical or practical interest until we know what it is we are looking at. And this requires a certain degree of local knowledge, of willingness to understand legal

---

[7] Mark Tushnet, *The Constitution of the United States of America: A Contextual Analysis* (Hart Publishing, 2009); Cheryl Saunders, *The Constitution of Australia: A Contextual Analysis* (Hart Publishing, 2010); Shigenori Matsui, *The Constitution of Japan: A Contextual Analysis* (Hart Publishing, 2010).

[8] Alexei Trochev, *Judging Russia: The Role of the Constitutional Court in Russian Politics 1990–2006* (Cambridge University Press, 2008).

[9] Lisa Hilbink, *Judges beyond Politics in Democracy and Dictatorship: Lessons from Chile* (Cambridge University Press, 2007).

[10] Tom Ginsburg, "Studying Japanese Law Because It's There," *American Journal of Comparative Law* 58 (2010): 15–25, 15.

systems on their own terms. There is therefore virtue in having a
group of scholars studying foreign legal systems for their own sake,
independent of the need to resolve any particular theoretical or practical question."[11]

A second, increasingly common mode of comparative constitutional
law is geared toward *self-reflection or betterment through analogy, distinction,
and contrast*. Scholarship in this mode may also be spurred by jurists'
quests for the "right" or "just" solution to a given constitutional
challenge their polity has been struggling with. In some cases, it echoes
comparative law's traditional search for "the best" or most suitable rule
across cultures.[12] In other instances, it serves as a valuable tool for what
Mark Tushnet refers to as the identification of "false necessities"—
constitutional measures that might appear necessary to maintain order,
but in fact are not necessary—thus advancing the idea that "doctrines
and institutions can accommodate much more change than we might
think."[13] The assumption informing this mode of comparative constitutional law is that although most relatively open, rule-of-law polities
face essentially the same constitutional challenges, they may adopt
quite different approaches to dealing them. By referring to constitutional jurisprudence, institutions, and practices of other presumably
similarly situated polities, we might gain a better understanding of
our own constitutional values and structures and thereby develop a
more cosmopolitan or universalist view of our constitutional discourse.
At a more concrete level, constitutional practice in a given polity might
be improved by emulating constitutional mechanisms employed elsewhere.[14] Likewise, comparative constitutional law has been offered as a
guide to constructing new constitutional provisions and institutions,
primarily in the context of "constitutional engineering" in the post-
authoritarian world or in ethnically divided polities.[15]

In legal academia, this type of comparative examination crops up in
the form of critical commentaries on contentious supreme court rulings

[11] Ginsburg, "Studying Japanese Law Because It's There" (n 10), 16.
[12] For an illustration of this way of thinking about comparative law, see, e.g., Bernhard
Grossfeld, *Core Questions of Comparative Law* (Carolina Academic Press, 2005).
[13] Mark Tushnet, *Weak Courts, Strong Rights* (Princeton University Press, 2007), 14.
[14] See, e.g., Mark Tushnet, "The Possibilities of Comparative Constitutional Law," *Yale
Law Journal* 108 (1999): 1225–309.
[15] The literature here is too vast to cite. A representative work of this genre is Andrew
Reynolds, ed., *The Architecture of Democracy: Constitutional Design, Conflict Management, and
Democracy* (Oxford University Press, 2002).

that draw on the treatment of roughly equivalent problems by courts in other jurisdictions. The most obvious manifestation of the comparative reference genre of comparative constitutional inquiry, however, takes place in the jurisprudential realm (see the discussion in Chapter 1). Constitutional courts worldwide are said increasingly to rely on comparative constitutional jurisprudence to frame and articulate their own position on a given constitutional question. In some instances, foreign case law is referenced as it reflects *jus cogens*-like norms; in others, it provides "a foil for further domestic self-understanding and self-evaluation."[16] As Rosalind Dixon suggests, "the key benefit of comparison is that it allows [U.S. courts] to gain insights about the moral conclusions of a large number of relatively independent constitutional decision-makers." This phenomenon is particularly evident with respect to constitutional rights jurisprudence.[17] As is well known, in its first landmark rights decision—in which it contemplated the constitutionality of the death penalty—the South African Constitutional Court examined in detail landmark rulings from Botswana, Canada, the European Court of Human Rights, Germany, Hong Kong, Hungary, India, Jamaica, Tanzania, the United Nations Committee on Human Rights, the United States (as a negative example), and Zimbabwe.[18] The purpose of this comparative inquiry was to draw the contours of an emerging global canon from which guidance could then be drawn.

Let us consider another illustrative example. In *Leyla Şahin v. Turkey* (2005), one of the most significant European cases to date dealing with the issue of religious attire in the education system, the European Court of Human Rights (ECtHR) was asked to determine whether restrictions on wearing Islamic headscarves in institutions of higher education in Turkey violated religious freedoms guaranteed under Article 9(2) of the European Convention on Human Rights (ECHR), as well as under Article 2 of Protocol No. 1 regarding the right to education.[19] In order to determine whether there is an

---

[16] Michel Rosenfeld, "Controversy over Citations to Foreign Authorities in American Constitutional Adjudication and the Conflict of Judicial Philosophies: A Reply to Professor Glendon," *Duquesne Law Review* 52 (2013): 25–68.

[17] Rosalind Dixon, "A Democratic Theory of Constitutional Comparison," *American Journal of Comparative Law* 56 (2008): 947–97, 956.

[18] *S v. Makwanyane*, 1995 (3) SA 391 (CC) [South Africa].

[19] *Şahin v. Turkey*, Applicaton No. 44774/98 (Grand Chamber, judgment of Nov. 10, 2005) [ECtHR].

emerging pan-European consensus on the wearing of religious attire by students in higher learning institutions, the ECtHR engaged in a comparative survey of constitutional practices across the continent.[20] The Court examined the relevant state of affairs in no less than 20 member states of the Council of Europe (in the order of their treatment in the judgment: Turkey, Azerbaijan, Albania, France, Belgium, Austria, Germany, the Netherlands, Spain, Finland, Sweden, Switzerland, the United Kingdom, Russia, Romania, Hungary, Greece, the Czech Republic, Slovakia, and Poland). Having determined that no consensus exists on the matter, the Court applied a generous "margin of appreciation" approach, essentially adopting the argument of (pre-AKP) Turkey that its situation was sufficiently unique to justify deference to its national authorities when it comes to regulating religious attire in Turkish institutions of higher learning. This ruling may well be strategic or culturally biased in some respects: however, viewed through the prism of comparative reference alone, the Court's look to member state law for guidance appears genuine, appropriate, and analytically justifiable, indeed required, given the stated goal of the inquiry. In contrast with the US Supreme Court where polarizing debates pivot around the very legitimacy and relevance of the use of comparative law, in the ECtHR's *Şahin* decision we find a disagreement over the *conclusion* to be drawn from the comparative evidence, not a challenge to the practice itself.[21]

While increasingly common and certainly more intuitively "comparative" than freestanding, single-country studies, the comparative reference approach is still lacking in methodological coherence. When executed poorly, it amounts to little more than result-oriented "cherry-picking" of favorable cases, which is precisely the kind of practice that opponents of reference to foreign law, most notably Justice Antonin Scalia of the US Supreme Court, base their objections on.[22] All too often, comparative reference entails seemingly unsystematic—and at times scant and superficial—reference to foreign constitutional jurisprudence. Case selection is seldom systematic, and it rarely pays due attention to the context and nuances that have given rise to alternative

---

[20] *Şahin v. Turkey* (n 19), paras. 55–65.

[21] *Şahin v. Turkey* (n 19), para. 3 (dissenting opinion of Judge Tulkens). Given that judges are masters of fine distinctions, disagreements over the actual lessons to be drawn from the comparative evidence are to be expected.

[22] See, e.g., Norman Dorsen, "The Relevance of Foreign Legal Materials in U.S. Constitutional Cases," *International Journal of Constitutional Law* 3 (2005): 519–41.

interpretations of constitutional norms. From a methodological standpoint, we have yet to encounter inter-court constitutional borrowing
that demonstrably transcends the accusation that it is merely an exercise
in rationalizing policy preferences.[23]

Comparative constitutional scholarship has more to offer than the
self-reflection and normatively driven advancement of cosmopolitan
values often seen in comparative reference works. Comparison is a
fundamental tool of scholarly analysis. It can sharpen our power of
description and can play a central role in concept formation by bringing into focus the similarities and differences between cases.[24] Indeed,
this is precisely the goal of a third and arguably more sophisticated type
of comparative inquiry that is meant to *generate concepts and analytical
frameworks for thinking critically about constitutional norms and practices*. This
mode of comparative constitutional scholarship involves a quest for
a detailed understanding of how people living in different cultural,
social, and political contexts deal with constitutional dilemmas
that are assumed to be common to most modern political systems. Its
focus is not on a single jurisdiction, but on a single practice (or a set of
closely related practices) as carried out in or encountered by different
jurisdictions.

More often than not, this third type of comparative scholarship takes
a universalist tone, emphasizing the broad similarity of constitutional
challenges and functions across many relatively open, rule-of-law
polities. By studying various manifestations of and solutions to roughly
analogous constitutional challenges, our understanding of key concepts
in constitutional law, such as separation of powers, statutory interpretation, or equality rights, becomes more sophisticated and analytically
sharp. The end often sought from this exercise is concept formation
through multiple description.

This approach serves as the organizing principle of most leading
textbooks in comparative constitutional law.[25] Each chapter in Vicki

---

[23] Similar concerns, in this case about the use of history in U.S. Supreme Court decisions
without sufficient concern for methodology, are raised in Alfred Kelly, "Clio and the Court:
An Illicit Love Affair," *Supreme Court Review* (1965): 119–58.

[24] David Collier, "The Comparative Method: Two Decades of Change," in Dankwart
Rustow and Kenneth Paul Erickson, eds., *Political Science: The State of the Discipline* (Harper-
Collins, 1991), 105.

[25] Vicki Jackson and Mark Tushnet, *Comparative Constitutional Law* (Foundation Press,
2006); see also, Norman Dorsen et al., *Comparative Constitutionalism* (West, 2003); Donald
Kommers et al., *American Constitutional Law: Essays, Cases, and Comparative Notes* (Rowman &
Littlefield, 2009).

Jackson and Mark Tushnet's *Comparative Constitutional Law*, for example, is devoted to a major aspect or concept of modern constitutional law as it manifests itself in a few pertinent polities. In David Beatty's *The Ultimate Rule of Law*, the author devotes chapters to comparative judicial interpretation of concepts such as liberty, equality, and proportionality.[26] Kent Roach's thorough book on the tension between national security needs and fundamental rights in the post-9/11 era analyzes concepts such as counterterrorism measures, the rule of law, and democracy in the United States, the United Kingdom, Australia, Canada, Egypt, Syria, Israel, Singapore, and Indonesia.[27] The same methodological approach also underlies recent collections of "country essays" on themes such as judicial independence or appointments;[28] gender equality;[29] and constitutional politics in regional settings where, presumably, the joint geographical context, political realities, and constitutional tradition possess some explanatory significance.[30]

Works dealing with innovative mechanisms designed to mitigate the tension between constitutionalism and democracy—mechanisms such as the Canadian Charter of Rights and Freedoms' "limitation" and "override" clauses, the New Zealand Bill of Rights Act's "preferential" model of judicial review, and the UK Human Rights Act's "declaration of incompatibility"—provide a good substantive illustration of the "concept formation through multiple description" approach. Drawing on a comparative examination of such mechanisms, comparativists like Stephen Gardbaum and Mark Tushnet have introduced the concept of the "Commonwealth model of judicial review" or "weak-form judicial review." In doing so, they have enriched and brought

---

[26] David Beatty, *The Ultimate Rule of Law* (Oxford University Press, 2004).

[27] Kent Roach, *The 9/11 Effect: Comparative Counter-Terrorism* (Cambridge University Press, 2011).

[28] See, e.g., Kate Malleson and Peter Russell, eds., *Appointing Judges in an Age of Judicial Power: Critical Perspectives from around the World* (University of Toronto Press, 2006); Peter Russell and David O'Brien, eds., *Judicial Independence in the Age of Democracy: Critical Perspectives from around the World* (University of Virginia Press, 2001).

[29] See, e.g., Beverly Baines and Ruth Rubio-Marin, eds., *The Gender of Constitutional Jurisprudence* (Oxford University Press, 2005).

[30] See, e.g., Nathan Brown, *Constitutions in a Non-Constitutional World: Arab Basic Laws and the Prospects for Accountable Government* (SUNY Press, 2002); Gretchen Helmke and Julio Rios-Figueroa, eds., *Courts in Latin America* (Cambridge University Press, 2011).

new life to the debate about the questionable democratic credentials of constitutionalism in the United States.[31]

Comparative studies have also successfully generated a more nuanced conception of inter-court borrowing of constitutional ideas by introducing a distinction between positive and negative borrowing. Positive borrowing refers to judicial use of foreign constitutional concepts to improve the borrowing polity's own constitutional practices; negative borrowing involves explicit contrast with other polities' imperfect constitutional experiences as a means to justify a given polity's advanced constitutional practices.[32]

The growth of high-quality comparative constitutional law scholarship produced by legal academics over the past decade has contributed tremendously not only to the mapping and taxonomy of the world of new constitutionalism, but also to the creation of conceptual frameworks for studying or understanding key aspects of comparative constitutionalism. Two of the most complete and integrative monographs on comparative constitutionalism that follow the "concept formation" methodological rationale are Vicki Jackson's *Constitutional Engagement in a Transnational Era*,[33] and Gary Jacobsohn's *Constitutional Identity*.[34]

Jackson's book introduces useful terminology, accompanied by ample illustrations, for understanding the various domestic constitutional reactions to transnational law. Jackson formulates three paradigmatic "postures" that domestic constitutions and constitutional courts may take vis-à-vis the emerging transnational legal environment: resistance, convergence, and, in between the two, engagement

---

[31] See, e.g., Stephen Gardbaum, *The New Commonwealth Model of Constitutionalism: Theory and Practice* (Cambridge University Press, 2013); Stephen Gardbaum, "Reassessing the New Commonwealth Model of Constitutionalism," *International Journal of Constitutional Law* 8 (2010): 167–206; Mark Tushnet, "Weak-Form Judicial Review and 'Core' Civil Liberties," *Harvard Civil Rights-Civil Liberties Law Review* 41 (2006): 1–22; Stephen Gardbaum, "The New Commonwealth Model of Constitutionalism," *American Journal of Comparative Law* 49 (2001): 707–60. See also Janet Hiebert, "New Constitutional Ideas: Can New Parliamentary Models Resist Judicial Dominance When Interpreting Rights?," *Texas Law Review* 82 (2004): 1963–87.

[32] Sujit Choudhry, "The Lochner Era and Comparative Constitutionalism," *International Journal of Constitutional Law* 2 (2004): 1–55; Kim Lane Scheppele, "Aspirational and Aversive Constitutionalism: The Case for Studying Cross-constitutional Influence through Negative Models," *International Journal of Constitutional Law* 1 (2003): 296–324.

[33] Vicki Jackson, *Constitutional Engagement in a Transnational Era* (Oxford University Press, 2010).

[34] Gary J. Jacobsohn, *Constitutional Identity* (Harvard University Press, 2010).

with transnational sources "founded on commitments to judicial deliberation and open to the possibilities of either harmony or disson-
ance."[35] At the book's core is the notion that constitutional law in
the United States and elsewhere now operates in an increasingly
transnational legal environment of international treaties and supranational human rights, trade, and monetary regimes. It is thus unrealistic, and indeed unwise, to assume that constitutional law in general,
and the strangely insular American constitutional law in particular, may
continue to defy universalism in favor of particularism. Engagement
with the emerging international legal and constitutional system is thus
preferable to full convergence or blanket resistance. Constitutional
courts—commonly thought of as the guardians of the nation's constitutional legacy and enduring values—*ought* to adjust and *are* adjusting,
admittedly faster in some places than in others. To prove her point,
Jackson conducts an impressive survey of comparative constitutional
jurisprudence (mostly from countries that are now considered the
"usual suspects" in such analyses) on a wide array of issues, ranging
from interpretive methods to reproductive freedoms, and from the
laws of federalism to gender equality. Taken as a whole, Jackson's
work is an exemplar of the best comparative constitutional law scholarship the non-explanatory mode can offer.

Gary Jacobsohn's majestic *Constitutional Identity* is an equally impressive comparative work within the concept formation mode of inquiry.
In this work, Jacobsohn develops the idea that a given polity may have
a "constitutional identity" that is deeper and considerably more idealist
in character than the day-to-day (constitutional) politics of that polity.
Through an exploration of constitutional development in India, Ireland, Israel, and the United States (with frequent reference to other
countries), Jacobsohn introduces the intriguing idea of "constitutional
disharmony" between a polity's deep and enduring constitutional
identity and its actual constitutional order, and discusses the near-
systemic quest to mitigate or resolve this disharmony. Constitutional
disharmony may emanate from a polity's commitment to apparently
conflicting values (e.g. Ireland's overarching Catholic morality whilst
also being a member state of the ECHR, or Israel's self-definition as
both a Jewish and a democratic state), or it may reflect a tension
between the values protected in a country's constitution and the

---

[35] Jackson, *Constitutional Engagement in a Transnational Era* (n 33), 9.

values prevalent among its populace (think of the tension between Turkey's constitutional legacy of militant secularism and the fact that the vast majority of Turks define themselves as devout Muslims). Jacobsohn then draws upon this concept to discuss foundational questions in constitutional theory such as the challenge of "unconstitutional" constitutional amendments, "militant" versus "acquiescent" constitutionalism, and the role of a nation's traditions, virtue, ethics, and ideas in the emergence of its constitutional identity. In short, the book illustrates how the "concept formation" mode of comparative constitutional law may be used effectively to advance novel thinking that may, in turn, lead to the formulation of testable hypotheses about the dynamics of constitutional stagnation and change. In some important respects, then, the type of grand conceptual exercise that both Jackson and Jacobsohn engage in represents the most sophisticated and potentially far-reaching contribution to theory-building in comparative constitutional law.

A fourth type of comparative constitutional studies differs from concept formation in that it aims to engage in *theory-testing and explanation through causal inference*. At the most abstract level, this type of scholarship is concerned with how two or more things or processes are related, why a certain phenomenon is happening, and why it is happening the way it is. Causation, however loosely or rigorously perceived, is a key element, perhaps even the main marker of identity of this scholarly enterprise.[36] This core concept is based on the notion that in the social universe things do not "fall from the sky" but have evolved in a certain way, fulfill a certain function, are constructed in a given form, or are treated in a particular way for a set of identifiable (and ideally testable) reasons or causes. A good theory requires elucidating concepts *as well as* offering causal explanations for observed phenomena, universal or particular as it may be.

Since their birth as autonomous academic disciplines, the social sciences have always been influenced by diverse approaches to social

---

[36] Causation, David Hume famously noted, is the cement of the universe: "surely, if there be any relation among objects which it imports to us to know perfectly, it is that of cause and effect. On this are founded all our reasonings concerning matter of fact or existence." See David Hume, *Treaties of Human Nature* (Oxford University Press, 1988); cited in John Gerring, *Social Science Methodology: A Unified Framework* (Cambridge University Press, 2012), 197. Hume's program of reform included a commitment to establishing a "science of human nature" that was based on observable fact and empirically-rooted inquiry. See *David Hume: An Enquiry concerning Human Understanding: A Critical Edition* (Tom L. Beauchamp, ed., Clarendon Press, 2000).

inquiry. While the inference-oriented goal of quantitative and qualitative methods in the social sciences is not uncontested, the aspiration to *explain* social (including legal) phenomena through the validation or refutation (some prefer less conclusive terms such as increase or lower our confidence in the explanatory power) of prepositions about the world is common to all quantitative and qualitative, small-N and large-N, behavioralist and historical-interpretive approaches to social inquiry used in disciplines such as sociology and political science, and certainly in generally more positivist disciplines such as social psychology and economics. These propositions may refer to or address social phenomena on any scale: a macro-level universal trend, a distinct manifestation of a widespread phenomenon, or a context-specific experience that calls for an explanation drawn from within that particular context.

Inference-oriented social science research, quantitative and/or qualitative, is often taken to mean: (i) formulation of testable hypotheses, models, or a priori plausible arguments concerning possible causal links among well-defined variables; (ii) support or disconfirmation (think Karl Popper) of these hypotheses, models, or arguments through pertinent research design, data collection, and analysis; and (iii) generation of conclusions that are likely to be true, based largely on inductive inference. Less rigid "realist philosophies of science"—essentially a-dogmatic, comparatively informed, reality- or commonsense-based approach to social inquiry—suggest a set of research principles that "impose fewer a priori constraints on scientific practice" than their rivals and thereby invite consideration of "a greater range of possible explanations."[37] Such realist accounts may thus be more effective than strictly behavioral approaches in addressing questions of power, consent, and other not easily observable forces that shape social (and legal) reality in given contexts.[38] Either way, controlled comparison and methodologically astute case selection and research design are critical to accomplishing any and all of these goals. There must also be a clear distinction between conditionality (a given phenomenon cannot occur without condition X, but that condition is not the *cause* of the

---

[37] Ian Shapiro and Alex Wendt, "The Difference that Realism Makes: Social Science and the Politics of Consent," in Ian Shapiro, *The Flight from Reality in the Human Sciences* (Princeton University Press, 2005), 20.

[38] Shapiro and Wendt as well as other authors who advocate a realist approach commonly cite John Gaventa's classic *Power and Powerlessness: Quiescence and Rebellion in an Appalachian Valley* (University of Illinois Press, 1982) as an illustration for a successful deployment of a realist approach to social inquiry.

phenomenon) and causality, as well as between direct factors and intervening factors, and between necessary and sufficient conditions.

It is precisely due to its traditional lack of attention to principles of controlled comparison, case selection, and causation, and its penchant for the familiar and easily accessible but not necessarily representative or generalizable, that comparative constitutional law scholarship, its tremendous development in recent years notwithstanding, often (though certainly not always) falls short of advancing knowledge in the manner sought by most social scientists. Whereas the third category of comparative scholarship does an excellent job of assessing the scope, extent, and nature of certain pertinent phenomena, it provides only limited "methodology-proof" insight into the origins and causes of such phenomena. To the extent that case selection receives any attention, the dominant principle informing it is usually that the cases chosen must involve current policy concerns in the author's own polity. While this is a legitimate case-selection criterion for many legal, pedagogical, or policy analysis tasks, it may not be so appropriate when one's goal is to advance a causal or an explanatory claim through comparative research. Here we can gain significant insight by exploring how other disciplines have developed the principles of case selection.

Principles of case selection in inference–oriented small–N comparative studies

Experimental research, statistical analysis (large-N), and systematic examination of a small number of cases (small-N) are the three major methods of causal inference and theory-testing within the "scientific" approach to the study of politics and society. The last category—small-N studies—is the most prevalent type of inquiry employed by social science scholars of comparative public law. In the following pages, I explain the basic principles of research design and case selection in the small-N method of theory testing.[39] These principles are: (i) the "most similar cases" principle; (ii) the "most different cases" principle; (iii) the

[39] A sophisticated body of literature in political science deals with inference-oriented case-selection principles in single-case study or small-N research designs. See, e.g., John Gerring, *Case Study Research: Principles and Practices* (Cambridge University Press, 2007); Charles Ragin, *Redesigning Social Inquiry: Fuzzy Sets and Beyond* (University of Chicago Press, 2008); Charles Ragin, *Fuzzy-Set Social Science* (University of Chicago Press, 2000).

"prototypical cases" principle; (iv) the "most difficult case" principle; and (v) the "outlier cases" principle.[40]

While legal scholars do occasionally follow one or more of these five principles, the majority of legal scholarship in the field of comparative constitutional law is either unaware of some of these principles or simply overlooks them altogether. In this section I illustrate the logic of these selection principles by reference to recent studies of the origins and consequences of judicial empowerment. My aim is to demonstrate how adherence to these simple principles of case selection may permit the field of comparative constitutional law to move beyond the third type of comparative examination—concept formation through multiple description—to the next level of comparative inquiry: causal inference through controlled comparison. Moreover, even those who prefer to engage with the first three types of comparative inquiry might still find it useful to have a grasp of these principles.

(i) The "most similar cases" principle

Initially put forth by John Stuart Mill in *A System of Logic* (1843), and later refined, confusingly renamed, and applied to the social sciences by a number of authors in the 1960s and 1970s, the "most similar cases" research-design method (Mill's "method of difference") and "most different cases" research design method (Mill's "method of agreement") are two standard case-selection principles used for inference-oriented, controlled comparison in qualitative, small-N studies.[41]

---

[40] Another type of inference-oriented small-N study focuses on cases of embedded insulation and isolation, whether geographical, social, or political. Think of studies of endemic flora and fauna specimens in Madagascar or the Galapagos Islands; studies of isolated hunting and gathering societies that have had no or minimal contact with the outer world; or situations of social isolation such as those witnessed by descendants of the Bounty mutineers on Pitcairn Island, or by Rudyard Kipling's Mowgli—an Indian child who gets lost in the jungle and is brought up by a family of wolves. Such cases constitute a natural "control group"; by comparing pertinent findings gathered in such enclaves of isolation against the benchmark of common knowledge or practices elsewhere, we are able to assess the net effect of domestic or "innate" characteristics versus the effect of external or acquired processes, ideas, and practices. This particular type of case study, however, is not easily transferable to the comparative constitutional law realm.

[41] See Adam Przeworski and Henry Teune, *The Logic of Comparative Social Inquiry* (Wiley-Interscience, 1970); Alexander George and Timothy McKeown, "Case Studies and Theories of Organizational Decision Making," in Robert Coulam and Richard Smith, eds., *Advances in Information Processing in Organization*, Vol. 2 (JAI Press, 1985); Charles Ragin, *The Comparative Method: Moving beyond Qualitative and Quantitative Strategies* (University of California Press,

Table 6.1. The "most similar cases" logic

	Possible explanation I	Possible explanation II	Possible explanation III	Possible explanation IV	Dependent variable
Case A	X_1	X_2	X_3	X_4	Y
Case B	X_1	X_2	X_3	Not X_4	Not Y

According to the "most similar cases" approach, researchers should compare cases that, as much as possible, are identical but for the factors of causal interest.[42] By controlling for variables or potential explanations that are not central to the study, the "most similar cases" principle helps to "isolate" the effect of the key independent variable on the dependent variable, creating a partial substitute for statistical or experimental control. Because the "most similar cases" principle is designed to hold non-key variables constant while isolating the explanatory power of the key independent variable, the methodological strengths of the approach are vividly illustrated by a comparison of the same polity at different times (e.g. a study of the impact of a certain change through a pre-change/post-change comparison).

Consider the hypothetical example outlined in Table 6.1. For the sake of simplicity, let us assume that all the pertinent variables are dichotomous (i.e. "Yes/No" or "X/Not X"), so that each possible explanation under consideration is either present or absent.[43] Case A and Case B are selected to test the hypothesis that explanation IV (X_4)—and not explanation I, II, or III—causes Y. If any of X_1, X_2, or X_3 were the cause of Y, then the result for Case B with respect to the dependent variable would have to be Y. Since the result in Case B is "not Y," X_1, X_2, and X_3 can be eliminated as causes of Y. However, in the column under "possible explanation IV," X_4 is

1989); Arend Lijphart, "Comparative Politics and Comparative Method," *American Political Science Review* 65 (1971): 682–93; Sidney Verba, "Some Dilemmas of Political Research," *World Politics* 20 (1967): 111–27.

[42] Selecting cases based on variance on the dependent variable alone may be problematic. See, e.g., Barbara Geddes, "How the Cases You Choose Affect the Answers You Get: Selection Bias in Comparative Politics," *Political Analysis* 2 (1990): 131–52.

[43] See, e.g., Stanley Lieberson, "Small N's and Big Conclusions: An Examination of the Reasoning in Comparative Studies Based on a Small Number of Cases," *Social Forces* 70 (1991): 307–20.

present for Case A but not for Case B. So, when X4 is present, the result is Y, but when "X4" is not present, the result is "not Y." It therefore appears that the presence of X4 (possibly in conjunction with other factors) is necessary to generate the result Y, and that the absence of X4 means that Y cannot result. This supports the hypothesis that of possible explanations X1, X2, X3, and X4, the most likely cause of Y is X4.

Put differently, because the first three possible explanations for the studied phenomenon are held constant across the two cases, possible explanation IV appears to be the most plausible explanation for the variance in the cases with respect to the dependent variable. Since the results "Y" and "Not Y" cannot be directly attributed to any of the first three possible explanations, explanation IV is the most likely to be the cause of the different outcomes in Case A and Case B. Conversely, if these readings for the four possible explanations led to *the same* outcome in both cases with respect to the dependent variable (i.e. if the readings for the dependent variable in the table were both "Y" or both "Not Y"), we could eliminate explanation IV as a significant determinant of the outcome or dependent variable.[44]

Consider the following simple illustrations of the "most similar cases" logic. First, imagine if we selected the United States and China as the two main cases for a study of the impact of judicial review on the status of civil rights and liberties. This choice would not make much sense. There are so many differences between the political institutions, cultural propensities, and constitutional legacies of these two countries that isolating the independent impact of judicial review on the status of civil rights and liberties within them would be virtually impossible. A far more productive tactic would be to select, say, the United States and the United Kingdom as our two main cases for this study.

Similarly, studying the status of civil liberties in the Netherlands—one of the few European countries that until recently stringently opposed the idea and practice of judicial review as it is commonly understood in North America—would be a logical choice for a researcher who wishes to establish that the independent impact of judicial review on the status of civil rights and liberties in a given polity

---

[44] This would not, however, eliminate X4 or its absence as a potentially necessary condition for Y. It would only mean that it is not a sufficient condition for Y.

has not been as significant as is often claimed. Comparing the Dominican Republic (which makes up the eastern two-thirds of the island of Hispaniola in the Caribbean) and Haiti (which covers the island's western end) would be prima facie a good strategy if one wishes to challenge Montesquieu's argument concerning the impact of environmental and material factors on a given polity's laws, but would not be ideal if one is interested in testing hypotheses concerning the impact of a given polity's religious creed, colonial heritage, economic development, and/or political stability on its constitutional practices, since the two countries vary significantly with respect to each of these parameters.

An effective application of the "most similar cases" logic to the study of comparative constitutional law and politics is provided by Tom Ginsburg's *Judicial Review in New Democracies*.[45] The book examines the evolution of independent constitutional courts during the early stages of democratic liberalization in post-authoritarian polities. Ginsburg argues that the establishment of constitutional review in new democracies is largely a function of politics and interests, not a reflection of macro-cultural or societal factors. Specifically, judicial review provides "insurance" for self-interested, risk-averse politicians, who are negotiating the terms of new constitutional arrangements under conditions of political deadlock or systemic uncertainty. At times of political transition, greater degrees of political deadlock and/or more diffused or decentralized political power increase the probability that uncertainty will be embedded in a polity's constitution-making process and subsequent electoral market. This in turn leads to a greater likelihood that a relatively powerful and independent constitutional court will be adopted by risk-averse participants as insurance in the constitutional negotiation game. In short, judicial review is a solution to the problem of uncertainty in constitutional design.

To substantiate these theoretical arguments, Ginsburg turns to an exploration of the constitutional courts, and the corresponding judicialization of politics, in three new Asian democracies: Taiwan, Mongolia, and Korea. The three countries share a roughly similar cultural context. Each underwent a transition to democracy in the late 1980s and early 1990s, and in each the newly established constitutional court

---

[45] Tom Ginsburg, *Judicial Review in New Democracies: Constitutional Courts in Asian Cases* (Cambridge University Press, 2003).

has struggled to maintain and enhance its stature within a political environment that lacks an established tradition of judicial independence and constitutional supremacy. And yet, despite these commonalities, there has been a significant variance in judicial independence among the three countries.

In Taiwan, the democratization process was governed by a single dominant party (KMT) with an overwhelmingly powerful leader (Chiang Kai-shek). The result has been a very gradual constitutional reform ("Confucian constitutionalism," as Ginsburg calls it) and the evolution of a relatively weak and politically dependent court (the Council of Grand Justices). In Mongolia, the former Communist Party was in a strong position during the constitutional negotiation stage, but was unable to dictate outcomes unilaterally because of a newly emergent set of opposition parties. This resulted in the creation of a "middle of the road," quasi-independent court (the Constitutional Tsets) in 1992. In Korea, constitutional transformation took place amidst heavy uncertainty stemming from political deadlock among three parties of roughly equal strength. As a result, a strong and relatively independent constitutional court emerged in 1998 as political insurance against electoral uncertainty.

Using the same case-selection logic, Pedro Magalhães points out that the transitions to democracy in Spain and Portugal in the mid-1970s were both characterized by the lack of a single core of post-authoritarian political power; consequently, each featured the rapid adoption of strong constitutional review mechanisms.[46] In Greece, by contrast, the post-authoritarian process was dominated by a single party: Constantine Karamanlis's New Democracy, which held over 70 percent of the assembly seats that did not have to face elections following the approval of the new constitution. The result, argues Magalhães, was that Greece, despite having authoritarian and civil law legacies similar to those of Spain and Portugal and an almost simultaneous democratic transition, remained the only Southern European democracy without constitutional judicial review of legislation.[47]

---

[46] Pedro Magalhães, *The Limits to Judicialization: Legislative Politics and Constitutional Review in the Iberian Democracies* (unpublished Ph.D. dissertation, Ohio State University, 2003).

[47] Other effective illustrations of the "most similar cases" logic in action are Carlo Guarnieri and Patrizia Pederzoli, *The Power of Judges: A Comparative Study of Courts and Democracy* (Oxford University Press, 2002)—a study of constitutional politics in Spain, France, and Italy; and, to a somewhat lesser degree, Alec Stone Sweet, *Governing with Judges:*

Another effective application of the "most similar cases" logic is David Kosar's work on the efficacy of new judicial accountability measures in the post-communist bloc.[48] Kosar uses a comparison of the Czech Republic and Slovakia to test the impact of a 2003 institutional reform that was designed to enhance judicial accountability in Slovakia by establishing a judicial council that would give judges a greater stake in making judicial appointments and monitoring judicial conduct. The two countries share the same essential features: a communist past, a civil law system, a career model of the judiciary, a centralized model of constitutional review outside the ordinary courts, and membership in the EU and the Council of Europe. In addition, Czechs and Slovaks shared a common institutional structure, almost uninterruptedly, from the independence of Czechoslovakia in 1918 until its dissolution in 1993. In other words, the Czech Republic and Slovakia share many important similarities, but vary on the key independent variable—the model of court administration. Whereas the Czech Republic has maintained its model of controlling the judiciary via the Ministry of Justice from 1993 to today, Slovakia, after initially going with a similar model, introduced a new institutional structure for judicial administration in 2003 with the establishment of the Judicial Council of the Slovak Republic. This turn of events provides Kosar with a ready-made natural experiment to test the impact of the institutional change in Slovakia while holding most other variables constant.[49]

Several key works in comparative constitutional studies innovatively use what might be called a proxy of the "most similar cases" research design. In their study of the reception of the ECHR in national legal systems, Helen Keller and Alec Stone Sweet present structured comparisons of 11 pairs of European countries, each pair sharing as many relevant features as possible.[50] The pairings include Norway and

Constitutional Politics in Europe (Oxford University Press, 2000)—a study of constitutional politics in Spain, France, Italy, Germany, and the EU.

[48] David Kosar, "Judicial Accountability in the (Post) Transitional Context: A Story of the Czech Republic and Slovakia," in Adam Czarnota and Stephan Parmentier, eds., *Transitional Justice, Rule of Law, and Institutional Design* (Intersentia, 2010).

[49] A well-known comparison of this type in political science is Robert Putnam's *Making Democracy Work: Civic Traditions in Modern Italy* (Princeton University Press, 1993), which compares the impact of institutional reforms in different sub-national regions in Italy over a 20-year period.

[50] Helen Keller and Alec Stone Sweet, *A Europe of Rights: The Impact of the ECHR on National Legal Systems* (Oxford University Press, 2008).

Sweden, Greece and Turkey, the Netherlands and Belgium, Russia and Ukraine, Ireland and the United Kingdom, and Spain and Italy. As the authors explain, the idea behind this unique design is "to develop appropriate theoretical concepts and to generate hypotheses" based on the assumption that "comparing two, relatively like cases offer a better opportunity to build more general theoretical frameworks.[51]

As indicated earlier, the requirement that comparable cases be selected so as to hold non-key variables constant while isolating the explanatory power of the key independent variable makes the "most similar cases" approach well suited to a diachronic comparison within the same polity. Because the comparison is carried out between two consecutive periods within the same polity, the researcher is able to control for potential intervening variables and explanations other than those he or she wishes to emphasize. This method has been employed with some success in the strategic approach to the study of judicial behavior, the basic insights of which I described in Chapter 4. According to the strategic approach, judges are not only precedent followers, framers of legal policies, or ideology-driven decision-makers, but also sophisticated strategic decision-makers who realize that the range of decisions they can reach is constrained by the preferences and anticipated reaction of the surrounding political sphere.[52] Accordingly, constitutional court rulings may be analyzed not only as mere acts of professional, apolitical jurisprudence or reflections of judicial ideology, but also as a reflection of judges' own strategic choices. Judges may vote strategically to minimize the chance that their decisions will be overridden; if the interpretation that the judges prefer is likely to lead to reversal by other branches, they will compromise by adopting the interpretation closest to their preference that is likely not to be reversed.[53] Likewise, judges in certain legal systems may vote strategically, especially in politically charged cases, in order not to diminish their chances for promotion.[54] Supreme court judges may also be viewed as

[51] Keller and Stone Sweet, *A Europe of Rights* (n 50), 18.

[52] Jeffrey Segal, "Judicial Behavior," in Keith Whittington et al., eds., *The Oxford Handbook of Law and Politics* (Oxford University Press, 2008), 19–33; Pablo Spiller and Rafael Gely, "Strategic Judicial Decision-Making," in Whittington et al., *The Oxford Handbook of Law and Politics* (ibid.), 34–45.

[53] Lawrence Baum, *The Puzzle of Judicial Behavior* (University of Michigan Press, 1997), 119.

[54] Mark Ramseyer and Eric Rasmusen, "Why Are Japanese Judges So Conservative in Politically Charged Cases?," *American Political Science Review* 95 (2001): 331–44.

strategic actors to the extent that they seek to maintain or enhance the court's independence and institutional position vis-à-vis other major national decision-making bodies.[55] In other words, they may recognize when the changing fates or preferences of influential political actors, or gaps in the institutional context within which they operate, might allow them to strengthen their own position by extending the ambit of their jurisprudence and fortifying their status as crucial national policymakers.

Gretchen Helmke demonstrates precisely this point via a diachronic study of judicial behavior in Argentina. While Argentine Supreme Court judges showed little resistance to the state's governing military junta at its zenith (1976–81), a significant increase in antigovernment decisions occurred between 1982 and 1983 after it became clear that the days of the military regime were numbered. The judges' willingness to issue antigovernment decisions was then relatively high during the years of weak democracy in Argentina (1983–89), primarily, Helmke argues, because the judges did not face a credible threat. However, as Carlos Menem became increasingly popular and it became more likely that he would be reelected, the percentage of antigovernment decisions declined.[56]

As is well known, in 1993 Russian president Boris Yeltsin reacted to the Constitutional Court's overactive involvement in Russia's political sphere by signing a decree suspending the Court until the adoption of a new constitution—an act that marked the demise of the first Constitutional Court and its controversial Chair, Valery Zorkin, and led to the establishment of the second Constitutional Court. Through a controlled comparison of the dockets of the first and second Constitutional Courts, Lee Epstein et al. show that the second Court, in a

---

[55] The establishment of an international rule of law in the EU, for example, was driven in no small part by national judges' attempts to enhance their independence, influence, and authority vis-à-vis other courts and political actors. For an elaboration of this point, see Karen Alter, *Establishing the Supremacy of European Law: The Making of an International Rule of Law in Europe* (Oxford University Press, 2001).

[56] Gretchen Helmke, "The Logic of Strategic Defection: Court–Executive Relations in Argentina under Dictatorship and Democracy," *American Political Science Review* 96 (2002): 291–303. For variations on the same theme, see Taavi Annus and Margit Tavits, "Judicial Behavior After a Change of Regime: The Effects of Judge and Defendant Characteristics," *Law and Society Review* 38 (2004): 711–36; Georg Vanberg, *The Politics of Constitutional Review in Germany* (Cambridge University Press, 2005); Gretchen Helmke, *Courts under Constraints: Judges, Generals, and Presidents in Argentina* (Cambridge University Press, 2005); Jeffrey Staton, *Judicial Power and Strategic Communication in Mexico* (Cambridge University Press, 2010).

marked departure from the first Court era when the docket was dominated by politically charged federalism and separation-of-powers cases, stuck largely to the "safe area" of individual rights jurisprudence and tended to avoid federalism or separation-of-powers disputes.[57] By applying the "most similar cases" principle to two consecutive periods in the same polity, the researchers illustrate another consequence of the strategic approach to judicial decision-making: harsh political responses to unwelcome activism or interventions on the part of the courts have a chilling effect on judicial decision-making patterns.

(ii) The "most different cases" principle

Under the "most different cases" approach to selecting comparable cases, researchers choose cases that are different for all variables that are not central to the study but similar for those that are. Doing so emphasizes the significance of the independent variables that are similar in both cases to the similar readings on the dependent variable. Consider the hypothetical example outlined in Table 6.2. Case A and Case B are selected to test the hypothesis that explanation IV (X_4)—and not explanation I, II, or III—causes Y. If the presence of any of the possible explanation I (X_1), II (X_2), or III (X_3) was necessary to cause result Y, then the result for Case B with respect to the dependent variable could not be "Y" and would instead have to be "Not Y." Since the result in both Case A and Case B is Y, possible explanations I, II, and III can be eliminated as direct causes of Y. By contrast, the reading for possible explanation IV, like the reading for the dependent variable, is the same in both cases. It therefore appears that the presence of X_4 is necessary

Table 6.2. The "most different cases" logic

	Possible explanation I	Possible explanation II	Possible explanation III	Possible explanation IV	Dependent variable
Case A	X_1	X_2	X_3	X_4	Y
Case B	Not X_1	Not X_2	Not X_3	X_4	Y

[57] Lee Epstein et al., "The Role of Constitutional Courts in the Establishment and Maintenance of Democratic Systems of Government," *Law and Society Review* 35 (2001): 117–63.

and sufficient to generate the result Y. This supports the hypothesis that of possible explanations X1, X2, X3, and X4, the most likely cause of Y is X4.

As we have seen, selecting comparable cases according to the "most similar cases" principle effectively emphasizes the explanatory power of an independent variable or variables that *vary* across the compared cases. By contrast, selecting comparable cases according to the "most different cases" principle emphasizes the explanatory power of independent variables with *similar* readings across the compared cases. Differently put, because independent variables I, II, and III vary significantly across the two cases while the readings for independent variable IV are similar, the most plausible explanation for the similarity in the dependent variable in the two cases is explanation IV—the only observed constant across the two instances. Conversely, if the same configuration of readings in the "possible explanations" columns led to a different result in Case A than in Case B with respect to the dependent variable, explanation IV would be eliminated as a determinant of the dependent variable.

Suppose a researcher is interested in studying the extent to which a polity's history of authoritarianism influences its constitutional court's interpretative approach to the "political question" doctrine. Selecting Chile and Argentina as the two lead cases for such a study would not be the most effective choice. Because these two countries share many pertinent features other than their authoritarian pasts (e.g. geographical circumstances, political realities, sociocultural propensities, and constitutional legacies), it would be difficult to determine whether any similarities in high court attitudes toward the executive branch are the result of these countries' similar histories of powerful military regimes and fragile transitions to democracy. It would make more sense to compare, say, Chile and Turkey, since these countries differ in almost all pertinent respects but do share a roughly similar history of military authoritarianism and fragile transition to democracy. Similarly, if a researcher were interested in drawing on comparative study to assess how a colonial legal legacy has shaped postcolonial constitutional arrangements, it would not be particularly effective to compare Mali and Niger, since these two countries share many features other than their joint French colonial heritage. It would be more useful to compare, say, Indonesia and Suriname—two former Dutch colonies with little in common besides their colonial past.

Consider the following application of this case-selection principle. In a recent book and accompanying set of articles, I explored the secularizing or religion-containing role of constitutional jurisprudence in several countries facing a deep secular/religious divide—Egypt, Israel, Malaysia, Nigeria, Pakistan, and Turkey.[58] In all these countries there has been a growth in the influence of religious political movements and in the level of popular support these movements receive. At the same time, these countries differ in their formal recognition of, and commitment to, religious values. In Pakistan, the law underwent full Islamization in 1973 and again in 1985 whereas the Egyptian Constitution, as amended in 1980, 2012, and 2013, states that principles of Muslim jurisprudence (the Shari'a) are *the* primary source of legislation in Egypt. Israel defines itself as a "Jewish and democratic" state while Malaysia is a federal country that endorses Islam as its official religion, and where political Islam has been continuously gaining support and clout at the state level. Nigeria is a secular federal country that grants some legislative autonomy to its states, thereby allowing the states to adopt religious-influenced laws and, finally, modern Turkey characterizes itself as secular, adhering to the Franco-American model of strict separation of state and religion. Accordingly, there are considerable differences in the interpretive approaches and practical solutions adopted by the six countries' respective high courts to deal with core questions of religion and state. Despite these dissimilarities, however, there are some striking parallels in the way that these constitutional courts have positioned themselves as important religion-containing forces within their respective societies. In all six countries, the increased popular support for principles of theocratic governance—principles which naturally were at odds with the cultural propensities and policy preferences of secular or moderate elites—resulted in a similar transfer of fundamental "religion and state" questions from the political sphere to the constitutional courts. By drawing on their disproportionate access to, and influence over, the legal arena, pragmatist political power-holders in these and other polities facing deep divisions along secular/religious lines look to ensure that their secular liberal views and policy preferences are less effectively contested. The result has been an unprecedented judicialization of collective identity (particularly

---

[58] Ran Hirschl, *Constitutional Theocracy* (Harvard University Press, 2010). See also Ran Hirschl, "Constitutional Courts vs. Religious Fundamentalism: Three Middle Eastern Tales," *Texas Law Review* 82 (2004): 1819–60.

"religion and state" questions) and the consequent emergence of constitutional courts as important guardians of secular interests in these countries.

(iii) The "prototypical cases" principle

The logic of the "prototypical cases" principle is fairly intuitive. If a researcher wishes to draw upon a limited number of case studies to test the validity of a theory or argument, these should feature as many key characteristics as possible that are found in a large number of cases. Unlike the cases chosen in most freestanding, insular, single-country studies of constitutional law, prototypical cases serve as exemplars of other cases with similar characteristics. The thinking is that theories that apply in prototypical cases are likely to apply in other analogous cases.[59] Indeed, the aspect of studies of prototypical cases that makes them methodologically superior to what political scientists call "country/area studies" is precisely the applicability of findings derived from proto-typical cases to other similar cases. In this respect, the underlying logic of the "prototypical cases" principle is that of reasoning by analogy. That is, the principle works on the logic that "if two units are the same in all relevant respects, similar values on the relevant explanatory variables will result in similar values on the dependent variable."[60]

The "prototypical cases" principle is the methodological basis of the work of pioneering comparative legal sociologists such as Henry Sumner Maine, Émile Durkheim, Max Weber, and more recently, Roberto Unger and Mirjan Damaška.[61] An illustration of an effective application of the principle is provided by Martin Shapiro's *Courts: A Comparative and Political Analysis*—the first thorough application of Robert Dahl's theory of courts as political institutions to the study of comparative public law.[62] Shapiro argues that courts worldwide

[59] Stephen Van Evera, *Guide to Methods for Students of Political Science* (Cornell University Press, 1997), 84.

[60] Gary King, Robert Keohane, and Sidney Verba, *Designing Social Inquiry* (Princeton University Press, 1994), 209–12.

[61] See, e.g., Henry Maine, *Ancient Law* (Book Jungle, 2000 [1861]); Émile Durkheim, *The Division of Labor in Society* (Free Press, 1997 [1893]); Max Weber, *Economy and Society: An Outline of Interpretive Sociology* (University of California Press, 1978 [1925]); Roberto Manga-beira Unger, *Law in Modern Society: Toward a Criticism of Social Theory* (Free Press, 1976); Mirjan Damaška, *The Faces of Justice and State Authority: A Comparative Approach to the Legal Process* (Yale University Press, 1991).

[62] Martin Shapiro, *Courts: A Comparative and Political Analysis* (University of Chicago Press, 1981).

should be thought of as political agencies of government and that judges should be perceived as political actors functioning largely in support of political regimes. "Most fundamentally," argues Shapiro, "the role of courts and judicial processes is to maintain the legitimacy of the regime, and most elements of the court system serve to advance this function."[63] Common characteristics of court systems worldwide (e.g. judicial independence, judicial selection processes, perceptions of impartiality and procedural fairness, appellate processes, etc.) are politically constructed to support political hierarchy, stability, and legitimacy.

In order to illustrate the applicability of his "courts as political institutions" argument to diverse legal contexts, Shapiro analyzes the main institutional, jurisprudential, and socio-legal characteristics of four prototypical cases, each representing a major and distinct legal tradition. He chooses the English legal system as a prototype of a common law system characterized by the political construction of judicial independence and the image of judicial impartiality. The legal systems of France and Italy serve as prototypical illustrations of civil law systems in which judges (who are commonly perceived as bound by pre-existing codes) adjust their jurisprudence to accord with regime interests. The legal system of Imperial China serves as a prototype of Asian systems that are characterized by Confucian ethics and non-litigious mediation. Finally, the Ottoman Empire's legal system serves as a prototypical example of a decentralized political system with a mosaic of secular and religious jurisprudence, and an absence of central political authority. Shapiro's conclusion is blunt: despite the variance in the legal cultures and traditions within which they operate, judicial tribunals in each of these prototypical cases—and by extension in many other cases—reflect and promote broad sociopolitical interests. Shapiro's study also demonstrates that research designs may actually incorporate multiple case-selection logics. While the four cases he chooses are more or less representative of their respective traditions, and in this way serve as prototypical cases, all four considered together exemplify the "most different cases" principle. Insofar as Shapiro's argument that courts are effective tools of social control is compelling, the marked variation among the cases he focuses on suggests that it is also widely applicable.

---

[63] Herbert Kritzer, "Martin Shapiro: Anticipating the New Institutionalism," in Nancy Maveety, ed., *The Pioneers of Judicial Behavior* (University of Michigan Press, 2002), 397.

Recent work in comparative constitutional reasoning suggests that methodologically astute small–N research design, in particular of the "prototypical cases" breed, is readily amenable to legal analysis. A couple of books that draw on such a design to question the supposed uniformity of proportionality analysis in comparative constitutional jurisprudence provide textbook illustrations. In their book *Proportionality and Constitutional Culture*, Moshe Cohen-Eliya and Iddo Porat present a detailed comparison of the origins and practice of proportionality analysis in Germany and balancing analysis in the United States to advance the argument that the scope and nature of proportionality/balancing analysis in a given polity may be affected by the concrete origins of the practice as well as the legal, political, and philosophical culture in that polity.[64] Whereas in Prussia, to pick one aspect of this comparative analysis, "proportionality stepped into the vacuum created by the absence of constitutional protection for rights, and introduced into administrative law an element of rights-protection through the notion of the rule of law," in the United States balancing emerged as a rights–limiting mechanism that, in lieu of limitations clause in the Bill of Rights, facilitated a pragmatic, rights-restricting jurisprudential approach in cases involving conflicting interests. The particular historical context, Cohen-Eliya and Porat show, "shaped the conception of these doctrines: proportionality as pro–rights and balancing as pragmatic and limiting rights."[65] They go on to illustrate that political culture accounts for the centrality and the intrinsic value accorded proportionality in German constitutional law as an effective means for shaping and optimizing German society's values, as opposed to the relative marginalization of balancing in American constitutional law and its conceptualization as a pragmatic exception to the construction of rights as categorical limitations on state power. In short, the conceptualization of proportionality analysis may vary from one polity to another; the differences may be culturally based.[66]

[64] Moshe Cohen-Eliya and Iddo Porat, *Proportionality and Constitutional Culture* (Cambridge University Press, 2013). For a similar research design, theme, and case studies, see Jacco Bomhoff, *Balancing Constitutional Rights: The Origins and Meanings of Postwar Legal Discourse* (Cambridge University Press, 2014).

[65] See Moshe Cohen-Eliya and Iddo Porat, "Is Proportionality Culturally-based?," *International Journal of Constitutional Law Blog* (Sept. 28, 2013), available at <http://www.iconnectblog.com/2013/09/is-proportionality-culturally-based>.

[66] Several classic comparative accounts of American legal and constitutional culture emphasize the adversarial nature of that culture, the uninhibited individualism (think Mary Ann Glendon's notion of "lone rights bearers"), and dyadic view of the society (Glendon's

Another illustration of the successful deployment of the "prototypical cases" principle to explore variance in comparative legal reasoning is provided by Mitchel Lasser's *Judicial Deliberations*—a study of inter-country differences in judicial discourse and styles of argumentation.[67] In Lasser's view, these differences reflect divergent ideological frameworks and national meta-narratives, and not merely well-rehearsed doctrinal distinctions among broad categories of legal traditions. His three case studies—the French Cour de cassation, the US Supreme Court, and the European Court of Justice (ECJ)—are prototypical of civil law, common law, and supranational law courts, respectively.[68] The Cour de cassation, Lasser argues, adheres to a formalistic or "grammatical" style of argumentation, whereby little or no reference is made to extrajudicial interpretive means, extra-textual arguments, etc. This is reflective, inter alia, of France's unified institutional and ideological framework, which is founded on both explicitly republican notions of meritocracy and managerial expertise and on the French legal system's longtime emphasis on control, hierarchy, and professionalism. The American judicial system, by contrast, derives its legitimacy from a more argumentative, engaging, "hermeneutic" style of judicial discourse that frequently resorts to extra-textual discursive contexts and interpretive means. This is reflective of the decentralized, multifocal nature of the American judicial system and the more deliberative or democratic political ethos within which it operates. Finally, Lasser argues that the ECJ's judicial discourse features elements of both the French "grammatical" approach and the American "hermeneutic" approach. This he sees as a result of the hierarchical, discursive-like structure on which the Court was originally patterned as well as its inherently fractured, transnational political and legal context. As with other works that follow the "prototypical cases" design, the explanation that Lasser offers with respect to the three courts he examines is

---

"right to be let alone") that characterize it, as opposed to European more communitarian conceptions of the person that are said to emphasize "dignity" and envision the rights-bearer as situated in family and community relationships. See Mary Ann Glendon, *Rights Talk: The Impoverishment of Political Discourse* (Free Press, 1991). See also Robert Kagan, *Adversarial Legalism: The American Way of Law* (Harvard University Press, 2001).

[67] Mitchel de S.-O.-L'E Lasser, *Judicial Deliberations: A Comparative Analysis of Judicial Transparency and Legitimacy* (Oxford University Press, 2004).

[68] On this, and for other methodologically astute observations concerning his own work and the field of comparative law more generally, see Mitchel de S.-O.-L'E. Lasser, "The Question of Understanding," in Pierre Legrand and Roderick Munday, eds., *Comparative Legal Studies: Traditions and Transitions* (Cambridge University Press, 2003).

said to elucidate styles of reasoning and argumentation employed by top courts operating within equivalent settings.

(iv) The "most difficult case" principle

Single case study research is not necessarily detrimental to causal inference. Indeed, it may even support it.[69] Consider the way in which the "most difficult case" principle can substantiate arguments made in a small-N or a single-country study.[70] The "most difficult case" principle is based on an idea known in formal logic as *ad absurdum*. It works on the logic that our confidence in the validity of a given claim, or in the explanatory power of a given hypothesis, is enhanced once it has been proven to hold true in a case that is, prima facie, the most challenging or least favorable to it. Put another way, "if the investigator chooses a case study that seems on a priori grounds unlikely to accord with theoretical predictions—a least likely observation—but the theory turns out to be correct regardless, the theory will have passed a difficult test, and we will have reason to support it with greater confidence."[71] Conversely, if a claim or hypothesis does not hold true in a "most likely" or a "most favorable" case, its plausibility is severely undermined. In short, a single crucial case may either positively validate a claim or, conversely, "score a clean knockout over a theory."[72] (A largely accepted Popperian insight is that it is generally easier to refute or disconfirm a hypothesis or inference than it is to substantiate or confirm the same hypothesis or inference, if indeed the latter is possible).

An effective application of the "most difficult case" principle helped to make Gerald Rosenberg's *The Hollow Hope* one of the most

---

[69] To be clear: a "case" in this context means a country, a jurisdiction, etc., not a single data point or observation, which cannot really be used to (dis)confirm a causal relationship. The underlying assumption is that a "crucial case study" would have several data points. The cases versus data points issue (and how to increase the number of data points in a case study) is discussed in Jason Seawright and John Gerring, "Case Selection Techniques in Case Study Research: A Menu of Qualitative and Quantitative Options," *Political Research Quarterly* 61 (2008): 294–308.

[70] The "most difficult case" method is sometimes referred to as the "crucial case" or "least likely case" method. See, e.g., Harry Eckstein, "Case Study and Theory in Political Science," in Fred Greenstein and Nelson Polsby, eds., *Handbook of Political Science* (Addison-Wesley, 1975); see also, John Gerring, "Is There a (Viable) Crucial-Case Method?," *Comparative Political Studies* 40 (2007): 231–53.

[71] King et al., *Designing Social Inquiry* (n 60), 209.

[72] Eckstein, "Case Study and Theory in Political Science" (n 70), 127.

influential works on the impact of landmark court rulings.[73] Rosenberg suggests in his polemic against the prevalent "dynamic court"
approach that the US Supreme Court's role in producing social
reforms, at least in the domains of racial desegregation and abortion,
has been far less significant than conventional wisdom would suggest.
In fact, hostile opposition forces were able to neutralize the Court's
seemingly groundbreaking and widely celebrated ruling in *Brown v.
Board of Education* (1954) for at least a decade following the decision.[74]
The limited progress eventually made after the ruling, argues Rosenberg, was due to a shift in political forces that had everything to do with
the changing economic role of African-Americans and their own
extra-legal activism, and little to do with the Supreme Court's ruling.
Because courts lack independent enforcement and implementation
powers, Rosenberg notes, they are institutionally constrained in their
efforts to bring about social change. Therefore, courts may affect
significant social reform only when extrajudicial political factors are
conducive to such reform, or when market forces offer positive incentives to induce compliance. By highlighting the surprisingly limited
direct effects of the most widely celebrated ruling in the history of the
US Supreme Court, Rosenberg uses the "most difficult case" strategy
to lend credence to his counterintuitive arguments.

Charles Epp's influential work on rights revolutions provides
another illustration of an effective use of the "most difficult case"
principle.[75] Epp suggests that the impact of constitutional catalogues of
rights may be limited by individuals' inability to invoke them through
strategic litigation. Hence, bills of rights matter only to the extent that
there is a well-developed support structure for legal mobilization—a
nexus of rights-advocacy organizations, rights-supportive lawyers and
law schools, and governmental rights-enforcement agencies and legal
aid schemes. In other words, while the existence of written constitutional provisions is necessary for the effective protection of rights
and liberties, it is certainly not a sufficient condition. The effectiveness
of rights provisions in planting the seeds of social change in a given

---

[73] Gerald Rosenberg, *The Hollow Hope: Can Courts Bring About Social Change?* (2nd edn,
University of Chicago Press, 2008).
[74] 347 U.S. 483 (1954) [United States].
[75] See Charles Epp, "Do Bills of Rights Matter? The Canadian Charter of Rights and
Freedoms," *American Political Science Review* 90 (1996): 765–79; and Charles Epp, *The Rights
Revolution: Lawyers, Activists, and Supreme Courts in Comparative Perspective* (University of
Chicago Press, 1998).

polity depends largely upon the existence of a support structure for legal mobilization and, more generally, hospitable sociocultural conditions.

To substantiate this claim, Epp engages in a comparative study of rights revolutions in several countries, most notably the United States, India, and Canada. The rights revolution in the United States occurred through a series of landmark Supreme Court rulings between 1961 and 1975, and was propelled largely by concerted pressure from well-organized rights advocates. In India, by contrast, "the interest group system is fragmented, the legal profession consists primarily of lawyers working individually, not collectively, and the availability of resources for noneconomic appellate litigation is limited."[76] Canada presents a "most difficult case" for Epp's thesis, as the Canadian rights revolution seems, on its face, to have an obvious, straightforward origin—the 1982 adoption of the Charter of Rights and Freedoms. However, Epp's analysis suggests that Canada's rights advocacy and rights litigation rates, as well as its "support structure for legal mobilization," started to gain momentum in the early 1970s, a decade prior to the adoption of the Charter.[77] In Canada, too, the rights revolution was largely contingent on the growth of a support structure for legal mobilization, and not merely on the formal protection of rights through constitutional provisions.

(v) The "outlier cases" principle

When an outcome is poorly explained by existing theories but may be explained with a new account or theory it is useful to study "outlier cases." In these cases, the values on the dependent variable are high (i.e. the result occurs frequently or in a significant fashion), but the known causes or existing explanations of this result on the dependent variable are absent (i.e. there ought to be another explanation).[78] This case-selection principle is designed to lend credence to a novel explanation for a given phenomenon through the negation of alternative explanations for that phenomenon. It draws upon a basic principle of formal logic: as long as a possible explanation for a given outcome is not proven irrelevant, it remains a possible explanation. Conversely,

---

[76] Epp, *The Rights Revolution* (n 75), 95.
[77] Epp, "Do Bills of Rights Matter?" (n 75).
[78] Van Evera, *Guide to Methods for Students of Political Science* (n 59), 86–7.

showing that a possible explanation for a given outcome is irrelevant to that outcome increases our confidence in other possible explanations. When using the "outlier cases" principle, we increase our confidence in a given explanation by selecting a case or cases that do not feature any possible explanation for the studied phenomenon other than the new explanation we wish to establish. In short, selecting a number of outlier cases that cannot be explained by existing theories helps to substantiate the new cause, explanation, or argument through the a priori elimination of alternative explanations.

Consider the following example of the "outlier cases" principle in action. The constitutionalization of rights and the corresponding establishment of judicial review are widely perceived as power-diffusing measures associated with liberal or egalitarian values. As a result, constitutionalization is portrayed in conventional theories of constitutional transformation as reflecting a polity's "pre-commitment" against its members' harmful future desires;[79] or as reflecting a polity's convergence toward an all-encompassing, post-WWII "thick" notion of democracy and of the universal prioritization of human rights and judicial review.[80] From a more functionalist standpoint, constitutionalization is often portrayed as reflecting a general waning of confidence in technocratic government and a consequent desire to restrict the discretionary power of the state.[81] Constitutionalization may also reflect an attempt to mitigate tensions in ethnically divided polities through the adoption of federalism and other power-sharing principles.[82] According to institutional economics and public choice theories of constitutional transformation, the constitutionalization of rights and the establishment of judicial review increase economic

---

[79] See, e.g., Jon Elster, *Ulysses and the Sirens: Studies in Rationality and Irrationality* (Cambridge University Press, 1984); and Stephen Holmes, *Passions and Constraint: On the Theory of Liberal Democracy* (University of Chicago Press, 1995).

[80] The most prominent proponent of this view is Ronald Dworkin. See, e.g., Ronald Dworkin, *A Bill of Rights for Britain* (Chatto & Windus, 1990).

[81] See Martin Shapiro, "The Success of Judicial Review and Democracy," in Martin Shapiro and Alec Stone Sweet, *On Law, Politics, and Judicialization* (Oxford University Press, 2002).

[82] The works that propose various versions of this "consociational" approach are too numerous to cite. Some of the most prominent exponents of this line of thought are Donald Horowitz, Arend Lijphart, and Yash Ghai. A helpful overview of these concepts is provided in Sujit Choudhry, "Bridging Comparative Politics and Comparative Constitutional Law: Constitutional Design in Divided Societies," in Sujit Choudhry, ed., *Constitutional Design for Divided Societies: Integration of Accommodation?* (Oxford University Press, 2008).

predictability and efficiently mitigate systemic collective-action problems such as coordination, commitment, and enforcement.[83]

Unfortunately, however, none of these theories of constitutional
transformation is based on a genuinely comparative, systematic analysis
of the political vectors informing any of the actual constitutional
revolutions of the past two decades. Additionally, the applicability of
some of these theories (e.g. the federalism/consociationalism theory of
constitutionalization) is limited to a small number of countries. More
importantly, if we apply any of these constitutional transformation
theories to any given "new constitutionalism" polity, it is still hard to
see why members of that polity chose to implement the post-WWII
constitutional supremacy model when they did, and not earlier. Likewise, if a given polity indeed requires efficient mitigation of systemic
collective-action problems, how can we explain the fact that earlier
attempts to resolve these problems through constitutionalization have
failed? Furthermore, conventional theories of constitutional transformation tend to focus exclusively on explaining constitutional change,
while overlooking constitutional continuity and stagnation. They
also ignore human agency and the important fact that constitutional
revolutions require constitutional innovators—stakeholders who make
concrete choices that affect the timing and scope of constitutional
reforms.

To address this lacuna, I devoted a substantial portion of an earlier
book of mine, *Towards Juristocracy*, to a comparative study of the
political origins of constitutionalization in established democracies.[84]
I argued that constitutionalization, and judicial empowerment more
generally, may provide an effective solution for those who have better
access to, and more influence on, the legal arena, and who, faced with
serious threats, real or perceived, to their political and cultural hegemony within the polity, wish to protect their worldviews and policy
preferences. In this fashion, threatened elites can obtain through the
constitutional domain what they cannot get through the electoral
market. Without debating the substantive merits of this "hegemonic
preservation" thesis, the "outlier cases" principle was a crucial aspect of

[83] See, e.g., Douglass North and Barry Weingast, "Constitutions and Commitment: The
Evolution of Institutions Governing Public Choice in Seventeenth Century England,"
Journal of Economic History 49 (1989): 803–32; Barry Weingast, "Constitutions as Governance
Structures: The Political Foundations of Secure Markets," *Journal of Institutional and Theoretical
Economics* 149 (1993): 286–311.

[84] Ran Hirschl, *Towards Juristocracy* (Harvard University Press, 2004).

the project's design.[85] At first glance, the possibilities for case selection seemed endless. Around the globe, in more than one hundred countries and in several supranational entities, fundamental constitutional reform has transferred an unprecedented amount of power from representative institutions to judiciaries. The countries that have witnessed this expansion of judicial power range from the Eastern Bloc to Canada, from Latin America to South Africa, and from the United Kingdom to Israel.

From an empirical perspective, the majority of constitutional revolutions over the past few decades follow one of five common scenarios. First, constitutionalization may stem from political reconstruction in the wake of an existential political crisis, as with the adoption of new, post-WWII constitutions in Japan in 1946, Italy in 1948, Germany in 1949, and France in 1958. Constitutionalization may also stem from decolonization processes, as with India in 1948 to 1950, or from a transition from an authoritarian to a democratic regime, as with the constitutional revolutions in Southern Europe in the 1970s and in Latin America in the late 1980s and early 1990s. Additionally, constitutionalization may occur in a "dual transition" scenario in which it is part of a transition to both a Western model of democracy and a market economy, as with the numerous constitutional revolutions of the post-communist and post-Soviet countries. Constitutionalization may also result from the incorporation of international and trans- or supranational legal standards into domestic law; consider the passage of the Human Rights Act 1998 in the United Kingdom, which effectively incorporated the provisions of the ECHR into British constitutional law, or the incorporation of ten international human rights treaties into Argentina's constitutional law in 1994 and Brazil's in 2004, or the similar development in Pakistan in 2008.

Each of these types of constitutional reform poses its own puzzles for scholars of public law and judicial politics. It is the fifth and final constitutional revolution scenario, however, which I call the "no apparent transition" scenario, that I find the most intriguing from a methodological standpoint. In this "none of the above" category,

---

[85] For a discussion of the merits of this thesis see, e.g., Leslie Goldstein, "From Democracy to Juristocracy," *Law and Society Review* 38 (2004): 611–29; Mark Graber, "Constructing Judicial Review," *Annual Review of Political Science* 8 (2005): 425–51. For additional discussion, see Jan Klabbers's review in *European Journal of International Law* 16 (2005): 160–3; and Mark Rush's review in *Law and Politics Book Review* 14 (2004): 552–7.

constitutional reforms are neither accompanied by, nor do they result from, any apparent fundamental change in political or economic regimes. The constitutional revolutions in Canada (1982) and Israel (1992–95) are prime examples; these revolutions provide an excellent testing ground for identifying the political origins and consequences of the constitutionalization of rights and the fortification of judicial review. Unlike the constitutional transformations in many former Eastern Bloc countries, South Africa (1995), or Egypt (2012 and 2013), the dramatic constitutional changes in Canada and Israel have not gone hand in hand with major shifts in the political regime. These revolutions therefore exemplify "ideal type" cases of constitutional revolution. Studying these cases makes it possible to disentangle the political motivations for constitutionalization per se from other possible motivations (e.g. reconstruction, independence, democratization, incorporation).

Moreover, these cases provide an effective response to efficiency-driven explanations which claim that constitutionalization occurs to mitigate problems of information, credible commitment, and effective enforcement, since it is unclear why these polities chose to adopt the mechanisms they adopted when they did, and not earlier. Likewise, these cases offer a cogent response to the broad "democratic proliferation," "constitutionalization in the wake of World War II," and "constitutionalization as pre-commitment" theses. It is unclear why members of the Canadian and Israeli public decided to commit themselves against their own imperfections or harmful future desires precisely in 1982 (Canada) or in 1992 (Israel), and not, say, a decade earlier or later. These timing choices are not explained by any of the broader explanations for constitutionalism. As "outlier" cases that are not easily explained by extant theories, the constitutional revolutions in these two countries may shed new light on the origins of constitutionalization.

But there is even more to consider in selecting these cases. When studying the political origins of constitutionalization (as well as the political origins of other institutional reforms), it is important also to take into account events that did *not* occur, and the reasons political power-holders did *not* behave in certain ways. In other words, the political origins of constitutional reform cannot be studied in isolation from the political origins of constitutional stagnation. By studying the origins of constitutional stagnation in the pre-constitutionalization eras in the selected countries, we can compare a series of "no cause/no effect" observations, at least with respect to the absence of the new explanation and of the independent variable (i.e. no reason to act/no action) with a series of combined "cause and effect" observations (i.e. clear presence of a reason to act/clear action). The selection of these outlier cases, therefore, helps to substantiate the hegemonic preservation thesis both by a priori elimination of other possible explanations and by the establishment of controlled comparison of "cause and effect" cases versus "no cause/no effect" cases.

The emergence of "large-N" and "multi-method" studies in comparative constitutionalism

One of the intuitive solutions to problems of heuristics and biases in case selection is a move away from single-case or small-N research toward analyses of large sets of observations, and ideally even the entire studied population. Such a move might provide a response to the limited generalizability associated with single-case and small-N research. With many phenomena, the sheer number of cases makes a complete analysis infeasible. However, when it comes to studying the world's constitutions, the full number of cases is still only in the hundreds. For many purposes this is a manageable number, and as long as quantitative studies limit themselves to what they can plausibly extract and deduce from constitutional texts (and possibly other cross-national indicators), they should be a most welcome addition to comparative constitutional studies. Large-N analyses would be particularly useful as a means to consider broader trends in constitutionalism—to focus on the forest rather than the trees. They may likewise help to empirically substantiate or refute some of the field's conventional wisdoms that, as is often the case, are based on the experience of a single, overanalyzed, and possibly exceptional constitutional setting (think the United States), or on the experience of a small number of "usual suspect" constitutions.

The apparent weaknesses of large-N studies have been addressed repeatedly, most notably (though not exclusively) by proponents of contextual, purportedly deeper research.[86] (Recall the discussion in Chapter 5 of the universalist/culturalist divide in comparative law).

---

[86] For a critique of economics' reliance on numbers to capture the complex nature of law in various contexts, see Pierre Legrand, "Econocentrism," *University of Toronto Law Journal* 59 (2009): 215–22. Legrand begins his powerful critique with an epigraph quote from Nietzsche: "the reduction of all qualities to quantities is nonsense."

Large statistical data sets, it is argued, overlook context or take it too lightly. They ignore the crucial "law on the ground" or "soft law" aspects. They sometimes rely on ready-made data sets or secondary sources that contain processed or formalized data and that require no or very little field work, no true acquaintance with various manifestations of the studied phenomenon, and no background knowledge, linguistic or otherwise. They may apply conceptual frameworks or variable classifications that incorrectly or arbitrarily classify phenomena as the same when they are not, or the reverse. Finally, they sometimes employ crude indices, leading to an inherent reduction of complexity. In short, large-N studies can become a mere numbers game, insensitive to details, stripped of nuance and context, and reliant on oversimplified or inherently biased coding schemes. The entire exercise, critics argue, "can only be based on fictional relationality across laws."[87]

Scientific behavioralism, upon which large-N quantitative studies are based, focuses on observable phenomena but lacks the tools to deal with non-observable ones. Consequently, quantitative studies tend to focus on questions and phenomena that lend themselves a priori to quantitative analysis of concrete observations. Tradition, culture, local knowledge, power relations, and other crucial yet fuzzy factors often get lost or are not adequately accounted for. This, in turn, may lead to what Ian Shapiro succinctly describes as "a flight from reality in the human sciences."[88] Problems of data mining, sample size, or info-glut and too much data are also common in large-N studies. They pour tremendous effort into sophisticated data-analysis techniques, some-times at the expense of net theoretical yield or substantive ingenuity. The inferences they draw from cross-cultural data may be problematic due to spurious (auto)correlation (i.e. initial dependence between apparently independent observations). Finally, there is an imperialist undercurrent to some statistical analysis and large-N jargon, manifested in part in a somewhat dismissive tone toward qualitative, hermeneutic, or normative accounts.

There is more than a kernel of truth in all these concerns. Yet, analyses of large data sets are still a very valuable addition to theory-building and testing in comparative constitutional studies. If properly executed, such analyses may go beyond the clichés, heuristics, and biases that emanate from the decades-long over-study of a handful of cases to actually test

---

[87] Legrand, "Econocentrism" (n 86).
[88] Shapiro, *The Flight from Reality in the Human Sciences* (n 37).

some of the canonical insights of constitutional theory or shed new light on causal links within the constitutional universe. (The reader may be reminded of the exposition in Chapter 5 of the "global south" critique, the "we are the world" attitude, and the question of how generalizable are insights that are drawn from the constitutional experience of a handful of prosperous, politically stable settings). Overcoming the so-called "availability heuristic," which occurs, essentially, when studies draw conclusions from an unrepresentative but readily available or well-known example is of particular importance here.

Consider the following simple, intuitive proposition: "constitutions adopted following a revolution or a coup d'état tend to be more militant in their outlook than constitutions adopted through gradual or negotiated transition." This is a perfectly plausible proposition, but what evidence is there of its accuracy? In order to substantiate it, a researcher could decide to draw on one of the small-N case-selection methods discussed earlier. However, given the broad nature of this proposition, it would probably be preferable if she analyzed an adequate sample of (or even all) revolutionary constitutions and constitutions adopted following extended and inclusive deliberation.

With the rise of the empirical legal studies movement in the American legal academy, comparative constitutional scholars have begun to use research methods, data gathering, and statistical analysis techniques that have been deployed in the social sciences since the 1970s in an attempt to address questions that may not be addressed through small-N analysis. The overall number of studies of this sort is still quite small, but the beginning of a general trend may be detected. Recent works that draw on statistical analyses of large data sets have addressed intriguing issues such as the extent of ideological convergence in constitutional jurisprudence worldwide, the role of inter-jurisdictional emulation in constitutional design, and the efficacy of constitutional power-sharing mechanisms in multiethnic states.[89]

Large-N work within the "legal origins" literature of the late 1990s and early 2000s is relatively well known.[90] Drawing on analysis of large

---

[89] See, e.g., David Law and Mila Versteeg, "The Evolution and Ideology of Global Constitutionalism," *California Law Review* 99 (2011): 1163–258; Zachary Elkins and John Sides, "Can Constitutions Build Unity in Multiethnic States?," *American Political Science Review* 101 (2007): 693–708.

[90] See, generally, Edward Glaeser and Andrei Shleifer, "Legal Origins," *Quarterly Journal of Economics* 117 (2002): 1193–230; and, more concretely, Rafael La Porta et al., "Legal Determinants of External Finance," *Journal of Finance* 52 (1997): 1131–50; Rafael La Porta et al.,

data sets concerning legal traditions (e.g. common law, civil law) and economic indicators in different countries, scholars of comparative law and economics have been able to assess what they define as the "efficiency" of legal systems, and to support the claim that a given country's economic development is greatly affected by the country's legal rules, where it received its law from (including the extent to which there has been colonial transplantation of laws), and the family into which its legal tradition falls. More recent studies offer a nuanced analysis of the "legal origins" thesis across various subfields of economic and business law.[91] Other large-N studies have established a positive correlation between the existence of institutional limitations on government action (e.g. constitutional provisions and judicial review) and economic growth.[92] Quantitative work has likewise become increasingly common in measuring and explaining performance in the area of human rights.[93]

A notable example of how large-N studies may contribute to comparative constitutional studies is *The Endurance of National Constitutions* by Zachary Elkins, Tom Ginsburg, and James Melton ("Melkinsburg").[94] At the core of this pioneering book is an ostensibly simple question: "why do the lifespans of national constitutions vary? Why is it that some live much longer than others?" To answer this, the authors build a data set of constitutions of the world from 1789 to 2005—a mere 216 years of modern constitutionalism. This leads them to some stunning results. First, they note that what is included in national constitutions varies tremendously across polities. So, although constitutional theory assigns certain tasks or functions to a constitution, the constitutions of the world in fact diverge in addressing these functions. While constitutions are written to last, they vary considerably

"Law and Finance," *Journal of Political Economy* 106 (1998): 1113–55; Rafael La Porta et al., "The Quality of Government," *Journal of Law, Economics and Organization* 15 (1999): 222–79; Paul Mahoney, "The Common Law and Economic Growth: Hayek Might Be Right," *Journal of Legal Studies* 30 (2001): 503–25; Andrei Shleifer et al., "Judicial Checks and Balances," *Journal of Political Economy* 112 (2004): 445–70.

[91] Anthony Niblett, Richard A. Posner, and Andrei Shleifer, "The Evolution of a Legal Rule," *Journal of Legal Studies* 39 (2010): 325–58.

[92] See, e.g., Torsten Persson and Guido Tabellini, *The Economic Effects of Constitutions* (MIT Press, 2005).

[93] See, e.g., Malcolm Langford and Sakiko Fukuda-Parr, "The Turn to Metrics," *Nordic Journal of Human Rights* 30 (2012): 222–38. See also, Beth Simmons, *Mobilizing for Human Rights: International Law in Domestic Politics* (Cambridge University Press, 2009).

[94] Zachary Elkins et al., *The Endurance of National Constitutions* (Cambridge University Press, 2009).

in terms of their endurance. Some constitutions are relatively long-lived. Besides the US Constitution, Norway's constitution was adopted in 1814 and is the second oldest constitution currently in existence, while Sweden's 1809 constitution was replaced in 1974 at the age of 165, and the 1874 constitution of Switzerland was replaced in 1999 at the age of 125. The life expectancy of other constitutions, however, is quite short. The authors find that only half of all constitutions last more than nine years, with an overall average of less than 20 years. Thus, the average citizen outside North America, they report, should expect to see her country cycle through four constitutions in her lifetime.

Why the variance in constitutional endurance? The authors group possible explanations into two main categories: "environmental" factors—non-institutional, "software"-like factors, including the social, political, and economic context within which constitutions operate; and "design" factors—matters of constitutional drafting and institutional design. Melkinsburg tend to emphasize the latter category; they argue that while extra-constitutional factors do affect a constitution's endurance, design choices matter more. Furthermore, their data support this claim that design factors are significant, which is itself a major development in the constitutional and institutional design literature. The authors see environmental factors, such as ethnic homogeneity/heterogeneity or a tradition of enduring constitutions, as manifest in the design process: the more heterogeneous a given polity's ethnic makeup, for instance, the greater the likelihood that the issue of ethnic cleavages will be addressed by constitutional framers (e.g. through protection of core group identity issues, limited sovereignty and jurisdictional autonomy, language rights, and so on). All in all, enduring constitutions tend to be specific, to emerge by virtue of a relatively open drafting stage that engenders "buy-in" by diverse constituencies, and to be adaptable as a result of amending formulae and provisions for incorporating modern practices. These three design choices "result from the constitution-making process itself, but are also features of ongoing practice. All three mutually reinforce each other to produce a vigorous constitutional politics in which groups have a stake in the survival of the constitution."[95]

---

[95] Elkins et al., *The Endurance of National Constitutions* (n 94), 89.

As in most large-N studies, Melkinsburg do not engage in exhaustive analysis of their cases. They treat their research subjects (constitutions of the world) much like a doctor in a triage system treats patients: with empathy and urgency, but ultimately in a distant, composed fashion. They conduct multivariate quantitative analysis in several chapters, while others are based on brief illustrative case studies. Their grasp of the pertinent constitutional theory arguments and political science literature is impressive. Perhaps most importantly, their project, even if somewhat overly a-contextual and "non-ethnographic" at times (Clifford Geertz's life expectancy certainly would not have increased had he read this book), opens up entirely new possibilities for research and constitutional drafting, notably the possibility of a "scientific," "planned," perhaps even computerized process of constitutional design—be it macro (e.g. containing pressures in a multiethnic polity) or micro (e.g. determining what is the most suitable judicial appointments strategy).[96]

Another captivating illustration of the possibilities of large-N comparative constitutional studies is Benedikt Goderis and Mila Versteeg's attempt to substantiate the transnational imitation or diffusion element informing the spread of constitutionalism throughout the world.[97] Constitutions are commonly described as inherently national products, shaped by domestic politics and reflecting the views and values of the nation. Goderis and Versteeg develop and empirically test a different hypothesis, which is that constitutions are also shaped by transnational influences, or "diffusion." Constitutional provisions, they argue, can diffuse through four possible mechanisms: competition, coercion, learning, and acculturation. Using a new data set based on the coding of 108 constitutional rights in 188 countries over the period 1946 to 2006, they find that constitution-makers are affected by the status of constitutional rights in countries with which they share a common legal origin, compete for foreign aid, share a common religion, and share colonial ties. By contrast, factors such as trade relationships and shared export markets, amongst others, do not generally explain the diffusion of constitutional rights. Zachary Elkins conducts a different

---

[96] On the possibility of computerized constitutional design see, e.g., David Law, "Constitutions," in Peter Cane and Herbert Kritzer, eds., *The Oxford Handbook of Empirical Legal Research* (Oxford University Press, 2010), 376.

[97] Benedikt Goderis and Mila Versteeg, *The Transnational Origins of Constitutions: An Empirical Investigation* (SSRN eLibrary, Aug. 2011).

empirical examination of the diffusion thesis. Drawing on an original set of data on the content of 19th-century European constitutions, Elkins shows that although Europe inherited its fundamental laws from a variety of sources, its constitutionalization was very much the result of diffusion. This finding disturbs some of the conventional thinking about European democratization, which tends to emphasize variation in *domestic* class structure and other important factors inside nation-states.[98]

Much has been written about the global convergence on constitutional supremacy, and the corresponding rise of an apparently universal constitutional discourse, primarily visible in the context of rights. Large-N studies may serve to assess the actual degree of such convergence. In a recent article, Courtney Jung, Evan Rosevear, and I examine the global constitutional homogeneity claim with respect to economic and social rights.[99] Based on a data set that identifies the status of 17 distinct economic and social rights in the world's constitutions (195 in total), we make four arguments that problematize the sweeping global convergence claim. First, although economic and social rights (ESRs) have grown increasingly common in national constitutions, not all ESRs are equally widespread. Whereas a right to education is so common as to be practically universal, rights to food or water are still very rare. Second, constitutions accord ESRs different statuses, or strengths. Roughly one-third of countries identify all ESRs as justiciable, another one-third identify all ESRs as aspirational, and the last one-third identify some ESRs as aspirational and some as justiciable. Third, legal tradition—whether a country has a tradition of civil, common, Islamic, or customary law—is a strong predictor of whether a constitution will have ESRs and whether those rights will be justiciable. Fourth, whereas regional differences partly confound the explanatory power of legal traditions, region and legal tradition retain an independent effect on constitutional entrenchment of ESRs. We conclude by suggesting that despite the prevalence of ESRs in national constitutions, as of 2013 there was still considerable variance with respect to the formal status, scope, and nature of such rights. Because the divergence reflects lasting determinants such as legal tradition and region, it is likely to persist.

---

[98] Zachary Elkins, "Diffusion and the Constitutionalization of Europe," *Comparative Political Studies* 43 (2010): 969–99.

[99] Courtney Jung, Ran Hirschl, and Evan Rosevear, "Economic and Social Rights in National Constitutions," *American Journal of Comparative Law* 62 (2014): 1043–1093.

In another article, David Law and Mila Versteeg test empirically the claim that the United States' constitutional legacy may be losing its influence over constitutionalism in other countries because it is increasingly dated, idiosyncratic, and generally out of step with an evolving global consensus on issues of human rights.[100] The authors find support for this proposition through an analysis of the content of the world's constitutions over the past 60 years. They argue that "there is a significant and growing generic component to global constitutionalism, in the form of a set of rights provisions that appear in nearly all formal constitutions." Using their data, they identify the world's most and least generic constitutions; placing the United States on the resulting continuum, they show that the US Constitution is increasingly distant from the global constitutional mainstream. Because of the method of inquiry they use, the authors cannot trace deeper, non-textual or invisible patterns of American constitutional influence on other countries' constitutional practice. But, that limitation aside, they are able to support empirically the prevalent intuition that the American influence on global constitutionalism is, by and large, on the decline.

Tom Ginsburg and Mila Versteeg's recent quantitative work on the origins of constitutional review provides another textbook illustration of how large-N statistical analysis may effectively complement and support the development of original constitutional thought.[101] Drawing on an original data set of over 200 countries from 1781 onward, Ginsburg and Versteeg put various existing explanations for why countries adopt constitutional review to a systematic empirical test. They find, in a nutshell, that the adoption of constitutional review is best explained by domestic politics and, in particular, uncertainties in the electoral market. This finding is in line with earlier qualitative or small-N work by Tom Ginsburg and myself that I discussed earlier in this chapter. Specifically, the authors find that electoral competition, as measured by the difference between the proportion of seats held by the first and second parties in the legislative branch, predicts the adoption of constitutional review. This phenomenon, they find, is present in autocracies and democracies alike. With respect to rival theories, Ginsburg and Versteeg do not find robust evidence to support theories of

---

[100] David Law and Mila Versteeg, "The Declining Influence of the United States Constitution," *NYU Law Review* 87 (2012): 762–858.

[101] Tom Ginsburg and Mila Versteeg, "Why Do Countries Adopt Constitutional Review?" *Journal of Law, Economics and Organization* 30 (2014): 587–622.

transnational diffusion, or the idea that constitutional review is adopted in response to previous adoption by other states. Although there is some evidence of diffusion in the sub-sample of democratic regimes, it is not identified as a main factor on a global scale.

To reiterate: large-N studies like those described here inevitably overlook certain details and nuances that may be crucial to understanding many of the individual cases. Existential constitutional battles in Malaysia over the place of Islam in law and politics, the impact of Confucian values on Korean constitutional identity, or how progressive norms with respect to reproductive freedoms or same-sex marriage are transforming rights jurisprudence in Latin America are not the kind of contextual nuances that are best captured by large-N studies of constitutions. In addition, a given polity's constitution is often considered one of the most ideational, context-dependent components of its law, and a reflection of its history, culture, worldviews, and aspirations. The preamble of Iraq's constitution, for instance, reads in part "We are the people of the land between the two rivers, the homeland of apostles and prophets . . . pioneers of civilization . . . Upon our land the first law made by man was passed." The preamble of the constitution of China emphasizes the accomplishments of a collective people. The Irish constitution invokes the "Most Holy Trinity," while the French constitution proclaims France a secular republic.[102] Over one billion people now live in "constitutional theocracies"—an apparently oxymoronic concept according to which a state enshrines a single religion and its interlocutors as *a* or *the* source of legislation and at the same time subscribes to most core principles of modern constitutionalism.[103] In Bosnia and Herzegovina, the Dayton Accords introduced a new constitution according to which the country's constitutional court must comprise two judges of Croat decent, two of Serb decent, two of Bosniak origin, and three international jurists appointed by the European Court of Human Rights who cannot be citizens of Bosnia and Herzegovina or any of its neighboring states. The list of unique constitutional creations goes on and on. Without attention to details of this nature, important nuances and idiosyncrasies are easily lost.

This, however, is not a sufficient reason to dismiss large-N studies of constitutionalism as overly broad or without value. Modern

---

[102] See Vicki Jackson, "Methodological Challenges in Comparative Constitutional Law," *Penn State International Law Review* 28 (2010): 319–26.

[103] Hirschl, *Constitutional Theocracy* (n 58).

constitutions do share many common features and functions, and the constitutional experience across polities does contain certain universal elements. Many political concepts—democracy, political participation, and responsible government, to pick just a few—are overly idealistic and often ring hollow without attention to the context within which they are exercised. But does that mean that no general account of any of these concepts is valid?

Consider the study of nutritious, healthy eating. The populations of the world vary considerably in what types of foods they consume and how they prepare and consume it. Cultural, environmental, genetic, and material factors all influence most people's diets. At first glance, then, what, how, and when people eat is very much a context-dependent activity. And yet, all people do eat. Indeed, despite all the important differences among them, most human beings feed on one combination or another of grains, dairy products, fruits and vegetables, and protein-rich foods. Thus, no one in their right mind would dismiss credible studies that highlight a general, cross-cultural risk in the frequent consumption of foods rich in trans fats. Likewise, a blanket dismissal of well-executed large-N studies of comparative constitutional law grounded solely in the fact that such studies "ignore context" is increasingly hard to justify. The truth is that these studies can be a useful addition to comparative constitutional studies provided that they acknowledge their embedded neglect of context and nuances. Tracing broad patterns and formulating general rules applicable across contexts is one of the meta-goals of modern scientific inquiry, and this is precisely what large-N studies attempt to do. For this reason, the new trend toward large-N studies in comparative constitutional law, however imperfect it may be, is to be loudly applauded.

Furthermore, small-N and large-N (and likewise, qualitative and quantitative) studies are not necessarily mutually exclusive; in fact, in many ways they are mutually supportive. Whereas small-N studies may be better for generating hypotheses and identifying possible causal links among pertinent variables, large-N studies more effectively test the validity and general applicability of such links. Indeed, the two types of studies may be combined in a single study, either by way of medium-N studies,[104] or through the creation of a multi- or mixed-method

---

[104] For an effective illustration of such an approach in action, see Diana Kapiszewski, "Tactical Balancing: High Court Decision Making on Politically Crucial Cases," *Law and Society Review* 45 (2011): 471–506.

research design that utilizes the advantages of two or more case-selection, data-collection, and analysis approaches.[105] Multi-method research is underpinned by the principle of triangulation (and in fact is often referred to as "triangulation"), which means that researchers should ensure they are not overreliant on a single research method, and should instead follow more than one measurement procedure when investigating a research problem. In this way, multi-method research enhances confidence in findings. In other words, the effects of the trade-off between contextual sensitivity and universal applicability may be mitigated by tackling a research question via a synthesis of a large-N statistical analysis *and* a detailed examination of crucial or indicative cases—or through any other effective combination of research styles at each stage of the process.[106] Research on the impact of constitutions, constitutional provisions, or constitutional jurisprudence might combine randomized examination, large-N analysis drawn from many constitutional settings, and in-depth case studies of particular provisions or rulings. Diversifying their approach to research design will allow comparative constitutional scholars to reach stronger, more meaningful conclusions about constitutional law and institutions worldwide.

Conclusion

Comparative study has emerged as the new frontier of constitutional law scholarship. Increasingly, jurists and legal scholars worldwide are accepting that "we are all comparativists now." Accordingly, the 21st century has been described the "era of comparative law."[107] And

---

[105] See, e.g., Evan Lieberman, "Nested Analysis," *American Political Science Review* 99 (2005): 435–52. An effective illustration of this approach in the area of comparative and international human rights is Simmons, *Mobilizing for Human Rights* (n 93).

[106] See, e.g., Rudra Sil and Peter Katzenstein, *Beyond Paradigms: Analytic Eclecticism in the Study of World Politics* (Palgrave Macmillan, 2010); Kristin Luker, *Salsa Dancing into the Social Sciences: Research in an Age of Info-glut* (Harvard University Press, 2008); James Mahoney and Gary Goertz, "A Tale of Two Cultures: Contrasting Quantitative and Qualitative Research," *Political Analysis* 14 (2006): 227–49.

[107] Esin Örücü, *The Enigma of Comparative Law: Variations on a Theme for the Twenty-first Century* (Martinus Nijhoff, 2004), 216.

yet, despite this tremendous renaissance, the "comparative" aspect of comparative constitutional law, as a method and a project, remains under-theorized and blurry.

Comparative constitutionalism has fascinated academics worldwide, but the decision to engage with it has not always led to methodologically astute research design.[108] Rather, the field of comparative constitutional law remains quite eclectic, and continues to lack coherent methodological and epistemological foundations. Fundamental questions concerning the very purpose and rationale of comparative inquiry and how it is to be undertaken remain largely unanswered in canonical constitutional law scholarship. While the field has made a remarkable leap forward over the past few years—primarily through comparative research aimed at generating thick, multifaceted descriptions, concepts, and tools for thinking—most leading works in comparative constitutional studies still lag behind the best of the social sciences in their ability to use controlled comparison to trace causal links among pertinent variables or phenomena, let alone in their ability to substantiate or refute testable hypotheses.

"I would rather discover a single causal connection than win the throne of Persia," said the Greek philosopher Democritus (c. 460–370 BCE) more than two millennia ago. Regrettably, tracing causal connections—one of the main goals of scientific inquiry, quantitative or qualitative, positive or hermeneutic—remains largely beyond the purview of comparative constitutional law scholarship. If we contrast the approaches of legal academics with the approaches of social scientists to the same sets of comparative constitutional phenomena, we find that the scholarship produced by legal academics often overlooks (or is unaware of) basic methodological principles of controlled comparison, research design, and case selection. And when we expand our lens beyond comparative constitutionalism to capture the entire comparative law enterprise, the methodological matrix becomes even more blurred.

This situation may be due in part to traditional doctrinal boundaries, varying trajectories of academic training, and the different epistemologies of social and legal inquiry. It is likely a reflection of the conceptualization of the constitutional domain as domestic and predominantly legal in nature, and a focus on context, meaning, and contingencies in the

---

[108] Barbara Geddes, *Paradigms, and Sand Castles: Theory Building and Research Design in Comparative Politics* (University of Michigan Press, 2003).

study of a given nation's constitutional development. Of those who do engage in constitutional comparison, too many still adhere to a "cherry-picking" approach to case selection while overlooking (or being unaware of) the basic methodological principles of controlled comparison and research design frequently drawn upon in the social sciences. Continued reliance on such an unsystematic, methodology-light practice of research design and case selection does not serve the cause of serious theory-building well. In fact, it is precisely because the concern over a-systematic "cherry-picking" case selection may not be easily dismissed that scholars who wish to engage in valuable comparative work ought to pay close attention to principles of case selection. Their response to this important concern should not be to abandon comparative work; rather, it should be to engage in comparative work while being mindful of key methodological considerations.

Comparative constitutionalists should also be attentive to analytical differences among empirical modes of inquiry (descriptive, taxonomical, and explanatory) and between data-based (*is*) claims and normative (*ought*) claims. These types and modes are not mutually exclusive, and may well be brought together to generate grand works of comparative constitutional studies. However, heedless conflation of them is not conducive to coherent theory-building in the field. In conducting and reporting research, we should try to clearly define their intended level of generalization and applicability—which may range from context-specific to universal and abstract. Once these ideals have been met, case-selection and data-analysis methods that match and are in concert with the inquiry's main goal and level of generalization are to be adopted.

Reliance on comparative research in the quest to *explain* variance in legal phenomena across polities is not foreign to the legal discipline. Explanation, as opposed to mere description or taxonomy, has long been a main objective of evolutionist and functionalist approaches to legal transformation, and of comparative law more generally.[109] It has also characterized various non-doctrinal approaches as well as the emerging trend toward empirical legal scholarship. There is no

---

[109] For a general survey of the evolutionist tradition in comparative law, see Peter Stein, *Legal Evolution: The Story of an Idea* (Cambridge University Press, 1980). For a general survey of the functionalist tradition in comparative law, see Michele Graziadei, "The Functionalist Heritage," in Pierre Legrand and Roderick Munday, eds., *Comparative Legal Studies: Traditions and Transitions* (Cambridge University Press, 2003).

apparent reason why the study of comparative constitutional law could not engage in a more explanation-oriented mode of scholarship.

Granted, detailed taxonomy and the formation of sophisticated concepts are fundamental to any academic endeavor, including the study of the yet under-charted terrain of comparative constitutional law. In addition, adherence to quasi-scientific, controlled comparison principles of research design is certainly not the only valuable mode of social, let alone legal inquiry. As Gary King, Robert Keohane, and Sidney Verba assert, research designs are necessarily imperfect, and involve trade-offs between valid, competing goals.[110] And any type of academic inquiry that advances our knowledge and understanding of the enterprise of public law in a meaningful way—be it qualitative or quantitative, normative or positivist, descriptive or analytical—is potentially of great value. But why compromise? As Law and Versteeg suggest, "methodological pluralism is healthy for any academic discipline, and constitutional law is no exception."[111] My own vision of social science methodology is similar to that articulated by Henry Brady's "workshop of tools" metaphor, in which all methods are "constantly being used and redesigned to fashion an understanding of reality," and where "there is no master tool, but there is constant attention to improving the relationship between the tools and the projects at hand."[112] In other words, methodological pluralism and well-thought-out analytical eclecticism ought to be endorsed provided that the research design and methods of comparison reflect the analytical aims or intellectual goals of the study, and that a rational, analytically adaptive connection exists between the research questions and the comparative methods used.

Accordingly, adherence to inference-oriented principles of research design and case selection is not required as long as one does not profess to determine causality or to develop explanatory knowledge. However, intellectual integrity warrants that when one aspires to establish meaningful causal claims or explanatory theories through comparative inquiry, she must follow inference-oriented research-design and case-selection principles. Neither advanced knowledge of the epistemological foundations of social inquiry nor mastery of complex research methods is

---

[110] King et al., *Designing Social Inquiry* (n 60).
[111] Law and Versteeg, "Evolution and Ideology" (n 89), 1248.
[112] Henry Brady, "Introduction to Symposium: Two Paths to a Science of Politics," *Perspectives on Politics* 2 (2004): 295–300, 297.

required. As we have seen, awareness of the methodological strengths and weaknesses of common research types, along with adherence to a few basic inference-oriented case-selection principles—such as the "most similar cases" and "most different cases" principles, the "prototypical cases" principle, the "most difficult case" principle, and the "outlier cases" principle—fill this gap.

To be perfectly clear, methodology concerns the means and not the ends of academic inquiry. Methods are employed to answer questions of interest and relevance to the contemporary world, and not for their own sake. The scholarly mission is to go forth seeking answers to problems and to use methods as an aid, not to choose problems because they can be answered by a favored method. That said, closer attention to, and more frequent deployment of, inference-oriented case-selection principles would be of particular value in the study of the transnational migration of constitutional ideas. After all, despite the general agreement that a large-scale migration of constitutional ideas has been taking place, we still know precious little about the actual extent of this phenomenon, let alone why, when, and how it has been occurring or is likely to occur. Why is the migration of constitutional ideas happening, and who are its main agents and advocates? Which polities and courts are the most and least receptive to transnational migration of constitutional ideas, and why? Which types of constitutional controversies are most conducive to inter-court borrowing? What makes certain cases canonical in comparative constitutional jurisprudence? What is the impact of the migration of constitutional ideas on methods of constitutional interpretation and reasoning? What links can be identified between the triumph of democracy, the emergence of an economic and cultural "global village," and the transnational migration of constitutional ideas? What accounts for the variance in scope, nature, and timing of various countries' and courts' convergence to the constitutional supremacy model? And what explains the variance among jurisdictions in government implementation or judicial enforcement of similar constitutional rights provisions? Answering these and other pertinent questions requires explaining and determining causality, writ small or large. Such questions cannot be answered with a juristic methodology or by legal argumentation alone. For this reason, the turn from comparative constitutional *law* to comparative constitutional *studies* is as urgently warranted as it is indisputably opportune.

Epilogue

Comparative Constitutional Law, Quo Vadis?

Our comparative constitutional journey reveals several insights, chief among them are three. First, the engagement with the constitutive laws of others has a long history. This engagement has taken place for a variety of reasons: out of necessity, out of curiosity, or as has often been the case (whether overtly acknowledged as such or not), as a means to a political end. From empires and communities long gone to timeless intellectuals and political visionaries, comparative constitutional encounters comprise a much richer field than is often captured in current scholarly conversations. Some of the purportedly fresh debates in comparative constitutional law have early equivalents: dilemmas of community and identity, tensions between the local and the universal, and convergence pressures and counter-resistance. These are all well known to historians of ideas, but have yet to be excavated and studied by constitutional scholars with a penchant for the contemporary and the "new."

Second, comparative constitutionalism is a political act as much as it is a legal or jurisprudential one. When it comes to constitutional law, we see an increasing uniformity across the world; but even so, it is clear that the domestic and particular persist. Virtually all constitutional settings—frequently studied or commonly overlooked—face frictions between the general and the contextual, the universal and the particular. In some settings, a rapid convergence upon global trends may be detected. In others, constitutional law's version of what has been termed *glocalization*—the process whereby the global and the local merge to form a new, perfectly authentic synthesis—has evolved. Engagement with the constitutive laws of others, near and far, is an important manifestation of these frictions and a key medium through which they play themselves out. From Antonin Scalia to Simón Bolívar to Jean Bodin, such engagements may include outright rejection, selective engagement with, or full endorsement of the comparative constitutional domain. Even so, a wider lens is needed. The epistemological, normative, and methodological grounds upon which these engagements take place cannot be understood without consideration of the social and political context within which they evolve.

Third, the dramatic political transformations of the past few decades and the "pax liberalis" that ensued has given rise to a stunning renaissance of comparative constitutional inquiry; this renaissance has of course been greatly facilitated by economic and technological interconnectedness. From constitution drafting in the Middle East to landmark rulings by apex courts in Germany, India, or Brazil and on to the publication of innovative scholarly accounts of comparative constitutionalism, not a week passes without a major development in the field. Comparative constitutional law now truly encompasses the world, real and academic. But for the latter to capture the former, a break-up of traditional disciplinary boundaries—already underway in some important respects—is required.[1] Given the inherently political nature of comparative engagement with the constitutive laws of others, a close dialogue with the social sciences is essential if we are to fully grasp, and then go on to explicate, the comparative constitutional enterprise, revealing in the process its various meanings, aims, and promises. Only a true conversation between pertinent research communities—legal, political, and philosophical—would ensure that such advancement occurs. The traditional intra-legal focus and "case law" method of instruction, or the accompanying normative persuasion that public law is a politics-free domain driven by analytical principles in defiance of everything we know about the world clearly cannot accomplish that goal by themselves. They must be complemented with pertinent insights and methods from the human sciences, qualitative and quantitative.

The means are readily available. In 1667, while completing his doctorate of law, Gottfried Wilhelm Leibniz—one of the great thinkers of all time—envisioned a utopian *theatrum legale mundi* ("theatre of the legal

---

[1] The manifesto of the recently launched International Society of Public Law, to pick one example, suggests that "some of the finest insights on public law come from social scientists deeply cognizant of law; also is there any legal scholarship that does not make at least some use of the theoretical and the empirical understandings and methodologies external to the 'legal discipline' *stricto sensu?*"

world"): an imagined repository that would include the entire corpus of the laws of all peoples at all places and in all times. This, Leibniz speculated, would be the driving engine of comparative legal inquiry and would allow for the discovery or articulation of universal principles of law. Nearly 350 years later, Leibniz's vision has become a reality, at least with respect to constitutional law. The universal aspiration is not shared by all, but extensive data sets and online information, powerful computer search engines, and an ever-expanding network of jurists and scholars allow those who are fascinated by the world of new constitutionalism easy and effective access to the constitutional laws, practices, and jurisprudence of virtually all countries in the world.

The modern materialization of such a *theatrum*—the rapid development of information technology and the tremendous improvement in the quality and accessibility of data sources on constitutional systems and jurisprudence worldwide—has already had an effect on the way in which comparative constitutional inquiries are pursued. In particular, thanks to the accessible, rich body of pertinent information, it is now possible—perhaps for the first time—to engage in serious, methodological, interdisciplinary dialogue between ideas and evidence, theory and data, normative claims and empirical analysis. It may well be that there is no appetite within certain disciplinary or epistemic communities to pursue such an interdisciplinary conversation. But from an open-minded and intellectually honest standpoint, it is the call of the hour.

Above all, it is the *comparative* element that separates comparative constitutional law from its older, more established, supposedly self-contained and undoubtedly less cosmopolitan sibling: constitutional law. Hence, an understanding of the "comparative" in comparative constitutional law—its various rationales, methods, limitations, and possibilities, alongside the contours and contents of the modern comparativist's toolkit—is essential for the field's renaissance to persist. It is my hope that this book contributes in some way toward the advent of such an understanding, and that en route it helps the fascinating, timely, and topical area of comparative constitutional inquiry to carve with confidence an intellectual home alongside other comparative undertakings.

Table of Cases

Canada

Chaoulli v. Quebec (AG), [2005] 1 SCR 791 183
Gosselin v. Quebec (AG), [2002] 4 SCR 429 184
Health Services and Support-Facilities Subsector Bargaining
    Assn v. British Columbia, [2007] 2 SCR 391 184
R v. Oakes, [1986] 1 SCR 103 139
R v. Prosper, [1994] 3 SCR 236 184
Reference re Secession of Quebec, [1998] 2 SCR 217 139

Egypt

Wassel v. Minister of Education (the niqab [veil] case), Case
    No. 8 of the 17th Judicial Year (May 18, 1996) 93

European Court of Human Rights

Lautsi and Others v. Italy, Application No. 30814/06 (ECtHR,
    Grand Chamber, judgment of Mar. 18, 2011) 202
Şahin v. Turkey, Application No. 44774/98 (ECtHR, Grand
    Chamber, judgment of Nov. 10, 2005) 236, 237
Sejdić and Finci v. Bosnia and Herzegovina, Application
    Nos. 27996/06 and 3483/06 (ECtHR, Grand Chamber,
    judgment of Dec. 22, 2009) 201

Germany

BverfG, 2 BvR 2134/92, and 2 BvR 2159/92 [1994]
    (Maastricht Case) 200
BVerfG, 2 BvE 2/08 [2009] (Lisbon Treaty Case) 168

India

Adithyan (N.) v. Travancore Devaswom Board AIR 2002
    SC 106 94
Commissioner, Hindu Religious Endowments, Madras v.
    Sri Lakshmindra Thirtha Swamiar AIR 1954 SC 282 96

Emmanuel (Bijoe) v. State of Kerala AIR 1987 SC 748 95
Jagdishwaranand (Acharya) v. Commissioner of Police,
    Calcutta AIR 1984 SC 51 94
Javed v. State of Haryana AIR 2003 SC 3057 96
Kaur (Gurleen) v. State of Punjab C.W.P. No. 14859/2008
    (decision released on May 30, 2009) [High Court of
    Punjab and Haryana] 95
Koushal (Suresh Kumar) and another v. Naz Foundation
    and others (2014) 1 SCC 1 74
Koushal v. NAZ Foundation, Civil Appeal 10972/2013
    (decision released Dec. 11, 2013) 74
Narayana (T. V.) v. Venkata Subbamma AIR 1996
    SC 1807 . . . . 94, 95
National Legal Services Authority v. Union of India and
    others, Writ Petition (Civil) 400/2012 and Writ Petition
    (Civil) 604/2013 (decision released Apr. 15, 2014) 73
Naz Foundation v. Government of NCT of Delhi, WP(C)
    No. 7455/2001 (decision released July 2, 2009)
    [High Court, Delhi] 73
Novartis v. Union of India & Others, Civil Appeal
    No. 2706-2716/2013 (decision released Apr. 1, 2013) 218
Qureshi (Mohd. Hanif) v. State of Bihar AIR 1958 SC 731 95
Saheb (Sardar Syedna Taher Saifuddin) v. State of Bombay
    AIR 1962 SC 853 96
State of Gujarat v. Mirzapur Moti Kureshi Kassab Jamat (2005)
    8 SCC 534 95
State of West Bengal v. Ashutosh Lahiri AIR 1995 SC 464 95

Israel

HCJ 7052/03 Adalah v. Minister of Interior, [2006] 2 TakEl
    1754 (Citizenship Law/Family Unification Case I) 44, 45, 58
HCJ 5507/96 Amir v. Haifa District Court, 50(3) P.D. 321
    (1997) 66
HCJ 1000/92 Bavli v. The Great Rabbinical Court, 48(2) P.D. 6
    (1995) 65, 66
HCJ 5227/97 David v. Great Rabbinical Court, 55(1) P.D. 453
    (1998) 66
HCJ 721/94 El Al Airlines Ltd. v. Danilowitch et al., 48 (5)
    P.D. 749 (1995) 61

CA 140/00 Ettinger Estate v. Jewish Quarter Co. [2004]
    IsrLR 97 (SCI) 46
HCJ 466/07 MK Zahava Gal-On (Meretz-Yahad) et al.
    v. Attorney General et al. (decision delivered on Jan. 11, 2012)
    (Citizenship Law/Family Unification Case II) 46
HCJ 1067/08 Noar Ke'Halacha v. Ministry of Education [2009]
    IsrLR 84 (decision delivered on Aug. 6, 2009) 64
CA 3077/90 Plonit ("Jane Doe") v. Ploni ("John Doe"), 49(2)
    P.D. 578 (1996) 65
HCJ 293/00 Plonit ("Jane Doe") v. The Great Rabbinical
    Court, 55(3) P.D. 318 (2001) 66
HCJ 8928/06 Plonit ("Jane Doe") v. The Great Rabbinical
    Court (decision delivered on Oct. 8, 2008) 66, 67
HCJ 746/07 Ragen v. Ministry of Transport (decision released
    on Jan. 5, 2011) 64
HCJ 2597/99 Thais-Rodriguez Tushbaim v. Minister of Interior,
    59(6) P.D. (2005) 64
CA 6821/93 United Mizrahi Bank v. Migdal Cooperative
    Village, 49(4) P.D. 221 (1995) (SCI) 44

Kuwait
Ministry of Islamic Affairs v. Rola Dashti and Aseel al-Awadhi,
    Constitutional Court of Kuwait, Decision of Oct. 28, 2009 . . . 94

Malaysia
Ishak (Meor Atiqulrahman) et al. v. Fatimah Sihi et al., 4 CLJ
    1 (2006) 96
Kamaruddin v. Public Services Commission Malaysia [1994]
    3 MLJ 61 96

Pakistan
Ahmed (Qazi Hussain) et al. v. General Pervez Musharraf, Chief
    Executive and Another, P.L.D. 2002 S.C. 853 70
Khan (Hakim) v. Government of Pakistan, P.L.D. 1992
    S.C. 595 69
Reference 2/2005 In Re: NWFP Hisba Bill, P.L.D. 2005
    S.C. 873 94
Shah (Syed Zafar Ali) v. Pervez Musharraf, P.L.D. 2000
    S.C. 869 169

Constitution Petition 9/2009 Sindh High Court Bar
   Association v. Federation of Pakistan, P.L.D. 2009
   S.C. 789 169

Philippines
G.R. 191200, Arturo M. De Castro v. Judicial and Bar Council,
   et al. (Mar. 17, 2010) 169

Romania
Constitutional Court Advisory Opinion No. 1/2012 (President
   Băsescu Suspension Case) [July 6, 2012] 56, 57
Constitutional Court Decision No. 334/2013 (Referendum
   Law Case) [June 26, 2013] 57

Singapore
Ramalingam Ravinthram v. Attorney General, [2012] SGCA 2 . . . 40

South Africa
S v. Makwanyane, 1995 (3) SA 391 (CC) 26, 236

Turkey
TCC Decision 116/2008 (Unconstitutional Constitutional
   Amendment Case), decision released June 5, 2008; legal
   reasoning released Oct. 22, 2008 . . . . 71, 168
TCC Decision 57/2001 (Virtue [Fazilet] Party Dissolution case),
   June 21, 2001 71
TCC Decision 1/1998 (Welfare [Refah] Party Dissolution case),
   Jan. 16, 1998 71

Uganda
Election Petition 1/2001, Rtd. Col. Dr. Besigye Kizza v. Yoweri
   Kaguta Museveni & The Electoral Commission, [2001]
   UGSC 3 (SC) 55
Election Petition 1/2006, Rtd. Col. Dr. Kizza Besigye v.
   Electoral Commission, Yoweri Kaguta Museveni, [2007]
   UGSC 24 (SC) 55, 169

United Kingdom
Borough of Hackney Case, 31 L.T.R. 69 (2 O'M. and H.77)
   [1874] 56
R (E) v. Governing Body of JFS [2009] UKSC 15 64

R (on the application of Shabina Begum) v. Headteacher and
    Governors of Denbigh High School [2006] UKHL 15 96

United States

Atkins v. Virginia, 536 U.S. 304 (2002) 27, 142
Awad (Muneer) et al. v. Paul Ziriax et al., Case No.
    CIV-10-1186-M (W.D. Okla. August 15, 2013)
Bowers v. Hardwick, 478 U.S. 186 (1986) 142
Brown v Board of Education, 347 U.S. 483 (1954) 27, 32, 261
Bush v. Gore, 531 U.S. 98 (2000) 143
Lawrence v. Texas, 539 U.S. 558 (2003) 26, 27, 142
Mapp v Ohio, 367 U.S. 643 (1961) 32
Marbury v. Madison, 5 U.S. 137 (1803) 44
Miranda v. Arizona, 384 U.S. 436 (1966) 32, 146
Roper v. Simmons, 543 U.S. 551 (2005) 26, 27, 142

Index

Introductory Note

References such as "178–9" indicate (not necessarily continuous) discussion of a topic across a range of pages. Wherever possible in the case of topics with many references, these have either been divided into sub-topics or only the most significant discussions of the topic are listed. Because the entire work is about 'comparative constitutional law', the use of this term (and certain others which occur constantly throughout the book) as an entry points has been minimized. Information will be found under the corresponding detailed topics.

accommodation 141, 201, 203, 213, 215, 263
accountability, judicial 250
Achenwall, Gottfried 11, 113, 126–7
Ackerman, Bruce 1, 171
active judicial review 2, 12, 139, 181
activism, judicial 45, 162, 172, 179, 216
adjudication, constitutional 19, 163, 233
affiliation, religious 45, 64, 68, 102, 174, 215
Afghanistan 87, 174, 209
Africa 25, 75, 130, 138, 140, 207, 212
AKP 71, 168
ALAC (American Laws for American Court) 146
al-Andalus 82, 105
American Laws for American Court (ALAC) 146
anthropology, social 189, 199, 227
apex courts, see peak courts
Arab Spring 149, 215
Ardashir I 89
Arendt, Hannah 51
Argentina 9, 73–4, 85, 167, 220, 252, 265
    Supreme Court 74, 252
Aristotle 73, 81
Arizona 32, 146–7

Aroney, Nicholas 36, 186, 227
Ashkenaz 78, 89, 100, 106
Asia 4, 138, 140, 160, 162, 212, 218–19
aspirations 13, 22, 43, 50, 74–5, 226, 231
Assyrians 108, 119
Athens 117–18
Atkins v. Virginia 27, 142
Australia 27–8, 31, 35–7, 43–4, 47–8, 73, 233–4
    Constitution 233–4
    High Court 36
Austria 38, 221, 237
authority 30–1, 33, 65–8, 81–4, 115–16, 122–3, 125–6
    constitutional 150, 200
    judicial 30, 145
    moral 110, 199
    persuasive 23–5
    religious 59, 82, 93, 98, 108
    ultimate 89, 107, 116
autonomy
    cultural 105
    jurisdictional 67, 90–1, 105, 271
    regional 134
    religious 89

Bacon, Francis 11, 113, 120
Bakr-Id 95

Balkin, Jack 147
Bangladesh 50, 181, 212
Barak, Aharon 22, 25, 45–9,
    58, 144
Bavli 65–7
Baxi, Upendra 205, 210, 214
Bayesian probability 18, 230
Beatty, David 239
Belgium 176, 237, 251
beliefs 14, 76, 91, 109, 158, 166
Berman, Harold 83–5
best practice 196, 225
Beza, Theodore 116–17
Bharatiya Janata Party (BJP) 215
biases 210, 212, 224, 267–8
    case selection 9, 23; *see also*
        cherry-picking
Bijoe Emmanuel v. State of Kerala 95
bilingualism 12, 49, 139
bills of rights 12, 139, 145, 171, 173,
    258, 263
bishops 85, 126
BJP (Bharatiya Janata Party) 215
blasphemy 85, 88
Boas, Franz 199
Bobek, Michal 25, 37
Bodin, Jean 7, 11–12, 113–20,
    149, 283
Bogdandy, Armin von 150, 152,
    190–1
Bolívar, Simón 7, 12, 114, 133–7, 149
borrowing 74–5, 101, 137, 143, 197,
    240, 281
Bosnia and Herzegovina 201–2, 275
Botswana 1, 26, 212, 236
Bourdieu, Pierre 53
Bowers v. Hardwick 142
Brady, Henry 186, 227, 280
Brazil 85, 134, 181, 184, 207,
    212, 220
BRICS 207
Britain, *see* United Kingdom
British Commonwealth 35–6, 157
Brown v. Board of Education 27, 32, 261
Bryce, James 155–6
Buddhism 74, 218–19
bureaucrats 119, 174
Burgess, John W. 154–5

Calabresi, Steven 29
Canada 26–8, 30–1, 35–7, 46–50,
    138–42, 178, 183–4
    Charter of Rights and Freedoms 28,
        49–50, 139, 141, 173, 183, 221
    Constitution 141
    Quebec 140, 183–4
    Supreme Court 27–8, 30–1, 47–9,
        74–5, 92, 139, 183–4
canon law 82–6, 106, 115, 117, 119,
    124–5
canonical scholarship 3, 17, 205–6
Carroll, Lewis 224
case selection 3, 9, 17, 155, 187, 192,
    224–81
    biases 9, 23; *see also* cherry-picking
    principles 15, 17, 224–5, 230, 244–5,
        255, 279–80
    inference-oriented 193,
        244–67, 281
Catholic Church 86, 115, 126
causal inference 224–6, 242,
    244–5, 260
causal links 5, 127, 130, 133, 229,
    269, 278
causality 186, 225, 228, 232, 244,
    280–1
Cézanne, Paul 224
cherry-picking 9, 19, 23, 98, 144,
    187, 279
Cheshin, Mishael 45, 58
Chiang Kai-shek 249
children 66, 101
Chile 207, 234, 254
China 33, 54, 130, 151, 181, 207, 233
choices 9, 12, 23–4, 41, 43, 76, 161–2
    design 177, 271
    judicial 9, 22, 24, 51–2, 75–6
    methodological 16, 206
Choudhry, Sujit 27, 43, 73, 80, 141,
    213, 263
church 59, 82, 84–5, 106
citation patterns, foreign 8, 20, 29,
    31, 37
citations 30–1, 33, 35–6, 38–9, 43,
    70–1, 75
    foreign 8, 20–1, 26, 28–30, 35–9,
        74, 76

citizenship 61, 85, 117, 135, 141,
        149, 153
civil law 35, 115, 259, 270
civil rights 247
classification 96, 128, 187, 196, 219,
        226–8, 230
coexistence of universal and
        particular law 123, 125
Cohen-Eliya, Moshe 258
Colombia 173, 183, 185, 214,
        216–17, 221
colonialism 35, 121, 208, 210, 220
common law 22, 34–6, 259, 270
    jurisdictions 31, 33, 40, 47
    traditions 35, 37
commonalities 18, 49, 187, 228,
        230, 249
commonwealths 59–60, 116–17, 120
    British Commonwealth 35–6, 157
communities 89–90, 99, 102, 113, 115,
        198, 282
    Jewish 62, 64, 78, 87, 90–1, 99–100,
        105–6
    religious 22, 65, 72, 82
comparative constitutional design
        112, 138–9, 158–9, 176, 179
comparative constitutional
        inquiry 5–7, 13, 18–19,
        113–15, 186–8, 191–3, 283–4
    drivers and study methodology 6–19
comparative constitutional
        jurisprudence 8, 20, 26, 31,
        201–3, 236, 241
    purveyors and consumers of 8, 20
comparative constitutional law, see also
        Introductory Note
    amorphous methodological
        matrix 186–9
    to constitutional studies 151–91
    universality 192–223
comparative constitutional
        studies 10–11, 13, 15, 17–18,
        160–1, 223–6, 230–1
comparative constitutional
        universe 12, 139
comparative constitutionalism 2–4,
        17–18, 153–5, 157, 164–5, 240,
        278–9

comparative inquiry 115, 117, 228–9,
        236, 238, 245, 278
    modes 17, 230, 232–44
comparative judicial imagination
        8, 20–76
comparative jurisprudence 9, 24, 36,
        120–1, 204
comparative law 3–4, 48, 130–1,
        193–7, 228–30, 233–7, 279
comparative legal studies 83, 133,
        195, 205, 226, 259, 279
comparative methods 18, 117, 125,
        157, 232, 238, 245–6
comparative politics 4, 6, 17, 156, 182,
        186, 190
comparative public law 19, 115,
        117–18, 120, 125, 127, 163
comparative reference 20, 60, 116,
        143, 237
comparative religion 4, 194, 227
comparative research 119, 127, 186,
        226–7, 231, 244, 278–9
computerized constitutional
        design 272
concept building through multiple
        description 117
concept formation 193–4, 226, 228,
        230, 238–9, 241–2, 245
Confucian constitutionalism 201, 249
consensus 49, 68, 93–4, 203, 237
Constable, Marianne 85
constitutional adjudication 19,
        163, 233
constitutional amendments 71, 86,
        168, 206
constitutional authority 150, 200
constitutional convergence 11, 150,
        172, 205
constitutional courts 1–4, 7–8, 20–2,
        162–3, 166, 173, 252–6
    Germany 8, 21, 27, 34, 44,
        46–8, 168
    Hungary 41
    independent 248–9
    Romania 39, 56
    Russia 39, 234
    South Africa 26, 75, 86, 216, 221, 236
    Turkey 71

constitutional democracy 47, 147, 174, 211
constitutional design 1, 14, 158–9, 166, 190, 269, 272
  comparative 112, 138–9, 158–9, 176, 179
  computerized 272
  literature 156, 160, 209
  as political science 176–9
constitutional engineering 113, 158, 176, 179, 235; *see also* constitutional design
constitutional entrenchment 160, 273
constitutional ethnographies 131, 225, 233
constitutional experiences 9, 16, 23, 192–3, 205–6, 214, 218–19
constitutional ideas, migration of 10, 25, 40, 75, 77, 80, 281
constitutional identity 50, 97, 117, 193
constitutional innovations 12, 133, 139
constitutional inquiry,
  comparative 5–7, 13, 18–19, 113–15, 186–8, 191–3, 283–4
constitutional interpretation 39, 41, 92, 108, 147, 153, 163
constitutional jurisprudence 1–2, 4, 14, 32, 42, 48–9, 232–3
  American 27, 31, 33, 35
  comparative 8, 20, 26, 31, 201–3, 236, 241
  foreign 13, 25, 30, 47, 72, 75, 114
constitutional legacies 232, 241–2, 247, 254, 274
constitutional monarchy 130, 133
constitutional north 206, 214–15, 220
constitutional orders 134–5, 148, 175, 177, 200, 202, 223
  new 175, 222
constitutional pluralism 150, 200
constitutional reforms 140, 161, 171, 173, 184, 264–6
constitutional review 172, 201, 249–50, 252, 274–5
  establishment of 173, 248
constitutional revolutions 12, 139, 173–4, 233, 264–6

constitutional rights 21, 25, 73, 80, 179, 182, 272
constitutional south 214, 218–20, 222
constitutional sovereignty 49, 144, 168, 203
constitutional studies 151–91, 210, 226
constitutional supremacy 171, 189, 249, 264, 273, 281
constitutional systems 4, 16, 24–5, 60, 225–6, 232–4, 241
constitutional theory 18, 32, 39, 134, 152, 166, 269–70
  normative 175, 199
constitutional thought 12, 33, 83, 125–6, 135–6, 138–9
  American 32, 135
constitutional transformation 1, 153, 160, 174, 233, 263–4, 266
constitutional universe 2, 7, 16, 18, 191, 223, 225
  comparative 12, 139
constitutionalism 1–4, 118–19, 171–2, 200–1, 211–12, 215–16, 239–40
  comparative 2–4, 17–18, 153–5, 157, 164–5, 240, 278–9
  Confucian 201, 249
  global 25, 163, 165, 201, 203, 210, 274
  liberal 171, 173
  modern 31, 189, 216, 270, 275
  new 16, 32, 63, 81, 148, 230, 240
  reasons for rise of 170–5
  transnational 80
constitutionality 73–4, 96, 218, 236
constitutionalization 152, 158, 161–2, 171–3, 175, 263–6, 273
  political origins of 264, 266
  of rights 54, 173, 180, 263, 266
constitutive laws of others, engagement with the, *see* engagement with the constitutive laws of others
contextualism 188–9, 192, 203, 231
control 84, 124, 132, 251, 259
controlled comparison 187, 193, 224, 226, 230, 243–5, 252
  basic methodological principles 278–9

convergence 6, 14, 16, 76, 80,
    240–1, 273
  constitutional 11, 150, 172, 205
  global 8, 21, 77, 171, 194, 273
Council of Europe 73, 201–3, 237, 250
Crane, William W. 154
creation of conceptual
    frameworks 187, 228, 230, 240
criminal law 16, 29, 90, 129, 201
crucifixes 202
cultural autonomy 105
cultural diversity 140, 211
cultural nationalism 140
cultural pluralism 64
cultural propensities 63, 247, 255
cultural rights 54, 210
culturalists 4, 188, 197, 231
culture wars 50, 53, 63, 68, 71,
    144, 147
cultures 38, 141, 152–3, 193, 196,
    198, 234–5
  legal 38, 198, 257
curiosity, intellectual 7, 112, 124,
    148–9
customary law 83, 151, 273
Czech Republic 37, 237, 250

Dahl, Robert 152, 163, 176,
    181, 256
Damaška, Mirjan 256
data sets, large 18, 230, 268–9
David, Rene 233
de jure discrimination 179, 182
de Tocqueville, Alexis 191, 234
death penalty 26–7, 142, 236
decision-making patterns 42,
    166–7, 253
democracy 48, 158–61, 170–1,
    179–82, 234–5, 239, 248–9
  liberal 9, 17, 23, 55, 205, 217
  stable 16, 56, 179, 182, 192
  transition to and consolidation
    of 159–60
democratic governance 133, 153
democratic regimes 265, 275
democratization 113, 138, 158–60,
    176, 266, 273
Denmark 127, 180–1

dependent variables 222, 246–7,
    253–4, 256, 262
description
  multiple 117, 120, 187, 193–4, 228,
    238–9, 245
  thick 5, 196, 225
design
  choices 177, 271
  constitutional, see constitutional
    design
  factors 271
  institutional 172, 250, 271
despotic colonialism 134
despotism 128–31, 171
Dicey, A.V. 155–7
diffusion 24, 54, 172, 272–3, 275
  transnational 172, 275
dignity 73–4, 88, 182, 189, 199,
    202, 259
dina de-malkhuta dina doctrine 89–90
discrimination 201, 217
disenfranchised groups 173, 179
diversity 100, 141, 211, 219
  cultural 140, 211
  legal 10, 81
Dixon, Rosalind 4, 36, 164,
    212–13, 236
domestic law 28, 30, 54, 86, 134,
    161, 265
domestic politics 270, 272,
    274, 277
Druze 60, 65–6, 86–7
Durkheim, Émile 127, 131–2, 256
Dworkin, Ronald 152, 171–2,
    188, 263
Dyzenhaus, David 214

Eastern Europe 56, 160, 162
ECJ (European Court of Justice) 26,
    46, 259
economic and social rights
    (ESRs) 222, 273
economic development 100, 133,
    207–8, 220, 248, 270
economic growth 100, 209, 270
economic rights 184–5, 221–2
economics 152, 176–7, 185, 187, 267,
    269–70, 274

education 27, 32, 41, 62, 64,
    181–4, 236
  legal 8, 21, 40, 212
Egypt 77, 81, 91–3, 100, 169, 174, 255
Eichmann trial 51
Ejima, Akiko 39
elections 54, 56, 185, 249
  presidential 55, 168–9, 177
Eliot, T.S. 192
elites 52–3, 63, 102, 169, 255, 264
  political 74, 174
Elkins, Zachary 152, 159–60, 172, 175,
    205, 269–73
Elon, Menachem 89, 99
empirical legal scholarship 187,
    228, 279
empirical legal studies
    movement 226, 269
enforcement 86, 90, 118, 145, 160,
    261, 264
engagement with the constitutive
    laws of others 5–7, 10–11, 79,
    110, 113–15, 147–8, 282–3
  comparative 6–7, 148, 283
  early 10–11, 77–111
  history 6, 11, 79, 113
  necessities, ideas, interests 112–50
  pragmatic 10, 78
  selective 6–7, 79–80, 148, 283
  social and political context 97–110
England, see United Kingdom
Enlightenment philosophy 72
environmental factors 271
epistemological leaps 11, 19, 115,
    148–50
Epp, Charles 182, 261–2
Epstein, Lee 42, 167–8, 186, 252–3
equality 34, 54, 64, 68, 73, 169, 201
  gender 65–6, 93, 103, 201,
    239, 241
Erastus 59, 124
ESRs (economic and social
    rights) 222, 273
Essenes 107
estrangement, principled 10, 78
ethnographies, constitutional 131,
    225, 233
EU, see European Union

Europe 1, 38, 84, 126, 202–3,
    211–13, 273
  Christian 100, 105, 121
  Eastern 56, 160, 162
  medieval 82–3
  Southern 138, 162, 265
European Court of Human Rights
    (ECtHR) 26–8, 44, 46, 73, 75,
    201–3, 236–7
European Court of Justice (ECJ) 26,
    46, 259
European Union 27, 138, 142, 148,
    200–1, 250, 252
exclusion 152, 183–4, 201, 208
excommunication 59, 102, 104, 123
expansion 63, 82–3, 161–2,
    189, 265
explanatory knowledge 228, 280
external interpretation 93, 104
extra-communal law 10, 78

faith 82, 91, 105, 108, 110
federalism 72, 135–6, 212, 233, 241,
    253, 263
Finland 180, 219, 237
flexible interpretation 108, 144
foreign citation patterns 8, 20, 29, 31, 37
foreign citations 8, 20–1, 26, 28–30,
    35–9, 74, 76
foreign constitutional
    jurisprudence 13, 25, 30, 47,
    72, 75, 114
foreign jurisprudence 8, 21, 26, 30,
    33–4, 40, 73
foreign law 24–6, 28–30, 34–7, 39–40,
    42–3, 85–6, 142–7
  judicial recourse to 9–10, 24, 47, 57,
    77, 85
foreign precedents 7, 10, 22–3, 28–31,
    33–6, 39, 42–3
foreign reference 9, 22, 74, 143–4
  choice of 52–3
  Israel as test case for 41–68
  patterns of 22, 24–41, 68
  trends outside Israel 68–75
foreign sources 25, 29, 38, 43, 45,
    55–8, 144–5
forum shopping 90

France 37–8, 116, 118, 126–7, 133–4, 156–7, 249–50
  law 116–17, 119
freedom 32, 34, 130, 136, 146, 171, 180
Friedrich, Carl 138, 151, 157–8
fundamental rights 61, 239

Galanter, Mark 208
Galligan, Denis J. 135, 162, 174–5
Gardbaum, Stephen 239–40
Geertz, Clifford 5, 196, 272
Gellner, Ernest 53
Gelter, Martin 38
gender equality 65–6, 93, 103, 201, 239, 241
genealogies 87, 127, 193–4, 208
gentile courts 90–1
Gering, John 186, 242, 244, 260
German Empire 119, 154
Germany 23, 36–8, 44, 46–51, 167–8, 232–3, 236–7
  constitutional court 8, 21, 27, 34, 44, 46–8, 75
  Weimar Republic 138, 156–7
Ginsburg, Tom 159–62, 164, 201, 212–13, 234–5, 248–9, 270–2, 274
Glendon, Mary Ann 33, 74, 236, 258–9
global constitutional north, see constitutional north
global constitutional south, see constitutional south
global constitutionalism 25, 163, 165, 201, 203, 210, 274
global convergence 8, 21, 77, 171, 194, 273
global north 16, 105–6, 206–9, 212, 216, 219–21, 223
global south 17, 106, 193, 207–9, 214
  critique 15–17, 193, 205–18, 220, 222, 269
  unravelling 217–23
globalization 13, 21, 30–1, 43, 74, 114, 204
God 59–60, 88, 91, 103, 123, 126, 128
governance 81, 124–5, 131, 154, 159, 177, 232
  democratic 133, 153

Graber, Mark 152, 153, 191, 265
Great Britain, see United Kingdom
Greece 136, 162, 203, 221, 237, 249, 251
Grimm, Dieter 46
Grotius, Hugo 59–60, 91–2, 121, 124

Ha-Levi, Yehudah 52
Hacker, Daphna 67, 103
Halakha 78, 88–9, 125
halakhic authorities 90, 99
Hasmonean Kingdom 107
HDI (Human Development Index) 181, 207
health care 147, 181–4
Hebrew 47, 51, 57, 88–9, 103, 107
Hellenized Judaism 78, 106–7
Helmke, Gretchen 42, 167, 239, 252
heresy 85–6
Herod, King 78, 100, 107
heuristics 267–8
hierarchy 82–3, 96, 199–200, 216, 257, 259
hijab 71, 93–4
Hilbink, Lisa 234
Hinduism 215, 218
holistic approach 15, 156, 185, 191
Holmes, Stephen 118, 119, 133, 160, 263
Hong Kong 26, 33–5, 54, 173, 181, 207, 236
Horowitz, Donald 159–60, 182, 263
Hotman, François 115–16
Howard, Dick 155–6
Hug, Walther 195
Huguenots 115–17
human development 181, 189, 207, 217, 220
Human Development Index (HDI) 181, 207
human dignity, see dignity
human rights 26–7, 37, 39, 46, 209–10, 236, 270
  discourse 163, 210
human sciences 199, 224, 243, 268, 283
Hume, David 242
Hungary 2, 26, 41, 173, 236–7
hunter-gatherer societies 161, 189
Huntington, Samuel 113, 160, 176

identity
    constitutional 50, 97, 117, 193
    construction 41–68
    national 22–3, 38, 51
    religious 82, 87–8, 102
idiographic knowledge 5, 197, 226
idolatry 88
IMF (International Monetary
        Fund) 100, 207
imperialism 208, 211, 220
incentives 40, 159, 161, 175, 209
independence 49, 68, 72, 84, 220,
        250, 252
    constitutions 12, 114, 133
    judicial 119, 169, 239, 249, 257
independent variables 180, 222, 246,
        250–1, 253–4, 267
India 26–8, 34–6, 72–4, 94–5, 183, 213,
        217–21
    Bharatiya Janata Party (BJP) 215
    Constitution 72–3, 94, 183, 221
    sodomy laws 73
    Supreme Court 34, 36, 70, 73–4,
        94–6, 216, 218
Indonesia 72, 93, 181, 212, 219–20,
        233, 239
inequalities 128, 207–8
inevitability 10, 13, 78, 114, 137
inference-oriented case-selection
        principles 193, 244–67, 281
inference-oriented principles of
        research design 228, 231, 280
inferences 98, 186, 193, 225, 228,
        260, 268
    causal 224–6, 242, 244–5, 260
inheritance 103, 122, 129, 151
innovations
    constitutional 12, 133, 139
    doctrinal 7, 10, 79
    theoretical 113, 138
inquisitiveness 6, 11, 13, 110, 113–15,
        148, 150
institutional design 172, 250, 271
institutions 81, 138, 151–2, 157–9,
        175–6, 205–6, 234–6
    legal 3, 35, 152, 164, 195, 225
    political 127, 129, 133–4, 138, 154,
        161, 163

instrumentalism 11, 19, 21, 112–13
insurance 161–2, 248–9
integration 104, 213, 233, 263
intellectual curiosity 7, 112, 124,
        148–9
intellectual goals 18, 224, 231, 280
international human rights 25, 54,
        161, 182, 265, 277
international law 54–5, 59, 121–3,
        145, 164–5, 208, 210
International Monetary Fund
        (IMF) 100, 207
international political economy 185,
        207, 233
interpretation 91, 93, 97–9, 109–11,
        197, 220–1, 251
    constitutional 39, 41, 92, 108, 147,
        153, 163
    external 93, 104
    flexible 108, 144
    purposive 24, 108
interpretive approaches 10, 41, 79,
        104, 108, 254–5
Iraq 102, 174, 209
Ireland 23, 38, 44, 72, 181–2, 241, 251
Islam 68–70, 86–7, 93–6, 105, 108,
        215, 218
    political 71, 255
Islamic Shari'a law 69, 78, 86, 92–3,
        101, 145–6, 215
Islamization 68–71, 255
Israel 22–3, 27–8, 173, 181–2, 213,
        255, 265–6
    courts 43, 46, 48, 58, 61, 67, 103
    Jewish law 9–10, 23, 57–61, 78–9,
        87–90, 99–104, 121–5
    Jews 59–61, 88–91, 99, 101, 105,
        107–8, 121–2
    Judaism 61, 64–5, 88, 107, 121–2
    non-Jews 60, 64, 88, 99–101
    rabbinical courts 61, 64–7
    self-definition 9, 23, 45, 241
    Supreme Court 22–3, 43–7, 50,
        52–3, 57–9, 63, 65–7
    as test case for foreign
        reference 41–68
Italy 86, 91, 134, 140, 177–8, 202,
        249–51

Jackson, Vicki 3, 6, 30, 80, 142, 204, 238–42
Jacobsohn, Gary J. 22, 24, 47, 50–1, 74–6, 153, 240–2
Jamaica 26, 173, 236
Japan 130, 174, 181, 207, 209, 219, 233–4
　Constitution 233–4
　Supreme Court 39
Jaspers, Karl 51
Jellinek, Georg 156
Jerusalem 46, 51–2, 100, 108
Jewish communities 62, 64, 78, 87, 90–1, 99–100, 105–6; see also Israel
Jewish holidays 61–2
Jewish law 9–10, 23, 57–61, 78–9, 87–90, 99–104, 121–5
Jewish Sabbath 62, 64, 101
Jews 59–61, 88–91, 99, 101, 105, 107–8, 121–2; see also Israel
Judaism 61, 64–5, 88, 107, 121–2
judicial activism 45, 162, 172, 179, 216
judicial authority 30, 145
judicial behavior 42, 163, 166–7, 170, 251–2, 257
　theories of 166–70
judicial choices 9, 22, 24, 51–2, 75–6
judicial independence 119, 169, 239, 249, 257
judicial recourse to foreign law 9–10, 24, 47, 57, 77, 85
judicial review 1–2, 4, 162–3, 171, 179–81, 247–8, 263
　active 2, 12, 139, 181
　reasons for rise of 170–5
　weak-form 239–40
jurisdictional autonomy 67, 90–1, 105, 271
jurisprudence 35–6, 47, 49–51, 70, 74–5, 221–2, 284
　actual effects 179–86
　comparative 9, 24, 36, 120–1, 204
　constitutional, see constitutional jurisprudence
　progressive 61, 221
　social rights 183–5

Kagan, Elena 144
Kalb, Johanna 55
Kamaruddin 96
Kant, Emanuel 73
Kantorowicz, Herman 195
Karzai, Hamid 70
kashrut 62, 64
Katz 66
Keller, Helen 250
Keohane, Robert 256, 280
khukot ha'goy 91, 102
King, Gary 186, 256, 280
kings 77, 90, 116, 118, 126, 260, 280
Kirby, Michael 36
knowledge 15, 17, 112, 117, 193, 195–6, 226–30
　explanatory 228, 280
　idiographic 5, 197, 226
　local 234, 268
　transportable 5, 197
Koh, Harold H. 145
Korea 72, 174, 248–9
　North 205, 219
Kosar, David 250
Kötz, Hein 196, 233
Koushal 73–4
Kumm, Mattias 200
Kuwait 93–4
Kymlicka, Will 141

landmark rulings 39, 41, 43, 64, 66, 69, 185
language 38, 41, 47, 49, 189, 220, 229
large data sets 18, 230, 268–9
large-N studies 18, 193–4, 223, 225–6, 230–1, 267–70, 272–7
Lasser, Mitchel 259
Latin America 133, 135, 138, 140, 207, 212, 239
Lautsi 202
Law, David 21, 27, 72, 172–3, 269, 272, 274
law schools 3, 40, 160, 164–5, 221, 261
Lawrence 26–7, 142
laws of nations 11, 81–2, 121, 123

laws of others
  engagement with, *see* engagement
    with the constitutive laws of
    others
  reference to, *see* foreign reference
  surviving 80–97
legal academia 30, 185–6, 192–3,
    229–30, 235, 240, 278
legal cultures 38, 198, 257
legal diversity 10, 81
legal education 8, 21, 40, 212
legal mobilization 261–2
legal scholarship 2, 127, 152, 187, 227,
    245, 283
  empirical 187, 228, 279
legal systems 37–8, 78–80, 83–4,
    88–90, 117, 193–7, 257
legal traditions 21–2, 35, 49–50,
    122–5, 233, 270, 273
  autonomous 10, 78
legitimacy 10, 37, 54–5, 78, 80–1,
    257, 259
Legrand, Pierre 195, 197–8, 205, 259,
    267–8, 279
Leibniz, Gottfried Wilhelm 11, 113,
    121, 283
Lerner, Max 147–8
Levinson, Sanford 98, 147, 177
Leviticus 91
L'Heureux-Dubé, Claire 31, 70, 141
liberal constitutionalism 171, 173
liberal democracies 9, 17, 23, 55,
    205, 217
Lijphart, Arend 159–60, 176,
    246, 263
Linz, Juan 156, 160, 176
litigation 78, 90, 100
  rights 172, 262
living tree approach 110, 147
local government 83, 125
local knowledge 234, 268
local traditions 12, 16, 92, 201–2, 204
Locke, John 73

Magalhães, Pedro 249
Maimonides 78, 99–100, 103–6, 124–5
Maine, Henry Sumner 131–2, 151, 256
Mak, Elaine 37–8

Makwanyane 26, 236
Malaysia 9, 23, 50, 72–3, 96, 179, 255
  Federal Court 50, 72, 95–6
Maldonado, Daniel Bonilla 216–17
Mannheim, Karl 112
marriage 45, 64–7, 122–3, 146
  same-sex 61, 218, 275
McCloskey, Robert 163
McCormick, Peter 30–1
McLachlin, Beverley 28, 30, 50
Mead, Margaret 189
medieval Europe 82–3
Melton, James 152, 159, 270–2
Menski, Werner 211
meta-narratives, national 13, 138, 259
methodological choices 16, 206
methodological pluralism 18, 231, 280
Mexico 39–40, 167, 181, 207,
    212, 221
Mian, Ajmal 69–70
migration
  of constitutional ideas 10, 25, 40, 75,
    77, 80, 281
  of interpretive methods 24
Mill, John Stuart 245
mobilization, legal 261–2
modern constitutionalism 31, 189,
    216, 270, 275
modes of comparative inquiry 17,
    230, 232–44
monarchy 115–17, 128–30
  constitutional 130, 133
Mongolia 162, 248–9
Montesquieu 11–12, 113–15, 136, 152,
    197, 234, 248
  as comparativist 125–33
moral authority 110, 199
moral principles 86, 106
Morrall, John 83–4
Moses, Bernard 154–5
most different cases principle 17, 230,
    244, 253–7, 281
most difficult case principle 17, 230,
    245, 260–2, 281
most similar cases principle 17, 230,
    244–50, 253–4
multi-method research 194, 267, 277
multiculturalism 12, 49, 139–41, 211

multiple description 117, 120, 187, 193–4, 228, 238–9, 245
Murphy, Walter 163
Musharraf, Pervez 54, 70, 169
Muslims 44, 60, 65, 68, 91, 95, 105; *see also* Islam

Nahmanides 106
national identity 22–3, 38, 51
national meta-narratives 13, 138, 259
nationalism 12, 53, 126
natural law 91, 123, 128, 130, 132
necessity 6, 13, 97, 102, 114–15, 120, 148–50
Nepal 45, 73, 87, 218
Netherlands 37, 73, 91, 180–1, 237, 247, 251
new democracies 162, 219, 248
New Zealand 27–8, 31, 35–7, 43, 47, 181, 207
Nigeria 106, 181, 212, 255
Noachide precepts 88, 121–3, 125
non-Jews 60, 64, 88, 99–101
Nordic countries 4, 181
normative constitutional theory 175, 199
North, Douglass 152, 161, 209, 264
north, global 16, 105–6, 206–9, 212, 216, 219–21, 223
North Korea 205, 219
Norway 133, 180–1, 219, 271

O'Donnell, Guillermo 160
originalism 10, 24, 37, 79, 107–8, 110–11, 147
outlier cases, principle 17, 230, 245, 262–7, 281

Pakistan 50, 68–70, 167, 169, 212, 214, 255
    Supreme Court 69–70, 94, 169
parliamentary elections 56, 169
particularism 6, 15–16, 111, 197, 199, 201–2, 241
patterns of foreign reference 22, 24–41, 68
peak courts 8–9, 21, 23, 39, 41, 44, 72–3

personal status 64–5, 82, 90, 103, 211
persuasive authority 23–5
Pharisees 107
Philippines 31, 45, 169, 212, 219
philosophy 10, 19, 104–5, 148, 187
Plonit ("Jane Doe") v. Ploni ("John Doe") 65–7
pluralism
    constitutional 150, 200
    cultural 64
    methodological 18, 231, 280
plurality 16, 141, 186, 200, 204
Poland 45, 50–1, 99, 118–19, 201, 203, 237
policy preferences 54, 63, 152, 162, 166, 175, 255
policymakers 2–3, 191, 204
political context 56, 60, 89, 97, 106, 115, 120
political economy 11, 79, 186, 270
political elites 74, 174
political institutions 127, 129, 133–4, 138, 154, 161, 163
political interests 7, 13, 115, 170, 185, 200
political Islam 71, 255
political market 161, 185
political realities 49, 78, 185, 239, 254
political reconstruction 178, 233, 265
political rights 33, 54, 210
political science 153–5, 160, 163–5, 167–8, 175–7, 243–4, 260
political sociology 41, 51
political sovereignty 10, 78, 118
political systems 119, 156, 158, 162, 169–70
political transformations 112, 117, 138, 283
political transition 54, 174, 248
politicians 142, 145–6, 161–2
politics 6–7, 148–50, 153–4, 170, 176–7, 248, 251
    domestic 270, 272, 274, 277
popes 84–5, 126
Porat, Iddo 43, 258
Portugal 72, 127, 134, 162, 218, 220, 249
positive obligations 183–4

positivism 17, 199, 225, 228, 280
post-authoritarian polities 9, 24, 34,
    162, 209, 248–9
post-colonialism 158
Pound, Roscoe 195
pragmatic engagement 10, 78
presidential elections 55, 168–9, 177
principled estrangement 10, 78
privacy 73–4, 146
privileges 146, 152–3
progressive jurisprudence 61, 221
property relations 67, 103
property rights 32, 100, 160, 209
prophets 87, 92, 108, 275
proportionality 12, 24–5, 66, 139,
    239, 258
  analysis 25, 149, 189, 258
prototypical cases principle 17, 230,
    245, 256–60, 281
Provence 78, 91, 103–4, 106
Pufendorf, Samuel von 11, 121, 124
purposive interpretation 24, 108
purveyors and consumers of
        comparative constitutional
        jurisprudence 8, 20

quasi-constitutional entities 16, 201
quasi-constitutional regimes 200, 206
Quebec 140, 183–4

rabbinical courts 61, 64–7
Rawls, John 73, 161
realist approach 243
reconstruction, political 178, 233, 265
reference 8–9, 21–2, 35, 39–46, 54–9,
    72, 142–4
  comparative 20, 60, 116, 143, 237
  epistemic communities of 42, 167
  voluntary 7, 10, 22, 25, 28, 42, 49
referenda 56–7, 92, 146
reforms, constitutional 140, 161, 171,
    173, 184, 264–6
religion 61–5, 94, 96–9, 108–11,
    215–16, 218–19, 255–6
  comparative 4, 194, 227
religion law 10, 79, 92, 97, 107, 110–11,
    121; see also religious law
religiosity 9, 23, 129

religious affiliation 45, 64, 68, 102,
    174, 215
religious attire 93, 236–7
religious authority 59, 82, 93, 98, 108
religious autonomy 89
religious communities 22, 65, 72, 82
religious diversity 211
religious identity 82, 87–8, 102
religious law 66, 78, 83, 98, 145
religious practices 94–5, 102
republics 59–60, 97, 128–9, 132, 137
research design 17–18, 155, 192, 223,
    224–81
  inference-oriented principles of 228,
    231, 280
  principles of 187, 230
research methods 18–19, 231, 269
revolutions, constitutional 12, 139,
    173–4, 233, 264–6
riba 101
rights 32–4, 54–5, 139–41, 171–3,
    179–84, 261–3, 273
  bills of 12, 139, 145, 171, 173,
    258, 263
  civil 247
  constitutional 21, 25, 73, 80, 179,
    182, 272
  constitutionalization 54, 173, 180,
    263, 266
  cultural 54, 210
  economic 184–5, 221–2
  fundamental 61, 239
  human, see human rights
  jurisprudence 143, 163, 179, 183–5,
    236, 253
  litigation 172, 262
  property 32, 100, 160, 209
  revolutions 261–2
  socioeconomic 185, 216, 221
  to vote 34, 135
Roach, Kent 141, 213, 239
Roman law 115–19, 125
Romania 24, 39, 56–7, 237
  Constitutional Court 39, 56
Rome 85, 117–18, 136, 138
Roper 26–7, 142
Rosenberg, Gerald 182, 260–1
Rosenfeld, Michel 34, 118, 153, 164, 236

Rousseau, Jean-Jacques 133, 153, 156
rule-of-law polities 235, 238
Russia 127, 160, 167, 182, 207, 212,
    251–2
  Constitutional Court 39, 234

Sabbath 99, 101
Sadducees 107
Sajó, András 34, 46, 118, 164
Sapir, Edward 189
Sartori, Giovanni 160
Saunders, Cheryl 36, 164,
    213, 233–4
Scalia, Antonin 30, 46, 142–3, 197,
    237, 282
Scheppele, Kim Lane 27, 56, 233, 240
Schubert, Glendon 163
SCI, see Israel, Supreme Court
Schwöbel, Christine 210
secularism 9, 23, 50, 71, 126, 203
Selden, John 11–12, 59, 91, 113–15,
    122–5, 149
selective engagement 6–7, 79–80,
    148, 283
self-estrangement 208
separation of powers 21, 73, 128,
    157, 238
Shachar, Ayelet 103, 141, 204
Shapiro, Ian 176, 243, 268
Shapiro, Martin 163, 256–7, 263
Siems, Matthias 38
Singapore 39–40, 162, 207, 239
single-country studies 193, 196, 232,
    237, 256
Slovakia 37, 45, 237, 250
small-N studies 193–4, 226, 228, 230,
    243–67, 269, 276
Smyth, Russell 36–7
social and political context of
    engagement with the
    constitutive laws of
    others 97–110
social anthropology 189, 199, 227
social rights 222, 273
  jurisprudence 183–5
  as parable 179–86
social sciences 6, 13–15, 166–91, 199,
    226–8, 242–3, 277–9

socioeconomic rights 185, 216, 221
sociology 53, 107, 131, 182, 199,
    226, 243
  political 41, 51
soft law 180, 268
south, constitutional 214,
    218–20, 222
South Africa 26–8, 35–6, 43–4, 183–5,
    217, 220–2, 233
  Constitutional Court 26, 75, 86, 216,
    221, 236
South Korea 162, 167, 181
Southern Europe 138, 162, 265
sovereignty 57, 68, 117–19, 208
  constitutional 49, 144, 168, 203
  political 10, 78, 118
Spain 106, 118, 127, 162, 233, 237,
    249–51
Sparta 118–19
Sri Lanka 50, 74, 215
statistical analyses 162, 193, 198,
    225–6, 268, 274, 277
Stepan, Alfred 156, 160
Stone Sweet, Alec 25, 249–50, 263
strategic-realist approach 162, 175
supranational entities 2, 265
supranational norms/entities 86, 123,
    200–1, 204, 206, 241, 265
supremacy, constitutional 171, 189,
    249, 264, 273, 281
Sweden 127, 180–2, 203, 220, 237,
    251, 271
Switzerland 72, 181, 203, 207,
    237, 271

Taiwan 40, 162, 167, 207, 248–9
Talmud 89–90, 99, 124–5
Tanzania 26, 236
taxonomies 128, 130, 225, 227, 230,
    233, 279–80
Taylor, Charles 126, 141, 215
Texas 26–7, 142, 200
textualism 10, 79, 108–9
Thailand 45, 87, 215
theocratic governance 255
thick description 5, 196, 225
Thomas, Robert 209
Timor-Leste 24, 72

Torah 104, 108
traditions 129, 195–6, 201–3, 205, 257,
        259, 271
    local 12, 16, 92, 201–2, 204
    religious 98, 103
transition to and consolidation of
        democracy 159–60
transitional societies 50, 53
transitions 158–60, 189, 195, 205,
        248–9, 259, 265
    fragile 254
    political 54, 174, 248
transnational constitutionalism 80
transnational convergence
        vectors 10, 77
transnational diffusion 172, 275
transportable knowledge 5, 197
Tripathi, P.K. 21, 27, 42
Trochev, Alexei 42, 167, 234
Trubek, David 208
Tully, James 141, 211
Tunisia 93, 215
turban 96
Turkey 23, 50, 71–2, 236–7, 242, 251,
        254–5
    AKP 71, 168
    Constitutional Court 71
Tushnet, Mark 2–3, 21, 147, 153,
        163–4, 233–5, 238–40

Uganda 24, 55–6, 168–9
ultimate authority 89, 107, 116
uncertainty 54, 161, 248, 274
UNDP (United Nations
        Development Programme)
        181, 207
Unger, Roberto 256
United Kingdom 27–8, 36–8, 46–8,
        72–3, 126–7, 136, 265
United States 25–31, 47–8, 73–5,
        140–7, 154, 180–1, 239–41
    Constitution 27, 74, 77, 143, 145–7,
        271, 274
    Supreme Court 26–7, 29–33, 46–7,
        142–3, 163, 237–8, 261

universal law 88, 117, 122
universalism 4, 15–16, 43–4, 59–60,
        192, 197, 199–203
universality 192–223
usual suspect settings 4, 16, 39, 119,
        192, 211, 241

Valcke, Catherine 204
variables
    dependent 222, 246–7, 253–4,
        256, 262
    independent 180, 222, 246, 250–1,
        253–4, 267
variance 99–100, 161–2, 172–3, 185–8,
        222, 246–7, 281
Venezuela 134–6, 160
Venice 20, 118–19
Verba, Sidney 246, 256, 280
Versteeg, Mila 27, 162, 172–5, 269,
        272, 274, 280
Vietnam 212, 219, 221, 234
voluntary reference 7, 10, 22, 25, 28,
        42, 49
vote, right to 34, 135

Watson, Alan 197
weak-form judicial review 239–40
Weber, Max 127, 133, 160,
        209, 256
Weiler, J.H.H. 1, 138, 200,
        202–3, 233
Weimar Republic 138, 156–7
Weingast, Barry 159–61, 264
Whorf, Benjamin Lee 189
Wigmore, John H. 151, 195
World Series syndrome 16, 192,
        205–6
worldviews 43, 49, 63, 148, 152,
        162, 171
worship 94, 104, 202

Zaring, David 28
Zimbabwe 26, 236
Zomia 87
Zweigert, Konrad 196, 233

Printed and bound by CPI Group (UK) Ltd, Croydon, CR0 4YY